Things and Thingness in European Literature and Visual Art, 700–1600

Sense, Matter, and Medium

New Approaches to Medieval Literary and Material Culture

Edited by
Fiona Griffiths, Beatrice Kitzinger, and Kathryn Starkey

Volume 7

Things and Thingness in European Literature and Visual Art, 700–1600

—

Edited by
Jutta Eming and Kathryn Starkey

DE GRUYTER

ISBN 978-3-11-074232-9
e-ISBN (PDF) 978-3-11-074298-5
e-ISBN (EPUB) 978-3-11-074308-1
ISSN 2367-0290

Library of Congress Control Number: 2021943981

Bibliographic information published by the Deutsche Nationalbibliothek
The Deutsche Nationalbibliothek lists this publication in the Deutsche Nationalbibliografie;
detailed bibliographic data are available on the Internet at http://dnb.dnb.de.

© 2022 Walter de Gruyter GmbH, Berlin/Boston
Cover image: Heinrich von Neustadt: Apollonius von Tyrland.
Oratio poetica ad BMV: Fragmentum. © ÖNB Wien: Cod. 2886, fol. 68v.
Printing and binding: CPI books GmbH, Leck

www.degruyter.com

In memory of Jacob Klingner (1973–2020), whose wise guidance and enthusiasm inspired this series.

Acknowledgments

Things and Thingness developed out of our interest in bringing together a group of young scholars from Germany and the United States to explore a topic that had been gaining traction in medieval and early modern studies: things. Our initial interactions were virtual – we shared an online library of scholarly books and articles. Finally, in September 2018 we met at the site of the "Episteme in Motion" Collaborative Research Center at the Freie Universität Berlin, where the participants presented the "things" that intrigued them, drawing on a variety of methodological and theoretical approaches. A visit to the medieval collection of the Kunstgewerbemuseum rounded out our discussions. Eight months later, in April 2019, the same group met at Stanford's Center for Spatial and Textual Analysis (CESTA), where they discussed and critiqued their precirculated papers. The meeting at Stanford was enriched by a hands-on exhibit of medieval and early modern manuscripts and incunabula at the Cecil H. Green Library organized for us by Kathleen Smith, curator of Germanic collections and medieval studies. This volume is thus the result of the participants' ongoing engagement with the topic and with the group assembled around it, over the span of several years. We would like to thank all participants in the project. Our discussions have been stimulating, far-ranging, and collegial, and our successive meetings have forged a scholarly network that has continued to flourish beyond this volume.

We are grateful to Elisabeth Kempf at De Gruyter for her continued support of the series, and this volume in particular. We also wish to thank Matt Gleeson for his editorial expertise and his careful attention to detail.

This book could not have been completed without financial and institutional support from Stanford University and the Freie Universität Berlin. At the Freie Universität Berlin we benefited from the generous support of the "Episteme in Motion" Collaborative Research Center. At Stanford, we are especially grateful to the senior associate dean for the humanities and arts, the Center for Spatial and Textual Analysis (CESTA), the Center for Medieval and Early Modern Studies (CMEMS), the Department of German Studies, and the Division of Literatures, Cultures and Languages (DLCL).

https://doi.org/10.1515/9783110742985-001

Contents

Illustrations

Figures

Plates

https://doi.org/10.1515/9783110742985-002

Jutta Eming and Kathryn Starkey
Introduction: The Materiality and Immateriality of Things

Toward the end of Gottfried von Straßburg's Middle High German fragmented romance *Tristan and Isolde* (ca. 1210), as the hero Tristan despairs at being separated
from his lover Isolde, his friend Duke Gilan, in an effort to cheer him up, shows him
a very peculiar creature: the magical little dog Petitcreiu (literally "little creature").[1]
Created by a "wise goddess" in the fairyland of Avalon and sent as a gift of love (line
15810), the dog is a marvel. It has shimmering fur as soft as silk and of a color that is
impossible to identify, for it changes hue depending on how one looks at it. The dog
wears a magical little bell on a golden chain, the sound of which alleviates all sad-
ness.[2] While one might hesitate to identify a dog as a "thing," Petitcreiu apparently
has none of the characteristic features of a living canine – it neither eats nor drinks
nor barks. It is Gilan's "heart's delight" (line 15798), and when he brings it out to
show Tristan, he places it on a priceless silk fabric to be admired – exactly like a precious object. Despite its seeming inanimateness, the dog has agency in the narrative:
it shapes the protagonists' emotions and actions, and it drives the story forward. Its
beauty and the joy it brings make Tristan desire it as a gift for Isolde to lessen her
sorrow at their separation, and he coerces Gilan into giving him the dog as a reward
for killing a giant.

For Isolde the dog takes on another meaning entirely: she does not wish to forget
the pain of her separation from Tristan, and so she removes the soothing little bell
and keeps the now-silent Petitcreiu with her at all times. Just as the shimmering of
Petitcreiu's fur makes it impossible to identify its color, the dog's function in the
story shifts and changes for the different characters – it is a token of love for
Gilan, an object of desire and delight for Tristan, and for Isolde a poignant reminder
of her pain and sorrow. Beyond its role in the narrative, scholars have interpreted
Petitcreiu as having a range of different figurative meanings for the poem. For
some, Petitcreiu symbolizes the perfection and singularity of the love between Tristan and Isolde, a love that has the capacity for both sorrow and joy, while for others
it symbolizes the multiperspectival nature of the poem as a whole, which Gottfried
acknowledges can be interpreted differently by different people. Petitcreiu thus func-

---

1 Gottfried von Straßburg, *Tristan und Isold*, ed. Walter Haug and Manfred Günter Scholz, 2 vols. (Berlin: Insel Verlag, 2012). *Tristan* is cited by line number in the running text. All translations in this
chapter are our own, unless otherwise stated.
2 On emotion in the Petitcreiu episode, see Jutta Eming, *Emotionen im "Tristan": Untersuchungen zu
ihrer Paradigmatik* (Göttingen: V&R Unipress, 2015), 155–177. On the Petitcreiu passage as an ekphrasis, see Kathryn Starkey, "From Enslavement to Discernment: Learning to See in Gottfried's *Tristan*,"
in *The Art of Vision: Ekphrasis in Medieval Literature and Culture*, ed. Ethan Knapp, Andrew James
Johnston, and Margitta Rouse (Columbus: Ohio State University Press, 2015), 124–148, at 138–142.

https://doi.org/10.1515/9783110742985-003

tions as a concrete thing in the narrative – it is an actual object in the diegetic world – and at the same time has immaterial, poetic qualities that invite interpretation. The dog's marvelous qualities, the evocative description given of it, its origin story, its shifting function in the narrative, the emotions it elicits in the characters, and its openness to interpretation are all characteristic features of things in medieval literature, which often function on multiple narrative levels (e. g., as plot devices, as material objects, as symbols, and as sites of intradiegetic and extradiegetic reflection).

While Petitcreiu may be unique in literary history, its role in the text and its astonishing qualities would have been familiar to the medieval audiences of *Tristan and Isolde*, who knew of wondrous things and their marvelous properties from stories both secular and religious. Yet wondrous things are just one class of objects that commonly feature in medieval and early modern texts. While some objects contribute primarily to creating a narrative setting (e. g., the fine tapestries that adorn a rich feast hall, or the bloody weapons that litter a battlefield), others more overtly intervene in and shape human perception and action. Many of the objects that feature in the chapters of this book do both.

This volume (comprising nine chapters by literary scholars and one by an art historian) developed out of a trans-Atlantic collaboration between scholars working in medieval and early modern literature and art history at Stanford University and the Freie Universität Berlin. In a series of workshops, participants presented their physical and textual things – all European in origin, ranging in date from the eighth to the sixteenth century – and discussed these in dialogue with a range of methodological approaches. Traditional literary and art historical analysis was deployed side by side with more recent theoretical work on things, including approaches from actor-network theory, object-oriented ontology, new materiality, ecocriticism, semiotics, and others. With each object we weighed different approaches, exploring the possibilities offered by both old and new interpretive paradigms. One central question emerged from our discussions and underlies all the chapters in this book, which otherwise differ widely in approach: How might we characterize and analyze the intersection and interplay between a thing's material and immaterial qualities?

Things and Thingness: A Brief Review

In recent years the "material turn" has focused scholarly attention on things and the importance of their materiality as a site of cultural production. Things have taken center stage in a wide variety of disciplines, including literary studies, art history, history, anthropology, and sociology. In all of these disciplinary approaches, including ours here, the distinction between a "thing" and an "object" and the relationship between things and humans are fundamental points of debate. Whereas an "object" is a passive recipient of subjective action, a "thing" is not defined by its relationship to a subject. But then how are we to define a "thing"? Is a thing necessarily inanimate, nonhuman, or materially concrete? It seems none of those characteristics must apply. "Things," according to political theorist Jane Bennett, are "vivid entities not entirely reducible to the contexts in which (human) subjects set them."[3] Yet, as literary theorist Bill Brown asserts, the conception of things *as* things implicates an object–human relationship. He distinguishes between things and objects by observing, in accord with Leo Stein, that an object's "thingness" comes to our attention when it stops working for us in its usual way. At such a juncture an object draws our focus to its physical properties and its usual role in our lives: "Forced to use a knife as a screwdriver, you achieve a new recognition of its thingness, its hardness, the shape and size of the handle."[4] The notion of entanglement, which anthropologist Ian Hodder developed as an interpretive concept, captures the "sticky" web of relationships – a kind of dialectic of dependence – that exists between humans and things (as well as things and other things).[5] In our opening example, the dog Petitcreiu exists as an object that can be shown and given, but it is also a thing, since its meaning is renegotiated in relation to each character and it is not fully subsumed within any single interpretation or relationship. Petitcreiu is no mere object; it is an actor that can change the state of human affairs by inspiring wonder, motivating action, or alleviating sorrow. Its thingness is thrown into high relief when Isolde breaks its little bell, whereby it ceases to perform its stated function of relieving sorrow and yet continues to play a role in the narrative.

The study of the agency of things and things as actors has developed in the past decade in the fields of archaeology, anthropology, and sociology to account for the importance of objects in human culture and their function not simply as products of creation or industry, but as constitutive of human relationships and of social action and interaction.[6] Actor-network theory (ANT), associated most closely with sociologist Bruno Latour, provides one framework for thinking about the importance of things and their essential role in the social assemblage that constitutes human society.[7] Indeed, several of the contributions to this volume engage explicitly with Latour's work (see, for example, the chapters by Martin Bleisteiner, Jan-Peer Hartmann, Falk Quenstedt, and Tilo Renz). ANT challenges the primacy of human action and

---

3 Jane Bennett, *Vibrant Matter: A Political Ecology of Things* (Durham, NC: Duke University Press, 2010), 5.

4 Bill Brown, *A Sense of Things* (Chicago: University of Chicago Press, 2004), 74–76, 78. See also Bill Brown, "Thing Theory," *Critical Inquiry* 28 (2001): 1–22.

5 Ian Hodder, *Entangled: An Archaeology of the Relationships between Humans and Things* (Malden, MA: Wiley-Blackwell, 2012).

6 For a general overview, see Dan Hicks, "The Material Cultural Turn: Event and Effects," in *The Oxford Handbook of Material Culture Studies*, ed. Dan Hicks and Mary C. Beaudry (Oxford: Oxford University Press, 2010), 25–98.

7 Bruno Latour, *Reassembling the Social: An Introduction to Actor-Network-Theory* (Oxford: Oxford University Press, 2007). See also earlier theories conceptualizing the idea of networks: Gilles Deleuze and Félix Guattari, *A Thousand Plateaus: Capitalism and Schizophrenia*, trans. Brian Massumi (Minneapolis: University of Minnesota Press, 1987); and Gilles Deleuze and Claire Parnet, *Dialogues* (New York: Columbia University Press, 1987).

agency. While Latour argues that things can have agency, such agency is not to be conflated with subjective or autonomous action. Instead, it means that inanimate things can effect and affect social processes and thus intervene profoundly in human society. No social action, according to Latour, has a primary agent; rather, it is constituted by many different entities that are associated with each other and, together, make up an actor network. It is this network, rather than any one part of it, that produces social (inter)action. Latour's aim is to show that social processes develop out of a hybrid collaboration between human and nonhuman entities, which stand in a symmetrical and nonhierarchical relation to one another.[8]

Psychologist James Gibson has developed the notion of affordance to explain how things can have agency without also having a soul or subjective ability.[9] Affordance theory assumes that things are materially disposed in a specific way and offer options for action. Or, as literary scholar Caroline Levine explains, affordance is the potential inherent or "latent in [a thing's] materials or design."[10] A dagger and a club are both designed to be held at one end and to inflict pain at the other: their physical qualities indicate how they are to be used without requiring further instruction. Gibson remarks: "An affordance is neither an objective property nor a subjective property; or it is both if you like. An affordance cuts across the dichotomy of subjective-objective and helps us to understand its inadequacy."[11] A thing's usage, immediate results, actions, consequences, and so on are the products of many different conditions and relationships.

Things in Literary Studies

Literary studies too have grappled with identifying, defining, and analyzing things. Literary scholar Barbara Johnson has argued for a new consideration of the boundaries between humans and things. Examining a variety of literary texts and artworks, she has shown how people / literary characters and things are closely intertwined and indeed dependent on one another, and she has developed the concepts of "the thingliness of persons" and "the personhood of things."[12] Her work has revealed that in many cultural contexts, the descriptive vocabulary used for things is equally used in reference to people, and vice versa, thus troubling – or even erasing – any boundary between the two. Such fluidity between persons and things is also a fea-

---

8 Latour, *Reassembling the Social*, 76–79.
9 James J. Gibson, *The Ecological Approach to Visual Perception* (Boston: Houghton Mifflin, 1979).
10 Caroline Levine, *Forms: Whole, Rhythm, Hierarchy, Network* (Princeton, NJ: Princeton University Press, 2015), 6. See also Richard Fox, Diamantis Panagiotopoulos, and Christina Tsouparapolou, "Affordanz," in *Materiale Textkulturen: Konzepte – Materialien – Praktiken*, ed. Thomas Meier, Michael R. Ott, and Rebecca Sauer (Berlin: De Gruyter, 2015), 63–70.
11 Gibson, *Ecological Approach*, 129.
12 Barbara Johnson, *Persons and Things* (Cambridge, MA: Harvard University Press, 2008), esp. 231.

ture in medieval and early modern literature. In Chrétien de Troyes's romance *Yvain*, for instance, it is a magic stone that poses the challenge that Yvain must overcome in order to win a wife; Yvain himself is later rendered senseless (rendered thingly?) from despair and must be reanimated by a magic salve.

In medieval and early modern literary studies, the "material turn" has created a shift from questions about human figures and their interactions and conflicts to investigations of the things that surround them. In German studies, Anna Mühlherr's influential work on the *Nibelungenlied* and the *Straßburger Alexander*, along with her coedited volume on *Dingkulturen* (cultures of things), shows how productive a thing-centered approach can be, making a convincing case for viewing plot and narrative not only from the perspective of the figures but also from the standpoint of things.[13] The recent book by Bettina Bildhauer, *Medieval Things* (2020), similarly adopts a thing-oriented perspective, uncovering new angles on familiar narratives and establishing "links between the narration, agency, and materiality of things in medieval German literature."[14]

Just as they do in the physical world, things in literature implicate the senses and can elicit or incite emotion – both for the characters within the diegetic world of the story (*histoire*) and for the audience.[15] Things evoke curiosity; they shock, astound, frighten, disgust, and delight; they can be auratic or mundane; and they can change their meaning and force, depending on character and context. In Wolfram von Eschenbach's *Parzival* (ca. 1210), the knight Gawan arrives at the court of King Vergulaht, who has challenged him to a duel for allegedly killing his father.[16] Gawan is hosted by the king's beautiful sister Antikonie while the king is out hunting. Their flirtation escalates, but as they are about to give in to their sexual attraction, they are rudely interrupted by a knight who calls the armed guard. Gawan and Antikonie flee to a tower, and the unarmed Gawan grabs the bar for securing the door to use as a weapon. Antikonie hands him a chessboard for a shield while she herself hurls chess pieces at the knights, bringing assailants to the ground with each successful strike. Gawan too kills several knights with his makeshift weapon. Thus, in this narrative context, the chess pieces and door bar – mundane objects in the intradiegetic courtly world – provide hope for the desperate lovers and pain and death for their assailants. At the same time, the poet plays with the common symbolism of chess as a game of love and war in a delightfully humorous way. In another example, in

---

13 Anna Mühlherr, Bruno Quast, Heike Sahm, and Monika Schausten, eds., *Dingkulturen: Objekte in Literatur, Kunst und Gesellschaft der Vormoderne* (Berlin: De Gruyter, 2016).

14 Bettina Bildhauer, *Medieval Things: Agency, Materiality, and Narratives of Objects in Medieval German Literature and Beyond* (Columbus: Ohio State University Press, 2020), 15.

15 See Fiona Griffiths and Kathryn Starkey, "Sensing through Objects," in *Sensory Reflections: Traces of Experience in Medieval Artifacts*, ed. Fiona Griffiths and Kathryn Starkey (Berlin: De Gruyter, 2018), 1–21.

16 Wolfram von Eschenbach, *Parzival*, ed. Karl Lachmann, Peter Knecht, and Bernd Schirok (Berlin: De Gruyter, 1998), lines 405,16–410,12.

Wernher der Gartenaere's *Helmbrecht* (after 1250), the peasant upstart Helmbrecht has a beautiful embroidered cap made with courtly scenes of dancing knights and ladies, literary heroes, and birds. Helmbrecht is proud of his cap, which, to him, constitutes his new chosen identity as a knight, but to the peasants around him it is a symbol of his arrogance and a source of anger and disgust, and the poem ends with an evocative image of the cap torn asunder, its embroidered little birds fluttering to the ground.[17] Medieval and early modern texts thus take full advantage not only of the rich thingness of objects with their interpretive possibilities, but also of their emotional and sensory potential. Joachim Knape has asserted that things represent an analogue entry to the world, by means of a rhetoric in which all the senses work together, functioning beyond speech ("jenseits der Sprachlichkeit").[18] In the example of Petitcreiu, the narrator's ability to capture the dog in words seems to break down (although Petitcreiu is actually described in detail), but Tristan's astonishment and the lengths to which he goes to acquire the dog are powerfully expressive of Petitcreiu's ability to trigger (or suppress) emotion even beyond the effect of its magical little bell.

Like the notion of agency, the materiality of things in literature has received much scholarly attention. In their recent collection of short essays on specific literary things, Peter Glasner, Sebastian Winkelsträter, and Birgit Zacke remind us that things in literature are not physical, real-world objects to be touched, held, and inspected, but rather signs that are comprised of words.[19] And yet in the diegetic world of the narrative, things *are* physical and exist concretely for the characters who interact with them, and their materiality is often crucial to the story. The thingness of such objects thus coexists with, and is essential to, their status as rhetorical and poetic figures. In the example of Petitcreiu, Tristan minutely inspects the dog, which is a material thing that he acquires and sends to Isolde, but its significance for the story also lies in its symbolic and poetic functions. Literary things can be highly complex: they are given material characteristics that refer to common objects or push the boundaries of the imagination; they function in a variety of ways immaterially as poetic figures such as metaphor, symbol, and allegory; and at the same time, they effect and affect social relationships in their narrative worlds.

---

17 Wernher der Gärtner, *Helmbrecht*, ed. Fritz Tschirch (Stuttgart: Reclam, 1986), lines 20–130, 1886–1889.

18 Joachim Knape, *Die Dinge: Ihr Bild, ihr Design und ihre Rhetorik* (Wiesbaden: Harrassowitz, 2019), 22.

19 Peter Glasner, Sebastian Winkelsträter, and Birgit Zacke, "Einführendes in das *Abecedarium* mittelalterlicher Dingkultur," in *Abecedarium: Erzählte Dinge im Mittelalter*, ed. Peter Glasner, Sebastian Winkelsträter, and Birgit Zacke (Berlin: Schwabe, 2019), 9–25. On the problem of the materiality of things in literary texts, see also Martina Wernli and Alexander Kling, "Von erzählten und erzählenden Dingen," in *Das Verhältnis von* res *und* verba: *Zu den Narrativen der Dinge*, ed. Martina Wernli and Alexander Kling (Freiburg: Rombach, 2018), 7–31.

In the visual arts too, which in the Middle Ages dealt primarily with religious themes, artists experimented with the material representation of the spiritual, using refined skills and strategies (framing, composition, gold leaf, interplay between text and image, etc.) not only to depict the ineffable power of God but also to help the devotee spiritually transcend the mortal realm (see the contribution by Iris Helffenstein). Unlike the things written about in literature, medieval artworks, and the materials used to produce them, have a concrete, physical reality and presence in the viewer's world, which poses different challenges and questions. Different aspects of the materials used and experimented with played a role in both the production and the reception of artworks: these materials' origin, their cost and value, their visual and haptic qualities, their physical qualities (how they can be tooled, shaped, and worked – their affordances), and the different meanings assigned to them not only in religious contexts but also in natural history or magical practices.[20] As scholars have shown, for reliquaries, paintings, sculptures, crucifixes, book illuminations, and other devotional objects, materiality played an important role in activating a devotee's experience or contemplation of the ineffable.[21] In art, as in literature, materiality and immateriality are two sides of the same coin.

To analyze things in literature and art is to consider them in their symbolic, representational, or semiotic function and in their material presence, and it is to query their agency in social processes and practices. An examination of the thingness of artifacts from the medieval and early modern past – that is, of how they intersected with and shaped human life – can productively complicate and enhance rhetorical and aesthetic analysis. E. Jane Burns's study of silk in medieval French literature, for example, uncovers networks of gendered cultural exchange and production that run parallel to aesthetic reflections on fine cloth in these texts.[22] In the epic narrative *King Rother*, the eponymous king secretly gives artfully crafted shoes to the princess he seeks to wed (against the wishes of her father). The gift of shoes in the context of Rother's wooing expedition invokes the customary ritual of a bride

---

20 See, for example, Christy Anderson, Anne Dunlop, and Pamela H. Smith, eds., *The Matter of Art: Materials, Practices, Cultural Logics, c. 1250–1750* (Manchester: Manchester University Press, 2015); Ann-Sophie Lehmann, "How Materials Make Meaning," in *Meaning in Materials, 1400–1800*, ed. Ann-Sophie Lehmann, Frits Scholten, and H. Perry Chapman (Leiden: Brill, 2013), 6–27; and Michael Baxandall, *The Limewood Sculptors of Renaissance Germany* (New Haven: Yale University Press, 1980).
21 Foundational studies include Herbert L. Kessler, *Spiritual Seeing: Picturing God's Invisibility in Medieval Art* (Philadelphia: University of Pennsylvania Press, 2000); Jeffrey F. Hamburger, *The Visual and the Visionary: Art and Female Spirituality in Late Medieval Germany* (New York: Zone Books, 1998); and Caroline Walker Bynum, *Christian Materiality: An Essay on Religion in Late Medieval Europe* (New York: Zone Books, 2011).
22 E. Jane Burns, *Sea of Silk: A Textile Geography of Women's Work in Medieval French Literature* (Philadelphia: University of Pennsylvania Press, 2009).

slipping into a new pair of shoes to symbolize her new role as wife.[23] What significance does this social practice, which is not explicitly addressed in the story, have for our understanding of the poem? At the very least, it complicates the narrative, raising a series of questions. Is the marriage between Rother and his princess bride formally sealed when she slips on the shoes? Do the princess's acceptance of the gift and her request to meet Rother indicate that she enters willingly into marriage negotiations, contrary to her father's wishes? Or are the gift and its acceptance merely a foreshadowing of the marriage to come, and are they even meant to be humorous – a perversion of ritual practice? Whatever the answer, the social significance of shoes in marriage practice enriches our understanding of the poem, which in turn plays with social norms in an aesthetically productive way. To return to our opening example of Petitcreiu, the little dog with its bell is fully entangled in its literary world and is an aesthetic object, but it also raises questions about, for instance, homosocial relationships, the power dynamics of gift giving, and the negotiation of desire – social concerns that point outside the text to conceptions of human relationships.

Materiality and Immateriality

Materiality, in the context of this book, refers to the physical qualities of things and the presence they have in a story or a work of art. But this is not to say that such material existence is simple, static, or passive. Instead, throughout this book the contributors reflect the notion that material objects are, as philosopher Manuel DeLanda writes with regard to the notion of a "new materiality," comprised of "active matter endowed with its own tendencies and capacities, engaged in its own divergent, open-ended evolution, animated from within by immanent patterns of being and becoming."[24] Meanwhile, the immateriality of things in text and the visual arts functions on two narrative levels. Within the diegetic world, represented objects – treated-as-real – have both material qualities (size, shape, physicality, etc.) and immaterial qualities (powers, roles played in social interactions, sacredness, etc.). At the same time, things in texts and images also exhibit another (extradiegetic) level of immaterial qualities including figurative meaning and semiotic functions, their roles as narrative tools, and so on.

The interplay between the materiality and immateriality of the things featured in this book is varied and complex. Moreover, sometimes the artists and authors who created the artworks and texts presented here seem to highlight this interplay. Some of the represented objects themselves raise the question that Christopher Hutchinson poses in his contribution: "What is the difference between a thing and

23 Kathryn Starkey, "Tristan Slippers: An Image of Adultery on a Symbol of Marriage?," in *Medieval Fabrications: Dress, Textiles, Clothwork and Other Cultural Imaginings*, ed. E. Jane Burns (New York: Palgrave, 2004), 35–53, at 41–44.
24 Manuel DeLanda, "The New Materiality," *Architectural Design* 85, no. 5 (2015): 16–21, at 16.

an image of a thing?" The image of the brick mold that he investigates both represents a physical thing – a brick mold – and *is* a (different) physical thing – the
paper page of a printed book. The format of the book and its text play with the in-
compatibility between these two physical things. In a different kind of interplay,
Hans Tucher's letter from Jerusalem, presented in the chapter by Mareike Reisch,
has such spiritual importance as a physical object sent from the Holy Land that it
is repeatedly handled and ultimately worn away. Additionally, the line between
what is material and what is immaterial does not always lie where we might expect
it to. In his chapter, Björn Buschbeck identifies a prayed mantle for the Virgin Mary
as an instance of "spiritual concreteness," an imagined thing that is made material
and present through devotional reading and practice. A further example can be seen
in Falk Quenstedt's chapter, which highlights Hartmann von Aue's comparison of
storytelling to saddle making, with the ingredients of narrative treated as raw materials to be shaped and crafted.

Literary things have long been a focus in work on rhetorical traditions, on practices of allegory and ekphrasis, on figural interpretation, and on the representational
and symbolic nature of objects.[25] From the perspective of some medievalists, such
work is fundamentally incompatible with approaches that consider the agency of
things or that follow the "material turn" in taking seriously the materiality of things
as physical objects and seeking to open up new perspectives on thing–human relationships.[26] But as our group discussed the various things that are the focus of these
chapters – panel paintings, landscapes, weapons, machines, knightly accoutrements, animals, books, intelligent staircases, and imagined cloaks – it became apparent that in each case both the immaterial *and* material qualities of a given object
were critical to the conceptualization of its thingness in its medieval or early modern
context.

As material objects, things perform a variety of roles in literature, including the
creation of an immersive environment and the setting of the scene for the story to
unfold. In this capacity, the representation of material objects goes hand in hand
with the emphasis on visuality, and sensory experience more generally, in medieval
and early modern literature.[27] In literary texts there is great attention paid to things
and their description, and this attention is essential to the creation of imaginary

---

25 See, for example, Friedrich Ohly, "Vom geistigen Sinn des Wortes im Mittelalter," in *Schriften zur mittelalterlichen Bedeutungsforschung*, ed. Friedrich Ohly (Darmstadt: Wissenschaftliche Buchgesell-schaft, 1977), 1–31; Kumler and Lakey, "*Res et significatio*: The Material Sense of Things in the Middle Ages," *Gesta* 51, no. 1 (2012): 1–17; and Haiko Wandhoff, *Ekphrasis: Kunstbeschreibungen und virtuelle Räume in der Literatur des Mittelalters* (Berlin: De Gruyter, 2003).
26 See Anna Mühlherr, "Einleitung," in Mühlherr et al., *Dingkulturen*, 1–20; and Christoph Schanze, "Dinge erzählen im Mittelalter: Zur narratologischen Analyse von Objekten in der höfischen Epik," *KulturPoetik: Zeitschrift für Kulturgeschichtliche Literaturwissenschaft* 16, no. 2 (2016): 153–172, esp. 170.
27 Kathryn Starkey and Horst Wenzel, "Visuality in German Courtly Literature," *Oxford German Stud-ies* 37 (2008): 130–159.

spaces and worlds.[28] Tapestries, furniture, architecture, linden trees, weapons, and magical objects are spatial markers that situate a story or a scene in a feast hall, a bedchamber, a chapel, a battlefield, or a *locus amoenus*.

Ekphrasis was a popular literary technique, often – at least in its medieval incarnation – used to describe particularly marvelous or beautiful objects, like Petitcreiu, or the horse's tack in Hartmann von Aue's *Erec* (see the contribution by Falk Quenstedt).[29] Ekphrasis immerses readers at extended length and in great detail in an imagined sensory, especially visual, experience, sometimes creating a world within a world.[30] In medieval narrative, ekphrases might be used to perform a whole host of literary functions – providing a different perspective on the story, creating suspense by delaying plot development, or even introducing an additional storyline or narrative time.[31] Ekphrastic things are immaterial in the sense that they only exist in the imagination, and yet ekphrases insist on the materiality of the thing described. In these scripted visual experiences, text and object are interdependent – one cannot exist without the other.

The function of literary things thus goes beyond helping to create an immersive literary experience: they are crucial for plot development, and they are constitutive of social relationships and agentive in their effect on human society. The agency of things becomes particularly apparent in scenes in which they fail. In *Parzival*, when the title hero finds his way to the Grail castle of Munsalvaesche the first time, he is witness to a ceremony featuring many things: a special sword, a beautiful mantle, exotic ivory pedestals for the table, candles, a bleeding lance, and even the Grail itself. In the Grail ceremony the presentation and proliferation of spectacular objects is supposed to motivate Parzival to ask his uncle a question. However, when these things fail to elicit the essential question, the Grail society is powerless to intervene.

Things in literature also have social meaning, as we see in the example of gift exchange, which is an important feature of medieval and early modern literature, just as it is in premodern real-world politics.[32] As art historian Cecily Hilsdale writes with regard to prestige objects given as gifts, they "operate on an optative register as

---

28 Wernli and Kling, "Von erzählten und erzählenden Dingen," 7.
29 See Wandhoff, *Ekphrasis*, 69–106.
30 Ruth Webb, *Ekphrasis, Imagination and Persuasion in Ancient Rhetorical Theory and Practice* (Farnham: Ashgate, 2009).
31 Kathryn Starkey, "Time Travel: Ekphrasis and Narrative in Medieval German Literature," in *Anschauung und Anschaulichkeit: Visualisierung im Wahrnehmen, Lesen und Denken*, ed. Hans Adler and Sabine Gross (Munich: Fink Verlag, 2015), 179–193.
32 See Marcel Mauss, *The Gift*, trans. Jane I. Guyer (Chicago: HAU Books, 2016). On gift exchange specifically in literary texts, see Gisela Ecker, *Giftige Gaben: Über Tauschprozesse in der Literatur* (Munich: Wilhelm Fink, 2008); and Gisela Ecker, "Gabe," in *Handbuch Literatur & materielle Kultur*, ed. Susanne Scholz and Ulrike Vedder (Berlin: De Gruyter, 2018), 403–405. With a special focus on gift exchange in medieval literature, see Marion Oswald, *Gabe und Gewalt: Studien zur Logik und Poetik der Gabe in der frühhöfischen Erzählliteratur* (Göttingen: Vandenhoeck & Ruprecht, 2004).

active agents of social bond and fracture and they oblige and orchestrate power relations among individuals and sacred economies."[33] In literary worlds, too, the act of
gift giving and the gifts themselves play a critical role in creating friendships, establishing social hierarchy, and achieving peace (or causing war) – the nature of the gift
is often key to its interpretation. The genre of the heroic epic is particularly preoccu-
pied with hierarchy, bonds of obligation, and social maneuvering, and gift giving in
this genre is fraught with anxiety because it is not just representative of these social
relations but constitutive of them.[34] In the Middle High German epic narrative *Ortnit*
(ca. 1230), King Ortnit's pagan father-in-law gives him the valuable and exotic gift of
three dragon eggs – seemingly an appropriate prestige gift between kings. But these
eggs hatch, and the dragons that emerge wreak havoc on Ortnit's lands, ultimately
killing the king – which also speaks to the weight such gifts can have as a narrative
plot point. In the courtly romance, by contrast, in which knights typically engage in a
series of quests to fulfill their potential, gifts often provide a key to their identity. In
Ulrich von Zatzikhoven's *Lanzelet* (after 1194), a fairy gives Lanzelet a magic tent that
is intended to prevent his loss of memory by reminding him of his past and informing
him about his future.[35] This tent constitutes a material connection to the fairyland
where he grew up, and it also indicates his destiny, showing him the identity of
his future wife Iblis by means of an integrated magic mirror.[36]

Real-World Things

Things also play important roles in texts traditionally categorized as nonfictional,
such as lapidaries, bestiaries, travelogues, chronicles, atlases, and encyclopedias.
In book 3 of the *Otia imperialia* (ca. 1210 – 1214), an encyclopedic tome written for
Emperor Otto IV (1175 – 1218), the cleric author Gervase of Tilbury presents a plethora
of natural and spiritual "marvels."[37] In compiling his material, Gervase drew on several antique sources but also added marvelous things of his own experience or invention. While the things he presents are diverse, they are all intended to elicit astonishment and fuel the reader's imagination.[38] Moreover, they are identified by
geographic origin and thus present a particular perspective on the world, offering

---

33 Cecily J. Hilsdale, "Gift," *Studies in Iconography* 33 (2012): 171–182, at 178.
34 William Ian Miller, "Gift, Sale, Payment, Raid: Case Studies in the Negotiation and Classification
of Exchange in Medieval Iceland," *Speculum* 61 (1986): 18–50, at 23.
35 Ulrich von Zatzikhoven, *Lanzelet: Text – Übersetzung – Kommentar*, ed. Florian Kragl (Berlin: De
Gruyter, 2013), lines 4705–4939.
36 See Pia Selmayr, *Der Lauf der Dinge: Wechselverhältnisse zwischen Raum, Ding und Figur bei der
narrativen Konstitution von Anderwelten im "Wigalois" und im "Lanzelet"* (Frankfurt: Lang, 2017), 180–
188.
37 Gervase of Tilbury, *Otia imperialia: Recreation for an Emperor*, ed. S. E. Banks and J. W. Binns, Oxford Medieval Texts (Oxford: Clarendon Press, 2002), 548–549.
38 Gervase of Tilbury, *Otia imperialia*, 558–559.

the reader a glimpse into its farthest reaches. In literary and nonliterary texts, things often provide a connection to, or lens through which to view, exotic and foreign realms. The French poem *Ordene de chevalerie* (ca. 1220), which Mae Velloso-Lyons discusses in her chapter, is one example: in it, Saladin's foreignness is made sense of through the depiction of his interactions with Christianized things.

The description of real-world things in texts, such as plants for distilling (see Christopher Hutchinson's contribution) or the planet Earth (see Leonardo Velloso-Lyons's contribution), provides entryways into the state of knowledge in the extratextual world at the time. Medieval clerical discourses expound on the nature of things – such as gemstones – that could be used for curing illnesses. Literature too drew on such scholarly discourses, contextualizing information and presenting it as part of a story. Thus, for example, in *Parzival* Wolfram von Eschenbach describes the Grail king Anfortas lying among specific gemstones that were thought to capture cosmic rays that could help him recover from his wound.[39] In Ulrich von Zatzikhoven's *Lanzelet*, the title hero's optimistic constitution is attributed to his environment as a young boy – he was brought up in a fairy castle, surrounded by certain gemstones that have the power to make people happy forever.[40] Gemstones, like other things of the natural world, were viewed as representative of the micro- and macrocosmos, and were thought to interact with or capture the forces of the cosmos in certain ways.[41] For readers of both nonfictional and narrative texts, things provide a point of entrance into such systems of knowledge and belief.

Medieval texts – literary and nonliterary alike – often focus precisely on the immaterial aspects of things: their histories, their effects, the emotions they engender, their cosmic place in the universe, and the senses they arouse. In their work on the history of science, Lorraine Daston and Katharine Park examine medieval and early modern marvels, identifying their epistemological status in the historical development of scientific discourse. They address the affective responses that things of this sort elicit, such as astonishment or curiosity – responses that are highly productive for the pursuit of knowledge. In their discussion of church treasuries in the High Middle Ages, they note that, in addition to reliquaries and liturgical objects, these treasuries held exotic things such as precious stones, ostrich eggs, and corals that were seamlessly integrated into a Christian context of symbolism.[42] Such exotic marvels can take on a variety of functions independent of their pricelessness or rarity: they can be carriers of magic properties and miracle stories, or they can have biblical

---

39 Wolfram von Eschenbach, *Parzival*, lines 790,18 – 792,5.
40 Ulrich von Zatzikhoven, *Lanzelet*, lines 206 – 240.
41 On gemstones in German medieval literature, see Ulrich Engelen, *Die Edelsteine in der deutschen Dichtung des 12. und 13. Jahrhunderts* (Munich: Wilhelm Fink, 1978), 216.
42 Lorraine Daston and Katharine Park, *Wonders and the Order of Nature 1150 – 1750* (New York: Zone Books, 2001), 67 – 69. See also Philippe Cordez, *Treasure, Memory, Nature: Church Objects in the Middle Ages* (London: Turnhout, 2020).

associations; as manifestations of God's creation, they can be used for meditation on the divine. In this way they mediate between the physical and spiritual worlds.[43]

Religious and Parareligious Things

Karl-Heinz Kohl has argued that sacral objects – crosses, reliquaries, amulets, religious panel paintings – are, in essence, pragmatically useless and often have no practical value. It is only within a discursive context or a ritual practice that their immaterial, spiritual function – their true value – is revealed.[44] In his study on the ways in which objects' meanings change as they are moved from church treasuries into museums, Stefan Laube examines the importance of context and particular spaces for creating the meaning of sacral and cult objects. He observes that sacral objects differ from profane ones primarily because they are viewed within spaces marked as sacral, which shapes their perception, and that when cult objects are moved from a sacral to a secular space, they can lose or change their immaterial qualities even while their material qualities remain intact.[45] The understanding of the immaterial qualities of such things is thus a dynamic and discursive process that takes context into account. For this reason, it is crucial to consider the specific devotional contexts of the panel painting, the letter from Jerusalem, and the communal prayers that Iris Helffenstein, Mareike Reisch, and Björn Buschbeck discuss respectively, in order to identify the particular forms of materiality and immateriality that lend these things their spiritual significance.

Things can also be important and significant because of qualities that draw from the parareligious context of magic.[46] In the Middle High German heroic epic *Nibelungenlied* (ca. 1200), Siegfried's cloak of invisibility is crucial to the story because of its powers, but the garment itself is not otherwise described in terms of its appearance or physical qualities.[47] Literary texts often tap into magical traditions, practices, and

---

43 Daston and Park, *Wonders*, 67–69, 75–77.

44 Karl-Heinz Kohl, *Die Macht der Dinge: Geschichte und Theorie sakraler Objekte* (Munich: C. H. Beck, 2003), 151–152.

45 Stefan Laube, *Von der Reliquie zum Ding: Heiliger Ort – Wunderkammer – Museum* (Berlin: Akademie-Verlag, 2012), 9.

46 Natalie Armitage and Ceri Houlbrook, eds., *The Materiality of Magic: An Artifactual Investigation into Ritual Practices and Popular Beliefs* (Oxford: Oxbow Books, 2015); Dietrich Boschung and Jan N. Bremmer, eds., *The Materiality of Magic* (Paderborn: Wilhelm Fink, 2015); Henry Maguire, *Rhetoric, Nature and Magic in Byzantine Art* (Aldershot: Ashgate, 1998). See also Genevra Alisoun Kornbluth, "Early Medieval Crystal Amulets: Secular Instruments of Protection and Healing," in *The Sacred and the Secular in Medieval Healing*, ed. Barbara S. Bowers and Linda Migl Keyser (London: Routledge, 2016), 143–181.

47 Anna Mühlherr has offered a convincing thing-oriented reading of the poem, analyzing the cloak of invisibility and uncovering its story independent of its use by Siegfried. Anna Mühlherr, "Nicht mit

beliefs, particularly with regard to such objects – magic swords, cloaks of invisibility, healing salves, stones or cloaks of virtue, and Petitcreiu's little bell are just a few examples. Such magic things function to transmit knowledge, invest characters with superhuman qualities, or create connections between human society and transcendent realms, such as the fairy world, the earthly paradise, or hell.[48] As their importance lies in their agency over human actions, the materiality and the physical presence of these magic things are often given short shrift in literary texts, while at the same time their "biography" is recounted in the story. The *Nibelungenlied* explains how Siegfried acquired the cloak of invisibility, although it is silent about the cloak's physical qualities. Similarly, we are told that the bandage used to heal Erec in Hartmann von Aue's Middle High German retelling of Chrétien de Troyes's courtly romance was created by the fairy Famurgan, and this spawns a ninety-line excursus about the fairy. Yet the bandage itself (its color, size, smell, feel), although crucial to Erec's healing, does not warrant a description – we do not even find out how it is applied.[49]

Anthropologist Igor Kopytoff first developed the idea of a "thing biography" as a way of thinking and writing about objects that anthropologists encounter. Composing such biographies of things means understanding artifacts – from their origins on – in their sociological contexts, even as these change over time.[50] The concept has been productively adopted by medievalists and early modernists in a variety of disciplines, including museum studies, art history, and literature.[51] Such "thing biographies" in medieval literature can contribute to things' material value and their immaterial significance as well as their power and agency within the text. Even mundane things take on significance if incorporated into hermeneutic practices. The knightly accoutrements that Mae Velloso-Lyons discusses in her contribution to this volume are both items that clothe the body of a knight and symbols that signify within a broader conceptual notion of knighthood – each item takes on symbolic or allegorical meaning. As Aden Kumler and Christopher Lakey have observed, the allegorizing and exegesis of such quotidian objects "recognize an expanded field of materialist hermeneutics, a medieval vision of the world in which not only *creatura* but also *artifacta* and *ornamenta* might signify, even in tropological or soteriological terms."[52] Yet, returning to our—albeit secular and non-quotidian—opening example

---

rechten Dingen, nicht mit dem rechten Ding, nicht am rechten Ort: Zur *tarnkappe* und zum *hort* im *Nibelungenlied*," *Beiträge zur Geschichte der deutschen Sprache und Literatur* 131 (2009): 461–492.
48 Britta Maria Wittchow, *Erzählte mediale Prozesse: Medientheoretische Perspektiven auf den "Reinfried von Braunschweig" und den "Apollonius von Tyrland"* (Berlin: De Gruyter, 2020).
49 Hartmann von Aue, *Erec: Text und Kommentar*, ed. Manfred Günter Scholz, trans. Susanne Held (Frankfurt: Deutscher Klassiker-Verlag, 2004), lines 5132–5255.
50 Igor Kopytoff, "The Cultural Biography of Things: Commoditization as Process," in *The Social Life of Things: Commodities in Cultural Perspective*, ed. Arjun Appadurai (Cambridge: Cambridge University Press, 1986), 64–91, at 66–67.
51 On its use in literature, see Bildhauer, *Medieval Things*, esp. 93–129 (ch. 3).
52 Kumler and Lakey, "*Res et significatio*," 6.

of Petitcreiu one final time, Gottfried's poem presents the dog's biography, explaining that it was made as a love-gift in the fairyland of Avalon by a "wise goddess." The dog's "thing biography" both establishes it as an object, and shapes its function, as well as its interpretation within the "new" context of Tristan and Isolde's story. Its magical and mythical origin further imbue it with a spiritual significance that transcends the story of Tristan and Isolde, placing their love story in a broader model of passionate love that Gottfried develops throughout his telling of the story.

Chapter Summaries

The medieval German examples invoked throughout this introduction establish the texture of many issues at stake in the book as a whole; the ten remaining chapters extend the discussion in various directions, uncovering new aspects of things in medieval European literature and visual arts and exploring the questions: When is an object a thing? In what sense are the imagined things of literature, or the diagrams of scientific discourse, things? When does a landscape become a thing? What is the relationship between a thing's thingness and its allegorical or symbolic meaning? What roles do narrated things play in the stories in which they appear? What dynamics come into play when human figures and things interact?

The first three chapters deal with things central to devotional practice. Iris Helfenstein examines the interplay between materiality and immateriality in a late medieval small-format panel painting by Lorenzo Monaco, now held in the Lindenau-Museum in Altenburg. The panel painting is representative of devotional objects created around 1400 in the context of monastic and mendicant orders. These fostered an affective model of devotion in which the devotee paid particular attention to the material and sensory aspects of the Passion, imagining it with emotional and physical intensity. Devotional objects were touched, kissed, and closely inspected; they were made to be handled. The Altenburg panel depicts Christ's lifeless body hanging limp on the cross and Saints Benedict, Romuald, and Francis of Assisi at his feet – the latter clutching the base of the cross with blood streaming from his stigmata. The techniques that Lorenzo uses – particularly his skilled illusionistic depiction of the cross and the rock, which makes the Crucifixion appear to protrude three-dimensionally into the space of the viewer; his use of the stippling technique to create unusual visual effects and evoke other forms of art; and his representation of blood at different stages of coagulation – emphasize the painting's materiality and insist on the physical presence of the divine. At the same time, however, the panel gestures toward Christ's eternal life after death, thus also invoking the immaterial realm of heaven. In this way, materials and techniques of painting create a devotional object that negotiates between the material and the immaterial.

In a much more pragmatic manner, as Mareike Reisch shows, the letter sent by the pilgrim Hans Tucher to his brother Endres from Jerusalem in 1479 mediates between Hans's experience of the Holy Land and the experience of his readers far away in his hometown of Nuremberg. Reisch's chapter raises questions about letters as things, and about the functions and meanings of their particular materiality. First, as an object from Jerusalem, the letter was a prized thing that transported with it, according to Reisch, the aura of holiness. The paper letter was handled so much that it quickly deteriorated, causing Endres to preserve its content by transcribing it and binding it into a book that also included a copy of the printed account of his brother's pilgrimage, a chronicle, and a drawing of the Via Dolorosa. Through a focus on the fate of the letter and its transcription by Endres, Reisch probes the relationship between the letter's content and its physical presence, and the relative importance of the one versus the other. Second, the letter describes the holy sites of Jerusalem by transposing the city's topography, particularly the layout of the Holy Sepulcher, onto the city of Nuremberg and its St. Sebaldus Church, thus attempting to make Hans Tucher's experience of the holy places "imaginatively tangible" to his Nuremberg readers. Finally, in his letter, Hans requests that Endres and others pray for his safe return home. Such intercessory prayers, sent across land and sea like the letter itself, create a spiritual connection between the pilgrim and his community at home. The content of the letter, its physical qualities as a thing associated with Jerusalem, and its request for prayers create a multifaceted experience for Hans Tucher's readers, one that connects them in different ways to the Holy Land and to the pilgrimage experience.

Like the chapter by Iris Helffenstein, Björn Buschbeck's chapter deals with the negotiation of materiality in devotional practice. But in contrast to Helffenstein, who begins with the physical object of the panel painting and traces the ways in which it evokes immaterial, transcendental truth, Buschbeck focuses on craft prayers, exercises in which devotees create imagined objects out of the raw material of prayers. Such devotional exercises conceive of themselves as a spiritual form of labor resulting in a material object. Buschbeck examines in detail the *Alemannic Coat of Mary*, a text proposing and describing an exercise whose purpose is to create a luxurious and detailed mantle for the Virgin Mary, arguing that this mantle, a thing created only in the devotees' minds and hearts, was understood to be "spiritually concrete" – and not a mere figment of the imagination. Such rare and costly prayed things were "sublime objects that transcend[ed] the border between the earthly and the heavenly." The Virgin's mantle and other such prayed things challenge our modern notion of materiality, positing a virtual materiality that is imbued with significance through Christian exegesis and interpretation. The devotees imagine the creation of Mary's cloak, in which each of them can participate through prayer; the time and effort they put into their prayers is envisioned as the work of fabricating some part of the cloak: a length of cloth, decoration, or braiding, for example. The text insists on the material nature of the cloak and the possibility of breaking it down into discrete acts of production, the result of which then provides the foundation for an imagined encounter with Mary herself, who wears the garment. Yet the immaterial nature of the mantle is equally important – its allegorical meaning and the devotion-

al environment of focused imagination it requires enable devotees to achieve spiritual access to the Virgin.

The next two chapters consider the significance and meaning given to battle gear
– especially attire and other personal accoutrements – in writings about knighthood.
Similar to Buschbeck, Mae Velloso-Lyons probes the relationship between material
objects and their symbolic significance. In the medieval French poem *Ordene de che-*
valerie, the sultan of Egypt and Syria, Saladin, asks his prisoner, Hugh II of St. Omer,
Prince of Tiberias, to teach him about the significance of objects associated with
knighthood. Hugh takes on a pedagogical role, itemizing the objects and interpreting
them according to Christian soteriology. The objects in question are mundane – undergarments, tunic, stockings, sword, spurs, etc. – falling into the category of objects
that can be worn or wielded rather than specific, unique things. The knight's accoutrements have a ritualized significance that lies in interpretive practice: Hugh
claims, for example, that the knight's black silk stockings expose man's mortality
and compel him to live humbly. Interestingly, Mae Velloso-Lyons questions whether
or not this poem can indeed be used as a source demonstrating commonly accepted
symbolic functions in actually practiced rites. Presented in the context of a discussion between a Christian and a pagan, the particular interpretation of these objects
establishes an epistemological divide that cannot be breached, since, as Velloso-
Lyons argues, these things are treated as "sensory manifestations of spiritual
truth," and understanding this truth requires a particular material "literacy" that
is specific to Christian practices. The presentation of this supposed epistemological
divide reveals the poem as being skewed toward Christian chauvinism, intolerant of
heretics (including the Albigensians/Cathars), and even intended to foment support
for violent crusade. This is done by speciously presenting a specific, situated material
literacy as if it were objective universal truth.

Martin Bleisteiner's chapter offers a rather different perspective on the trappings
of chivalry presented in the early fifteenth-century Middle English *Alliterative Morte*
Arthure. Whereas the *Ordene de chevalerie* focuses on the significance of things and
their correct interpretation in terms of Christian knighthood in the context of the Crusades, the *Alliterative Morte Arthure* undercuts any attempt to glorify knighthood and
chivalry. The poem is replete with material objects of all kinds, especially weapons
and armor. Yet despite the *Morte*'s obvious fascination with these items and their aesthetic appeal, no allegorical description or interpretation elevates these tools of battle. Instead, they become part of a blood-soaked landscape filled with maimed and
dead bodies, in which martial accoutrements, knights, and horses turn into assemb-
lages in the Latourian sense, hybrid entities united in the pursuit of war and destruction. Ultimately the things of battle do not protect their human wielders, but instead
threaten to overwhelm them. The effect of this mass of weapons and the countless
acts of violence in which they are implicated is utterly depersonalizing: death is inevitable and comes for everyone. In the *Morte*, the excess of objects (and, we might
say, paucity of things) reveals the fragility of the Arthurian world, exposes its de-

structive potential, and ultimately showcases the end of an era – or at least the end of a genre.

A different kind of landscape is the focus of Jan-Peer Hartmann's chapter on the eighth-century *Vita Guthlaci*. Drawing on Latour's notion of the assemblage and the new materialisms of thinkers such as Karen Barad, Hartmann views the desolate English fenland to which the hermit Guthlac retreats as a conglomerate of different material and immaterial forces and entities in dynamic relation to one another. The actors in this hybrid scenario even include literature and imagination themselves: the *Vita Guthlaci*, according to Hartmann, subtly depicts potential signs of prior human presence in the landscape and, at the same time, the construction of this landscape as an eremitic desert thanks partly to the influence of hagiographical literature. The *Vita* focuses on the process by which Guthlac achieves integration into (as opposed to colonization of) the landscape and on its transformation into a holy space: "the mechanisms by which the *Vita* imagines [the fenland's] physical and semiotic transformation from a peripheral border region into an integrated part of an imagined early-medieval British religious landscape." As such, the *Vita* provides an account of the process by which an assemblage is transformed. However, this representation of the Fens of eastern England stands in contrast to historical reality: the Fens were radically changed by human intervention before, during, and after the composition of the text, making the *Vita* the narrative of an alternate "agential possibility" that never came to be.

The next two chapters focus our attention on the narrative and social functions of specific things in literary texts. Falk Quenstedt draws on ANT in his analysis of a much-debated passage in Hartmann von Aue's *Erec*, in which the narrator engages in a lengthy excursus on a marvelous horse and its tack. The passage is generally regarded as a reflection on fictionality, but Quenstedt's interpretation of it has broader implications for our understanding of courtly narrative in general. He argues that the passage constitutes a disturbance, in the Latourian sense, that reveals the specific components, or figurations, of narrative. Courtly narrative, according to Quenstedt, is a network, and the processes of narrative production are its actors. As a network, narrative has its own characteristics and its own governing principles – and this is particularly important when it comes to truth claims and the incorporation of marvelous objects, both points of contention for medieval critics of the courtly romance. Latour's notion of the network thus seems to map onto Hartmann's digression in a productive way to reveal a critical moment of medieval theorizing about courtly narrative. Moreover, while one might consider narrative itself to be medium rather than matter, as Quenstedt observes, analogies made to other crafts in the passage – for example, goldsmithing and saddle making – present narrative as a craft in which a story is manufactured from the "raw" materials of time, processes of oral or written narration, imagination, etc. It is thus conceived as something material, even independent of any actual physical manifestation in a manuscript.

In the next chapter, Tilo Renz explores the essential roles that objects play in the formation of the utopian medieval community of Crisa in Heinrich of Neustadt's

Apollonius von Tyrland. He shows that ANT's claims that objects both gain agency within networks of different actors and contribute to community building hold true for ideal societies developed in medieval literature as well. Heinrich took poetic license in his translation of a late antique source, adding the lengthy passage about Crisa, a utopian society to which marvelous objects – a wheel, a fountain, a stair-case, and a pillar – contribute in a significant way by controlling the borders and preserving the community's integrity, allowing strangers to enter only if they fulfill certain moral and ethical conditions. Unexpectedly, through their important role in migratory processes, objects also foster the community's evolution. The objects have these effects, as Renz shows, not by acting on their own, but by acting together with human and divine agents (the goddess Venus) as part of a larger network.

Two final essays focus on the printed book and ways of reading in the early modern period. As mentioned above, Christopher Hutchinson starts his chapter with the deceptively simple question, "What is the difference between a thing and an image of a thing?" He identifies a paradox in Hieronymus Brunschwig's innovative distillation handbook, a printed book that instructs its readers to cut a depicted mold out of its pages and use it to make bricks for building a distillation furnace. Yet cutting out this mold, which is printed on a double-sided page, will create a hole in the book, dis-rupting its text and, in a sense, drawing attention to its particular thingness as the page of a book. Hutchinson uses this image of a mold as an opening to explore "how printed books represent the materiality of things" – this is a particularly com-plex question in the case of Brunschwig, whose ambivalent notion of materiality was informed by alchemy, itself viewed as a means to transform and even transcend mat-ter. Indeed, as Hutchinson reveals, Brunschwig's book is not only a treatise on the practical aspects of distilling – an example of the popular genre of the artisanal man-ual – but also a reflection on "the material and immaterial components that inhabit things." Although it purports to present real-world objects and practices in ways that allow readers to pragmatically engage with them, many of its images instead present idealized forms and improbable things that are not reflective of actual artisanal prac-tice. Throughout the book, images thus invoke not only the material qualities of things but also the immaterial qualities that matter is "inflected by" (mythic associ-ations, aesthetics, etc.) – a tension that imbues the brick mold.

Leonardo Velloso-Lyons too considers the intersection between physical things, imagined things, and reading in the context of scientific discourses that emerge in the sixteenth century. He places Abraham Ortelius's atlas *Theatrum orbis terrarum* (1570) into dialogue with the "machine of the world" imagined in canto 10 of Luís de Camões's *Os Lusíadas* (1572). The highly complex poetic description of the ma-chine of the world not only invites readers to imagine the world from a "God-like" perspective but provides a model for reading the world that is relevant to six-teenth-century atlases, such as the one by Ortelius. Crucial to Leonardo Velloso-Lyons's analysis is the fact that both Camões's and Ortelius's texts were distributed in books. The book market provided a critical connection between the Portuguese and Spanish kingdoms and their colonies, creating a shared culture and knowledge base, and indeed the distribution of books was a colonizing mechanism. The two books at the center of Velloso-Lyons's study present a view of the world that differs from the more "static" and less engaging diagrams that had come before. Creating a book that could be easily handled was, for Ortelius, an important part of the reading experience. He presented at first an overview of the world before addressing its different parts – all in a manageable format that enabled the reader to flip back and forth, creating in his or her mind a comprehensive understanding of the parts and how they fit into the whole, by means of a dynamic reading experience that aimed not merely at the transmission of abstract knowledge but at interactive immersion. Velloso-Lyons argues that Camões's depiction of the machine of the world is a poetic rendering of just such an immersive reading experience.

In the chapters of this book, the importance of the interplay between materiality and immateriality in interpreting objects is exemplified in several ways. In all of these forms of interplay, the immaterial is shown to have effect on the material and vice versa. First, physical objects, such as the accoutrements of knighthood, as Mae Velloso-Lyons shows, or techniques, such as those used to create the panel painting that Iris Helffenstein presents, often have symbolic or allegorical meaning that must be interpreted and understood in a particular heuristic context. Second, things are often the focus of literary ekphrasis – such as the marvelous objects in *Apollonius von Tyrland* that Tilo Renz discusses, the saddle and tack in Hartmann von Aue's *Erec* that are the focus of Falk Quenstedt's analysis, or the devastating things of battle that Martin Bleisteiner addresses in the *Alliterative Morte Arthure*. Ekphrases have as much to do with the narrative and temporal unfolding of a story as they do with the imagined material objects they describe. Yet they also highlight things, focusing our attention on them and immersing us in contemplation of their nature and the possibilities they provide for interpretation of the frame narrative. Third, as Mareike Reisch shows, the relationship between the meaning of things and their physical presence is complex. The letter from Jerusalem that she discusses continues to signify as a text long after the letter itself has been worn to shreds and lost, but it loses its aura. Similarly, the brick mold that Christopher Hutchinson discusses plays on its status as an image of an object in a book, and this invites reflection on the reading process as well as the real-life status of printed things. Indeed – and this is the fourth way in which immateriality features in the discussions of objects in this volume – many of the medieval objects that our authors discuss are imagined: the cloak of Mary in Björn Buschbeck's chapter and the machine of the world that Leonardo Velloso-Lyons discusses are just two such objects, whose imagined nature is critical to their meaning and significance. While many of our objects are literary objects, and therefore inherently immaterial, they are integrated as things into literary worlds where they engage with human figures, asserting themselves and demanding particular responses, interpretations, and perspectives. The things that are addressed in this volume are varied, and they are embedded, or entangled, in different contexts and societies, yet they share a concerted engagement in human life – a claim to thingness.

Iris Helffenstein

1 Intermedial Practice, Multisensory Perception: Lorenzo Monaco and the *lavorii di mano* around 1400

In 1374, the Camaldolese monk Fra Leonardo bequeathed a considerable sum of money to Sta. Maria degli Angeli, his monastery in Florence. This inheritance was invested in liturgical church equipment; among other items, it financed several choir books, known as graduals, and a lectern to place these books upon during Mass. The lectern displayed the books' contents to the choir of monks who stood before it: a "leggiò di chiesa, dove si chanta," as noted in a corresponding document from 1375.[1] Perhaps it is this very lectern that is depicted within an initial *C* (plate 1) in an early fifteenth-century gradual deriving from Sta. Maria degli Angeli and now preserved in the Biblioteca Medicea Laurenziana, Florence.[2] In the illumination, a group of monks, their white robes identifying them as members of the Camaldolese order, gathers around an opened gradual on the lectern. Most of them have turned their attention to the book, some of them singing, others waiting their turn, thereby visualizing the dynamic performance of the group. The scene painted here thus reflects in miniature the actual situation in which the gradual itself must have been used. Indeed, the song text in the painted book is identical to the one on the page of the real book: a song assigned to the fourth Sunday after Easter and beginning with the verse "Cantate Domino, Canticum Novum" (Psalm 96:1) (figure 1.1).

This small illumination, then, opens a perspective on the complex sensual and material environment it belonged to: an environment shaped by practices that connected the monastic community to deceased donors or external patrons; to the church and convent as architectural, liturgical, and symbolic spaces; to words,

Acknowledgements: I would like to thank the editors Jutta Eming and Kathryn Starkey as well as the participants of the workshops in Berlin and Stanford for stimulating conversations and thoughtful comments. I am grateful to Matt Gleeson and the two anonymous readers of this chapter for helpful comments and suggestions. Thanks also to Caroline Geide for her help in obtaining images and rights. An initial version of this chapter was translated by Gabriella Gabrielle; it has been revised several times since.

1 "A church lectern, where we chant." Gaudenz Freuler, "Don Silvestro dei Gherarducci," in *Painting and Illumination in Early Renaissance Florence 1300–1450*, ed. Laurence B. Kanter, exh. cat. (New York: Abrams, 1994), 124–176, at 131–132.
2 Florence, Biblioteca Medicea Laurenziana, Cod. Cor. 3, dated 1409 in a colophon on fol. 3r, indicating the completion of the text as well as the Lombard and filigree initials. The miniature on fol. 41v is variously attributed to Zanobi Strozzi or Battista di Biagio Sanguigni and dated to the 1420s. For both the manuscript and the miniature, see Kanter, *Painting and Illumination*, 283–287, cat. no. 37 (Laurence B. Kanter).

https://doi.org/10.1515/9783110742985-004

Figure 1.1: Gradual from Sta. Maria degli Angeli, Florence, text completed by 1409, illumination dated to the 1420s. Ink, tempera, and gold leaf on parchment. Florence, Biblioteca Medicea Laurenziana, Ms. Corale 3, fol. 41v. Reproduced by kind permission of the MiBACT. Any reproduction in any form is prohibited.

song, and the scent of oil lamps and incense; and to artifacts including altarpieces, devotional paintings, and choir books.

A scriptorium for the production of manuscripts had been set up in the monastery and may have been in operation as early as 1332.[3] The Florentine gradual thus attests not only to the liturgical practice of the monastic community of Sta. Maria degli Angeli but also to the production and use of the necessary artifacts. Book *illuminations* like the one just described, however, were not produced in the scriptorium in question; rather, they were subcontracted to external painting workshops.[4] One such workshop was run by Lorenzo Monaco (born Piero di Giovanni, documented 1391–1422), to whom some of the illuminations in the aforementioned gradual are attributed.[5] Himself a Camaldolese monk from Sta. Maria degli Angeli, he left the

---

3 For the scriptorium of Sta. Maria degli Angeli and the manuscript production there, see George R. Bent, *Monastic Art in Lorenzo Monaco's Florence: Painting and Patronage in Santa Maria degli Angeli, 1300–1415* (Lewiston: Edwin Mellen Press, 2006), 71–76 and ch. 5.

4 George Bent has convincingly argued against a separate artist workshop in Sta. Maria degli Angeli, the existence of which Giorgio Vasari had assumed in the second edition of his compilation of artists' lives (1568). Cf. Giorgio Vasari, *Le vite de' più eccellenti pittori, scultori ed architettori*, ed. Gaetano Milanesi, Le opere di Giorgio Vasari 2 (Florence: G. C. Sansoni, 1878), 2:21–26. See Bent, *Monastic Art*, 181–194, for the methods, functioning, and operation of the scriptorium.

5 The illuminations in Cod. Cor. 3 attributed to Lorenzo Monaco are dated to around 1409–1410, but he seems to have left the gradual unfinished. The remaining illuminations, including the one with the

monastery after his ordination as deacon in 1396 to set up a painting business in the city. He remained connected to the Camaldolese and created both panel paintings and book illuminations for the order.[6]

This connection is attested by Lorenzo Monaco's small Crucifixion panel now in the Lindenau-Museum in Altenburg, even though it cannot be established with certainty whether it was commissioned by a Camaldolese monk or a lay patron associated with the order.[7] The painting shows the crucified Christ surrounded by three saints, who demonstrate different responses to the scene they are witnessing: awestruck, fervent, or contemplative (figure 1.2, plate 2).[8] Similar to the miniature with the singing monks, the painting thus thematizes its own reception and the practices that would have gone along with it. The singing of a group of monks at a lectern or the act of praying in front of a painting were multisensory, intermedial experiences in which material objects, more specifically works of art, played a central role.[9] These practices, and the objects to which they were connected, shaped a perceptual space that could embrace visual, haptic, acoustic, and olfactory elements. The artworks themselves were embedded in an artistic and aesthetic practice that, in the period around 1400, was characterized by intermediality.[10]

---

singing monks on fol. 41v, are commonly thought to have been executed after Lorenzo Monaco's death, in the 1420s. See Kanter, *Painting and Illumination*, 283–287, cat. no. 37 (Laurence B. Kanter).
6 For Lorenzo Monaco and his relationship to the Camaldolese, see Miklós Boskovits, "Su Don Lorenzo, pittore camaldolese," *Arte Cristiana* 82, no. 764–765 (1994): 351–364, at 351; Laurence B. Kanter, "Lorenzo Monaco," in Kanter, *Painting and Illumination*, 220–222, at 220–221; and Bent, *Monastic Art*, 194–202.
7 The question of the panel's patron will be further discussed below.
8 Altenburg, Lindenau-Museum, inv. no. 23, ca. 1405–1407, tempera and gold leaf on poplar, 56.4 x 42 x 2.8 cm. On the panel, see Miklós Boskovits and Daniela Parenti, eds., *Da Bernardo Daddi al Beato Angelico a Botticelli: Dipinti fiorentini del Lindenau-Museum di Altenburg*, exh. cat. (Florence: Giunti, 2005), 110–111, cat. no. 22 (Sonia Chiodo); Ortrud Westheider and Michael Philipp, eds., *Die Erfindung des Bildes: Frühe italienische Meister bis Botticelli*, Publikationen des Bucerius-Kunst-Forums, exh. cat. (Munich: Hirmer, 2011), 156, cat. no. 17 (Wolf-Dietrich Löhr); and Klaus Krüger, *Bildpräsenz – Heilspräsenz: Ästhetik der Liminalität*, Figura 6 (Göttingen: Wallstein, 2018), 82–97. The painting is slightly cropped on all sides and was probably sawn out of the wooden frame initially attached to the panel. As the technical investigation conducted by Holger Manzke in 2010 shows, the various traces of processing on the verso are inconclusive regarding the question of whether the painting has always been a single panel or whether it previously belonged to a diptych or a polyptych. I would like to thank Benjamin Rux of the Lindenau-Museum for giving me access to the technical report and for allowing me to inspect the painting so closely.
9 For Christian liturgy in the Middle Ages as a multisensory, synesthetic experience, see Eric Palazzo, "Art, Liturgy, and the Five Senses in the Early Middle Ages," *Viator* 41, no. 1 (2010): 25–56; and Béatrice Caseau, "The Senses in Religion: Liturgy, Devotion, and Deprivation," in *A Cultural History of the Senses in the Middle Ages*, ed. Richard Newhauser, A Cultural History of the Senses 2 (London: Bloomsbury Academic, 2014), 89–110.
10 The term *intermediality* here refers in a broad sense to artistic practices in which at least two media that are commonly perceived as distinct from one another interact. For a general introduction, see Irina O. Rajewsky, *Intermedialität*, UTB für Wissenschaft 2261 (Tübingen: A. Francke, 2002). In the

In this chapter, I will explore this web of interrelations in the case of the Altenburg panel, focusing on the relevance of materiality and (inter)mediality for the production as well as the reception of the painting. In so doing, my chapter engages in a recent current in various fields of medieval studies that concerns itself with the role of things and thingness in the negotiation between the material and the immaterial, especially in devotional practices.[11] While this larger discussion encompasses objects ranging from prayer beads to bleeding hosts to liturgical cradles and Christ dolls, here I examine the specific ways in which artworks, artistic practices, and aesthetic strategies can take part in, inform, and determine this process of negotiation. Lorenzo Monaco renders the subject of the Crucifixion with its inherent promise of salvation in a way that highlights the material character of both the sacred events depicted and the painting itself, while also playing on modes of reception and experience. This original treatment of a core theme of Christian faith – and iconography – raises questions about the relationships between materiality and mediality, matter and meaning, presence and evocation, artistic practice and sensory perception. In what follows, I will analyze how the Altenburg panel creatively exploits the capacities of painting, including intermedial references, to manifest in visual and material form the theme of resurrection and eternal life that is implicit in the Crucifixion

---

time around 1400, this interaction could take place on various levels: the scope of intermedial practices thus ranges from the combination of different media in artworks, such as sculpture and painting in funerary monuments or altarpieces, to the imitation or evocation of one medium in another – and everything in between. See Iris Helffenstein, "Intermediale Verfahren im *studietto:* Zu Materialästhetik und Medialität von Verre églomisé und Goldgrund im italienischen Spätmittelalter bis Lorenzo Monaco," in *Gezeichnete Evidenz auf kolorierten Papieren in Süd und Nord von 1400 bis 1650*, ed. Iris Brahms and Klaus Krüger (Berlin: Walter de Gruyter, forthcoming). For case studies of and methodological approaches to media combinations, see Iris Wenderholm, *Bild und Berührung: Skulptur und Malerei auf dem Altar der italienischen Frührenaissance*, Italienische Forschungen des Kunsthistorischen Institutes in Florenz, I Mandorli 5 (Munich: Deutscher Kunstverlag, 2006); and Britta Dümpelmann, *Veit Stoß und das Krakauer Marienretabel: Mediale Zugänge, mediale Perspektiven*, Medienwandel – Medienwechsel – Medienwissen 24 (Zurich: Chronos, 2012). On the evocation of different media, see the section on intermedial practices below. Preliminary overviews of intermedial techniques in the Tre- and Quattrocento are given in John Pope-Hennessy, "The Interaction of Painting and Sculpture in Florence in the Fifteenth Century," *The Journal of the Royal Society for the Encouragement of Arts, Manufactures and Commerce* 117, no. 5154 (1969): 406 – 424; Marco Collareta, "Il primato del disegno: Un percorso attraverso le arti minori," in *L'eredità di Giotto: Arte a Firenze 1340 – 1375*, ed. Angelo Tartuferi, exh. cat. (Florence: Giunti, 2008), 57 – 65; and Machtelt Israëls, "'Sculpted Painting' in Early Renaissance Florence," in *The Springtime of the Renaissance: Sculpture and the Arts in Florence 1400 – 60*, ed. Beatrice Paolozzi Strozzi and Marc Bormand, exh. cat. (Florence: Mandragora, 2013), 151 – 157.

11 For the fundamental, productive interconnection of the material and the immaterial in Christian practices of the late Middle Ages, see Caroline Walker Bynum, *Christian Materiality: An Essay on Religion in Late Medieval Europe* (New York: Zone Books, 2011); and the overview in Christian Kiening, "Einleitung," in *Medialität des Heils im späten Mittelalter*, ed. Carla Dauven-van Knippenberg, Cornelia Herberichs, and Christian Kiening, Medienwandel – Medienwechsel – Medienwissen 10 (Zurich: Chronos, 2009), 7 – 20.

scene; to appeal to the senses, especially the sense of touch; and to engage the painting's viewers and users in the construction of meaning.

Lorenzo Monaco's Altenburg Crucifixion and the Tradition of Panel Paintings for Personal Devotion

Lorenzo Monaco's panel in Altenburg, dated to around 1405–1407 and measuring 56.4 by 42 cm, shows Christ on the cross (figure 1.2, plate 2): his limp body is caved in, yet strained and stretched, held by the nails that fix his hands and feet to the cross. Small angels, stippled into the gold ground, hold bowls ready to catch the blood from the Savior's wounds. At the foot of the cross, three hermit saints crouch on the rock, each the founder of an order. Benedict and Romuald, the latter the historical founder of the Camaldolese order, flank Christ to the left and right, while Francis of Assisi passionately embraces the cross. Although the commission is not documented, the fact that the panel was painted by Lorenzo Monaco and the presence of St. Romuald in the image suggest that the patron was a member of, or at least close to, the Camaldolese order, which was distinguished in Florence around 1400 by a combination of mystical piety and cultural, urban sophistication.[12]

Figure 1.2: Lorenzo Monaco, Christ on the Cross with Saints Benedict, Francis of Assisi, and Romuald, ca. 1405–1407. Tempera and gold leaf on poplar, 56.4 x 42 x 2.8 cm. Altenburg, Lindenau-Museum, inv. no. 23. © Lindenau-Museum Altenburg. Photo: Bernd Sinterhauf.

---

12 For the Camaldolese order and Sta. Maria degli Angeli, see Bent, *Monastic Art*, esp. chs. 1–4. For the likely affiliation of the patron with a Camaldolese convent, see Krüger, *Bildpräsenz*, 83–85.

Such small-scale panel paintings, in the form of individual panels, diptychs, triptychs, or polyptychs, had been produced in large numbers since the late thirteenth century. They most likely served as objects of personal devotion.[13] In this respect, the small size is not a trivial fact; rather, it has consequences for both the physical and mental engagement of the devotee. These objects were handled: put into and taken out of storage chests or cases, opened or turned, at times touched and kissed.[14] Moreover, the small scale, which requires up-close viewing and thus creates a reception situation of great intimacy, invites a dedicated contemplation that can have emotional, spiritual, and intellectual components.

Where identifiable, the patrons of these pieces were often high-ranking, elite personalities.[15] Accordingly, these panels should also be seen as precious "connoisseur's" objects to be shown and admired.[16] They were particularly widespread in the first half of the fourteenth century, especially in the Tuscan cities of Florence and Siena. By 1400, their popularity had reached a second peak. In this period, they often had a retrospective character, following the standards established during the first half of the fourteenth century.[17] This also applies to the work of Lorenzo Monaco, who appropriated this tradition in an original way by updating and intensifying its aesthetic strategies through iconographic, formal, and technical experiments.

---

13 On small-scale panels used for personal devotion, see Victor M. Schmidt, *Painted Piety: Panel Paintings for Personal Devotion in Tuscany, 1250–1400*, Italia e Paesi Bassi 8 (Florence: Centro Di, 2005), with a discussion of the concept of "personal" or "individual devotion" as opposed to "private devotion," which Schmidt considers to be an anachronistic term, at 190–192. See also Stefan Weppelmann, "Kollektives Ritual und persönliche Andacht: Kleinformate in der Tafelmalerei des Trecento," in *Kult Bild: Das Altar- und Andachtsbild von Duccio bis Perugino*, ed. Jochen Sander, exh. cat. (Petersberg: Imhof, 2006), 212–249; Andrea De Marchi, "Oggetti da maneggiare tra sacro e profano," in *Da Jacopo della Quercia a Donatello: Le arti a Siena nel primo Rinascimento*, ed. Max Seidel, exh. cat. (Milan: F. Motta, 2010), 356–361.
14 For a discussion of the medial characteristics of small-scale panels and their handling, see David G. Wilkins, "Opening the Doors of Devotion: Trecento Triptychs and Suggestions concerning Images and Domestic Practice in Florence," in *Italian Panel Painting of the Duecento and Trecento*, ed. Victor M. Schmidt, Studies in the History of Art 61, Symposium Papers 38 (Washington, D.C.: National Gallery of Art, 2002), 370–393, esp. 376, 380. See also V. Schmidt, *Painted Piety*, esp. 95–101; Marius Rimmele, "(Ver-)Führung durch Scharniere: Zur Instrumentalisierung kleinformatiger Klappbilder in der Passionsmeditation," in Dauven-van Knippenberg, Herberichs, and Kiening, *Medialität*, 111–130; De Marchi, "Oggetti," 356–361; and Marius Rimmele, *Das Triptychon als Metapher, Körper und Ort: Semantisierungen eines Bildträgers* (Munich: Wilhelm Fink, 2010), 11–13, 42–51, 195–198, and passim.
15 On the patrons of small-scale panels, see V. Schmidt, *Painted Piety*, ch. 7.
16 See Weppelmann, "Kollektives Ritual," 225, 228; Victor M. Schmidt, "Der Maler und seine Kunst: Über Pietro Lorenzettis Diptychon in Altenburg," in Westheider and Philipp, *Erfindung des Bildes*, 46–57, esp. 52–55. See also Julian Gardner, "The Back of the Panel of Christ Discovered in the Temple by Simone Martini," *Arte Cristiana*, n.s., 78, no. 741 (1990): 389–398, at 393, for a consideration of a small-scale panel by Simone Martini as a "connoisseur's painting."
17 See De Marchi, "Oggetti," 357.

Devotional Practice and Sensuality

The emergence of these small-scale panels for individual worship at the end of the thirteenth century has been associated with changes in the practice of religious devotion, particularly ones connected to the relation between the material and the immaterial and the role of artworks in devotional practice. A brief discussion of these shifts is useful to help evaluate the aspect of materiality in the Altenburg Crucifixion: its treatment by the artist, its relation to the sacramental subject matter, and its impact on the reception of the panel.

The changes in devotional practices began in the twelfth century with writings from the Bernardine and Cistercian ambit and unfolded principally among the mendicant orders of the thirteenth and fourteenth centuries.[18] As scholars have noted, these changes entailed a thematic concentration on the life of Christ, and especially the Passion, which devotees were meant to envision, even co-experience, with great emotional and physical intensity. In the development and dissemination of this form of Passion piety, the mendicant orders in general and the Franciscans in particular played an essential role – for example, through sermons and Passion literature. An important example is the *Meditationes vitae Christi* (*Meditations on the Life of Christ*), attributed to a Franciscan friar and dated to around 1300. This text calls for intense inner contemplation of the Passion, using evocative and emotional descriptions of the events to position the recipient in the role of an eyewitness and appeal to all the senses.[19] Besides texts, artworks played a crucial role in contemplative immersion and experiential involvement at that time, as is documented in biographical accounts of saints and mystically gifted persons, as well as in sources pertaining to brotherhoods and laypeople: in these accounts, the crucifixes, statues, or panel

---

18 See Jeffrey F. Hamburger, "The Visual and the Visionary: The Image in Late Medieval Monastic Devotions," *Viator* 20 (1989): 161–182; Klaus Krüger, "Bildandacht und Bergeinsamkeit: Der Eremit als Rollenspiel in der städtischen Gesellschaft," in *Malerei und Stadtkultur in der Dantezeit: Die Argumentation der Bilder*, ed. Hans Belting and Dieter Blume (Munich: Hirmer, 1989), 187–200; Miklós Boskovits, "Immagine e preghiera nel tardo Medioevo: Osservazioni preliminari," in Miklós Boskovits, *Immagini da meditare: Ricerche su dipinti di tema religioso nei secoli XII–XV*, Arti e scritture 5 (Milan: Vita e Pensiero, 1994), 73–106; Peter Dinzelbacher, "Religiöses Erleben von bildender Kunst in autobiographischen und biographischen Zeugnissen des Hoch- und Spätmittelalters," in *Images of Cult and Devotion: Function and Reception of Christian Images in Medieval and Post-Medieval Europe*, ed. Søren Kaspersen and Ulla Haastrup (Copenhagen: Museum Tusculanum Press, 2004), 61–88. For an overview of this subject, see Ulrich Köpf, "Kreuz IV: Mittelalter," in *Theologische Realenzyklopädie*, vol. 19, *Kirchenrechtsquellen–Kreuz* (Berlin: Walter de Gruyter, 1990), 732–761, at 752–756.
19 Wilkins, "Doors of Devotion," 377; Tobias A. Kemper, *Die Kreuzigung Christi: Motivgeschichtliche Studien zu lateinischen und deutschen Passionstraktaten des Spätmittelalters*, Münchener Texte und Untersuchungen zur deutschen Literatur des Mittelalters 131 (Tübingen: Niemeyer, 2006), 79–109, with a detailed discussion of attribution and dating.

paintings the protagonists contemplate might come alive, communicate, or physically interact with the devotee.[20]

From a strict theological point of view, the goal of these practices was traditionally to overcome bodily forms of perception in an anagogic ascent (*per visibilia ad invisibilia*), based on the hierarchical progression from corporeal seeing (the viewing of present objects with the physical eye) to spiritual seeing (recollections and imaginations within the spirit) to intellectual seeing (the perception of intelligible things within the intellect), as established by the church father Augustine of Hippo.[21] However, the writings connected to devotional practice rather than theological thought reveal time and again that the contemplated works of art did more than simply serve as arbitrary and interchangeable starting points for meditation practices. Rather, their presence as real objects and their material and aesthetic qualities were essential for the sensual experience of the supernatural.[22] Similarly, the devotional practices and forms of reception described in (auto)biographical texts as well as sources regarding liturgy, homily, and prayer techniques are often strongly informed by physical and sensual experiences.[23]

---

20 In addition to the literature in note 18, see the numerous examples in Millard Meiss, *Painting in Florence and Siena after the Black Death* (Princeton, NJ: Princeton University Press, 1951), 105–121; and Sixten Ringbom, "Devotional Images and Imaginative Devotions: Notes on the Place of Art in Late Medieval Private Piety," *Gazette des Beaux-Arts* 73 (1969): 159–170. See also Klaus Krüger, *Der frühe Bildkult des Franziskus in Italien: Gestalt- und Funktionswandel des Tafelbildes im 13. und 14. Jahrhundert* (Berlin: Mann, 1992), 154–155, which includes particulars about corresponding practices in the ambit of the Franciscans.

21 For Augustine, his influence on late medieval conceptions of visionary experience, and the question of the actual practicability of this approach, see Ringbom, "Devotional Images"; and Barbara Newman, "What Did It Mean to Say 'I Saw'? The Clash between Theory and Practice in Medieval Visionary Culture," *Speculum* 80, no. 1 (2005): 1–43, at 6–7.

22 See, with different emphases and findings, Ringbom, "Devotional Images"; Hamburger, "Monastic Devotions"; Krüger, "Bildandacht"; Klaus Krüger, "Mimesis als Bildlichkeit des Scheins: Zur Fiktionalität religiöser Bildkunst im Trecento," in *Künstlerischer Austausch: Artistic Exchange*, ed. Thomas W. Gaehtgens (Berlin: Akademie Verlag, 1993), 2:423–436; Boskovits, "Immagine e preghiera"; Lars Raymond Jones, "Visio Divina? Donor Figures and Representations of Imagistic Devotion; The Copy of the 'Virgin of Bagnolo' in the Museo dell'Opera del Duomo, Florence," in V. Schmidt, *Italian Panel Painting*, 30–55; Dinzelbacher, "Religiöses Erleben"; Klaus Krüger, "Bild und Bühne: Dispositive des imaginären Blicks," in *Transformationen des Religiösen: Performativität und Textualität im geistlichen Spiel*, ed. Ingrid Kasten and Erika Fischer-Lichte, Trends in Medieval Philology 11 (Berlin: Walter de Gruyter, 2007), 218–248, at 218–222; Wolf-Dietrich Löhr, "Die Perle im Acker: Francesco di Vannuccios Berliner 'Kreuzigung' und die Eröffnung der Wunden," in *Zeremoniell und Raum in der frühen italienischen Malerei*, ed. Stefan Weppelmann, Studien zur internationalen Architektur- und Kunstgeschichte 60 (Petersberg: Imhof, 2007), 160–183; Bynum, *Christian Materiality*, esp. 101–104; and Krüger, *Bildpräsenz*, esp. ch. 3. It is understood that the forms of sensual devotional practice described in each case do not follow a uniform conceptualization and vary from text to text.

23 In addition to the literature in note 20, see B. Newman, "Visionary Culture"; Wenderholm, *Bild und Berührung*, esp. 177–182; and David Ganz, *Medien der Offenbarung: Visionsdarstellungen im Mittelalter* (Berlin: Reimer, 2008), chs. 10–12. On the difficulty of reconstructing the reception of art-

Within this interplay of material presence and immaterial realms in devotional practices, the aspect of tactility could play a crucial role.[24] This is evident in a much-cited passage from the *Trattato della perfezione* (*Treatise on Perfection*), by the Franciscan mystic Ugo Panziera da Prato, from about 1320. In this treatise, Panziera illustrates the method of inner visualization of Christ by comparing it with the process of painting. According to this technique, Christ should first appear inscribed ("scritto") in the thoughts and the imagination of the devotee, then sketched ("disegnato"), filled in with underdrawing and shading ("disegnato e ombrato"), then painted with color and flesh tones ("colorato e incarnato").[25] Finally, his presence in the imagination of the believer should appear incarnated ("incarnato") and in relief. Panziera here uses the word "rilevato," whose polysemy is crucial to the passage.[26] In the context of artistic practice, the word *rilievo* and its derivatives designated both raised elements in the present-day sense of "relief" and the three-

---

works in everyday life, see Wilkins, "Doors of Devotion," 377–378; and V. Schmidt, *Painted Piety*, ch. 3.

24 Although there was no binding hierarchy of the senses in the Christian Middle Ages, sight was usually regarded as the most noble sense. Nevertheless, the sense of touch was also given a prominent place. Since it is distributed throughout the body, authors like Aristotle and, following him, Thomas Aquinas, considered it to be the basis for sense perception as a whole. See David Summers, *The Judgement of Sense: Renaissance Naturalism and the Rise of Aesthetics*, Ideas in Context (1987; repr., Cambridge: Cambridge University Press, 1994), ch. 1 and pp. 103–104. Accordingly, recent studies increasingly consider the tactile components of devotional practices as well as the aural, olfactory, or synesthetic ones. See, for example, Jacqueline E. Jung, "The Tactile and the Visionary: Notes on the Place of Sculpture in the Medieval Religious Imagination," in *Looking Beyond: Visions, Dreams, and Insights in Medieval Art and History*, ed. Colum Hourihane, Index of Christian Art, Occasional Papers 11 (Princeton, NJ: Index of Christian Art, Princeton University / Penn State University Press, 2010), 203–240, esp. 206–209; Bynum, *Christian Materiality*, esp. 38, 65–67, 101–104; Richard Newhauser, "The Senses, the Medieval Sensorium, and Sensing (in) the Middle Ages," in *Handbook of Medieval Culture: Fundamental Aspects and Conditions of the European Middle Ages*, ed. Albrecht Classen (Berlin: Walter de Gruyter, 2015), 3:1559–1575, at 1565–1566; Fiona Griffiths and Kathryn Starkey, eds., *Sensory Reflections: Traces of Experience in Medieval Artifacts*, Sense, Matter, and Medium 1 (Berlin: Walter de Gruyter, 2018).

25 For the term *incarnare*, which denotes the process of painting flesh and skin, see note 41 below.

26 Panziera uses and repeats several polysemous terms, such as "disegnato" and "incarnato," apparently playing on the shifts in meaning. I mostly follow the translation proposed by Jones, who also cites the only surviving source text. See Jones, "Visio Divina?," 44, 53n39, with further analysis and information on the source. This passage in Panziera's treatise has been cited in connection with intermedial artworks in Wenderholm, *Bild und Berührung*, 172; Christopher R. Lakey, "The Materiality of Light in Medieval Italian Painting," in "Medieval Materiality," special issue, *English Language Notes* 53, no. 2 (2015): 119–136, at 127; Britta Dümpelmann, "Presence as Display: Carved Altarpieces on the Threshold to Eternity," in *Temporality and Mediality in Late Medieval and Early Modern Culture*, ed. Christian Kiening and Martina Stercken, Cursor Mundi 32 (Turnhout: Brepols, 2018), 75–113, at 80; and Beth Williamson, "Matter and Materiality in an Italian Reliquary Triptych," *Gesta* 57, no. 1 (2018): 23–42, at 39–40.

dimensional qualities that are produced in painting by chiaroscuro modeling.[27] In the Christian context, however, the term could also mean "lifted," and thus designate Christ resurrected (*ri-levato*).[28]

While Panziera describes the technique and effect of painting, the logic of progressive intensification he employs attests to the importance of three-dimensional values in devotional practices: whether actually sculptural or created by the illusionist methods of the painter, they approximate reality, create the effect of actuality, appeal to the verifying sense of touch, and suggest an immediate sensory experience.[29]

Figure 1.3: Sienese or Pisan painter and Nino Pisano, Crucifixion, ca. 1365. Tempera and gold leaf on wood panel, polychrome wooden crucifix, 72 x 30 x 10.5 cm (overall). Florence, private collection. Photo: in Kreytenberg 2000.

---

27 In the artist's handbook by the painter Cennino Cennini, *Il libro dell'arte*, written ca. 1400, the words *rilievo*, *rilevare*, and *rilevato* are used with both meanings discussed here. See Cennino Cennini, *Il libro dell'arte*, ed. Fabio Frezzato, 2nd ed. (Vicenza: Pozza, 2004). In the sense of real three-dimensional reliefs, they appear, for example, in chapters 4, 102, and 124–131. For the sense of the highest or brightest parts of painted figures or objects, and the figure's volume, see, for example, chapters 31, 67, and [145]. For further discussion of Cennini's use of the terms, see Wolf-Dietrich Löhr, "Dantes Täfelchen, Cenninis Zeichenkiste: *Ritratto, disegno* und *fantasia* als Instrumente der Bilderzeugung im Trecento," *Das Mittelalter* 13 (2008): 148–179, at 176–178. On Cennini's *Libro*, see also note 41 below.

28 Jones, "Visio Divina?," 44.

29 On the importance of three-dimensional works, such as carved crucifixes, and both imagined and actual touch in devotional practices of the Middle Ages, see Geraldine A. Johnson, "Touch, Tactility, and the Reception of Sculpture," in *A Companion to Art Theory*, ed. Carolyn Wilde and Paul Smith,

Artistic production may have followed a similar motivation in such works as a small tabernacle from the second half of the Trecento in a private collection in Florence (figure 1.3, plate 4). Here, as in a small number of similar works that have been preserved, a sculptural crucifix is set against a gold-ground panel with painted figures.[30] Painting on its own, however, also developed techniques to evoke a kind of tangible presence.

Modes of Reception: Matter and Materiality of the Passion

Lorenzo Monaco's painting (figure 1.2, plate 2) is dedicated to one of the central mysteries of Christianity: the Crucifixion, with its inherent promise of resurrection and eternal life. As the culmination of the paradoxical union of spirit and matter in the Incarnation, this scene was also a vital site of Christian reflection on questions of materiality. While the sacred truths at the heart of the subject transcended the physical world and the capacity of human perception, they were intrinsically bound to historical sites, fleshly suffering, and tangible instruments. In the Altenburg panel, Lorenzo Monaco explores this notion through his aesthetic strategies, notably by accentuating the paradoxical matter and materiality of both the Passion and the painting. The scene suggests different modes of reception pertaining to three interrelated categories: it provides role models for compassionate Passion piety; calls attention to the material, sensory aspects of the Passion in an affect-stimulating manner; and foregrounds these material stimuli in a peculiar way in order to sensually convey the ineffable.

While we cannot reconstruct just how reverent or exuberant the actual devotional practices taking place in front of this object would have been, we can ask which reactions might have been suggested by the painting itself. The varied responses of the three saints before Christ invoke different forms of contemplation. Thus, SS. Benedict and Romuald serve as historical representatives of a reformed monastic and

---

Blackwell Companions in Cultural Studies 5 (Oxford: Blackwell, 2002), 61–74; Wenderholm, *Bild und Berührung*, esp. 57–64, 109–114, and ch. 5; Jung, "Tactile"; and Adrian W. B. Randolph, *Touching Objects: Intimate Experiences of Italian Fifteenth-Century Art* (New Haven: Yale University Press, 2014).
30 Florence, private collection, Sienese or Pisan painter and Nino Pisano, Crucifixion, ca. 1365, tempera and gold leaf on wood panel, polychrome wooden crucifix, 72 x 30 x 10.5 cm (overall). See Gert Kreytenberg, "Ein Tabernakel mit Kruzifix von Nino Pisano und Luca di Tommè," *Pantheon* 58 (2000): 9–12; Wenderholm, *Bild und Berührung*, 160 and cat. no. 25, as well as ch. 5 on the combination of three-dimensional crucifixes with painting, cf. also cat. no. 23 and cat. no. 128. For the media-reflexive dimension of this group of works and the concomitant relationship between artwork and viewer, see Krüger, "Mimesis," 425–426.

hermitic life.[31] With their internalized contemplation of Christ on the cross, they function as role models for meditation on Christ's Passion. So does St. Francis, but his approach, by contrast, is one of physical engagement.

Francis's response corresponds to his role as a central figure in the history of Passion piety, the development of which was significantly advanced by the Franciscan order. His life, as described by his early biographers, was an important source of particularly intense interactions with appearances of Christ, both in visions and in artworks. These episodes influenced hagiographical writing and pictorial depictions throughout the fourteenth century.[32] From the middle of the thirteenth century onward, painted crucifixes and paintings of the Crucifixion showed Francis kneeling next to the cross and embracing, touching, or kissing Christ's feet, as in the case of an Umbrian crucifix in Arezzo (figures 1.4a–1.4b).[33]

In the Altenburg panel, Francis is seen from behind and positioned in the middle of the group, thus inviting the beholder kneeling in front of the painting to identify with him.[34] Tightly embracing the cross, he comes so close to the legs of Christ that he almost touches them. Red streaks spurting out of Francis's feet and hands – the bodily locations where he received the stigmata in a vision – testify to the saint's *compassio* with and *imitatio* of Christ. Thick drops of blood flow downward from the nail wounds of Christ himself. More blood gushes out of the wound in his side, as if he has been freshly pierced. It drips down over his feet, runs under Francis's arms as they embrace the cross, and flows over the Golgotha rock out to the very edge of the painting. Its bright red color stands out in stark contrast against the pale hue of the stone (figure 1.5, plate 3c).

The blood and wounds of Christ were especially worshiped in the context of Passion piety. Christ's blood sacrifice bears a strong affective potential: it signifies redemption and therefore the possibility of human salvation. At the same time, it serves as evidence of Christ's suffering, allowing this suffering to be experienced

---

31 See Bent, *Monastic Art*, 19–32; Westheider and Philipp, *Erfindung des Bildes*, 156, cat. no. 17 (Wolf-Dietrich Löhr).

32 See Krüger, *Bildkult des Franziskus*, esp. 149–155; Ganz, *Medien*, chs. 10–12.

33 Arezzo, Basilica di San Francesco, Umbrian Master, Painted Crucifix with Saint Francis, second half of the thirteenth century, with later restorations, gold leaf and tempera on wood. For the motif of the mystical embrace of the cross or the crucified Christ, including the example in Arezzo, see Boskovits, "Immagine e preghiera," 87–89. For its relevance in popular devotion, see also Ketti Neil, "St. Francis of Assisi, the Penitent Magdalen, and the Patron at the Foot of the Cross," *Rutgers Art Review* 9/10 (1988/1989): 83–110. For depictions of Francis at the foot of the cross, see also Krüger, *Bildkult des Franziskus*, 155–161; and V. Schmidt, *Painted Piety*, 219–230. About the same time, depictions of Mary Magdalene at the foot of the cross started to appear. For this iconography, see, in addition to Neil's study, Frank O. Büttner, *Imitatio pietatis: Motive der christlichen Ikonographie als Modelle zur Verähnlichung* (Berlin: Mann, 1983), 142–157. See also Krüger, *Bildpräsenz*, 94–95.

34 Wolf-Dietrich Löhr suggests that St. Francis might have been the patron saint of the painting's patron: see Westheider and Philipp, *Erfindung des Bildes*, 156, cat. no. 17. For a detailed discussion of the relation between the depicted saints and the viewer, see Krüger, *Bildpräsenz*, 82–97.

Figures 1.4a and 1.4b. Umbrian master, Painted Crucifix with Saint Francis, second half of the thirteenth century, with later restorations. Gold leaf and tempera on wood. Arezzo, Basilica di San Francesco. Reproduced by kind permission of the Ministero per i Beni e le Attività Culturali e per il Turismo – Soprintendenza Archeologia Belle Arti e Paesaggio per le province di Siena Grosseto e Arezzo. Photo: Alessandro Benci. Any reproduction in any form is prohibited.

Figure 1.5: Lorenzo Monaco, Christ on the Cross with Saints Benedict, Francis of Assisi, and Romuald, ca. 1405–1407 (detail). Tempera and gold leaf on poplar, 56.4 x 42 x 2.8 cm. Altenburg, Lindenau-Museum, inv. no. 23. © Lindenau-Museum Altenburg. Photo: Bernd Sinterhauf.

in a sensory way and to engender the devotee's *compassio*.[35] In the Altenburg panel, the angels collecting Christ's blood allude to the presence of the blood in the Eucharist, in the form of the wine in the chalice. However, mystical texts from the thirteenth and fourteenth centuries also describe visionary encounters in which visual, tactile, and gustatory interactions with the blood of Christ happen independently of a Eucharistic context and can take on a literal meaning. Not infrequently, such encounters result from the contemplation of a crucifix or other artworks. From the end of the thirteenth century onward, realistic depictions of the crucified Christ also called greater attention to the bleeding wounds. In turn, these depictions could be integrated performatively into devotional and liturgical practices.[36]

As in these texts and depictions, the materiality of the blood is also emphasized in the Altenburg Crucifixion. Using different shades of red color, Lorenzo Monaco differentiates between freshly flowing and already coagulated blood.[37] He thus makes deliberate use of his artistic resources to present mysteries of faith and theological discourses in an experiential manner. For, as Beate Fricke has shown, artists around 1400 experimented with the depiction of blood in different stages of coagulation in order to confront the viewer with a paradox: "The more imminent Christ's death appears to be, the more vividly his blood appears to flow."[38] Lorenzo Monaco employs a similar strategy when he combines the naturalistic depiction of a dead body with an illusionistic suggestion of eternally flowing blood. Here as in other examples, the paradox of the simultaneously dead and animated body evokes the paradox of the double nature of Christ and his promise of eternal life.[39]

But the paradox also resides in the panel's materiality, as well as its artificial nature. The blood emanating from the nail wounds on Christ's hands drips from his forearms, flows downward, and coagulates into thick beads. Dripping down in vertical streams, parallel to the picture plane, the blood seems to be running down

---

35 See Wenderholm, *Bild und Berührung*, 179–180.

36 See Peter Dinzelbacher, "Das Blut Christi in der Religiosität des Mittelalters," in *900 Jahre Heilig-Blut-Verehrung in Weingarten, 1094–1994*, ed. Norbert Kruse and Hans U. Rudolf (Sigmaringen: Jan Thorbecke Verlag, 1994), 1:415–434, esp. 421–429; Johannes Tripps, *Das handelnde Bildwerk in der Gotik: Forschungen zu den Bedeutungsschichten und der Funktion des Kirchengebäudes und seiner Ausstattung in der Hoch- und Spätgotik* (Berlin: Mann, 1998); and Dinzelbacher, "Religiöses Erleben." See also Caroline Walker Bynum, "The Blood of Christ in the Later Middle Ages," *Studies in Christianity and Culture* 71 (2002): 685–714.

37 Beate Fricke, "A Liquid History: Blood and Animation in Late Medieval Art," *RES: Anthropology and Aesthetics* 63/64 (2013): 53–69, at 64–65. The use of different shades of red is also described by Cennino Cennini in the chapter devoted to the depiction of wounds in his artist's handbook. Cennini, *Il libro dell'arte*, 172 (ch. [149]).

38 Fricke, "Liquid History," 54.

39 Beate Fricke, "Matter and Meaning of Mother-of-Pearl: The Origins of Allegory in the Spheres of Things," *Gesta* 51, no. 1 (2012): 35–53, at 42–43; Fricke, "Liquid History." See also Bynum, *Christian Materiality*, 61–65.

the gold ground itself: matter on matter (figure 1.6, plate 3a).[40] The connection between blood-red color and the effect of animation is also established by Cennino Cennini, himself a painter and the author of an artist's handbook. In his *Il Libro dell'arte*, written shortly after 1400, he describes the red pigment – or more precisely the "flesh color" ("incarnazion") – made from different shades of rose as the key component of the painting process through which an accomplished painter distinguishes living from dead figures. He instructs his reader not to use red pigments for depicting a dead figure, "because a dead person has no colour."[41] In this passage, as in Lorenzo Monaco's painting, blood, discussed as the elixir of life by contemporary natural philosophy and medical writings, and the animating power of red paint coincide.[42]

The fact that the blood seems to form thick droplets on the surface of the panel and is shown in different stages of coagulation introduces both spatial and temporal components into the perception of the image. Other elements of the painting also foreground the aspect of materiality and address the beholder's tactile perception. A painted decorative frame surrounds the image, but the painted scene seems to be located in front of it rather than behind it (see figure 1.6, plates 2 and 3a). The crossbeam overlaps the frame at the top and the whole cross is subtly rotated toward the viewer, giving the impression of leaning out of the pictorial space. At the bottom of the painting, the frame seems to disappear completely. The figures of the saints and the starkly highlighted, naturalistic stone ground extend almost aggressively into the viewer's space.[43]

---

40 For this observation, see also Westheider and Philipp, *Erfindung des Bildes*, 156, cat. no. 17 (Wolf-Dietrich Löhr); and Krüger, *Bildpräsenz*, 87.

41 Cennini, *Il libro dell'arte*, 172 (ch. [148]): "E non dare rossetta alchuna, che 'l morto nonn-à nullo colore." English translation from Cennino Cennini, *Cennino Cennini's Il libro dell'arte: A New English Translation and Commentary with Italian Transcription*, trans. Lara Broecke (London: Archetype, 2015), 192. For Cennino Cennini and *Il libro dell'arte*, see Wolf-Dietrich Löhr and Stefan Weppelmann, eds., *Fantasie und Handwerk: Cennino Cennini und die Tradition der toskanischen Malerei von Giotto bis Lorenzo Monaco*, exh. cat. (Munich: Hirmer, 2008). For the procedure and terminology of *incarnazione* – i.e., the painting of flesh or skin – in Cennini's *Libro*, see Christiane Kruse, *Wozu Menschen malen: Historische Begründungen eines Bildmediums* (Munich: Wilhelm Fink, 2003), 175–190; and Löhr, "Dantes Täfelchen," 174n112.

42 For the medical discourse, see Fricke, "Liquid History," 54–56. It is only in the Cinquecento that the relation between the seeming animation of painted or sculpted human figures and their color, particularly with regard to the color red, is discussed in art-theoretical writing. However, sporadic text passages from the Middle Ages and the early Renaissance also make this connection. On this subject, see Frank Fehrenbach, "'Eine Zartheit am Horizont unseres Sehvermögens': Bildwissenschaft und Lebendigkeit," *kritische berichte* 38, no. 3 (2010): 33–44, at 40. For the discourse in the sixteenth century, see Verena Krieger, "Die Farbe als 'Seele' der Malerei: Transformationen eines Topos vom 16. Jahrhundert zur Moderne," *Marburger Jahrbuch für Kunstwissenschaft* 33 (2006): 91–112.

43 For instances of spatial ambivalence and pictorial paradoxes, see also Westheider and Philipp, *Erfindung des Bildes*, 156, cat. no. 17 (Wolf-Dietrich Löhr); and Krüger, *Bildpräsenz*, 86–89.

Figure 1.6: Lorenzo Monaco, Christ on the Cross with Saints Benedict, Francis of Assisi, and Romuald, ca. 1405–1407 (detail). Tempera and gold leaf on poplar, 56.4 x 42 x 2.8 cm. Altenburg, Lindenau-Museum, inv. no. 23. © Lindenau-Museum Altenburg. Photo: Bernd Sinterhauf.

The rock on which the Crucifixion takes place protrudes outside the frame and is shown in cross section, thus acting as a tactile stimulus. As in the case of the blood, several connotations are attached to the materiality of the rock. The stones of Golgotha were venerated as contact relics, since they had come in contact with Christ's blood and the cross on which he was crucified. Starting in the twelfth century, the motif of the cleft in Calvary had become increasingly important. In the exegesis of the Bible and the Song of Songs, Christ was identified with the rock and his wounds with the clefts in the stone, an idea that became widespread. As part of their devotional practices at the site believed to be the rock of Golgotha, pilgrims touched and even entered the rock crevices.[44] In the thirteenth and fourteenth centuries, stone fragments from Calvary – as well as wooden fragments from the cross – were inserted into reliquary tabernacles, such as the one by Naddo Ceccarelli currently in Baltimore (figure 1.7). These tabernacles combined figurative representations with relics that were visibly presented in small compartments behind glass.[45]

---

[44] See the contributions by Yamit Rachman Schrire and Bruno Reudenbach in Hans Aurenhammer and Daniela Bohde, eds., *Räume der Passion: Raumvisionen, Erinnerungsorte und Topographien des Leidens Christi in Mittelalter und Früher Neuzeit*, Vestigia bibliae 32/33 (Bern: Peter Lang, 2015). For the significance of contact relics in general, see also Bynum, *Christian Materiality*, 131–139.
[45] Baltimore, The Walters Art Museum, 37.1159, Naddo Ceccarelli, Reliquary Tabernacle with the Virgin and Child, ca. 1350, tempera and gold leaf on wood panel with glass, paper, and relics, 62 x 43.1 x 9.4 cm. On Naddo Ceccarelli's reliquary tabernacle, including a discussion of the stone relics, see C.

Figure 1.7: Naddo Ceccarelli, Reliquary Tabernacle with the Virgin and Child, ca. 1350. Tempera and gold leaf on wood panel with glass, paper, and relics, 62 x 43.1 x 9.4 cm. Baltimore, The Walters Art Museum, 37.1159. Photo: The Walters Art Museum, Baltimore.

In the Altenburg panel, the wound-cleaved rock and the grained wood of the cross are literally foregrounded (see figure 1.2, plate 2). Lorenzo Monaco's painting techniques emphasize these material witnesses of the Crucifixion by seemingly projecting them into the viewer's space and endowing them with a materiality that has a disturbingly tactile quality. He thus explores the paradoxical nature and sacred essence of the crucifixion scene by means of materialities that themselves have paradoxical implications.

lavorii di mano: Intermedial Practices

As we have seen, Lorenzo Monaco combines naturalism and illusionism with paradoxical pictorial strategies, thereby intertwining material qualities, sensory stimuli, and transcendental truths. This effect is further enhanced by intermedial references, which, as the following analysis will show, capture the beholder's attention, add a further layer of meaning, and highlight the thingness of the panel.[46]

Griffiths Mann, "Relics, Reliquaries, and the Limitations of Trecento Painting: Naddo Ceccarelli's Reliquary Tabernacle in the Walters Art Museum," *Word & Image* 22, no. 3 (2006): 251–259, at 253–257. For the group of reliquary tabernacles in general, see Dagmar Preising, "Bild und Reliquie: Gestalt und Funktion gotischer Reliquientafeln und -altärchen," *Aachener Kunstblätter* 61 (1995/1997): 13–84.
46 For a definition of intermediality and introductory literature concerning the concept, see note 10 above.

Lorenzo Monaco's works attest to his creative handling of the techniques and materials of the artisan, as can be seen in the depiction of blood described above. His working methods are rooted in late medieval workshop practice, which was far more interdisciplinary than today's museum exhibits would suggest when they present panel paintings and sculptures on their own and show all other objects separately, labeling them as "decorative arts" or "crafts." In the workshops of the Trecento, however, there was not such a clear separation of media. Lorenzo Monaco is a case in point, even though the intermedial aspect of his work has not received the scholarly attention it deserves.[47] Indeed, he created mural paintings, panel paintings, book illuminations, and so-called *verre églomisé* panels as well as works that elude classification, such as sheets – neither strictly drawings nor illuminations – executed with pen and brush using ink, paint, and white lead on colored parchment. His monumental two-sided crucifix panels are another example: because their contours coincide with the cross they depict and Christ is shown from both the front and the back, these panels create a three-dimensional effect even though they are essentially flat.[48]

Cennini, in his *Il libro dell'arte*, summarizes the diverse range of tasks in a painter's workshop as "lavorii di mano," literally meaning "works of the hand."[49] With this designation he is referring above all to the individual steps of drawing and painting on paper, walls, and panels, but he also describes tasks such as the gilding of sculptures, the application of plaster reliefs to panels, and techniques of painting and drawing on glass.[50]

In this latter context, Cennini also explains how to make a kind of engraving on the reverse of a gilded glass sheet, commonly referred to as *verre églomisé* (plates 5,

47 A dedicated study of Lorenzo Monaco as an intermedial artist remains to be written. While the comprehensive catalogue of a recent exhibition assembles all relevant works, these are still primarily considered together in terms of stylistic comparisons: Angelo Tartuferi and Daniela Parenti, eds., *Lorenzo Monaco: A Bridge from Giotto's Heritage to the Renaissance*, exh. cat. (Florence: Giunti, 2006).
48 For the *verre églomisé* panels, see below. For the parchment sheets, see Löhr and Weppelmann, *Fantasie und Handwerk*, 294–299, cat. nos. 14 and 15 (Lorenza Melli); and Brahms and Krüger, *Gezeichnete Evidenz*. For the crucifixes, see Boskovits, "Su Don Lorenzo"; and Tartuferi and Parenti, *Lorenzo Monaco*, 118–119, cat. no. 7 (Gaudenz Freuler), and 175–176, cat. no 25 (Daniela Parenti).
49 Cennini, *Il libro dell'arte*, 64 (ch. 4). For the emphasis on the importance of the hand and the handmade in Cennini's conceptualization of artistic creation, see Wolf-Dietrich Löhr, "Handwerk und Denkwerk des Malers: Kontexte für Cenninis Theorie der Praxis," in Löhr and Weppelmann, *Fantasie und Handwerk*, 152–177.
50 For intermedial workshop practice, see also Wolf-Dietrich Löhr and Stefan Weppelmann, "'Glieder in der Kunst der Malerei': Cennino Cenninis Genealogie und die Suche nach Kontinuität zwischen Handwerkstradition, Werkstattpraxis und Historiographie," in Löhr and Weppelmann, *Fantasie und Handwerk*, 13–43, at 23. See also Erling Skaug, "Painters, Punchers, Gilders or Goldbeaters? A Critical Survey Report of Discussions in Recent Literature about Early Italian Painting," *Zeitschrift für Kunstgeschichte* 71, no. 4 (2008): 571–582, dealing with sophisticated gold-tooling techniques, for which, as Skaug argues convincingly, the painters themselves were responsible.

6, and 7).[51] In this process, gold foil is applied to the back of a glass panel, then a needle is used to scratch the depiction into the gold, while blank spaces are scraped away. In the next step, the back is painted over with opaque paint, creating a strong visual contrast with the gold foil, as we see in the example of a Man of Sorrows panel in Fiesole (figure 1.8, plate 6).[52] With an enthusiasm that is quite rare in his book, Cennini describes this technique as "vaga, gientile e perlegrina quanto più dir si può."[53] He defines it as "a branch of great devotion" and deems it suitable for the production of reliquaries.[54] Indeed, most of the *verre églomisé* panels preserved have a reliquary function.[55]

Verre églomisé works, both with and without reliquary function, also survive from Lorenzo Monaco's workshop, among them a tabernacle in Lyon and a Madonna of Humility in Turin (plates 5 and 7).[56] A typical framing decoration for these glass panels depicts tendrils with leaves and blossoms, either in gold against a dark back-

---

51 Cennini, *Il libro dell'arte*, 192–195 (ch. [172]). For this technique and its history, see Frieder Ryser, *Verzauberte Bilder: Die Kunst der Malerei hinter Glas von der Antike bis zum 18. Jahrhundert* (Munich: Klinkhardt & Biermann, 1991); and Cristina De Benedictis, *Devozione e produzione artistica in Umbria: Vetri dorati dipinti e graffiti del XIV e XV secolo* (Florence: Edizioni Firenze, 2010), 9–13. For the rather anachronistic term *verre églomisé*, coined in the nineteenth century, see also Georg Swarzenski, "The Localization of Medieval Verre Eglomisé in the Walters Collections," *The Journal of the Walters Art Gallery* 3 (1940): 55–68, at 55; and Rudy Eswarin, "Terminology of *Verre Églomisé*," *Journal of Glass Studies* 21 (1979): 98–101. For the corpus of works preserved, see, in addition to the studies mentioned, Pietro Toesca, "Vetri italiani a oro con graffiti," *L'Arte* 11 (1908): 247–261; Silvana Pettenati, "Vetri a oro del Trecento padano," *Paragone: Arte* 24, no. 275 (1973): 71–80; Silvana Pettenati, *I vetri dorati graffiti e i vetri dipinti* (Turin: Museo Civico, 1978); Silvana Pettenati, *Vetri dorati e graffiti dal XIV al XVI secolo: Vetri rinascimentali*, Lo specchio del Bargello 20 (Florence: Museo nazionale del Bargello, 1986); Irene Hueck, "Ein umbrisches Reliquiar im Kunstgewerbemuseum Schloß Köpenick," *Forschungen und Berichte* 31 (1991): 183–188; Dillian Gordon, "The Mass Production of Franciscan Piety: Another Look at Some Umbrian verres églomisés," *Apollo* 140, no. 394 (1994): 33–42; and De Benedictis, *Devozione*.
52 Fiesole, Museo Bandini, Florentine artist, Man of Sorrows, ca. 1315–1325, *verre églomisé*, 24 x 30 cm. See Angelo Tartuferi, ed., *Giotto: Bilancio critico di sessant'anni di studi e ricerche*, exh. cat. (Florence: Giunti, 2000), 218–220, cat. no. 35 (Magnolia Scudieri).
53 Cennini, *Il libro dell'arte*, 192 (ch. [172]). On the ambiguous vocabulary used in this passage, see also Frezzato's etymological comment at 192, note b. Translated by Lara Broecke as "beautiful, refined and rare as it is possible to describe" (Cennini, trans. Broecke, 226), and by Daniel V. Thompson Jr. as "indescribably attractive, fine and unusual." Cennino d'Andrea Cennini, *The Craftman's Handbook: The Italian "Il libro dell'arte,"* trans. Daniel V. Thompson Jr. (1933; repr., New York: Dover, 1960), 112.
54 Cennini, *Il libro dell'arte*, 192 (ch. [172]): "membro di gran divozione per adornamento d'orlique sante." Translation in Cennini, trans. Broecke, 226.
55 See Gordon, "Mass Production"; and Preising, "Bild und Reliquie," 25–29.
56 The preserved *verre églomisé* panels attributed to Lorenzo Monaco, or his workshop, are: Lyon, Musée des Beaux-Arts, D698, Reliquary Tabernacle with Saint, ca. 1400–1410, gilded wood, *verre églomisé* (relics lost), 47 x 28.3 x 16 cm; Paris, Musée du Louvre, the Virgin and Child with Saints, ca. 1400, 17.1 x 17.5 cm; and Turin, Palazzo Madama – Museo Civico d'Arte Antica, 0140/VD, the Virgin and Child with Saints, 1408, 29.5 x 23 cm (overall). For these panels, see Kanter, *Painting and Illumination*, 223–226, cat. no. 27 (Laurence B. Kanter).

Figure 1.8: Florentine artist, Man of Sorrows, ca. 1315–1325. *Verre églomisé*, 24 x 30 cm. Fiesole, Museo Bandini. Photo: Museo Bandini.

ground or vice versa (see figure 1.8, plates 6 and 7). Just such a border also frames the Crucifixion in the Altenburg panel. It is not, however, engraved into gilded glass, but rather evoked by sgraffito. In this technique, gold leaf applied to a panel is painted over with opaque paint and a pattern is scratched out, showing the gold ground beneath it (see figure 1.6, plate 3a).[57] With this kind of decorative border, which was uncommon in panel painting, Lorenzo Monaco evokes the sumptuous and delicate technique of *verre églomisé* and, together with it, the sacred dignity and material authenticity of the objects for which it was typically used. With its concentration on gold, white, black, and brown shades, Lorenzo Monaco's Crucifixion is also reminiscent of the aesthetic appearance of these reverse-painted and gilded glass panels, characterized by their necessarily limited range of colors. In *verre églomisé* works, red – the only chromatic pigment in the Crucifixion panel – is often used as a color accent.

---

57 For the sgraffito technique in general, see Norman E. Muller, "The Development of Sgraffito in Sienese Painting," in *Simone Martini: Atti del Convegno*, ed. Luciano Bellosi (Florence: Centro Di, 1988), 147–150. Without using this term, Cennini discusses this technique in his chapters on the depiction of textiles on gold ground. Cennini, *Il libro dell'arte*, 162–165 (chs. [141]–[143]).

Material preciousness is also introduced by the gold ground of the Altenburg panel (see figure 1.2, plate 2).[58] In late medieval panel painting, as is well known, the materiality of the gold ground was ever present – namely, its economic, natural, semantic, and aesthetic aspects.[59] The monetary value of gold made it an appropriate choice for the portrayal of saints.[60] At the same time, its natural material qualities of durability, permanence, and purity could also be interpreted as virtues of the saints depicted. Its aesthetic quality of luminosity, seen within the context of the metaphysics of light, could be understood as representing the essence of the divine.[61]

Additionally, gold grounds and frames in Italian panel painting were often decorated with punchwork and *pastiglia* elements in relief, which undoubtedly generated an intermedial reference to metalwork objects – not only in terms of formal and aesthetic criteria but also because the concrete materials, instruments, and techniques of the goldsmith were used.[62] This is, however, not to suggest that painting was dependent on or imitated metalwork, since both art forms had a long-standing tradition of tooling techniques.[63] Rather, a familiar category of objects with specific

---

58 For gold-ground tooling, see Skaug, "Painters."

59 The increased research on gold and gold ground in recent decades has clearly shown that it is not possible to speak in a general way about evaluations and interpretations of this material. On this question in general and the material character of gold ground in particular, see Ellen J. Beer, "Marginalien zum Thema Goldgrund," *Zeitschrift für Kunstgeschichte* 46 (1983): 271–286. See also Iris Wenderholm, "Aura, Licht und schöner Schein: Wertungen und Umwertungen des Goldgrunds," in *Geschichten auf Gold: Bilderzählungen in der frühen italienischen Malerei*, ed. Stefan Weppelmann, exh. cat. (Berlin: SMB-DuMont, 2005), 100–113, esp. 100–104; Michael Philipp, "Vom Kultbild zum Abbild der Wirklichkeit: Zur Entwicklung der Malerei in Italien 1250–1500," in Westheider and Philipp, *Erfindung des Bildes*, 12–33, esp. 13–15, 22–24; Anna Degler and Iris Wenderholm, eds., "Der Wert des Goldes – der Wert der Golde," special issue, *Zeitschrift für Kunstgeschichte* 79, no. 4 (2016). For the insistent materiality of late medieval Christian art per se and its significance and semantics, see also Bynum, *Christian Materiality*, 53–59 and passim.

60 For the criterion of appropriateness, see Victor M. Schmidt, "The Lunette-Shaped Panel and Some Characteristics of Panel Painting," in V. Schmidt, *Italian Panel Painting*, 83–101, at 93–96. Schmidt also cites pertinent passages in Cennini.

61 See Beer, "Marginalien," 273–274.

62 See Beer, "Marginalien," 276–278. Cf. Mann, "Relics," 251; De Marchi, "Oggetti," 356. According to Bastian Eclercy, the techniques for gold-ground tooling in panel painting, as described by Cennini – namely, incision, stippling, and punchwork – are "borrowed" from the practice of the goldsmiths. Bastian Eclercy, "'Granare': Zur historischen Terminologie des Goldgrunddekors im Traktat des Cennino Cennini," *Mitteilungen des Kunsthistorischen Institutes in Florenz* 51, no. 3/4 (2007): 539–554, at 539 and passim. Cf. Cennini, *Il libro dell'arte*, 162–165 (chs. [141]–[143]).

63 Cf. Erling Skaug, "Stippled Angels and 'Forgotten Haloes,'" in "Das Göttinger Barfüßerretabel von 1424," special issue, *Niederdeutsche Beiträge zur Kunstgeschichte*, n.s., 1 (2015): 395–402, at 398–401. Skaug points to the long tradition of various tooling techniques for gold grounds in panel painting as well as related techniques in drawings and (in the fifteenth century) prints. In this way, he argues against the idea that painting is influenced by metalwork, instead suggesting a parallel development provoked by the material common to both genres – burnished gold – and its potentials.

connotations, such as reliquaries or liturgical instruments, was evoked in a latent way to enrich the aesthetic appearance of panel paintings and elevate their status.

The painters' treatment of the gold ground thus created intermedial references by virtue of similarities in tooling techniques, decorative patterns, and aesthetics. The nature of these criteria, in turn, called attention to gold as matter: as a material that was applied deliberately, worked diligently, and appropriated creatively. At the same time, the materiality of the gold ground and its tooling emphasize the artificial nature of the image itself, the illusionistic representation of which is disrupted by the insistent presence of the material. Like other artists around 1400, Lorenzo Monaco developed strategies to use this tension creatively to explore the connotations of the scene depicted, while subordinating the tooling techniques to the domain of painting.[64] For while gold tooling in the form of punching or stippling was commonly used for halos and ornamental decorations within paintings, Lorenzo Monaco applied it also to the figurative depiction of the Altenburg panel, specifically to the representation of the angels – in other words, to the figures that mediate between the earthly and the heavenly realms.

For these angels, he used the tooling technique of stippling together with the painted application of dark shadows and white highlights, in order to achieve an effect of corporeality (see figures 1.6 and 1.9, plates 3a – 3b). At the same time, the light reflected and scattered in varied ways by the indentations of the gold ground lends the angels an elusive and ephemeral quality.[65] The stippling treatment of the burnished gold causes the surface to shimmer, creating an effect of movement, which would have been increased when the panel was illuminated by candlelight. Depending on the direction from which light comes – and on the recipient's position and movement – the indentations made in a burnished gold surface will either shine brightly and seem to protrude or else appear darkly shaded and seem to recede behind the surface.[66] Cennini, too, explains how to apply tooling techniques to create

---

64 For the tension between gold ground and figurative representation, see Beer, "Marginalien," 279; and Philipp, "Kultbild," 15. See also the examples in Andrea De Marchi, "Angels Stippled in Gold: The Perugia Madonna," in *Gentile da Fabriano and the Other Renaissance*, ed. Laura Laureati and Lorenza Mochi Onori, exh. cat. (Milan: Electa, 2006), 94–95; and Andrea De Marchi, "Oro come luce, luce come oro: L'operazione delle lamine metalliche da Simone Martini a Pisanello, fra mimesi e anagogia," in *Medioevo: Natura e figura; La raffigurazione dell'uomo e della natura nell'arte medievale*, ed. Arturo Carlo Quintavalle (Milan: Skira Editore, 2015), 701–715. For the productive tension between figurative representation and emphatic material presence, see also Krüger, "Mimesis," 424–428; and V. Schmidt, *Painted Piety*, ch. 5.
65 According to the catalogue entry in Boskovits and Parenti, *Da Bernardo Daddi al Beato Angelico*, 110, cat. no. 22 (Sonia Chiodo), red color was used, which today has darkened to a bluish black. For the chiaroscuro modeling, see Fricke, "Liquid History," 65. For the related technique of applying punch marks in clusters of varying density to achieve the effect of relief, fittingly called *granare a rilievo* in Cennini's treatise, see Cennini, *Il libro dell'arte*, 161–162 (ch. 140); Eclercy, "Granare," 544; and Skaug, "Stippled Angels," which includes consideration of its purposeful use for the depiction of angels, which Cennini also cites as one of the main subjects to employ this technique for.
66 Skaug, "Stippled Angels," 395.

different light effects on a gold surface. According to his instructions, stippling, as employed by Lorenzo Monaco for his angels, is to be done with tiny punches, so that the indentations, paradoxically, "sparkle like millet grain."[67]

Figure 1.9: Lorenzo Monaco, Christ on the Cross with Saints Benedict, Francis of Assisi, and Romuald, ca. 1405–1407 (detail). Tempera and gold leaf on poplar, 56.4 x 42 x 2.8 cm. Altenburg, Lindenau-Museum, inv. no. 23. © Lindenau-Museum Altenburg. Photo: Bernd Sinterhauf.

The tooling techniques in the Altenburg panel thus continue Lorenzo Monaco's exploration of the gold ground as a paradoxical site of pictorial space, as witnessed in his treatment of frame and ground. In this case, however, the transgression of the pictorial plane is achieved both optically, by the effect of highlights created by stippling, and physically, by the punch marks engraved into the gold ground. Consequently, transcendental otherworldliness and shimmering immateriality come into tension with the perceived three-dimensionality as well as the actual material. In this way, Lorenzo Monaco's gold tooling techniques complement the previously described effects of the tempera painting – effects of spatial and sensory disorientation, of tangibility combined with withdrawal.

The (im)materiality of the angels, as well as of the material witnesses of the Passion and even Christ on the cross, thus would have engaged the recipient's attention and imagination: it might have encouraged viewers to contemplate the respective natures of the figures depicted and to think about the various materials and substances – be they real, painted, or evoked. This ties in with the overall creative handling of artistic materials, iconographic choices, and suggestive tactility through which Lorenzo Monaco's painting triggers various modes of reception and reflection. Rooted in the tradition of small-scale panel paintings, the Altenburg Crucifixion can be situated within a wider practice of individual devotion: a practice in which the material and the immaterial were intrinsically linked and paradoxically intertwined. However, this interdependence of the material and the immaterial concerns artistic practices in addition to religious ones, and not only because paintings were used in acts of devotion, which is true for many other material objects as well. Rather, this interplay is also negotiated within the paintings themselves, as the sacramental subject and

---

67 Cennini, *Il libro dell'arte*, 162 (ch. 140): "istampe minute che brillino come panicho." Translation in Cennini, trans. Broecke, 157. See Eclercy, "Granare," 543–544.

the recipient's imagination are interconnected with the emphatic presence of painting materials, the calculated use of artistic techniques, and sensory stimuli that suggest physical engagement.

Focusing closely on a painting that is both exemplary and highly original, this chapter has traced how concrete materials, painting and tooling techniques, and intermedial practices may all partake in the negotiation of sacred truths. Encouraged by the intimacy of the reception situation, the contemplation of such a small-scale panel can thus generate dynamic, relational, and productive connections between artistic and devotional practices, between painting materials and painted matter, and between sensory experiences and immaterial realms.

Mareike E. Reisch

2 Transporting the Holy City: Hans Tucher's Letter from Jerusalem as Medium and Material Object

A Letter: More Than Ink and Paper

On 6 August 1479, Hans Tucher the Elder, a Jerusalem pilgrim, wrote a letter to his brother Endres II Tucher, a Carthusian lay brother in Nuremberg. In it, he informed his brother that he had reached the Holy City safe and sound on 2 August. While most of his fellow pilgrims were already preparing to embark again on the galley to sail back to Venice after only a few days in the Holy Land, he and his companion Sebald Rieter the Younger had decided to prolong their pilgrimage. They were planning to cross the desert on foot and by camel in order to visit the Monastery of St. Catherine at Mount Sinai, and they hoped to catch another ship to Venice in Alexandria.[1] Mirroring Hans Tucher's outbound journey by returning on the same galley that he had taken to Jaffa, the message arrived in Nuremberg twelve weeks after it was written.[2] Once in Franconia, the letter appears to have sparked great interest on the part of its recipient as well as his relatives, friends, and acquaintances.

While the original letter does not survive, since it was, as I explore below, apparently destroyed by too much wear and tear, its content survives today in one single copy made by Endres Tucher. Endres bound this transcript of the Jerusalem letter, together with a chronicle and a sketch of the Via Dolorosa, into his personal copy of the 1482 edition of his brother's pilgrimage account, printed by Johann Schönsperger in Augsburg.[3] This transmission situation does not allow for definite state-

Acknowledgements: I warmly thank Rev. Dr. Petra Seegets, pastor at St. Sebaldus Church in Nuremberg, and Alexandra Fritsch, the church's master builder, for their generous help with understanding the architectural history of St. Sebaldus, and particularly the church's late medieval history.

1 The second still-surviving letter that Hans Tucher wrote from Jerusalem is addressed to his cousin Anton Tucher and is dated 8 August 1479. According to this letter, the other pilgrims were planning to return to Jaffa either on the same day or on 9 August. This indicates that the pilgrims stayed no longer than a week in the Holy Land after their arrival in Jerusalem. See Hans Tucher, *Die "Reise ins Gelobte Land" Hans Tuchers des Älteren (1479–1480): Untersuchungen zur Überlieferung und kritische Edition eines spätmittelalterlichen Reiseberichts*, ed. Randall Herz, Wissensliteratur im Mittelalter 38 (Wiesbaden: Dr. Ludwig Reichert Verlag, 2002), p. 655, lines 12–13. Both of Hans Tucher's letters are appended to the modern edition of his *Reise ins Gelobte Land* and are cited from this source.
2 Regarding the time it took the letter to reach Nuremberg, see H. Tucher, *Reise*, p. 648, lines 1–4.
3 Today, the Bibliothèque nationale de France houses Endres Tucher's personal copy of Hans Tucher's pilgrimage account: Paris, BnF, Rés. 4° O²f. 13. See Randall Herz, *Studien zur Drucküberlieferung*

https://doi.org/10.1515/9783110742985-005

ments about the materiality of the original letter. Still, Hans Tucher provides us with enough insight into the luggage he took with him on pilgrimage to allow us to assume that the letter was written with ink on paper.[4]

The body of the letter can be divided into three parts: First, it informed Endres Tucher about his brother's well-being and whereabouts. Second, it tried to render the holy places Hans Tucher had visited during his stay imaginatively tangible to his brother and other potential readers. Third, Hans Tucher asked his brother and other potential readers of the letter for intercessory prayers to secure his safe return to Franconia. In this chapter, I will focus on the last two points, which aim to produce a connection between the recipient of the written document and its author as well as between Nuremberg and the Holy City.

However, to focus solely on the content of the letter would mean ignoring its particular materiality: having been produced in Jerusalem, I will argue here, the letter had the Holy City inscribed in its materiality and was indeed a part of the city itself.[5] In the form of this letter, a piece of Jerusalem came to Franconia and into the hands of its receiver.[6] In other words, Jerusalem is part of the letter's aura, as Walter Benjamin notably called it.[7] The missive thus contains the Holy City both in its semantics and in its physicality.

---

der "Reise ins Gelobte Land" Hans Tuchers des Älteren: Bestandsaufnahme und historische Auswertung der Inkunabeln unter Berücksichtigung der späteren Drucküberlieferung, Quellen und Forschungen zur Geschichte und Kultur der Stadt Nürnberg 34 (Nuremberg: Selbstverlag des Stadtarchivs Nürnberg, 2005), 156–161.

4 At the end of his pilgrimage account, Hans Tucher provides a packing list for aspiring Jerusalem pilgrims. In that list we find a note about writing tools: "Jtem kauf auch ein schreibzeug, papir, vnd dintten, das einer vntterwegen fur die langen weil schreiben mug, vnd was einer vntterwegen auch sicht." H. Tucher, Reise, p. 633, lines 9–10.

5 In this sense, the letter functioned similarly to the pilgrim badges that were sewn into books of hours. "The close association of badge to place allowed such souvenirs," Shayne Aaron Legassie has argued, "to be used as mnemonic prompts." Shayne Aaron Legassie, The Medieval Invention of Travel (Chicago: University of Chicago Press, 2017), 114–115.

6 The Jerusalem letter functions differently in this sense from other objects, such as ritualistic objects, that signify something beyond their objectness. In his book Die Macht der Dinge, Karl-Heinz Kohl shows that objects can often have a semiotic character and thus signify something else: "Die distinkte, sprachlich erfaßbare Einheit des Objekts ist zugleich Bedingung der Möglichkeit, daß es selbst Zeichencharakter erhalten und für ein anderes als es selbst stehen kann." Karl-Heinz Kohl, Die Macht der Dinge: Geschichte und Theorie sakraler Objekte (Munich: C. H. Beck, 2003), 120. Kathryn Rudy has argued that in the ritualistic handling of books in religious and legal contexts, "books symbolise power." Kathryn M. Rudy, "Touching the Book Again: The Passional of Abbess Kunigunde of Bohemia," in Codex und Material, ed. Patrizia Carmassi and Gia Toussaint, Wolfenbütteler Mittelalter-Studien 34 (Wiesbaden: Harrassowitz Verlag, 2018), 247–257, at 248.

7 In this chapter, I will use the term aura according to Walter Benjamin's notion of the aura as that which is inscribed in the materiality of a piece of art and which describes the object's history, its material changes, and its changing ownership. See Walter Benjamin, "The Work of Art in the Age of Its Technological Reproducibility: Second Version," in The Work of Art in the Age of Its Technological Reproducibility, and Other Writings on Media, by Walter Benjamin, ed. Michael W. Jennings, Brigid Doh-

If we pay close attention to this double inscription of Jerusalem in the written document, a number of questions are raised regarding the ways in which the letter makes the Holy City tangible for its readers: In what ways does the object bridge – or maybe even overcome – the geographical distance between Franconia and the Holy Land, between Nuremberg and Jerusalem, and finally between its readers and its author Hans Tucher? How does it render faraway things and places perceivable to its readers? Does it invite its readers to participate in the pilgrimage? And if so, how are the readers able to take part from afar in Hans Tucher's endeavor?

The semantics and the materiality, I will argue in the following, worked together in Tucher's Jerusalem letter in order to connect the geographically removed cities in the mind's eye of the recipient. Furthermore, I will argue that by traveling from one place to the other and by implying a simultaneity between the act of reading and the events described in it, the letter allowed and even asked for its recipient's active participation in the pilgrimage from afar through intercessory prayers.

Experiencing the Church of the Holy Sepulcher in Nuremberg's St. Sebaldus Church: The Content of the Letter

Purely on the level of content, Hans Tucher's letter works to connect the cities of Nuremberg and Jerusalem, specifically through the technique of layering the two cities' topographies on top of each other. Tucher intertwines certain places in the two cities so that they appear to merge into one, causing parts of the Holy City to become vividly tangible in the cityscape of Nuremberg.[8] This becomes particularly evident in Tucher's rendering of the Church of the Holy Sepulcher, one of the most sacred places of Christianity. In preparing readers for this highlight of the letter, he begins by mentioning that the Mameluke authorities granted his travel group entrance to the Church of the Holy Sepulcher one evening:

> And at the time of Vespers they let us enter the temple. There they counted us and eventually locked us overnight in the temple.

---

erty, and Thomas Y. Levin (Cambridge, MA: The Belknap Press of Harvard University Press, 2008), 19–55, at 21.

8 By rendering the Holy City in a tangible way for its recipients, the letter might be seen as belonging to the *synthetic tradition* that Shayne Aaron Legassie establishes in his monograph *The Medieval Invention of Travel*. In connecting Hans Tucher's own pilgrimage experiences in Jerusalem to the St. Sebaldus Church in Nuremberg, the letter "not only preserves knowledge and experience, it also – and perhaps more importantly – *transforms* knowledge and experience in a way that makes it valuable to readers." Legassie, *Medieval Invention of Travel*, 123 (italics in original).

About this, I want to write a little and give a comparison to St. Sebaldus Church, although the temple is not as long, and it is also wider, etc.[9]

Before he immerses his readers in his visit to the church, Tucher stops to reflect on the rhetorical device he is going to employ in order to provide them with a description of the Church of the Holy Sepulcher that is as vividly imaginable as possible.[10] A comparison with St. Sebaldus Church in Nuremberg, Tucher implies here, is the best way to convey the architectural structure of the church in Jerusalem, even though the two churches differ in size and thus a comparison between them must remain approximate.[11] Such a link between the two churches, as I will show below, furthermore elevates St. Sebaldus in Nuremberg by highlighting a supposed correlation with one of the most sacred places of Christianity.

In late medieval pilgrimage literature, comparisons are, along with illustrations, among the most common rhetorical devices for rendering the foreign and unknown understandable to the audience.[12] In the attempt to make new objects, unknown traditions, and foreign animals and landscapes imaginable for readers who were unlikely to ever see them with their own eyes, composers of late medieval pilgrimage literature referred to comparatively well-known objects and used these as a basis

---

9 H. Tucher, *Reise*, p. 650, lines 15–19:

    Vnd vmb vesper czeÿt, do burde wir jn den thempel gelossen. Do czalet man vns alle ein vnd versloß vns erstlich die nacht jn dem thempel.

    Do von wil jch ein wiennÿg schreÿben ein geleichnuß von Sant Sebolcz kirchen, wie wol der thempel nicht als langk ist, so ist er doch weÿtter etc.

    All translations in this chapter are my own, unless otherwise stated.

10 For immersion as an effect of medieval religious literature, see Björn Klaus Buschbeck, "Sprechen mit dem Heiligen und Eintauchen in den Text: Zur Wirkungsästhetik eines Passionsgebets aus dem 'Engelberger Gebetbuch,'" *Das Mittelalter* 24, no. 2 (2019): 390–408, at 401.

11 In his later pilgrimage account, Tucher also employs the method of comparison in order to describe the Church of the Holy Sepulcher to his reader. There he reasons that a comparison between the two churches will help his audience better remember the architectural structure of the Church of the Holy Sepulcher. See H. Tucher, *Reise*, p. 390, line 12–p. 391, line 5. About the seeming resemblance of the Church of the Holy Sepulcher and St. Sebaldus in Tucher's comparison, see Kathryn Blair Moore, *The Architecture of the Christian Holy Land: Reception from Late Antiquity through the Renaissance* (Cambridge: Cambridge University Press, 2017), 196. About resemblances in premodern times in a more general sense, see Michel Foucault, *The Order of Things: An Archaeology of the Human Sciences* (New York: Vintage Books, 1994), 17–30.

12 See Arnold Esch, "Anschauung und Begriff: Die Bewältigung fremder Wirklichkeit durch den Vergleich in Reiseberichten des späten Mittelalters," *Historische Zeitschrift* 253, no. 2 (1991): 281–312. As both Stephan Matter and Arnold Esch have shown, comparisons were often employed when writers tried to describe something for which there was no specialized terminology in the vernacular, such as in descriptions of buildings. See Esch, 308; and Stefan Matter, "Zur Poetik mittelalterlicher Architekturbeschreibungen," *Mittellateinisches Jahrbuch: Internationale Zeitschrift für Mediävistik und Humanismusforschung* 47, no. 3 (2012): 387–413, at 389.

for their explanations.[13] Consequently, many fifteenth-century pilgrims to Jerusalem compared the Church of the Holy Sepulcher with their hometown parish churches.[14] In so doing, they put the church in Jerusalem in direct relation with the church they had to assume was most familiar to their audience. Such a comparison would allow their readers to gain a vivid impression of the unknown church.[15]

In comparing the church in Jerusalem with St. Sebaldus in Nuremberg, then, "he [Hans Tucher] is drawing," as Kathryn Blair Moore points out, "upon a technique of description that uses the audience's collective experience of a shared architectural environment, in order to bring to mind otherwise unseen buildings."[16] St. Sebaldus might have been a particularly fruitful basis of comparison, given that during medieval times Tucher's parish church was a pivotal element in some of the major processions of the city of Nuremberg, such as the Corpus Christi procession, the procession on St. Sebaldus's feast day, and different processions of the Cross.[17] Oftentimes, especially for the Corpus Christi processions, St. Sebaldus served as both starting and end point: the participants walked from there through large parts of the city and back to the church.[18] During these processions, various locations inside and outside St. Sebaldus were used as stations for devotion and prayer. Relievos depicting various stations of the Passion of Christ – starting with Christ's entry into Jerusalem and ending with the Resurrection – run around the exterior façade of the church, indicating where the processions stopped.[19] As active members of the parish of St. Sebaldus, Tucher's brother and other potential readers of the letter were thus used to employing specific locations in the church in Nuremberg to envision the Passion of Christ and the associated places in Jerusalem. In this way, Tucher ties his comparison closely to the religious experience that his readership already associates with the church in Nuremberg. He invites his audience to do once more what they are already used to

---

13 See Esch, "Anschauung und Begriff," 289; and Georgia Clarke, "Diverse, Synoptic, and Synchronous Descriptions of the Church of the Holy Sepulchre in Jerusalem in Fifteenth-Century Accounts," *Città e Storia* 7, no. 1 (2012): 43–75, at 55.
14 See Moore, *Architecture of the Christian Holy Land*, 196.
15 This meant, however, that the audience being addressed in these comparative descriptions of foreign objects was very clearly defined and often rather small, given that they had to relate to the same knowledge and experience in order to appreciate the comparison. See Esch, "Anschauung und Begriff," 290.
16 Moore, *Architecture of the Christian Holy Land*, 196. Arnold Esch understands Tucher's comparison a little differently when he argues that Tucher is not primarily concerned with conveying an architectural structure but rather a "topographie religieuse en miniature." Esch, "Anschauung und Begriff," 294.
17 See Gerhard Weilandt, *Die Sebalduskirche in Nürnberg: Bild und Gesellschaft im Zeitalter der Gotik und Renaissance*, Studien zur internationalen Architektur- und Kunstgeschichte 47 (Petersberg: Michael Imhof Verlag, 2007), 301.
18 See Weilandt, *Sebalduskirche*, 301; and Andrea Löther, *Prozessionen in spätmittelalterlichen Städten: Politische Partizipation, obrigkeitliche Inszenierung, städtische Einheit*, Norm und Struktur 12 (Cologne: Böhlau Verlag, 1999), 105–107.
19 See Weilandt, *Sebalduskirche*, 301–305.

doing: to allow the St. Sebaldus Church to function as a gateway through which they can vividly imagine the Passion of Christ, or, in the context of the letter, the site where it took place – the Church of the Holy Sepulcher in Jerusalem.

Not only did Tucher's comparison draw on his readers' experience to facilitate a vivid image of the Church of the Holy Sepulcher, it also elevated his congregational church by putting it in direct relation with the holiness of Christ's final resting place. Such an enhancement of the status of St. Sebaldus Church had, as Bernhard Jahn has argued, a direct impact for Hans Tucher and his family, as well as many other Nuremberg patrons: St. Sebaldus was not just Tucher's parish church but also the site of the Tucher family grave, or, if you wish, his own Church of the Sepulcher.[20] The comparison thus directly related his own tomb with Christ's tomb.

In his letter, Hans Tucher goes on to invite his readers to vividly experience the Church of the Holy Sepulcher by imaginatively walking through St. Sebaldus, effectively merging two geographically distant spaces. This connection between the two churches evokes the impression of a (nonexistent) architectural resemblance between them:

> Item: the temple has just one portal where you enter; the heathens lock and seal it at all times. [...] Item: the portal leads into the temple as if it were the door at St. Sebaldus Church that leads into the church through the Portal of Our Lady. And if one enters [the church] straight away, there is the place [the stone of anointment], where they laid down our dear Lord, when he was taken down from the Holy Cross. Behind it, where the choir of St. Catherine is located, is a round church that looks from the outside similar to the one that stands in Eichstätt outside of the city. It [the church] is hence built in the middle of the same church. There stands the Holy Sepulcher.[21]

As he invites his readers to imaginatively walk through St. Sebaldus Church, Tucher pauses at each important architectural structure, directly linking sites in the church

---

20 See Bernhard Jahn, *Raumkonzepte in der Frühen Neuzeit: Zur Konstruktion von Wirklichkeit in Pilgerberichten, Amerikareisebeschreibungen und Prosaerzählungen* (Frankfurt: Peter Lang, 1993), 74–76. Tucher's comparison, Jahn concludes, is not only invested in rendering the place imaginatively tangible: "Tuchers Vergleich ist weit mehr als ein pragmatisches Mittel, um einen räumlichen Sachverhalt zu veranschaulichen. Er stellt eine religiöse Handlung dar, die Tuchers Grabesstätte heiligt und die eigene Auferstehung von den Toten erleichtern möchte" (76).

21 H. Tucher, *Reise*, p. 650, line 20–p. 651, line 3: "Jtem der thempel hot nëwer ein tor, do man hin ein get, das versliessen und versigelen die heÿden albegen. [...] Jtem das thor get jn den thempel, als wer es die thur czw Sant Sebolcz kirchen, die do vntter vnsser lieben Frawen thur jn die kirchen get. Vnd als man gerichcz hin ein get, do ist die stat, do vnsser lieber Here hin gelegt wardt, als er von dem heÿligen kreucz gennumen waß. Dor noch, do Sant Kathreyn kor stet, do ist ein sinbelle kirch hin auß geleich, wie die ist czw Eÿstet, die vor der stat stet. Die ist dor noch gemacht mÿtten jn der selben kirchen. Do stet das Heÿlige Grab." With "Portal of Our Lady," Hans Tucher refers to the portal of the Three Magi. The name "Our Lady" originates in the image of a nursing Madonna that hangs over the portal on the inside of the church. Originally the wooden tympanum decorated the outside façade of the portal. Only in 1657 was it turned so as to be displayed on the inside of the church, where it remains today. See Weilandt, *Sebalduskirche*, 344; and H. Tucher, *Reise*, 391.

in Nuremberg to locations in the church in Jerusalem. Laying the floor plans of both churches on top of each other and using doors, choirs, and chapels as the anchors connecting the two spaces, the letter produces the opportunity to imaginatively be in two geographically separate and distant places at once (see figures 2.1 and 2.2).[22] The choir of St. Catherine in Nuremberg and the Aedicule in Jerusalem have, according to the letter, the same coordinates in the respective spaces they inhabit. After giving the position of the Aedicule, Tucher alludes to its architectural shape. He mentions a model of this structure in Eichstätt, a town close to Nuremberg. The *tertium comparationis* of the altar and the Aedicule hence is their identical location in two spaces layered on top of each other rather than a resemblance in appearance. By sharing the same position in the spaces of the two distant churches, the two objects strengthen the impression that the parallel spaces occupied by St. Sebaldus and the Church of the Holy Sepulcher are analogous.

After establishing this seeming spatial connection which invites the readers to experience each church in the other, the letter moves beyond a mere comparison by merging the Church of the Holy Sepulcher and St. Sebaldus Church into one single space:

> Afterward, one starts walking again, and as if walking down from the choir of St. Catherine, and leaving the church through the portal of baptism, one enters into a chapel. This chapel is approximately as big as the Church of the Twelve Brothers and is called the chapel of Our Dear Lady. In this chapel, the father prior started a beautiful procession and all pilgrims joined it. And everyone bought a candle worth two, three, four, or five silver shillings in Venetian currency. And everyone joined in to sing the litany. And thus, they started the procession at this location. This chapel is the place where Our Dear Lord after his resurrection first appeared to his dear mother.[23]

Guiding its readers through the baptism portal and seemingly out into the cityscape of Nuremberg, the letter actually leads its audience into the Chapel of Our Dear Lady – a side chapel adjacent to the main aisle of the Church of the Holy Sepulcher. It is here, with the description of a fictitious chapel attached to St. Sebaldus yet located in

---

22 See Matter, "Architekturbeschreibungen," 392. Although copies of Hans Tucher's sketches depicting the Via Dolorosa are extant, no drawing meant as an aid to visualize the laying of the two floor plans on top of each other survives today. Furthermore, Tucher does not mention that such a drawing ever existed. We thus have to assume that the visualization is solely relying on verbal description.
23 H. Tucher, *Reise*, p. 651, lines 3–11: "Dor noch get man wider, als ob man von Sant Kathreyn kor herab ging, vnd als peÿ der thawff thur man hin auß gÿng jn ein kapellen. Die selbige kapelle ist als groß als vngeferlich der Czwelf Pruder Kirch vnd heÿst vnsser lieben Frawen kapellen. Jn disser kapellen hub der vatter gardian an ein schune proczeß, vnd gingen die pilgrame mit. Vnd jeder kauffet ein kerczen von ij iij, iiij oder v schilling venediger munczen. Vnd gingen alle mit der letteneÿ singen. Vnd huben also an der selben stat mit der proczessen an. Die selbe kapelle ist die stat, do vnsser lieber Here seyner lieben mutter erscheÿnn, des ersten noch seÿner vrstende etc." With the "Church of the Twelve Brothers," Tucher is referring to the chapel of the House of the Twelve Brothers, which was endowed in 1388 by Konrad Mendel. See Günther P. Fehring and Anton Ress, *Die Stadt Nürnberg: Kurzinventar*, Bayerische Kunstdenkmale 10 (Munich: Deutscher Kunstverlag, 1961), 154.

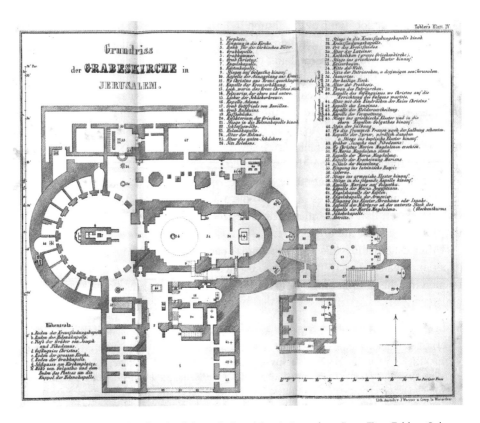

Figure 2.1: Floor plan of the Church of the Holy Sepulcher in Jerusalem. From Titus Tobler, *Golgatha: Seine Kirchen und Klöster; Nach Quellen und Anschau; Mit Ansichten und Plänen* (St. Gallen: Huber, 1851), appendix, sheet 4.

Jerusalem, that the constant oscillation between the two similar and connected spaces turns into a blending of the two churches in Jerusalem and Nuremberg. The space of St. Sebaldus Church is extended in such a way that it morphs into a church that is simultaneously St. Sebaldus and the Church of the Holy Sepulcher, and which is furthermore located both in Nuremberg and in Jerusalem. The floor plan of this new space is based on the shape of St. Sebaldus in Nuremberg, with amplifications in height, depth, and width.

Besides evoking a change in spatial perception, the letter furthermore invites the readers to perceive present and past simultaneously by intertwining different layers of time. Once the two floor plans have been merged, the letter offers information about the pilgrimage procession through the Church of the Holy Sepulcher: the readers learn where the procession starts, the fact that every participant buys a candle, and the fact that the guardian leads the procession through the church while singing a litany. With this description, Hans Tucher asks his readers to follow him and his pilgrimage companions on this procession through the church in Jerusalem. Thus, the letter produces here a temporal simultaneity as well – one that I will explore

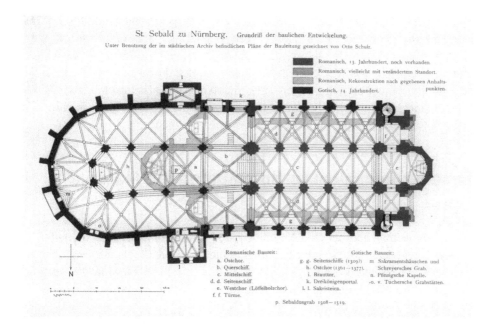

Figure 2.2: Floor plan of St. Sebaldus Church in Nuremberg. From Otto Schulz, "Die Wiederherstellung der St. Sebaldkirche in Nürnberg 1888–1905," *Mitteilungen des Vereins für Geschichte der Stadt Nürnberg* 17 (1906): 246–281, at 281. Nuremberg, Stadtarchiv Nürnberg, A4/XI Nr. 46. Reproduced by permission of Stadtarchiv Nürnberg.

in greater detail below – which allows the readers to experience an event from the author's past as if it were occurring in their own present time.[24] On a second level, the letter produces a temporal connection between its readers, Hans Tucher, and the events of the New Testament by reminding the readers which events of Christ's Passion and Crucifixion happened at each of the places they imaginatively visit. This correlates to Christian Kiening's observations:

> The re-memorization of the Passion takes place in a complex memorial space: one in which Jerusalem and Nuremberg are superimposed on top of one another; one in which the origin of Mass celebrations appears in the present ceremony; one in which the historical origins of salvation coincide with one's own salvational hopes.[25]

---

24 The temporal discrepancy between reading about an experience, writing about the experience, and actually having the experience is an inherent feature of the epistolary conversation over distances. See Christine Wand-Wittkowski, *Briefe im Mittelalter: Der deutschsprachige Brief als weltliche und religiöse Literatur* (Herne: Verlag für Wissenschaft und Kunst, 2000), 22–23.

25 Christian Kiening, "Mediating the Passion in Time and Space," in *Temporality and Mediality in Late Medieval and Early Modern Culture*, ed. Christian Kiening and Martina Stercken, Cursor Mundi 32 (Turnhout: Brepols, 2018), 116–146, at 128–129.

By employing another object – St. Sebaldus Church – on the semantic level of his letter, Tucher produces a connection between the two churches that transcends temporal and spatial boundaries. Salvation history, the time of Tucher's visit to the Church of the Holy Sepulcher, and the moment in which the recipient reads the letter or hears its content all collapse into one singular instant. The spatial distance between Franconia and the Holy Land diminishes and the spaces of the two churches merge into one before the mind's eye of the letter's audience.[26]

Sending Jerusalem to Nuremberg: The Material Letter

The spatial connection between Nuremberg and Jerusalem evoked by the letter is, however, not bound to the letter's content alone: the Holy City is also inscribed in the materiality of the letter in the form of an aura, as I will argue in this section. By coming from Jerusalem to Nuremberg, the missive brought a material piece of the Holy City to its recipient.

A letter, by definition, bridges the distance between sender and addressee by creating the impression of a direct conversation.[27] This seemingly direct dialogue between two or more interlocutors is enabled through different processes of production, transmission, and reception, which are all linked to the letter as a material object. As such, a letter entails an operation of writing and an operation of reading, and connected to these operations are at least two separate places, one of production and one of reception, as well as the various partners in the dialogue. In order to get from one place to another and from composer to recipient(s), the missive has to travel. It is this last process which leads to a time delay between the writing of the letter's

26 On the mind's eye in late medieval religion and piety, see Thomas Lentes, "Inneres Auge, äußerer Blick und heilige Schau: Ein Diskussionsbeitrag zur visuellen Praxis in Frömmigkeit und Moraldidaxe des späten Mittelalters," in *Frömmigkeit im Mittelalter: Politisch-soziale Kontexte, visuelle Praxis, körperliche Ausdrucksformen,* ed. Klaus Schreiner (Munich: Wilhelm Fink Verlag, 2002), 179–220; and Niklaus Largier, *Die Kunst des Begehrens: Dekadenz, Sinnlichkeit und Askese* (Munich: C. H. Beck, 2007), 34–38. On the mind's eye in the context of late medieval pilgrimage narratives, see Kathryne Beebe, "The Jerusalem of the Mind's Eye: Imagined Pilgrimage in the Late Fifteenth Century," in *Visual Constructs of Jerusalem,* ed. Bianca Kühnel, Galit Noga-Banai, and Hanna Vorholt, Cultural Encounters in Late Antiquity and the Middle Ages 18 (Turnhout: Brepols, 2014), 409–420.
27 See Wand-Wittkowski, *Briefe im Mittelalter,* 22; Janet Gurkin Altman, *Epistolarity: Approaches to a Form* (Columbus: Ohio State University Press, 1982), 13; and Astrid Bußmann, "Versehrte Briefe, unversehrte Siegel – Zur Materialität des Briefes in der Brieffälschungs-Episode von Philippes de Remi *Roman de La Manekine,*" in *Der Brief – Ereignis & Objekt: Frankfurter Tagung,* ed. Waltraud Wiethölter and Anne Bohnenkamp (Frankfurt: Stroemfeld, 2010), 72–91, at 72–73.

message, and its reception.[28] This is especially true for the medieval period, considering that it took the Jerusalem letter a quarter of a year to reach Endres Tucher.

However, a letter is more than a medium that makes it possible to communicate over distances: the materiality of the letter is an indispensable factor in its successful functioning as a carrier of information. It is the letter as a material object, consisting of ink and paper and carrying a message, which is in direct contact with all the interlocutors and which physically traverses the space separating them.[29] The letter as an object is furthermore a witness of the passing of time. As such, a letter is both a medium and an object: "As an ensemble of text and material, letters are never just text. In fact, without their material substratum, they lack what makes them letters."[30] Consequently, once the original materiality of a letter is gone – for example, when the letter is copied – it is no longer a letter in its proper sense, but rather a text.[31]

That a letter is a material object is also stressed by Endres Tucher, who took great interest in his brother's pilgrimage and wrote a chronicle of it.[32] As mentioned in the introduction, he attached this chronicle, together with a copy of the Jerusalem letter and other documents, to his personal copy of Hans Tucher's printed pilgrimage account.[33] In the chronicle, Endres Tucher noted all the places from which his brother had sent letters to his family and friends in Nuremberg, including the original letter from Jerusalem:

> Item: on Friday, October 28, [the feast day of] St. Simon and St. Jude, I received here in Nuremberg the long letter from Hans Tucher senior, copied above. It was posted at Jerusalem on Friday, the feast day of St. Sixtus, the sixth day of the month of August. And it took twelve weeks for the letter to get from Jerusalem to our monastery, etc.[34]

---

28 See Gottfried Honnefelder, *Der Brief im Roman: Untersuchungen zur erzähltechnischen Verwendung des Briefes im deutschen Roman*, Bonner Arbeiten zur deutschen Literatur 28 (Bonn: Bouvier, 1975), 4–5. See also Wand-Wittkowski, who bases her observations on Honnefelder: Wand-Wittkowski, *Briefe im Mittelalter*, 22–23.

29 In this sense, a letter might well be viewed in the context of more recent theories about the agency of objects and their entanglement with other actors – both humans and objects. See Bruno Latour, *Reassembling the Social: An Introduction to Actor-Network-Theory* (Oxford: Oxford University Press, 2005); and Ian Hodder, *Entangled: An Archaeology of the Relationships between Humans and Things* (Malden, MA: Wiley-Blackwell, 2012).

30 Bußmann, "Versehrte Briefe," 73: "Als Ensemble aus Text und Material sind Briefe nie bloßer Text. Ohne ihr materielles Substrat fehlt ihnen vielmehr das, was sie zu Briefen macht."

31 See Bußmann, 73.

32 Randall Eugene Herz, the editor of Hans Tucher's pilgrimage account, the Jerusalem letter, and Endres Tucher's chronicle, states with respect to the chronicle: "Aus seinen Angaben wird ersichtlich, wie stolz Endres auf die Briefe aus der Fremde war." Randall Herz, "Briefe Hans Tuchers aus dem Heiligen Land und andere Aufzeichnungen," *Mitteilungen des Vereins für Geschichte der Stadt Nürnberg* 84 (1997): 61–92, at 82.

33 See Herz, 81.

34 Endres Tucher, in Herz, "Briefe Hans Tuchers," p. 82, lines 16–20: "Item an dem achtundczweinczigsten tag des manacz Octobri am freitag noch Simoniß et Jude, do kum mir der vorgeschriben lang prieff von Hanssen Tucher senior her gen Nurmbergk. Der waß geben zu Jerusalem am freitag Sant

By focusing on the time and place of departure and arrival, Endres Tucher emphasizes the material nature of the letter and the fact that it took a certain amount of time to physically traverse the space between the composer and the reader. He thus underlines the fact that the letter as a material object connects Jerusalem and Nuremberg – or, to be more precise, Endres's monastery – through its journey.

The arrival of the written message coming from Jerusalem appears to have been an event that was out of the ordinary:

> Item: after the letter copied above arrived here, everyone, both clerical and secular people, wanted to hear it, and therefore it was completely torn and damaged, so that I finally copied it and added it here for the sake of remembrance.[35]

Such an eager and rather public reception of a written message, as Rolf Köhn has shown, was not uncommon in the Middle Ages.[36] This type of open reception, however, did not mean that letters were read to a general public. The circle of potential readers remained rather contained: the composer of a letter could, according to Köhn, often make quite exact assumptions about who belonged to this circle.[37] Part of the reason for such a public reception may well have been the event-like character of the arrival of letters from afar.[38] This holds particularly true for the Jerusalem letter, which came from the supposed center of the world, where Christ had walked the earth and worked his miracles. The heightened interest in this letter becomes apparent in Endres Tucher's description of the reaction to it, but it is also evident from the fact that Endres deemed it important enough to preserve its text after the material substratum was badly damaged.

That the arrival of a letter from Jerusalem was an extraordinary event in which the letter's character as a material object played a dominant role is also demonstrated by another letter Hans Tucher sent from Jerusalem to Nuremberg. On August 8, two days after he wrote to his brother Endres, Hans Tucher wrote another letter addressed to his cousin Anton Tucher in Nuremberg. The content of this second letter is rather personal: Hans asks Anton to take care of his family and business while he

---

Sixtuß tag, den sechsten tag des monacz Augusti. Und der prieff kum in zwelff wochen von Jerusalem piß her in unser kloster etc."

35 Endres Tucher, in H. Tucher, *Reise*, p. 654, lines 30–33: "Jtem noch dem der hie vorgeschriben prieff also her kum, wolt jn jederman horen von geistlichen vnd weltlichen persunnen also, das er gancz zw rÿssen vnd beschediget wardt, das ich jn doch abgeschriben vnd do her czw eÿner gedechtnuß geseczet hab."

36 See Rolf Köhn, "Dimensionen und Funktionen des Öffentlichen und Privaten in der mittelalterlichen Korrespondenz," in *Das Öffentliche und Private in der Vormoderne*, ed. Gert Melville and Peter von Moos (Cologne: Böhlau Verlag, 1998), 309–357, at 320.

37 "Allerdings kann hier mit 'öffentlich' [...] sinnvollerweise nur ein mehr oder weniger großer, ziemlich eindeutig zu bestimmender Kreis von Personen gemeint sein, denen der Empfänger seinen gerade erhaltenen Brief zeigte oder vorlas oder vorlesen ließ." Köhn, "Dimensionen und Funktionen," 320–321.

38 See Köhn, 320.

continues his pilgrimage to Mount Sinai. Instead of describing the holy sites, in this second letter Hans Tucher expresses his fatigue due to an overly busy travel schedule which hardly allows for any rest. This shorter, more personal letter, less focused on the description of the holy sites in Jerusalem and more on practical matters of life in Nuremberg during its author's absence, survives today in its original form and in a copy.[39] A letter from Jerusalem, even if its content was mundane, appears to have been important enough to be preserved in its original form as a material object.

The fact that the Jerusalem letter addressed to Endres Tucher survives only as text and no longer as an object has to be seen as a consequence of the attention paid to it by a broader circle of recipients. As Endres Tucher remarks, because so many people wanted to hear it, the letter was "completely torn and damaged" ("gancz zw rÿssen vnd beschediget"). Those interested in the missive were apparently not only interested in a summary or report of its contents. Rather, it seems that they wanted to hear or read the actual content of the letter, see it, and probably touch it and hold it in their hands. While we can only speculate about the exact ways in which the circle of recipients interacted with the letter, Endres's remark shows us that the continued physical handling led to damage and likely at some point to the destruction of the original document.[40] As Kathryn Rudy has shown, the physical handling of manuscripts, in forms that went beyond simple holding with the hands, was a common medieval practice, especially in religious and legal contexts. She argues that the kissing and touching of manuscripts by priests, which could be observed in liturgical celebrations, was imitated by many laypeople: "Members of the laity began kissing images of Christ crucified in their books of hours, in imitation of priests who did so during the Mass. Laypeople were copying what Marcel Mauss would call a 'technique of the body,' that is, a particular culturally learned corporeal behavior."[41] While the question of whether the recipients engaged in a bodily interaction with the letter that went beyond opening, reading, and folding it must remain speculation, Rudy's argument may suggest a desire to interact similarly with a textual object coming from Jerusalem.

The fact that the letter to Endres Tucher was posted in Jerusalem might indeed be one reason for this heightened "public" interest in it. In this regard, the letter is different from late medieval pilgrimage narratives such as Hans Tucher's *Reise ins Gelobte Land*, which he composed and published after his return: while both the printed pilgrimage account and the letter try to render the Holy Land and its sacred sites vividly imaginable and often do so in a very similar manner, only the letter has

---

39 The letter was also edited by Randall Herz: see Hans Tucher, *Reise*, 655. For an image of the original letter, see Hans Tucher, appendix, fig. 2. The original letter is today in Schloss Eschenbach under the shelf mark Nr 57. The copy of the letter is housed in Nuremberg, Stadtarchiv Nürnberg, Rep. F 10 (FA Ebner).

40 For the changing nature of objects, see Hodder, *Entangled*, 4–5.

41 Rudy, "Touching the Book Again," 249.

physically been to Jerusalem.[42] Hence, it does something that the pilgrimage narrative cannot do: it is a piece of the Holy Land that has traveled across the Mediterranean Sea to its recipient and the others who read and interact with it upon its arrival.

In his essay "The Work of Art in the Age of Its Technological Reproducibility," Walter Benjamin speaks of how each piece of art is embedded in a specific spatial and temporal context that constitutes its being, tells its history, and proves its authenticity:

> It is this unique existence – and nothing else – that bears the mark of the history to which the work has been subject. This history includes changes to the physical structure of the work over time, together with any changes in ownership. [...] The here and now of the original underlies the concept of its authenticity.[43]

Benjamin refers to these traces of history, inscribed in the materiality of an object and defining a work of art as exceptional, as aura.[44] According to him, in processes of reproduction, meaning the transferral of content or depiction from one material to another, the aura gets lost, because it is bound to the materiality of the original work of art.[45]

Tucher's letter, even though it does not qualify as a work of art, has an aura in the Benjaminian sense. As the letter was produced in the Holy Land and traveled from there to Nuremberg, the Holy City forms an essential part of the written document, "the history to which [it] has been subject."[46] This particular manifestation of the city is not immediately obvious, given that it requires the recipients to know the history of the object or to be able to engage with it in the proper manner – that is, to read it – and thus allow the textual object to reveal its own history.[47]

In this sense, one might argue that the Jerusalem letter functioned similarly to the stones and crumbs of earth that many pilgrims brought back home from their pilgrimages to Jerusalem. Hans Tucher's letter has Jerusalem inscribed in its material,

---

42 See Herz, "Briefe Hans Tuchers," 63.

43 Benjamin, "Work of Art," 21.

44 Benjamin, 23.

45 Although I use Walter Benjamin's term *aura* to refer to layers of meaning that manifest themselves in the materiality of an object, such as the history of the object, the circumstances of production, etc., here I detach the term from Benjamin's critique of the notion of aura, his call for its deconstruction through technical reproduction, and the process of democratization of art that he sees in direct correlation with the destruction of the aura. Cf., for example, Benjamin, 24–25.

46 Benjamin, 21. Given that the letter only survives as a copy, it is difficult to make definite statements about the paper on which the letter was written. However, we have to assume that the letter was likely written on paper produced in Venice. At the end of his pilgrimage account, Tucher adds a list of all the things that pilgrims should buy in Venice before embarking to Jaffa. Among these items, he lists paper and other writing utensils. See H. Tucher, *Reise*, p. 633, lines 9–10.

47 Following the *salutatio* the letter states when and where it was written; in this way it directly brings its own history of production to the attention of its recipients: "Jn nomine Jhesu Christÿ, amen, 1479, adj vj. augusto jn der heÿligen stat Jerusalem." H. Tucher, *Reise*, p. 649, lines 3–4.

and thus it is a piece of the Holy City that has been sent to Nuremberg. Handling the letter meant, consequently, physically interacting with a piece of Jerusalem.[48] However, unlike the content of the letter preserved through Endres's copying of the text, the aura of the letter is bound to its materiality, and it vanishes together with this materiality.

Intercessory Prayers: Participating in Your Relative's Pilgrimage from Home

A letter, as I have established above, is a medium of communication enabling two or more people to engage in seemingly direct conversation even though they are in geographically distant places and their dialogue is temporally delayed.[49] This holds true for Tucher's Jerusalem letter: besides rendering Jerusalem vividly tangible in its content and being itself a piece of the Holy City arriving to Nuremberg, the letter also opens up the possibility of communication between Hans Tucher and his brother Endres. As Endres Tucher's chronicle illustrates, it was not just a monologue in which Hans Tucher updated his family about his well-being and his whereabouts: the two brothers actually engaged in dialogue with each other. Four galleys from Venice reached Alexandria on 13 January 1480. "On the same galleys," Endres writes, "I sent a letter to Hans Tucher Senior and wrote him how things were here [Nuremberg]. Also sent were a letter from his wife, and likewise a letter to Sebald Rieter from his wife."[50] Endres Tucher and the wives of Hans Tucher and Sebald Rieter appear here not only as mere recipients of letters but also as active participants in a written conversation with their relatives and husbands who were far away on pilgrimage.[51]

This long-distance dialogue allowed for far more than occasional checking in. It also opened up the possibility of active participation in the pilgrimage from afar. In his letter, after providing his brother with detailed information regarding his plan to

---

48 Natural materials coming from the Holy Land were often treated as relics of *loca sancta*. By comparing the letter to these natural materials, I do not want to imply that the recipients considered the Jerusalem letter to be a relic. Rather, I would like to suggest that in a mitigated way the letter, like natural materials, brought the Holy City to Franconia. About natural materials and their relic-like nature, see Renana Bartal, Neta Bodner, and Bianca Kühnel, "Natural Materials, Place, and Representation," in *Natural Materials of the Holy Land and the Visual Translation of Place, 500–1500*, ed. Renana Bartal, Neta Bodner, and Bianca Kühnel (London: Routledge, 2017), xxiii–xxxiii, at xxiv.
49 Wand-Wittkowski, *Briefe im Mittelalter*, 22–23.
50 Endres Tucher, in Herz, "Briefe Hans Tuchers," p. 83, lines 1–5: "Pei den selben golein sant ich prieff dem Hans Tucher senior und schreib im wie es hie stundt. Auch waren do pei prieff von seiner hausfrawen, des geleichen auch prieff an Sebolt Rietter von seiner hawßfrawen." For the date of the galleys' arrival, see lines 1–5.
51 Endres Tucher furthermore states in his chronicle that, once they had returned to Nuremberg, both Hans Tucher and Sebald Rieter expressed how delighted they were to receive these letters in Alexandria. See Herz, "Briefe Hans Tuchers," p. 83, lines 5–6.

cross the desert, Hans Tucher asks Endres to continue praying for him, thus encouraging him to contribute to the success of his dangerous undertaking:

> Item: we have in Doctor Otto Spiegel, knight, a good companion for our journey to Saint Catherine. He wants to trek with us and has a servant. The same is true for Sebald Rieter and me, we have also a servant. [...] And each of us will have a camel that will carry the food and also the water and the wine and a servant who will come with us and who will take care of each of our camels and donkeys, so that I hope that, with God's help, we will manage well. And my heart is lightened thereby. I console myself with your and your cousin's and brother's daily prayer that so far has led me well. Therefore, I beg you to not cease [to pray]. I have thought of all of you at the holy sites with my little prayer, where it will please God.[52]

At the end of the letter, he reiterates this request:

> Let all of you be instructed [regarding one] thing, so that I do not quail. I surrender myself to your prayer. And send my regards to the worthy father prior and to [our] cousin and [our] brother, all diligent, and ask them not to cease to think of me in their prayers. So that God the almighty keep us healthy, so that we may happily see each other again. Amen.[53]

In light of the dangers awaiting Hans Tucher in the desert, he seeks his brother's support in the form of intercessory prayers, along with the support of others he knows in Nuremberg. In return for Endres's spiritual help in crossing the wasteland, Hans offers his own spiritual support to his brother by praying for him at the holy sites he visits during his pilgrimage. The letter serves here as a medium through which to communicate this call for mutual spiritual endorsement.

Through the letter, then, Endres Tucher takes part in a phenomenon that Berndt Hamm has described, in the context of a fifteenth-century broadsheet, in the following way: "The latent contractual structure that filters through here is basically a mode of usage of the highly expandable axiom of late medieval theology: God can-

52 H. Tucher, *Reise*, p. 654, lines 6–15: "Jtem so haben wir eÿnen gutten geferten gen Sant Katherina an docktor Otten Spiegel, rÿtter. Der will mit vns czihen vnd hot ein knecht. So ist Sebolt Rÿtter und ich, haben auch ein knecht. [...] Vnd wirt jeder haben ein kamel, das die speÿß auch wasser vnd weyn tregt, vnd ein knecht, der mit get, der jeder seinß kamelß vnd essel wartet, das ich hoff, wir wollen wol außkumen mit Gotz hilff. Vnd mir ist das hercz gering dor czw. Jch thröste mich ewr vnd eẅr vetter vnd pruder teglicheß gepecz, das mich piß her wol gefurdert hot. Dor vmb so pitte jch euch, ir losset nit ab. Jch hab eẅr aller auch gedocht an den heÿligen stetten, wo es Got angeneme wer, mit meÿnem klein gepet."
53 H. Tucher, p. 654, lines 20–24: "Dan lost euch alle sach befolhen ßein, als mir nit czweiffelt. Jch befilch mich jn eẅr gepet. Vnd grust mir den wirdigen vatter prior vnd vetter vnd pruder alle fleissig, vnd pitt sie nit noch czw lossen, meÿn czw gedencken mit jrem gepet. Do mit spar vns Got der almechtÿg gesunt, das wir mit freẅden wieder an einander sehen mugen. Amen." The "brother" referred to here may be Hans and Endres's brother Berthold Tucher. While it is also conceivable that Hans could be referring to the friars of Endres's monastery, the use of "brother" in the singular seems to more likely indicate Berthold. For the Tucher family lineage, see Johann Gottfried Biedermann, *Geschlechtsregister des hochadelichen Patriciats zu Nürnberg [...]* (Bayreuth: Dietzel, 1748), p. Sss2, table 507.

not deny his grace to the human who does what they can (*homini facienti quod in se est deus non denegat gratiam*)."[54] By praying for Hans Tucher, his brother attempts to access the grace of God and secure him a safe journey. In this sense, Endres Tucher and the others who pray for Hans participate directly from Nuremberg in the successful outcome of the pilgrimage.

In return for this participation in the pilgrimage through prayer, Tucher offers his own prayers for them at the holy sites he visits. Even though the letter's recipients do not join Tucher in the Holy Land, they are still present at the holy sites in his prayers.[55] In this way, the prayers reverse the act of sending the letter, bringing the recipients to Jerusalem instead of Jerusalem to the recipients. The letter thus offers here a third way to bridge the distance between Nuremberg and Jerusalem, and between sender and addressees, which one might call closeness through prayer.

However, this participation is of a particular, even limited, kind. Although Hans Tucher asks those who have stayed behind in Franconia to participate in his pilgrimage and offers to bring his brother to Jerusalem in prayers, the letter does not function as a guidebook to spiritual pilgrimage. A spiritual or mental pilgrimage is a devotional practice in which the devotee imagines actually traveling to holy sites.[56] Though one does not physically embark on a journey, the experience has all the phe-

---

54 Berndt Hamm, "Die Medialität der nahen Gnade im späten Mittelalter," in *Medialität des Heils im späten Mittelalter*, ed. Carla Dauven-van Knippenberg, Cornelia Herberichs, and Christian Kiening (Zurich: Chronos, 2009), 46: "Die latente Vertragsstruktur, die hier durchscheint, ist im Grunde eine Anwendungsweise des sehr dehnbaren Axioms spätmittelalterlicher Theologie: Dem Menschen, der tut, was er kann, wird und kann Gott seine Gnade nicht verweigern (*homini facienti quod in se est deus non denegat gratiam*)."

55 In Hans Tucher's second letter from Jerusalem to Franconia, he also creates a tit-for-tat situation that allows his addressee, in this case his cousin Anton Tucher, to participate in the successful outcome of the pilgrimage. There, however, he does not ask for prayers but instead asks his cousin to take care of his household and his business while he continues his pilgrimage. Anton Tucher's contribution to the successful pilgrimage is thus more concerned with ensuring that Hans Tucher's absence from Nuremberg will not be the cause of unforeseen problems. In return Hans Tucher again offers prayers at the holy sites. See H. Tucher's letter in Herz, "Briefe Hans Tuchers," p. 74, lines 7–11.

56 See Lutz Kaelber, "Spiritual Pilgrimage," in *Encyclopedia of Medieval Pilgrimage*, ed. Larissa J. Taylor et al. (Leiden: Brill, 2010), 693–695. Kathryn Rudy refers to it as virtual pilgrimage. See Kathryn M. Rudy, "Virtual Pilgrimage through the Jerusalem Cityspace," in *Visual Constructs of Jerusalem*, ed. Bianca Kühnel, Galit Noga-Banai, and Hanna Vorholt, Cultural Encounters in Late Antiquity and the Middle Ages 18 (Turnhout: Brepols, 2014), 381–396, at 381; Kathryn M. Rudy, *Virtual Pilgrimages in the Convent: Imagining Jerusalem in the Late Middle Ages*, Disciplina Monastica: Studies on Medieval Monastic Life 8 (Turnhout: Brepols, 2011), 19. Kathryne Beebe also employs the term "virtual pilgrimage." See Kathryne Beebe, *Pilgrim and Preacher: The Audiences and Observant Spirituality of Friar Felix Fabri (1437/8–1502)*, Oxford Historical Monographs (Oxford: Oxford University Press, 2014), 79. On other occasions Beebe uses the terms "mental pilgrimage" and "imagined pilgrimage"; both Kathryn Rudy and Kathryne Beebe, in their usage of "virtual pilgrimage," refer to Wieland Carls, who suggested in the German-speaking context the term "geistliche Pilgerfahrt." See Wieland Carls's introduction in Felix Fabri, *Felix Fabri, Die Sionpilger*, ed. Wieland Carls, Texte des späten Mittelalters und der Frühen Neuzeit 39 (Berlin: Erich Schmidt Verlag, 1999), 22–23.

nomenal qualities of a physical trip to a pilgrimage destination.[57] One of the most well-known late-medieval spiritual pilgrimage guidebooks written in the German vernacular might well be Felix Fabri's *Die Sionpilger*. This guidebook intended for nuns living in cloister offers not only a description of the journey to the Holy Land and its holy sites, but also clear instructions for the devotees to follow during their mental pilgrimage as well as prayers and songs. All of these measures are intended to help the mental pilgrim in their spiritual journey.[58] In contrast to this, Tucher does not offer his readers a chance to mentally embark on the pilgrimage together with him and Sebald Rieter. He invites the recipients of his letter to help him successfully finish his pilgrimage with their prayers, but the audience's participation does not lead them on their own mental journey to Jerusalem. Instead, they endorse the success of Tucher's pilgrimage from afar, an endorsement mediated through the communicative function of the letter and the salvific effects of intercessory prayer.

Conclusion

At first glance, on the level of content, Hans Tucher's Jerusalem letter foreshadows many topics and motifs that the author would later expand on in his pilgrimage narrative, which he wrote after returning home to Franconia.[59] Yet, even though there are obvious parallels between the two texts, the letter functions quite differently from the pilgrimage account. This is mostly due to the fact that, firstly, the letter and the pilgrimage narrative are different media that pursue different communicative aims, and, secondly, the two texts are bound to distinct types of textual materiality.

As I have shown in this chapter, Tucher's letter first creates a connection between sender and addressee and between the two geographically distant cities Nuremberg and Jerusalem through its content. By comparing and semantically layering those two spaces, Hans Tucher even imaginatively merges his Franconian hometown and the Holy Land, evoking a sacred space that constitutes a mental synthesis of the Church of the Holy Sepulcher in Jerusalem and St. Sebaldus in Nuremberg. Furthermore, with regard to its materiality, the letter bridges the distance between Germany and the Levant by physically coming from Jerusalem, and thus having the Holy City inscribed into its material origins. It thus transports a piece of Tucher's pilgrimage destination to Nuremberg. Finally, the letter asks for intercessory prayer and offers equivalent prayers in return. It thus stimulates the recipients to engage in a form of spiritual participation in the sender's religious travels and shows them a way to share in both the successful outcome and the salvific effects of Tucher's pilgrimage

---

57 "Als geistliche Pilgerfahrt ist jeder Text zu verstehen, der darauf ausgerichtet ist, den Rezipienten in Form einer im Geiste vollzogenen Reise an bestimmte Orte des Heils zu führen." Carls, Geistliche Pilgerfahrt, in Fabri, *Sionpilger*, 23.
58 See Beebe, *Pilgrim and Preacher*, 188.
59 See Herz, "Briefe Hans Tuchers," 63.

effort. Pilgrimage narratives written and published after the pilgrim's return do none of these things. While such texts narrate a past event and often allow for different types of imaginary reperformance, the letter, as a traveling text bound to a specific and unique material substratum, bridges geographical distance both semantically and physically and enables long-distance communication as well as participation.

A closer look at Hans Tucher's Jerusalem letter therefore opens up two inter-twined new perspectives on fifteenth-century Christian pilgrimage literature. First of all, it illustrates the crucial importance of the material substratum of epistolary media in a pilgrimage context. The letter's materiality is, I argue, far more than just a vessel for transporting information – it is meaningful in itself, makes the claims and instructions of the text plausible, and lies at the core of the document's specific aura. Additionally, it offers insights into how late-medieval pilgrims to Jeru-salem stayed in contact with their friends and relatives over the course of the for-mer's travels, and it shows how those who stayed at home could nonetheless spiri-tually participate in their relatives' travels by means of prayer and written communication.

Björn Klaus Buschbeck

3 Producing Spiritual Concreteness: Prayed Coats for Mary in the German Late Middle Ages

Artworks of Devotion: Craft Prayer in Late Medieval Germany

Late medieval Christians saw their prayers and other acts of piety as capable of crafting almost anything. Browsing through the enormous and to a large extent still-unstudied corpus of fifteenth-century German devotional literature, the modern reader encounters a surprisingly large subgenre of texts giving detailed instructions on how to spiritually manufacture a great variety of objects ranging from gardens, houses, and cloisters to jewels, garments, and crowns, from ships for St. Ursula to wreaths of flowers for the Holy Virgin, from complete banquets to crullers fried in the devotee's religious virtues.[1]

These texts are artifacts of the widespread late-medieval religious practice of "craft prayer."[2] In the most general terms, the principle of such religious exercises can be characterized as follows: A single devotee or a community of devotees produces, usually according to instructions given by a text, an imagined object that is seen as being manufactured out of the raw material of a prescribed number of prayers, Masses, virtuous deeds, or ascetic exercises.[3] Following this spiritual handiwork,

---

1 In my dissertation, which I am currently preparing for publication, I am analyzing a selection of such texts, among them the *Alemannic Coat of Mary* and Dominic of Prussia's *Pallium gloriosae virginis Mariae*, which are discussed in this chapter. The archival research necessary for this chapter has been made possible by a generous travel grant from the Europe Center at Stanford University.

2 For a discussion of craft prayer focusing on wreaths of flowers and garments, see the pivotal article by Thomas Lentes, "Die Gewänder der Heiligen: Ein Diskussionsbeitrag zum Verhältnis von Gebet, Bild und Imagination," in *Hagiographie und Kunst: Der Heiligenkult in Schrift, Bild und Architektur*, ed. Gottfried Kerscher (Berlin: Reimer, 1993), 120–151. For a study of textile craft prayer in Helfta mysticism, see Racha Kirakosian, *From the Material to the Mystical: The Vernacular Transmission of Gertrude of Helfta's Visions* (Cambridge: University Press, 2021), 196–204. I would like to thank the author for letting me read her manuscript prior to publication. A detailed discussion of prayed gardens can be found in Dietrich Schmidtke, *Studien zur dingallegorischen Erbauungsliteratur des Spätmittelalters: Am Beispiel der Gartenallegorie* (Tübingen: Max Niemeyer, 1982).

3 See the discussion in Jeffrey F. Hamburger, *Nuns as Artists: The Visual Culture of a Medieval Convent* (Berkeley: University of California Press, 1997), 75. Hamburger describes how "in the tradition of prayers known as *Handwerkliches Beten* [...], supplicants offered up make-believe gifts fashioned, not from gold, silk, or beads, but from prayer formulas reiterated so often that the words took on the char-

https://doi.org/10.1515/9783110742985-006

the devotees give the prayed object to Christ, Mary, or a specific saint, usually in combination with a plea for a salvific gift in return. The final product of craft prayer is, on the one hand, evoked as an aesthetically impressive and agentive thing; on the other hand, it often has an allegorical quality as well.

Prayed textiles constitute – together with, for example, rosaries and spiritual houses – a particularly widespread type of craft prayer.[4] Texts that provide instructions for such devotional exercises, often written in the vernacular, draw on a strong medieval association of textile imagery with Christian devotion. This association is particularly strong with Marian piety. Over the course of the thirteenth century, the motif of the Virgin of Mercy (Schutzmantelmadonna) spreading her coat and sheltering those who seek refuge became a topos in religious writing and visual arts.[5] As Christa Belting-Ihm shows, this image draws on legends about textile relics which spread to the Christian West in the early 1200s, as well as on the legal gesture of adopting premarital children by taking them under one's coat during the marriage ceremony.[6] In addition, depictions of Mary spinning and weaving are widespread, and recent scholarship has highlighted the meditative function of late medieval textile work.[7]

In this chapter, I look at devotional exercises that somewhat reverse the usual dynamic in which the use and manufacture of textiles is depicted as having devotional purposes: instead, they conceptualize prayer and other acts of piety as a spiritual form of textile labor. In the 1400s, the motif of the Schutzmantelmadonna was already connected to prayer and reflected an idea that, in heaven, Mary and the

---

acter of an incantation." Often, a divine figure such as Jesus Christ or a specific saint is invoked to help the devotees in the process of manufacturing the prayed object.

4 For a study of the evolution of the rosary, which originally meant praying a wreath of roses for Mary, see Anne Winston-Allen, *Stories of the Rose: The Making of the Rosary in the Middle Ages* (University Park: Pennsylvania State University Press, 1997). The motif of the *claustrum animae* is discussed in Mirko Breitenstein, "Das 'Haus des Gewissens': Zur Konstruktion und Bedeutung innerer Räume im Religiosentum des hohen Mittelalters," in *Geist und Gestalt: Monastische Raumkonzepte als Ausdrucksformen religiöser Leitideen im Mittelalter*, ed. Jörg Sonntag (Berlin: LIT Verlag, 2016), 19–55.

5 A rich selection of sources is given and discussed in Vera Sussmann, "Maria mit dem Schutzmantel," *Marburger Jahrbuch für Kunstwissenschaft* 5 (1929): 285–351.

6 See Christa Belting-Ihm, *"Sub matris tutela": Untersuchungen zur Vorgeschichte der Schutzmantelmadonna* (Heidelberg: Carl Winter, 1976), 38–57. On the legal tradition of mantle adoptions, see Adalbert Erler, "Mantelkinder," in *Handwörterbuch zur deutschen Rechtsgeschichte*, ed. Adalbert Erler and Ekkehard Kaufmann, vol. 3 (Berlin: Schmidt Verlag, 1984), 255–258.

7 For an introduction to the religious and particularly Marian significance of textiles and textile labor, see Kathryn M. Rudy, "Introduction: Miraculous Textiles in 'Exempla' and Images from the Low Countries," in *Weaving, Veiling, and Dressing: Textiles and Their Metaphors in the Late Middle Ages*, ed. Kathryn M. Rudy and Barbara Baert (Turnhout: Brepols, 2007), 1–35. On meditative textile work, see, for example, Anna Dlabačová, "Spinning with Passion: The Distaff as an Object for Contemplative Meditation in Netherlandish Religious Culture," *The Medieval Low Countries: History, Archaeology, Art and Literature* 4 (2018): 177–209.

saints are dressed in the prayers of the faithful.[8] As Anne Margreet W. As-Vijvers argues, in textile craft prayer, words become the raw material for a spiritual garment and prayer is understood as a type of spiritual handiwork: "praying the *Ave Maria* yielded the fabrics, the threads, and the decorations to manufacture the Virgin a mantle."[9]

Such spiritual garments draw on a range of preexisting motifs and literary traditions. As Anne Winston-Allen notes, the "act of constructing and giving spiritual gifts for the Virgin – especially clothing and jewelry (even a temple) – made out of words is an old and particularly attractive idea."[10] For example, the *Marienmirakel* by Heinrich Clûsenêre, an otherwise unattested author active around 1300, tells the story of a young devotee dressing the Holy Virgin in a set of clothes made from prayers.[11] The underlying idea of spiritual garments appears to have been widespread by that time. The Helfta corpus, to name just one example, contains several references to such miraculous dresses: Gertrude of Helfta describes how her own religious life appears to her in a vision as a spiritual dress she wove for herself, and Mechthild of Hackeborn records a vision of Mary wearing a mirrorlike heavenly dress in which the saints recognize all their virtuous deeds.[12]

A distinct subgenre of vernacular devotional texts giving instructions for textile craft prayer evolved in the mid-fifteenth century, with one particularly early and influential example being the *Alemannic Coat of Mary*, which I discuss in detail in this chapter. The number and variety of texts belonging to this tradition is enormous – they range from relatively simple lists that name the individual elements of the spiritual garment and their respective "prices" to instructions on how to dress Mary on every single day of the church year, from short prayers for specific feast days to early printed booklets presumably aimed at confraternities of pious laypeople.[13] If we want

---

8 Marius Rimmele discusses "eine prägende Vorstellung spätmittelalterlicher, quantifizierender Frömmigkeit [...], dass nämlich Gebete im Himmel zu Kleidung der Heiligen werden." Marius Rimmele, "Memlings Mantelteilung: Der Marienmantel als Schwellenmotiv," in *Bild-Riss: Textile Öffnungen im ästhetischen Diskurs*, ed. Mateusz Kapustka (Berlin: Edition Imorde, 2015), 101–126, at 120.
9 Anne Margreet W. As-Vijvers, "Weaving Mary's Chaplet: The Representation of the Rosary in Late Medieval Flemish Manuscript Illumination," in Rudy and Baert, *Weaving, Veiling, and Dressing*, 41–79, at 62. Especially in the Middle Dutch tradition, legends and exempla about prayed garments are numerous; a selection of texts is discussed in Rudy, "Introduction."
10 Winston-Allen, *Stories of the Rose*, 103.
11 Published as [Heinrich Clûsenêre], "Marienlegende," in *Mitteldeutsche Gedichte*, ed. Karl Bartsch (Stuttgart: Litterarischer Verein, 1860), 1–39.
12 See Gertrude d'Helfta, *Le héraut*, 4.28, vol. 4 of *Œuvres spirituelles*, ed. and trans. Jean-Marie Clément and Bernard de Vregille (Paris: Éditions du Cerf, 1978), 268; and [Mechthild of Hackeborn], *Sanctae Mechtildis virginis ordinis Sancti Benedicti Liber specialis gratiae [...]*, in *Revelationes Gertrudianae ac Mechtildianae*, ed. Solesmensium O.S.B. monachorum, vol. 2 (Paris: H. Oudin, 1877), 1–421, at 91.
13 Lists of "prices": See, for example, a later fifteenth-century manuscript from the Dominican convent Unterlinden in Colmar which contains such a list: Colmar, Les Dominicains, Ms. 267bis, fols. 68r–69v; edited in Thomas Lentes, "Gebetbuch und Gebärde: Religiöses Ausdrucksverhalten in Gebetbüchern aus dem Dominikanerinnen-Kloster St. Nikolaus in undis zu Straßburg (1350–1550)"

to analyze just what type of thing these textiles might be, the idea of spiritual artisanship that lies at the core of such devotional exercises requires further explanation. First of all, although the products of craft prayer were thought of and treated as objects, they do not fall into the category of things that Caroline Walker Bynum describes as "holy matter." Things made from prayer do not "speak or act their physicality in particularly intense ways that call attention to their per se 'stuffness'" – on the contrary, they distinctly lack the type of physical "stuffness" Bynum and others focus on.[14]

Yet, as I argue in this essay, textiles made from prayer were believed to make up for this absence of physical concreteness with a claim to something that I will characterize as "spiritual concreteness." I use the term *concreteness* with a particular emphasis on the physical metaphor at its roots. Derived from the Latin verb *concrescere*, it points to all things that have been thickened, stiffened, or congealed into the form of an object, whether they are made from cloth, gold, pearls, and fur, from prayers and devotions, or from any other sort of material.[15] This metaphor of thickness

(PhD diss., Westfälische Wilhelms-Universität Münster, 1996), 1085–1086. The manuscript also contains a longer devotional exercise for a single nun that gives instructions on how to dress Mary and Jesus in prayers and devotional acts (Ms. 267bis, fols. 84r–98v), and afterward invite them into a spiritual house equipped with different household items also made from prayers and meditations (fols. 98v–116v). Instructions on daily dressing: An example transmitted in a manuscript presumably written for the Franciscan nuns of Valduna in Voralberg (Freiburg, UB, HS 1500,30, fols. 190v–198r) gives instructions for a simple spiritual dress made from sixty-three Ave Marias for normal days, as well as more sophisticated and costly Marian garments for different feast days. On this manuscript and its context, see Ina Serif, "…*wie dz ich ain súnderin bin:* Überlegungen zu Text und Kontext eines spätmittelalterlichen Gebetbuchs aus einem franziskanischen Frauenkloster in Vorarlberg," in *Handschriften als Quellen der Sprach- und Kulturwissenschaft: Aktuelle Fragestellungen – Methoden – Probleme*, ed. Anette Kremer and Vincenz Schwab (Bamberg: University of Bamberg Press, 2018), 177–199. Short prayers: See, for example, a Marian dress for Candlemas in a sixteenth-century manuscript from the Dominican convent St. Margareta and St. Agnes in Strasbourg (Munich, BSB, cgm 856, fol. 210r). Longer prayers: See the early print *Unserer Frauen Mantel* (Ulm: Johann Zainer the Younger, [ca. 1500]) (GW M20668).

14 Caroline Walker Bynum, *Christian Materiality: An Essay on Religion in Late Medieval Europe* (New York: Zone Books, 2015), 29. For a survey of recent applications of material perspectives to literary studies, see Susanne Scholz and Ulrike Vedder, eds., *Handbuch Literatur & Materielle Kultur* (Berlin: De Gruyter, 2016). Medievalist approaches to materiality are discussed in Anna Mühlherr, Bruno Quast, Heike Sahm, and Monika Schausten, eds., *Dingkulturen: Objekte in Literatur, Kunst und Gesellschaft der Vormoderne* (Berlin: De Gruyter, 2016).

15 See P. G. W. Glare, ed., *Oxford Latin Dictionary* (Oxford: Clarendon Press, 1982), s.v. "concrescere": "To be formed by hardening or condensation, to harden, to set, coalesce"; "(of liquids) to congeal, coagulate, solidify, freeze solid." Drawing on Erich Auerbach's idea of an "Evidenz des Dargestellten" evoked by literary descriptions of reality (Erich Auerbach, *Dante als Dichter der irdischen Welt*, 2nd ed. [Berlin: De Gruyter, 2001], 6), Niklaus Largier speaks of a "konkrete Darstellung der Naturdinge" in medieval devotional literature. Such concrete depictions are "nicht im modernen Sinne 'symbolisch' zu lesen" but aim at a "Herstellung sinnlicher Evidenz," which in turn meaningfully orients the reader toward the divine, mirrored by what thus becomes concretely evident. Niklaus Largier, *Spekulative Sinnlichkeit: Kontemplation und Spekulation im Mittelalter* (Zurich: Chronos, 2019), 26–27. My

and densification appears to offer more precise insights into the relation between prayed and physical objects and their aesthetic effects than does a mere discussion and comparison of their respective materialities in the sense of their basic elements.

Made and obtained from the raw material of the devotee's words, virtuous deeds, and ascetic exercises, and crafted, usually under divine guidance, into an incommensurable artwork, spiritual garments constituted, at least in the minds of the late medieval devotees involved in their manufacture, more than just mental images or visualized ideas. As I propose below, they are better understood as things of the spirit, as densifications of the aesthetic impressions and religious meanings evoked and constructed by the words and instructions of devotional texts, as sublime objects that transcend the border between the earthly and the heavenly.

As illustrated by the *Pallium gloriosae virginis Mariae*, a treatise on prayed garments written by the fifteenth-century Carthusian monk Dominic of Prussia (1384– 1460), which I discuss in greater detail below, prayed objects were even thought to possess a higher form of materiality and "thingness." According to Dominic, things crafted from the matter of the spirit surpass things made from the matter of the world in quality, splendor, and efficiency.[16] Prayed things thus challenge modern notions of medieval religious materiality. When medieval devotees crafted items from prayer, instead of categorizing them as unthingly and immaterial, they attributed an intensified and more precious material quality and object status to them.

This main point leads us to two additional questions. First, we might ask how such spiritual things were thought to be crafted from prayer, how this process of production was performed and taught, and what role devotional literature played in it. Second, what was the perceived relationship between the aesthetically present objects that were produced and their abstract significance? Here especially, the interplay between the vivid imagining of prayed objects and their allegorical interpretation is crucial. Focusing on the comparatively early and influential *Alemannic Coat of Mary* and its instructions on how to pray a coat for the Holy Virgin, the following section tries to shed light on these two questions with regard to textile craft prayer.

---

own notion of concreteness is strongly influenced by Largier's proposal but attempts to slightly broaden the term by applying it both to the aesthetic effects of late medieval prayed objects and their production and conceptualization as spiritual things.

16 When employing the term *thing* in this chapter, I am using it according to the broad definition suggested by Ian Hodder: "a thing is an entity that has a presence by which I mean it has a configuration that endures, however briefly." This definition includes "words, thoughts, institutions, events and materials," as well as prayed objects, since they all "create bundles of presence or duration in the continual flows of matter, energy and information." Ian Hodder, *Entangled: An Archaeology of the Relationships between Humans and Things* (Malden, MA: Wiley-Blackwell, 2012), 7.

Producing Spiritual Concreteness: The *Alemannic Coat of Mary*

The precarious thingness of the products of craft prayer lies at the core of the devotional manual that, in the absence of a medieval title, I am referring to as the *Alemannic Coat of Mary*.[17] This text prompts its readers to manufacture a coat for the Holy Virgin from prayers and other exercises, including literary stimuli that encourage material imagination and meditative immersion together with allegorical imagery and a conceptualization of the emerging spiritual object as an efficacious gift for Mary. Thus it instructs its readers not only to visualize or think of this Marian mantle but to see themselves as creating a spiritually concrete artwork, a crystallization of devotional labor into an object that has aesthetic presence, religious meaning, and salvific agency. Despite not being made of physical matter, the spiritual garment can be imaginatively treated, perceived, and relied upon as if it were physically real.

Summarized in the most general terms, the *Alemannic Coat of Mary* explains how to produce a lavish mantle for the Virgin Mary from a total of "53 Masses, 6 Psalters, 600,000 Ave Marias, 300 Salve Reginas, 6,000 Ave Marias accompanied by cruciform *veniae*, 31 Paternosters with an Ave Maria and the Gloria Patri, and 1,800 acts of self-denial, three of which are particularly great."[18] Considering these vast numbers as

---

17 The *Alemannic Coat of Mary* is transmitted in Heidelberg, UB, cod. pal. germ. 108, fols. 86r–90r (H); Karlsruhe, Badische Landesbibliothek, Cod. Lichtenthal 87, fols. 215r–220v (K); Munich, BSB, cgm 783, fols. 168r–173r (M); and St. Gallen, StiftsB, Cod. 591, pp. 265–289 (S). The manuscript in St. Gallen stems from a Franciscan convent in Freiburg, the one in Munich most likely from a female Franciscan house in Unlingen. In this chapter I cite, for simplicity's sake, from the manuscript held in Karlsruhe – the earliest of the four, probably written in Strasbourg around 1450. It is hereafter cited as Cod. Lich. 87. Unless otherwise noted, all transcriptions and translations in this chapter are my own. In all German quotations from manuscripts, I follow the general orthography of my source but add modern punctuation and capitalization in order to enhance legibility. The orthography of Latin texts is normalized.

For the title of the work, see Hardo Hilg, "Mantel Unserer Lieben Frau," in ²VL 5 (1985), 1221–1225. Hilg proposes the provisional German title *Alemannische Marienmantelallegorese*, which, although the text indeed employs allegorical strategies rather prominently, is somewhat misleading. I discuss the question of allegory in greater detail below.

18 Cod. Lich. 87, fol. 220v: "drige und fúnfftzig Messen, sechs selter, sechs werbe hundert werbe tusent Ave Maria, drihundert Salve Regina, sechs tusent Ave Maria, die mit crútz venien gesprochen sint, und eins und drissig Pater Noster und Ave Maria und Gloria Patri und tusent fúnffhundert und drúhundert willen brechen und sunder drige grosse." A "cruciform *venia*" is a bodily devotional exercise which consists of prostrating oneself or kneeling on the floor with outspread arms, creating a cruciform shape. The term "willen brechen" refers to an ascetic exercise. Whether it describes a more specific religious practice in this context cannot be said with certainty. The text also refers to the "drige grosse willen brechen" as "gelossen" (fol. 217r), drawing on the term *gelassenheit*, coined by Meister Eckhart. This term is prominent in German late-medieval mystical writing and roughly translates as "detachment" or "letting go of oneself." Here it probably signifies a particularly severe act of asceticism. On the complex meaning and history of *gelassenheit*, see Burkhard Hasebrink, Sus-

well as the different types of pious efforts demanded, it is quite clear that the text was written to be used not by a single person but by a whole group of people who prayed this Marian mantle as a collaborative exercise. Such a group most likely included mendicant nuns but, as further discussed below, was also open to priests and laypeople.[19] Although the text does not provide specific instructions on how to divide up the great number of prayers, comparable exercises, such as the spiritual ship prayed by the Strasbourg confraternity of St. Ursula founded in 1476, shed some light on how such acts of communal devotion were organized by allotting specific devotional tasks to diverse participants and keeping meticulous records of their respective contributions.[20] In such exercises, the devotees did not pray together or simultaneously, but attended to their individual "spiritual workload" over a given period of time. This allowed devotees at geographically distant places to join and participate – a fact that might have contributed to the circulation of the *Alemannic Coat of Mary*, which, as its manuscript transmission and reception show, was not specific to a single convent or place but was disseminated from Strasbourg to Freiburg, Trier, and beyond. In 1458, for example, Dominic of Prussia mentions that this exercise had already spread widely.[21]

A total of four extant manuscripts transmit this short text, two of which are known to have been produced for female Franciscan communities in the Upper

---

anne Bernhardt, and Imke Früh, eds., *Semantik der Gelassenheit: Generierung, Etablierung, Transformation* (Göttingen: Vandenhoeck & Ruprecht, 2012).

19 The *Alemannic Coat of Mary* relies, for example, on the participation of priests who celebrate the number of Masses demanded by the text. As Dominic of Prussia highlights (see the discussion below), monks, nuns, clerics, and even laypeople of both genders are invited to join in the production of this spiritual garment. Textile craft prayer is at the same time, at least to some degree, a gendered religious practice. Religious women were often the primary recipients and copyists of devotional texts that contained instructions on how to pray spiritual garments. Nonetheless, Dominic's explanations and the nature of the spiritual contributions demanded in the text show that other social groups must have taken part in this devotional exercise too. There is not enough evidence to make speculations about the proportion of men to women, or of monks, nuns, priests, and laypeople in this heterogeneous devotional community, rendering any global thesis about textile prayer, religious status, and gender unstable. Also, most devotional literature is transmitted anonymously and thus does not allow for claims about authorship.

20 See André Schnyder, *Die Ursulabruderschaften des Spätmittelalters: Ein Beitrag zur Erforschung der religiösen Literatur des 15. Jahrhunderts* (Bern: Haupt, 1986), 191–242. A sixteenth-century text for constructing a spiritual house from prayers and ascetic exercises (Berlin, SB, ms. germ. qu. 762, fols. 125r–129v) includes exact instructions for how to organize such an exercise in the context of a female convent and gives details on, for example, exceptions for participating children, lay sisters, or nuns who at the same time have to fulfill essential duties such as taking care of the sick. It appears reasonable to assume that in devotional practice, the exercise instructed by the *Alemannic Coat of Mary* was organized in a similar fashion.

21 "Pallium quoque eius hic conscriptum ad honorem ipsius etiam in pluribus locis iam habetur et conficitur, sicut intelleximus." Dominicus de Prussia, *Liber experientiae II*, ed. James Hogg, Alain Girard, and Daniel Le Blévec (Salzburg: s.n., 2013), 32.

Rhine region.[22] Although the remaining two manuscripts cannot be attributed with certainty to a specific monastery, their composition, script, and content suggest a similar provenance, indicating that the *Alemannic Coat of Mary* was used and circulated in the vibrant literary culture of female mendicant monasteries in the southwestern German-speaking regions. The use of distinctly regional lexemes common to all manuscript witnesses, such as the word *trotteboum* for "winepress," further supports this localization and might even point to a specifically Alsatian provenance.[23] The earliest extant manuscript, today kept in Karlsruhe, was probably written in Strasbourg and dates to around 1450–1454.[24] The other three were copied in the following four decades. If the origin story advanced by Dominic of Prussia, discussed in detail below, holds true, the *Alemannic Coat of Mary* must have been composed in or close to Strasbourg in the early to mid-1440s.[25] The Carthusian link, along with the fact that the three oldest manuscripts also contain a compendium of devotional and hagiographic texts on St. Ursula, allows us to presume a possible connection to the Strasbourg charterhouse.[26] This monastery was a regional center of the cult of St. Ursula and in 1476 initiated the foundation of the abovementioned confraternity of this saint, which practiced praying a coat for Mary as part of its communal exercises.[27]

This makes the *Alemannic Coat of Mary* part of the abundant corpus of German devotional literature that emerged in the fifteenth century. Although books of prayers and meditations in the vernacular language were transmitted as early as the twelfth century, this genre remained comparatively scarce until the drastic late-medieval increase in literary production and manuscript copying that coincided with the spread

---

22 See note 17 for the four manuscripts.

23 For this localization, see Charles Schmidt, *Historisches Wörterbuch der elsässischen Mundart: Mit besonderer Berücksichtigung der früh-neuhochdeutschen Periode* (Strasbourg: J. H. E. Heitz, 1901), 360–361.

24 This date and location are established in Felix Heinzer and Gerhard Stamm, *Die Handschriften der Badischen Landesbibliothek Karlsruhe XI: Die Handschriften von Lichtenthal* (Wiesbaden: Otto Harrassowitz, 1987), 204–208.

25 This date roughly correlates to the spread of the Observant reform in the Franciscan convents of the German-speaking southwest. In his *Pallium gloriosae virginis Mariae*, which constitutes a commentary on and praising of the *Alemannic Coat of Mary* and can be dated with relative certainty to around 1445, Dominic of Prussia states that this devotional exercise was invented in Strasbourg two years before the composition of his own work. The emphasis on the new and innovative character of the *Alemannic Coat of Mary* is part of Dominic's rhetorical strategy in promoting textile craft prayer, but there is no reason to fundamentally doubt the general veracity of his claims.

26 The manuscripts in Heidelberg, Karlsruhe, and St. Gallen all transmit, in addition to the *Alemannic Coat of Mary*, prose legends about St. Ursula, a German version of Elisabeth of Schönau's visions of this saint, and other texts connected to the cult of St. Ursula. In addition, the manuscripts also contain different selections of devotional texts, prayers, and excerpts related neither to textile craft prayer nor to St. Ursula.

27 See A. Schnyder, *Ursulabruderschaften*, 52, 198, and 203.

of the Observance Movement.[28] As Peter Ochsenbein summarizes, there are only nineteen known and extant private books of prayers in German written before 1400, whereas the number of extant manuscripts for the following century ranges in the hundreds or even thousands.[29] Until recently, this extensive field of late medieval literature in the German vernacular has attracted little scholarly attention.[30] Most of the texts are still unpublished and unstudied. Although recent years have seen some important pioneering research, a suitable survey that would allow us to navigate the plethora of literary forms, traditions, and subgenres found in devotional miscellanies still remains a scholarly desideratum.[31] The *Alemannic Coat of Mary* belongs in this literary and historical context, and more specifically it is a key text in the evolution of a distinct literary tradition of vernacular textile craft prayer.

This devotional exercise, which can be characterized as an "exercise of imagination," gives detailed descriptions of the individual materials and elements from which the vestment for Mary is made, including golden cloth, splendidly decorated braids, different embroideries, and a variety of jewels, pearls, and golden clasps that attach to the garment.[32] The devotees are supposed to "manufacture," or in some

---

28 An early example of the genre in the vernacular is discussed in Christian Kiening, "Gebete und Benediktionen von Muri (um 1150/1180)," in *Literarische Performativität: Lektüren vormoderner Texte*, ed. Cornelia Herberichs and Christian Kiening (Zurich: Chronos, 2008), 100–118. For an overview of the cultural changes and dynamics brought about by Observant reform, see James Mixson, "Introduction," in *A Companion to Observant Reform in the Late Middle Ages and Beyond*, ed. James D. Mixson and Bert Roest (Leiden: Brill, 2015), 1–20. For a discussion of the impact of the Observance Movement on literary culture, see Werner Williams-Krapp, "Observanzbewegungen, monastische Spiritualität und geistliche Literatur im 15. Jahrhundert," *Internationales Archiv für Sozialgeschichte der deutschen Literatur* 20, no. 1 (1995): 1–15; as well as Regina D. Schiewer, "Sermons for Nuns of the Dominican Observance Movement," in *Medieval Monastic Preaching*, ed. Carolyn A. Muessig (Leiden: Brill, 1998), 75–96.
29 See Peter Ochsenbein, "Deutschsprachige Gebetbücher vor 1400," in *Deutsche Handschriften 1100–1400: Oxforder Kolloquium 1985*, ed. Volker Honemann and Nigel F. Palmer (Tübingen: Max Niemeyer Verlag, 1988), 379–398, at 383.
30 When using the terms *literature* and *literary* in this chapter, I am drawing on an expanded notion of literature (*erweiterter Literaturbegriff*) that, instead of denoting only texts with an aesthetic or artistic claim, encompasses all texts transmitted in writing, the "Schrifttum in allen seinen Erscheinungsformen" (Kurt Ruh, "Vorwort," in ²VL 1 [1978], v–vii, at vi). For a recent discussion of this expanded notion of literature with regard to medieval religious texts, see Burkhard Hasebrink and Peter Strohschneider, "Religiöse Schriftkultur und säkulare Textwissenschaft: Germanistische Mediävistik in postsäkularem Kontext," *Poetica* 46, no. 3–4 (2015): 278–291.
31 Recent contributions to the study of late medieval German prayer and the aesthetics of devotional literature include Jeffrey F. Hamburger and Nigel F. Palmer, eds., *The Prayer Book of Ursula Begerin*, 2 vols. (Dietikon: Urs-Graf Verlag, 2015); Ruth Wiederkehr, *Das Hermetschwiler Gebetbuch: Studien zur deutschsprachigen Gebetbuchliteratur der Nord- und Zentralschweiz im Spätmittelalter; Mit einer Edition* (Berlin: De Gruyter, 2013); Roy Hammerling, ed., *A History of Prayer: The First to the Fifteenth Century* (Leiden: Brill, 2008); and Johanna Thali, "Strategien der Heilsvermittlung in der spätmittelalterlichen Gebetskultur," in *Medialität des Heils im späten Mittelalter*, ed. Carla Dauven-van Knippenberg, Cornelia Herberichs, and Christian Kiening (Zurich: Chronos, 2009), 241–278.
32 The German term *Imaginationsübung* is suggested in Lentes, "Gebetbuch," 460–465.

cases "purchase," each of these items from a set number of prayers and devotional exercises. As they do so, they are instructed to vividly visualize the items and, as discussed in detail below, to meditate on their allegorical meaning. Finally, the finished coat is presented to the Holy Virgin, who, in an extensive meditative passage concluding the text, wears it on her way to the presentation of Jesus at the temple. Different saints, angels, and biblical figures accompany Mary as her entourage, and the devotees are instructed to "pay" them in prayers and ascetic exercises for their services.

Thomas Lentes convincingly characterizes the imaginative process that such texts aim at as "inner painting."[33] As the following passage illustrates, interior visualization and creation of images indeed play a central role in the devotional practice prescribed by the *Alemannic Coat of Mary:*

> This coat shall be made from ten ells of the most precious golden cloth one can have, and each ell shall cost 15,000 Ave Marias. This golden cloth signifies the true divine love which inflamed her heart so ardently. The lining of this coat shall be made from white ermine fur in order to show her maidenly purity. The lining shall cost 100,000 Ave Marias.[34]

While engaging in the otherwise repetitive and potentially monotonous activity of praying the same memorized words over and over again, the devotees following these instructions must imagine the golden cloth and the white ermine lining created and purchased by their prayers in all their lavish materiality and visual splendor.[35] Every single detail of the textile object constructed by means of prayers is named and described in this way. The devotional text stimulates its readers to immerse themselves, as Niklaus Largier puts it, in a textually constructed "space of experience" in which the objects evoked in writing appear in present form.[36]

---

33 Lentes, "Gewänder," 126: "Das Gebet wird zum Malvorgang, bei dem in der Vorstellungskraft der Beter der Kranz entsteht."

34 Cod. Lich. 87, fol. 215r–v: "Diser mantel sol sin geordent von x elen das kostberlichen guldin tůches, das man gehaben mag, und je die ele sol kosten xv tusent Ave Maria. Dis gúldin tuch bezeichent uns die wore gôtliche mynne, in der ir hertze so kreffteclichen entzúndet was. Das fůter under disem mantel sol sin von wissen hermelin zů einer bezeichnunge ir megtlichen luterkeit. Dis fůter sol kosten hundert tusent Ave Maria."

35 This intensified material imagination draws on a fundamental meditative technique of medieval devotional culture. As Johanna Thali shows, the verb *betrachten,* a key word in late medieval piety, is "zur Beschreibung einer Technik des Betens verwendet. Demnach bedeutet *betrachten,* sich etwas innerlich so lange und intensiv vorzustellen, bis es gegenwärtig wird." A thing, person, or action imagined that way is experienced not merely "als eine mentale Vorstellung [...] – es wird zur erfahrbaren Wirklichkeit." Johanna Thali, "*andacht* und *betrachtung:* Zur Semantik zweier Leitvokabeln der spätmittelalterlichen Frömmigkeitskultur," in Hasebrink, Bernhardt, and Früh, *Semantik der Gelassenheit,* 226–267, at 246.

36 As Largier argues, prayers as a literary genre aim at the "Konstruktion von Wahrnehmungs- bzw. Erfahrungsräumen und auf damit verbundene Formen der Animation der Sinne und der Emotionen."

In this way, the devotees imaginatively enter a virtually real space populated by an interdependent network of materials and things which combine into the Marian coat that the devotional exercise aims to construct. Cloth, border, embroideries, lining, clasps, and brooches belong together and relate to each other in meaningful ways. This interdependency of different parts is crucial both for the *Alemannic Coat of Mary*'s character as a set of instructions for a communal devotional exercise, to which each member of a group of devotees can quite literally contribute their part, and for the thingly status of the prayed garment. Viewing this relation through the lens provided by the theoretical work of Ian Hodder, we see here the "dependences and dependencies of things on each other, all of which draw humans into a skein of tangles, sticky or tightly woven relations."[37] Applied to the garment devised by the *Alemannic Coat of Mary*, Hodder's notion of entanglement opens up an insightful perspective: the different parts of the prayed mantle depend on each other; the imagined textile object as a whole relies on these parts as well as on the devotees producing it; and the devotees in turn hope for and depend on the assumed salvific power of the thing they manufacture from their acts of piety, while also being connected to each other through the shared effort of producing the garment. By thus presenting it as a thing made up of other things, all of which are strongly entangled in their functional and semantic relations, the text firmly anchors Mary's coat in the realm of objects. However, this depiction cannot hide the fact that this textile has no physical manifestation. In the course of the devotional exercise, it is woven from words, thoughts, and pious deeds, not tailored from cloth, thread, fur, and gold. Yet one might ask: Does the coat's lack of physical "stuffness" create any impediment to establishing it as "real" – that is, as the manifestation of a *res*?

This question necessitates a closer look at the construction and qualities of the prayed vestment. Though evocations of visuality, as mentioned above, play an important part in it, the devotional practice of craft prayer outlined here doesn't just aim at wallowing in imagined, lavish imagery, which could be understood as a form of "willing suspension of disbelief" with regard to the objects mentioned in the text.[38] Going far beyond the mere creation of interior images, the text claims to produce an actual thing from prayers and devotional exercises – a thing that, though lacking any physical concreteness outside of the devotees' minds, (1) can be treated as an object in the processes of production and gifting, (2) is embedded in a network

---

Niklaus Largier, *Die Kunst des Begehrens: Dekadenz, Sinnlichkeit und Askese* (Munich: C. H. Beck, 2007), 30.

37 Hodder, *Entangled*, 59.

38 The phrase was coined by Coleridge, who discussed the ability of literary texts to cause their readers "to transfer from our inward nature a human interest and a semblance of truth sufficient to procure for these shadows of imagination that willing suspension of disbelief for the moment, which constitutes poetic faith." Samuel Taylor Coleridge, *Biographia Literaria, or Biographical Sketches of My Literary Life and Opinions II*, ed. James Engell and Jackson Bate, vol. 7 of *The Collected Works* (New York: Princeton University Press, 1983), 6.

of interdependent things, and (3) possesses a specific type of agency. When following the instructions of the *Alemannic Coat of Mary*, the devotees not only collectively visualize a precious textile object, they also create and produce it in and from their thoughts and words.

On the one hand, this constitutes a form of interiorization, which, instead of positing a physically concrete object, posits an equipollent mental one.[39] The latter, though consisting of prayed words and devotional exercises, is attributed a spiritual concreteness that makes it at least as real as the former. Keeping in mind that the Latin *res* ("thing") lies at the etymological root of the English word *real*, craft prayer can be understood as the construction of an interior reality. The underlying idea of producing an inner object to which a specific spiritual concreteness appertains is in line with contemporaneous theories about the "real" quality of mental images: as Mary Carruthers shows, Thomas Aquinas, for example, thought of memories as "an actual physical imprint that permanently affects the brain tissue."[40] Following this understanding of interior images, the prayed garment is not abstract; rather, it is "really" brought into existence within the devotees. On the other hand, this interiorization is also an act of exteriorization. By quantifying the prayers and devotions that make up the Marian coat and conceptualizing them as a sort of raw material, the devotees reify their acts of piety. These eventually crystallize into an object which can be detached from the devotees by being given away to the Virgin Mary. The text thus inextricably combines the creation of an interiorized reality with a reification and exteriorization of the numerous acts of piety this demands.

Not only does the prayed coat consist of imaginatively concrete and aesthetically impressive parts, it is also presented as intensely meaningful, and thus significance and material appearance are indissolubly blended. On one level, most of the materials mentioned can be understood in terms of medieval fashion and dress codes. Often their meaning is rather obvious. Ermine fur, for example, was a material reserved for royalty and thus symbolizes Mary's status as queen of heaven.[41] Golden cloth signifies splendor and costliness, and, in combination with the white fur, it might also point to the liturgical colors appropriate for the feast days of holy virgins, especially Mary.[42] Most parts of the prayed mantle possess some significance in terms of contemporaneous textile and material culture.

---

39 Though less complex, this interiorization is in some ways analogous to the interiorization of the concept of poverty analyzed by Burkhard Hasebrink in "Selbstüberschreitung der Religion in der Mystik: 'Höchste Armut' bei Meister Eckhart," *Beiträge zur Geschichte der deutschen Sprache und Literatur* 137 (2015): 446–460.

40 Mary J. Carruthers, *The Book of Memory: A Study of Memory in Medieval Culture* (Cambridge: Cambridge University Press, 1990), 55.

41 For a discussion of the social significance of ermine fur, see Herbert Norris, *Medieval Costume and Fashion* (Mineola, NY: Dover, 1999), 283.

42 See Innocent III, *De sacro altaris mysterio*, 1.65, in PL 217:773–916, esp. col. 799–802. Although the practice of supplementing white with gold or silver on high feast days was officially approved

Yet the text adds an additional and more sophisticated layer of meaning by presenting the prayed garment and its individual components as a complex Marian allegory whose different parts signify and bear witness to the Virgin's virtues and her
role in the unfolding of the history of salvation. As shown by the examples of the
cloth and the lining, which stand for Mary's love and purity, the references found
in some elements of the coat are relatively simple. Other parts, though, involve
more complex structures of signification. This becomes apparent, for example, in
the portrayal of the coat's embroidered hem:

> The border at the hem of this coat shall be made from red gold and embroidered with a bloom-
> ing vine and its grapes. The grape signifies Our Lady, who has brought into this world the noble
> grape of Cyprus, who for our sake has been trodden and pressed in the winepress of the Holy
> Cross. And from his loving heart, he gave us the two living rivers. And we wish for the two living
> rivers to make fertile all hearts which have ever contributed to this coat. The grapes on this vine
> shall be made from all the tears of love which have been shed during this exercise. The leaves on
> this vine shall be all the devout words which are spoken during this exercise. This border shall
> cost two Psalters and 15,000 Ave Marias.[43]

This border, worked from gold thread and decorated with figurative needlework, unfolds the story of the Incarnation and Passion of Christ before the devotees' eyes. Its
floral pattern of vines and grapes constitutes a cluster of biblical references, explained and resolved by the devotional text. In an allusion to the Song of Solomon,
Mary is presented as a vine bearing the fruit of Jesus Christ.[44] Two further biblical

---

of only after the period discussed in this chapter, it appears to have been common in the late Middle
Ages too.

43 Cod. Lich. 87, fol. 215v: "Das bort unden umb disen mantel sol sin von rotem golde, und darin
gewúrcket ein blůgende rebe mit iren frúchten. Dise rebe bezeichent uns unser liebe frŏwe, die
uns den edelen trúbel von zyppern hett brocht an dise welte, der durch unsern willen getretten
und getrottet ist under dem trotbŏme des heiligen crútzes. Und uns uß sinem minnen hertzen ge-
schencket het zwen lebendige flússe. Und begerent, das die zwen lebendige flússe fruchtber machent
alle die hertzen, die je zů disem mantel gestúret hant. Die trúbel an diser reben sŏllent sin geordenet
von allen den mynnetrehen, die in disem dienste vergossen sint. Die bletter an diser reben söllent sin
alle die andechtigen wort, die in disem dienst gesprochen sint. Diser porte sol kosten zwen selter und
xv tusent Ave Maria."

44 This Marian motif is widespread in the German Middle Ages. For a detailed discussion, see Jutta
Seibert, *Lexikon christlicher Kunst: Themen, Gestalten, Symbole* (Freiburg: Herder, 1980), 333–334; as
well as Alois Thomas, *Maria der Acker und die Weinrebe in der Symbolvorstellung des Mittelalters*
(Trier: Habil, 1952). The motif is based on Song 4:12–13: "Hortus conclusus soror mea, sponsa, hortus
conclusus, fons signatus. Emissiones tuæ paradisus malorum punicorum, cum pomorum fructibus,
cypri cum nardo." ("A garden locked is my sister, my bride, a spring locked, a fountain sealed. Your
shoots are an orchard of pomegranates with all choicest fruits, henna with nard.") This passage has a
long tradition of Marian exegesis. The word *cyprus*, which in current biblical philology is understood
to refer to henna, is interpreted as a reference to Cypriot wine in the *Alemannic Coat of Mary*, a common medieval reading stemming from the mentioning of both *cypri* and vineyards in Song 1:14: "Bo-
trus cypri dilectus meus mihi in vineis Engaddi" ("My beloved is to me a cluster of henna blossoms in

references elaborate on this image. In addition to the parable of the true vine, the text also alludes to John 7:38: "Whoever believes in me, as the Scripture has said, 'Out of his heart will flow rivers of living water.'"[45] The text also hints at a related visual motif known as "Christ in the winepress," which was widespread in late medieval religious art.[46] Taken together, these points of reference depict Christ as the grape growing on the vine of Mary. The wine produced from the grape stands for the blood shed during the Passion: Jesus nourishes mankind with salvific substance. The Eucharistic undertones of this allegory of wine and blood are obvious and fit well into the general framework of late medieval piety.[47]

When embroidering the border of Mary's coat with prayers, the devotees thus produce an image which is embedded in a web of textual and visual connections and associations. If we understand allegory along with Angus Fletcher as the characteristic quality of a cultural object, image, or narrative that "manifestly has two or more levels of meaning" and whose apprehension hence "must require at least two attitudes of mind," then the allegorical quality of prayed garments speaks to both the devotees' material imagination and to their ability to read objects and texts through the interpretive lens of Christian exegesis.[48]

Yet the embroidered image is not simply a conjunction of two levels of meaning. Rather, it constitutes a complex hub where different texts, images, things, and religious doctrines come together and intersect. The hem constructed by and through the devotional text is thus an imagined thing (the textile object) that is made from words and depicts yet another thing (the grapevine). This second thing has to be understood as a complex sign that draws on a certain iconographic tradition and the events of the Bible, as well as their Marian interpretation. Insofar as this is not a simple allegorical combination of sign and signified, but must rather be understood as a complex semantic chain in which a spiritually constructed and concrete object in the present is tied back to real events and persons in the past and at the same time con-

---

the vineyards of Engedi"). When quoting from the Bible in this chapter, I use both the Vulgate and the English Standard Version.

45 "Qui credit in me, sicut dicit Scriptura, flumina de ventre ejus fluent aquae vivae." The parable of the true vine is found in John 15:1–17. The central sentence of this parable, "ego sum vitis vera, et Pater meus agricola est" (John 15:1; "I am the true vine, and my Father is the vinedresser"), lies at the root of the motif of Christ as the true vine, which is often found in both medieval literature and visual arts.

46 For a discussion of this motif and an exemplary image, see Bynum, *Christian Materiality*, 83–84. A detailed discussion of the motif's evolution and significance is given by Alfred Weckwerth, "Christus in der Kelter: Ursprung und Wandlung eines Bildmotivs," in *Beiträge zur Kunstgeschichte: Eine Festgabe für Heinz Rudolf Rosemann zum 9. Oktober 1960*, ed. Ernst Guldan (Munich: Deutscher Kunstverlag, 1960), 95–108.

47 For a detailed study of late medieval Eucharistic piety, see Miri Rubin, *Corpus Christi: The Eucharist in Late Medieval Culture* (Cambridge: Cambridge University Press, 2006).

48 Angus Fletcher, *Allegory: The Theory of a Symbolic Mode*, foreword by Harold Bloom (Princeton, NJ: Princeton University Press, 2012), 18.

sidered to be the meaning they point to, the *Alemannic Coat of Mary* here borders on typological modes of signification, which, as Hennig Brinkmann and others have argued, were not categorically distinguished from other forms of allegory by medieval writers.[49] The prayed garment is at once a thing and a sign that points to, is determined by, and makes present the events and figures in salvation history which it evokes through its thingness.

This multilayered and mutually dependent interweaving of thingness and significance might be understood in terms of what Erich Auerbach, in his famous discussion of typological exegesis, calls a "figura," meaning "something real and historical which announces something else that is also real and historical."[50] Although Auerbach focuses on readings of the Old Testament as "phenomenal prophecy" (*Realprophetie*) of the events of the New Testament, a mode of interpretation that hardly fits the relation between Mary, Christ, and the prayed garment, his analysis of the dynamic of a real, historical event or thing prefiguring another equally real thing or event that at the same time points back to the former and contributes to its fulfillment seems quite applicable to the *Alemannic Coat of Mary*. Employing a figura's characteristic quality of simultaneously appearing as an aesthetically present thing that fulfills prefigurations found in past historical reality and as a sign that unfolds meaning and itself prefigures a salvific future, this devotional text merges object, image, and word into a density of both impressiveness and meaning – the prayed thing thus becomes spiritually concrete.[51]

This construction of concreteness aims at different effects of reader response. In the passage discussed above, the combination of allegorical or even typological meaning and aesthetically intense, imagined thingness illustrates the central events of salvation history – that is, the Incarnation and Passion of Christ – and highlights Mary's part in this history. In some passages of the text, allegory has a strongly catechetical function, while in other instances the significant things produced by prayer might also serve as mnemonic devices. Yet, though the text thus aims at a whole spectrum of effects of signification, the ambivalent character of the prayed thing remains stable: from their acts of piety, the devotees manufacture a creation that, all at once, is made aesthetically present by means of meditative visualization and imagination, functions as a hub of referential meaning, and ultimately is treated as an

---

49 See Hennig Brinkmann, *Mittelalterliche Hermeneutik* (Tübingen: Max Niemeyer, 1980), 251–256.
50 Erich Auerbach, "Figura," trans. Ralph Manheim, in *Scenes from the Drama of European Literature* (Minneapolis: University of Minnesota Press, 1984), 11–79, at 29.
51 In this understanding of "figura," I draw on Niklaus Largier, "Zwischen Ereignis und Medium: Sinnlichkeit, Rhetorik und Hermeneutik in Auerbachs Konzept der *figura*," in *Figura: Dynamiken der Zeiten und Zeichen im Mittelalter*, ed. Christian Kiening and Katharina Mertens Fleury (Würzburg: Königshausen & Neumann, 2013), 51–70. Christian Kiening describes a somewhat comparable phenomenon "einer wechselseitigen Implikation von Präsenz und Sinn, von materialisierender und spiritualisierender Dimension," in his reading of the *Herzmaere* by Konrad of Würzburg. See Christian Kiening, *Fülle und Mangel: Medialität im Mittelalter* (Zurich: Chronos Verlag, 2016), 155–157.

object that can be detached from its producers' minds – more precisely, as a gift which, in the culminating final part of the *Alemannic Coat of Mary*, is presented to the Holy Virgin together with a plea for intercession and gracious protection.

The principle of giving a gift and expecting a salvific reward in return is key to craft prayer, and, if it is to be given, the product of the pious exercise needs to be thought of and treated as a concrete thing and not an idea. In the *Alemannic Coat of Mary*, this becomes apparent when, after its laborious manufacture, the finished garment is presented to and paraded by the Holy Virgin. Different late-medieval motif traditions provide the background for this imagined procession and the coat's role in it. Mary's coat, drawing on the widespread motif of the Schutzmantelmadonna, is first an agential object that allows the Holy Virgin to adopt, protect, and shelter the devotees as her children. Second, it is also a royal garment worn by Mary, portrayed as the queen of heaven, on her way to the presentation of Jesus at the temple (see Luke 2:22–38), which is described as a sort of royal *adventus*.[52] Finally, the coat also evokes liturgical associations. Although the text does not situate the devotional exercise in a specific liturgical context, the references to the Marian feast day of Candlemas, celebrated on February 2, are quite obvious.[53] The white lining and golden adornments of the prayed coat visually allude to the liturgical vestments used on Marian feast days, and Mary's way to the temple can also be read as a liturgical procession.

All these layers of reference come together and are connected in the devotional exercise taught by the *Alemannic Coat of Mary*. From their prayers and other acts of piety, the devotees who follow this text, supported by the soul of Christ, collectively craft an imagined thing which is at once aesthetically present, exuberantly significant, and expected to have a salvific effect. Although the prayed garment lacks physical concreteness, its density of impressiveness, meaning, and agency renders it spiritually concrete – at least to those who take part in the communal religious practice of producing it.

---

[52] On the idea of Mary as queen of heaven, see Rachel Fulton Brown, *Mary and the Art of Prayer: The Hours of the Virgin in Medieval Christian Life and Thought* (New York: Columbia University Press, 2018), 266–268.

[53] Neither the *Alemannic Coat of Mary* nor Dominic of Prussia give any instructions to do this spiritual exercise on a specific date or for a particular feast day. There appears to be a general connection of textile craft prayer to Candlemas, though. Two comparable sixteenth-century texts on textile craft prayer, one transmitted in a manuscript from Strasbourg (Munich, BSB, cgm 856, fol. 210r) and the other from a female northern German Benedictine or Cistercian monastery (Berlin, SB, ms. germ. qu. 762, fols. 129v–132r), specifically instruct the praying of a spiritual garment for Candlemas.

A Higher Materiality: Dominic of Prussia and the *Pallium gloriosae virginis Mariae*

The *Alemannic Coat of Mary* doesn't explicitly address questions of the ontological status of prayed textiles and how they compare to physically concrete things. In a contemporaneous text written around 1445, though, we find a detailed theorization of craft prayer. With the *Pallium gloriosae virginis Mariae*, Dominic of Prussia, whose literary activity spanned the years from around 1409 to his death in 1461, authored a text praising and explaining the religious practice of praying a coat for the Holy Virgin.[54] This still-unedited Latin work, which is transmitted in two extant manuscripts, offers insight into how late medieval devotees might have understood the spiritual things they crafted in and through their pious practice.[55]

Based in Trier, the Carthusian monk Dominic took his inspiration to write this work directly from the *Alemannic Coat of Mary*. He begins his text by explaining that "in southwestern Germany, in particular in Strasbourg and the surrounding regions," there were religious people whose pious devotion was so intense that they would faint, overwhelmed by divine love and a desire for heaven.[56] From this regional center of intensified piety he reports having received a "new, good and devout exercise" which he now intends to spread in his hometown Trier and other places.[57]

---

54 On the biography and works of Dominic of Prussia, see Karl Joseph Klinkhammer, *Adolf von Essen und seine Werke: Der Rosenkranz in der geschichtlichen Situation seiner Entstehung und in seinem bleibenden Anliegen; Eine Quellenforschung* (Frankfurt: Josef Knecht, 1972), 7–22. See also Karl Joseph Klinkhammer, "Dominikus von Preußen," in ²VL 2 (1980), 190–192.

55 Cologne, Historisches Archiv, Ms. GBf 129, fols. 9r–12v (K1); Cologne, Historisches Archiv, Ms. Wkf 119, fols. 73r–77r (K2). These are subsequently cited as Ms. GBf 129 and Ms. Wkf 119. Apart from a short discussion in Klinkhammer, *Adolf von Essen*, 16, the text is briefly treated in Lentes, "Gewänder," 140, as well as in Klaus Schreiner, "Gebildete Analphabeten? Spätmittelalterliche Laienbrüder als Leser und Schreiber wissensvermittelnder und frömmigkeitsbildender Literatur," in *Wissensliteratur im Mittelalter und in der Frühen Neuzeit: Bedingungen, Typen, Publikum, Sprache*, ed. Horst Brunner and Norbert Richard Wolf (Wiesbaden: Ludwig Reichert, 1993), 296–317. For a discussion and addition of the Marian Te Deum, which constitutes a sort of appendix to Dominic's hymns on textile craft prayer, see Andreas Heinz, "Das marianische Te Deum des Trierer Kartäusers Dominikus von Preußen (†1461): Ein spätmittelalterlicher Lobgesang auf Maria als Vorlage für ein Marienlied Friedrich Spees," *Spee-Jahrbuch* 15 (2008): 93–114.

56 Ms. Wkf 119, fol. 73r: "In Alamania superiori, Argentine videlicet et in partibus circum adiacentibus, personae quaedam religiosae in tantum, pro ut audivimus, in Christi caritate et devotione sancta profecerunt, ut nulla prorsus alia cogente infirmitate lectulis decumbant, solo divino languentes, amore desiderioque patriae caelestis accensi." (In southwestern Germany, in particular in Strasbourg and the surrounding regions, certain religious people have, as we have heard, made such progress in their love for Christ and in holy devotion that for no other reason, they swooned and sank down into their beds, fainting from holy love and inflamed by desire for the heavenly realm.)

57 Ms. Wkf 119, fol. 73r: "Ibidem et exercitium novum bonum atque devotum nuper, videlicet ante biennium, inchoatum est nobisque huc Treverim et aliis in partes alias est transmissum, ut quemadmodum ipsi illic ita et nos hic similiter faciamus." (In the same place, a new, good and devout exer-

The highly detailed description of the exercise that the Carthusian monk is promoting leaves very little doubt that it was indeed the *Alemannic Coat of Mary* that made its way from Alsace and spurred him to write his *Pallium*. Dominic's work can be seen as a sort of promotional theological commentary meant to popularize the religious practice of textile craft prayer beyond the Upper Rhine region.[58]

According to Dominic, two years earlier some religious people in Strasbourg had begun to weave a "sort of mystical and most precious coat" for the Virgin Mary.[59] Now it was the task of all other faithful Christians to continue enhancing this extraordinary piece of spiritual handiwork. Drawing on the *Alemannic Coat of Mary*, Dominic of Prussia envisions manufacturing this coat for Mary as a communal exercise. Yet the community he has in mind is not limited to a single specific convent or group of nuns. For him, it at least potentially includes all pious Christians: all who are faithful can join the collaborative network of spiritual labor and contribute to the production of the Marian coat. Explaining the different devotional exercises mentioned in the vernacular text, he describes how a community of laypeople, monks, nuns, and priests contributed to the original devotional exercise when it was started in Strasbourg:

> Those who were able to read recited Psalters, Songs of Songs, and other devout prayers from the Holy Scriptures. Priests read Masses, but in even greater number, laypeople contributed truly innumerable thousands of Ave Marias to the coat, just as though they were thus buying most precious cloth as well as golden braids and different other embellishments attached to the garment, [and] for each single piece, many thousands of angelic salutations were spoken steadily. Furthermore, they also added many of the exercises familiar to those serving in the faith [i.e., monks and nuns] in order to decorate the coat of the most virtuous Virgin.[60]

For Dominic of Prussia, textile craft prayer is a devotional exercise specifically tailored to tie together a heterogeneous community of faithful Christians: together

---

cise was started a short while, more precisely two years, ago, and it was sent to us here in Trier and to others in other places, so that we can start to make start to make it [i.e., the coat] similarly to how they made it there [i.e., in Strasbourg].)

58 Several very specific details, among them the close description of the garment, the detailed discussion of the different prayers and devotional exercises contributed by the devotees, and, most idiosyncratically, the election of the soul of Jesus Christ as the Marian coat's master artificer, match exactly in the *Alemannic Coat of Mary* and the exercise commented on in Dominic of Prussia's *Pallium gloriosae virginis Mariae*. Though it is of course possible that Dominic received, for example, a nonextant variant or translation of the vernacular text, his *Pallium* is certainly referring to the emerging tradition of this devotional exercise.

59 Ms. Wkf 119, fol. 73r: "pallium misticum quoddam preciosissimum."

60 Ms. Wkf 119, fol. 74r–v: "Qui enim litterati fuerunt psalteria, cantica canticorum seu alias orationes devotas ex scriptis dixerunt. Sacerdotes missas legerunt, quam plures laici vero innumeras milia Ave Maria ad pallium hoc obtulerunt, ementes quasi preciosissimum pannum et fimbrias aureas et reliqua varia ornamenta ad ornatum pertinentia, multis semper milibus angelicis salutationibus pro singulis dictis. Insuper exercitia multa in religione militantibus consueta inserverunt ad ornandum pallium virtuosissimae virginis."

they share in the production of the Marian garment, conjure up its aesthetically impressive spiritual concreteness and allegorical significance, and finally hope to share the salvific reward of the Virgin Mary's intercession and protection. Comparable to the characteristic pious exercises performed by many types of religious confraternities that flourished in the late Middle Ages, the production of a Marian garment from prayer and other pious acts relied on the collective effort of people of varying status and identity who were united by this spiritually concrete object.[61] It is not surprising that, for example, the confraternity of St. Ursula at Strasbourg, founded in 1476, included textile craft prayer and even a "coat of Our Lady" (*vnser frawen mantel*) in its prayers.[62] The connective quality that the spiritual garment has points to a central characteristic of objects: as Ian Hodder demonstrates, "the thing ties people together, and into relations."[63]

As exemplified by the *Alemannic Coat of Mary*, there is a different quality, strange and miraculous, to the imagined materiality of objects made from prayer. Dominic's text sheds some light on how medieval devotees conceptualized prayed garments and integrated them into the framework of material culture. "Yet, this coat is not made from the matter of this world nor from any other corruptible material, neither from gold nor from silver, neither from purple nor from blue linen," Dominic asserts – it is impossible to craft clothes for the Holy Virgin from the matter of this world or from any other perishable material.[64] Gold, silver, and precious cloth simply do not suffice. Similarly, all complicated worldly crafts are useless when it comes to the task of clothing Mary. With visible literary delight, drawing on the Old Testament story of the construction of the tent of the congregation (Exodus 25 – 40) as the biblical model for the even more sublime communal production of Mary's coat, Dominic lists all the types of artisans whose elaborate skills are incapable of contributing to this highest of artworks:

> In the whole world, no mortal craftsman could be found who was able enough to execute such a magnificent handiwork. Even if Bezalel and his companion Aholiab [Exodus 31:2 – 6, 35:30 – 34] were still in this world together with every erudite man whom God ever gave the wisdom and intellect to work with gold and silver, with purple cloth, with fine linen, with jewelry and woven damask, and to produce all the things for furnishing the tabernacle, which was erected in the times of Moses – they would not suffice to make a mantle worthy of the most holy Mother of God.[65]

---

61 For other confraternities and their pious exercises, see Konrad Eisenbichler, ed., *A Companion to Medieval and Early Modern Confraternities* (Leiden: Brill, 2019).

62 A. Schnyder, *Ursulabruderschaften*, 198. "Many beautiful garments" ("etliche schöne cleydünge") and other items of clothing made for St. Ursula and her virgins are mentioned in A. Schnyder, 199.

63 Hodder, *Entangled*, 9.

64 Ms. Wkf 119, fol. 73r: "Fit autem hoc idem pallium non de mundi huius seu alia qualicumque corruptibili materia, auri videlicet vel argenti, purpurae bissini aut iacincti."

65 Ms. Wkf 119, fol. 73r–v: "nemo mortalium artificum ad opus tam magnificum idoneus reperiri posset in terris. Beseleel et socius eius Ooliab hic adhuc essent in mundo et omnis vir eruditus, cui deus dederat sapientiam et intelligentiam ad operandum in auro et argento, in purpura, bisso, opere gem-

Yet if no worldly artisan is able to contribute to the intended religious garment, how can it be produced at all? How can mortal humans succeed in crafting an artwork that surpasses all other artworks and requires a material that surpasses all other materials? Faced with the futility of all human efforts, the would-be creators of the prayed mantle turned to the soul of Jesus Christ and elected it as their work's master artificer ("operatrix").[66] Under this divine patronage, the pious undertaking finally comes to seem possible: it takes the form of a spiritualization of the produced thing. Instead of precious worldly materials and sophisticated artisanal skills, the faithful have to contribute Masses, prayers, and pious deeds to the garment, and thus, following Paul's words in his First Epistle to the Corinthians, achieve spiritual things by spiritual means ("spiritualibus spiritualia comparantes"; see 1 Corinthians 2:13).[67] These devotional exercises constitute a material higher than all other materials, and with the aid of Christ they combine to make Mary's protective coat, which shelters all of humanity.

The underlying idea that Dominic of Prussia sketches out here appears rather unusual to modern readers used to categorical distinctions between purely mental thoughts and things that have existence outside of the mind.[68] In a condensed form, it could be summarized as follows: While physically concrete things are made from the corruptible material of the world, prayed things are made from the incorruptible – and thus superior – material of the spirit. Prayed things are comprised of and obtained through words, virtuous deeds, and pious thoughts offered by a community of devotees that is open to wider participation. They are, therefore, things above all other things, and they can appear to be thingly and simultaneously transcend this thingness by belonging to the sphere of the superphysical. They mediate between the world of things and the world of the spirit, and in so doing they have the potential to elicit salvific effects in the world.

---

mario ac polinitario, ad faciendum omne opus ad cultum tabernaculi illius, quod tempore Moisi fabricatum fuit, non sufficerent ad faciendum pallium dignum sanctissimae dei genitricis." The *opus ad cultum tabernaculi* here describes the liturgical devices and vestments made for the tent of the congregation. According to the Old Testament (Exodus 31:1–6, 36–39), Bezalel and Aholiab were the artisans in charge of constructing the Ark of the Covenant. The connection to the tent of the congregation here is based on a long-standing medieval exegetic tradition of typologically reading the tabernacle and the Ark of the Covenant stored in it as prefigurations of Mary; some crucial sources for the development of this motif are given in Fulton Brown, *Mary*, 156–157.

66 "de omni humana industria desperantes." Ms. Wkf 119, fol. 73v.

67 "Sed offerunt ad hoc homines pii atque devoti preces varias, missas et virtuosas operationes: spiritualia, ut docet apostolus, spiritualibus comparantes." (Instead, pious and devout people contribute different prayers, Masses, and virtuous deeds, earning, as the Apostle teaches, spiritual things by spiritual means.) Ms. Wkf 119, fol. 73r.

68 Yet, as Carruthers argues in *Book of Memory*, 46–60, the idea of thoughts as real things within a person's mind would have been familiar to a learned medieval audience acquainted with contemporaneous theories of memory and cognition. For a related but more modern notion of thingness that includes mental objects, see note 16.

The idea of a human community of devotees creating such an instrument of divine intercession by contributing prayers and other pious exercises, giving it to Mary, and expecting a salvific reward in return is fraught with theological tensions. As Arnold Angenendt shows, the notion of a salvific "gift economy," based on principles of balance and compensation, can hardly be reconciled with the New Testament notion of a God who freely gives his grace and whose mercy does not stand in any relation of equivalence to human merit.[69] Yet medieval devotional culture was saturated with ideas of "counting piety" and "measuring grace," which come down to exchanging pious efforts for divine favors.[70] The theological tensions created by this contradiction were immense, and it is no coincidence that the learned theologian Dominic went to great lengths in attempting to relativize the ideas of equivalent gifts and gifts in return that informed the exercises in textile craft prayer which he sought to promote.[71]

The *Alemannic Coat of Mary*, which the *Pallium* comments on, generally frames the devotees' pious acts as a sort of spiritual raw material and currency. In a first instance of giving and giving in return, the devotees entrust their prayers and devotional exercises to the soul of Christ, who, "paid" with additional prayers, combines them into a superphysical garment. In a second act of giving, this prayed cloak is afterward offered to Mary, who in return is asked to protect and intercede for all those who helped to produce this textile artwork.

But why, one could ask in the first place, should the omnipotent and omniscient soul of Christ need the contributions of the faithful in order to fashion a coat for Mary?[72] Dominic of Prussia is acutely aware of this question, and he attempts to solve it by arguing that Christ indeed neither lacks nor needs the offered prayers;

---

69 Arnold Angenendt, *Geschichte der Religiosität im Mittelalter*, 4th ed. (Darmstadt: Primus Verlag, 2009), 373–378. Drawing on the terminological framework of Marcel Mauss's gift theory, Angenendt briefly describes the evolution and theological tensions of a religious "gift economy" in the Middle Ages. From the perspective of literary studies and with a focus on hagiographical texts, these productive contradictions are discussed in Margreth Egidi, "Gabe, Tausch und *êre* in der Alexiuslegende," in *Anerkennung und Gabe: Literaturwissenschaftliche Beiträge*, ed. Martin Baisch (Frankfurt: Peter Lang, 2017), 353–370.

70 See the survey of quantified acts of piety given in Arnold Angenendt et al., "Gezählte Frömmigkeit," *Frühmittelalterliche Studien* 29 (1995): 1–71.

71 Berndt Hamm, for example, speaks of a "groß[e] mittelalterlich[e] Spannung zwischen einem verdienstorientierten *virtus*-Ideal des Heiligen und der Gegenkonzeption einer radikalen Gnadenhaftigkeit von Heil und Heiligkeit." Berndt Hamm, "Heiligkeit im Mittelalter: Theoretische Annäherungen an ein interdisziplinäres Forschungsvorhaben," in *Literatur – Geschichte – Literaturgeschichte: Beiträge zur mediävistischen Literaturwissenschaft; Festschrift für Volker Honemann zum 60. Geburtstag*, ed. Nine Miedema and Rudolf Suntrup (Frankfurt: Peter Lang, 2003), 627–645, at 639.

72 According to Hugh of St. Victor, for example, "ist die Weisheit der Seele Christi der Weisheit Gottes gleich, da ein u. dieselbe Weisheit gegeben ist. [...] Neben der Allwissenheit hat die Seele Christi auch die Allmacht, Ewigkeit, Unermeßlichkeit Gottes." A. Grillmeier, "Jesus Christus. II. Die nachbiblische Christologie. A: Dogmengeschichte der kirchl. Christologie," in *Lexikon für Theologie und Kirche*, 2nd ed., ed. Josef Höfer and Karl Rahner, vol. 5 (Freiburg: Herder, 1960), 941–953, at 950.

he demands them from the devotees, however, in an act of grace that allows them to lead a devout life and thus contribute to their own salvation:

> The soul of Jesus Christ, who is elected to complete this coat, does not lack our goods. But we simply give a sign of our good will that we, if we were able to contribute anything good to this work, would gladly do so, searching for any pious opportunity to serve, if we can, so that we will in this way earn protection under her coat and thus be freed by her from all evil. Yet, although the soul of Jesus Christ has incomparable treasures and, since he is given all power in heaven and on earth, lacks nothing, he still demands the fruits of our efforts and pious labor for our own sake.[73]

The true master artificer (*operatrix*) of the spiritual garment is thus the soul of Christ, who does not depend on the help of the human devotees but generously allows them to participate in the task and thus share in its salvific effects. There is no equivalence between the human contributions, the lavish spiritual garment, and the divine grace mediated by this garment. In a way, then, Dominic breaks here with the problematic logic of a sacral gift economy while still maintaining that the pious exercise of praying a coat for Mary would allow the devotees to "earn" her intercession and protection.

The latter point becomes especially apparent in a set of two hymnal poems, one in Ripuarian and the other in Latin, that Dominic wrote to accompany and summarize the *Pallium gloriosae virginis Mariae*.[74] Writing in the vernacular is somewhat unusual for a Carthusian author, but in this case it might be explained by the explicitly mentioned fact that this devotional exercise is open to laypeople.[75] As an auxiliary medium, Dominic's writings on textile craft prayer aim to instruct and guide readers in a religious practice of participation in the divine grace brought into the world by

---

73 Ms. Wkf 119, fol. 73v: "Nostrorum bonorum non eget anima Iesu Christi, quae ad pallium hoc perficiendum electa est. Sed nutum tantummodo benivolentiae nostrae ostendimus, ut si quid boni ad opus hoc agere vel prestare possemus libenter faceremus, quaerentes piam quandam occasionem, qua applicare nos sic valeamus ad matrem ipsam misericordiae, quatenus eius protecti pallio a malis omnibus per eam liberari mereamur. Quantumvis enim Iesu Cristi anima thesauros habeat incomparabilis et nullius eget, quia data est ei omnis potestas in caelo et in terra, fructum tamen nostrae industriae et fidelis laboris requirit propter nos."
74 These two poems, while not direct translations of each other, are mostly identical in content. Both are accompanied by a Marian Te Deum supposedly meant to be sung as part of constructing the spiritual garment; see Heinz, "Das marianische Te Deum." The Ripuarian version, written in rhymed couplets, is only transmitted in Ms. GBf 129, fols. 63r–67v, while the Latin double poem in four-verse stanzas is transmitted in Ms. Wkf 119, fols. 77v–79v (including the Marian Te Deum), and in a much later, presumably late-sixteenth- or even seventeenth-century hand, as an addendum to Ms. GBf 129, fols. 89v–90r (without the Marian Te Deum). The short discussions of these texts in Klinkhammer, *Adolf von Essen*, 16 and 20, and in Lentes, "Gewänder," 140, are somewhat misleading: the poems aren't translations of the *Pallium* or works independent from it but rather lyric summaries of this learned treatise.
75 See the discussion above, as well as the discussion in Schreiner, "Gebildete Analphabeten," 317–318.

Jesus Christ, and also by Mary and the saints.[76] In order to open this participation to as many faithful Christians as possible, different versions of the *Pallium* and the poems summarizing it are tailored to the needs and skills of different audiences.

The Ripuarian poem, written in rhymed couplets, addresses the effects of praying a coat for Mary quite explicitly. The coat "will be made so long and big, so wide and broad that it shelters all of your children, all of them: nobody shall be left in the open."[77] These verses evoke the abovementioned motif of the Virgin of Mercy spreading her cloak for those who seek her protection. Thus, the prayed coat has a specific function: it is meant to shelter and protect the devotees from evil and eventually obtain God's grace for them. Mary's ability to obtain this grace is illustrated by a series of short visions and exempla attached to the Ripuarian poetic summary, including the following:

> A religious person heard the evil spirits complain about the Virgin Mary. And one of them told the other, "Alas, it's a shame that the mighty one causes us so much trouble. She steals so many souls from us! No matter what a great sinner someone is and how many bad things he has done, if he lit a candle for her, fasted a day, ever greeted her or said a little prayer, or invoked her name in his hour of death, or did something else for her sake, she wants to keep him. And she says, 'He has been my servant.' And no matter how much we plead to the just judge, it won't help us: she gets whatever she wants when she intercedes with God, who once was at all times a stern and strict judge. Thus, the sinners' souls are taken from us if they stay with the mighty one."[78]

---

76 The idea of devotional literature as an auxiliary medium that allows participation is based on the typology of late medieval religious media developed in Berndt Hamm, "Die Medialität der nahen Gnade im späten Mittelalter," in Dauven-van Knippenberg, Herberichs, and Kiening, *Medialität des Heils*, 21–60.

77 Ms. GBf 129, fol. 63r: "Hey sall werden also bereyt, / So lanck, so gross, so wydt ind breyt, / Dat hie bedecke alle dyne kynder / Myt allen: geyner bleyue dar hynder."

78 Ms. GBf 129, fol. 65r–v: "Eyn geistliche mynsche horte, wie die boese geisten klagenten van der junckfrauwen marien. Ind sprachen eyn zo dem andern: 'Ach we vnss, dat die breite vnss so vil groissen schaden doet! Sy berouffet vnss also vil selen! Wie groiss nu eyn sunder is, ind wie vil bosheit hait gedaen – eyn kertze gebrant, eynen dach geuast, sy ye gegrust ader eyn gebetgyn gesprochen, ader eren namen an roufft an syme lesten ende, ader ander eyt vmb eren willen gedaen, den wilt sy hauen ind sprich: "Hey is myn diener gewest." Ind wat wir den gerechten richter an roiffen, dat en hilpt vns allit neit. Sy beheldet eren willen, wie sy wil vur gaen vur gode, der doch vur was allit eyn strenger richter ind ernster. Also werden vns die selen der sundere genomen, als sy blyuen zo der breyten.'" A total of seven exempla in prose accompany the rhymed Ripuarian work, all of which illustrate the salvific and protective properties of Mary's prayed coat. Some of these exempla appear to have been adapted from the *Dialogus miraculorum* by Caesarius of Heisterbach; for an English translation, see Caesarius of Heisterbach, *The Dialogue on Miracles*, trans. E. Scott and C. C. Swinton Bland, introduction by G. G. Coulton, 2 vols. (London: G. Routledge & Sons, 1929). The example of the vision of a Cistercian monk seeing his brothers sheltered under Mary's mantle, a version of which Dominic includes in his collection of exempla (Ms. GBf 129, fols. 64v–65r) and mentions in the *Pallium*, has also been translated and discussed in Renata E. Wolff, "Selected Marian Stories from *The Dialogue of Miracles* of Cesarius of Heisterbach," *Cistercian Studies Quarterly* 33, no. 2 (1998): 191–210, at 209–210.

Mary's power as an intercessor with God is unrivaled. As Rachel Fulton Brown describes, "Mary is a mediator (*mediatrix*) because she mediates between God and humankind [...], reconciling sinners to God, interceding for them daily and communicating between those who are still in the world and the saints who are already on the way to heaven."[79] Here sinners who pray to her or do other things in her honor may hope for her intercession to protect them from God's stern judgment.

But what role does Mary's coat play in obtaining her salvific intercession? A short explanation following the passage above sheds light on this matter:

> Therefore, we sinful people do wisely when we lengthen, enlarge, widen and broaden Mary's coat as much as we can, and decorate it with all good things that we can give or make. Thus, we can with greater security seek refuge with the Mother of Mercy, whom God gave the power to help the sinners and to receive those that seek refuge with her, and to shelter them from God's wrath under the coat of her grace.[80]

Here the mantle functions as an instrument of grace: much of Mary's intercessory power is delegated to it. This spiritual object protects the devotees, and in its protective function it has an agency of its own. Mary shelters sinners under it, and in order to help her perform this task, earn a place under the protective coat, and strengthen this textile rampart against God's just wrath, the devotee might contribute to it.

Although the following comparison holds a high risk of profaning religious ideas and beliefs, the Marian mantle, at least in the imagination of those who contribute to it, works similarly to the physically concrete nonhuman actors analyzed by Bruno Latour: a religious task that otherwise would have to be fulfilled by a human or supernatural actor is delegated to the cloak, which in turn prescribes a certain program of quantified prayer and piety to the devotees.[81] The spiritual garment protects the devotees from divine judgment, while they in turn contribute thousands of Ave Marias to the construction of this object. At least for those who believe in Marian intercession, the prayed coat has a very real effect on their hopes for salvation and thus shapes both social and spiritual reality.

---

79 Fulton Brown, *Mary*, 96.

80 Ms. GBf 129, fol. 65v: "Dar vmb doen wir sundige mynschen wijslichen, dat wir marien mantel na vnsem vermogen lengen, groissen, wijden ind breyten, tzieren myt allem guede, dat wir dar zo geuen ader gedoen kunnen, vp dat wir mit merrer sicherheit zo der moder der barmhertzicheit fluwen, der van gode dat ampt beuolen is, dat sy den sunderen helppen mach ind sall entfangen, die zo ir vleynt, ind vnder dem mantel erer gnaden bedecken vur dem zorne godes."

81 In an article on the social role of the door-closer, Latour, under the pseudonym Jim Johnson, argues that social action is delegated to nonhuman actors (things), who in turn prescribe certain types of behavior and knowledge and thus have agentive character. Latour considers that religion plays a role here. After appeals to humans and things fail, religious people tend to turn to God as the "supreme court of appeal, that is, to a nonhuman who regularly and conveniently does the job in place of unfaithful humans." Jim Johnson, "Mixing Humans and Nonhumans Together: The Sociology of a Door-Closer," *Social Problems* 35, no. 3 (1988): 298–310, at 304.

Physical concreteness is not necessary for this effect; as outlined above, its absence even enhances the status of the prayed object. Yet this does not mean that texts instructing textile craft prayer cannot use intensely visual imagery. Dominic's Ripuarian poem, for example, on the one hand emphasizes the spiritual raw materials from which the prayed object is crafted: "From Masses, from prayers, from psalmodies, from many thousand Ave Marias the coat and its lining are made for you, oh worthy Mother!"[82] At the same time, the coat and the process of its production are described using the imagery and vocabulary of textile labor and material culture. "Now we shall all work together in order to finish the precious coat with clasps and with golden borders," the text exhorts, prompting its readers' imagination with material images, only to continue by highlighting the spiritual quality of the garment: "I mean, with good and godly words. We will adorn it with all good things we can imagine."[83] Christian Kiening fittingly characterizes such effects of devotional literature as "oscillating between material appearance and a spirituality which transcends the material" – the fact that Mary's coat consists not of cloth and gold but of prayers and devout exercises might even intensify this dynamic.[84]

Conclusion

Many other examples of prayed coats could be mentioned and studied in detail, and they would in all likelihood allow further fascinating insights into the devotional literary culture of the late Middle Ages. Yet, although this chapter has merely scratched the surface of the vast corpus of medieval craft prayer and leaves many questions open, I would like to conclude by summarizing the observations made above in three tentative theses.

First, textile craft prayer not only instructs the devotee on how to visualize Marian garments, but it also allows that person to produce these objects from pious words and deeds. Interweaving vivid imagination and dense networks of allegorical meaning, this religious practice creates things that can be gifted, used, and experienced – at least in the minds of those who engage in it. Written texts are crucial for this process of production. Functioning as auxiliary media that facilitate and enable craft prayer, they prompt and guide the reader's imagination and, by prescribing set numbers and types of prayers and devotional exercises, provide a controlled framework for devotion.

---

82 Ms. GBf 129, fol. 63r: "Van missen, van gebeden, van psalmodyen, / Van vyl dusent Aue marien / Wyrt der mantel ind dat foeder / Dyr gemacht, o wirdige moder."

83 Ms. GBf 129, fol. 64r: "Nu willen wir alle zo samen schyssen / Ind den tuwern mantel besleissen / Myt vurspannen ind myt gulden borden: / Ich meyne myt guden goetlichen worden. / Myt allem gueden willen wir yn tzieren, / Dat wir koennen ymaginieren."

84 Kiening, *Fülle*, 261: "Oszillieren zwischen materiellen Erscheinungsformen und einer das Materielle transzendierenden Spiritualität."

Second, the material that prayed objects are made of, if one accepts the notion that devotional words and exercises are just another form of matter, is categorically different from physical matter outside of the devotees' minds. Physically concrete objects are made from worldly, corruptible, imperfect stuff, while the products of prayer consist of flawless, eternally splendid spiritual material.[85] In their concreteness, though, both types of objects are comparable, albeit with the somewhat unexpected difference that spiritual concreteness is deemed more real, in the literal sense of more "thingly," than physical concreteness.

Finally, prayed garments, usually produced as gifts for Mary, are thought to have a specific agency. In return for the spiritual textile, the Holy Virgin is asked to shelter the devotees under the cloak that has been produced for her. While garments made of cloth can protect the wearer from cold, damp, and physical harm, spiritual garments protect those who manufacture them from divine wrath and a subsequent fall into hell. Though it might appear strange to many modern readers, we have to assume that most fifteenth-century Christians believed the latter capacity to be more pivotal for both their life and afterlife, and that they valued the spiritual object fulfilling this function accordingly.

---

85 On this idea of textile prayer as a "perfect spiritual craft," see my forthcoming article: Björn Klaus Buschbeck, "Ein vollkommenes Handwerk des Geistes? Gebet und Andacht als produktive Tätigkeiten im Alemannischen Marienmantel und bei Dominikus von Preußen," in *Vita perfecta? Zum Umgang mit divergierenden Ansprüchen an religiöse Lebensformen in der Vormoderne*, ed. Henrike Manuwald, Daniel Eder, and Christian Schmidt (Tübingen: Mohr Siebeck, 2021) 245–278.

Mae Velloso-Lyons

4 How to Make a Knight: Reading Objects in the *Ordene de chevalerie*

In his 2010 memoir *Decision Points*, former US president George W. Bush recalls his attempt to "forge a connection" with Russian president Vladimir Putin on the occasion of their first meeting.[1] Interrupting Putin's prepared remarks on Soviet-era debt, Bush asks him about a cross which the Russian leader had apparently been given by his mother and had blessed in Jerusalem. Putin recounts, with great emotion, how the cross was rescued from a fire at his dacha, observing that its survival seemed "meant to be." "Vladimir," affirms Bush, "that is the story of the cross. Things are meant to be." Their discussion of Putin's cross is what Bush claims to have been thinking of when he subsequently told journalists that he "was able to get a sense of [Putin's] soul" and could vouch for his trustworthiness.[2]

Given the widely noted deterioration of Russian–American relations during the presidency of the younger Bush, this small anecdote has an outsize role to play in the memoir as both explanation and excuse. On one level, it exemplifies how objects are often relied upon to facilitate cross-cultural communication (think of the elaborate gift-giving between heads of state at international gatherings). Objects constitute a particularly alluring touchstone in such settings: they are seemingly passive, stable, neutral, safe, accessible, and legible – at least in comparison to the humans who discuss them.[3] In the case of Putin's cross, the significance of the object seems evident: a symbol of faith and family, two values which the leaders could bond over and which would provide a stable basis for thornier interactions in the future. Except, in this case, the object did not unlock the man, and constructive conversations did not become the rule. Despite Bush's initial confidence in the insight yielded by their discussion of the cross, his account concludes with a recognition of just how flimsy that insight proved to be: he notes that, in the years which followed, he would have "reasons to revise" his assessment of his Russian counterpart.[4]

On a second level, therefore, Bush's anecdote exploits the rhetorical power of showing the failure of object-predicated communication. By shifting attention from an abstract and tendentious subject (state debt) to a concrete, semiotically pure object (Putin's family cross), Bush seeks a common ground upon which the two leaders can speak plainly and clearly to one another. The failure of this strategy to bear fruit

---

1 George W. Bush, *Decision Points* (New York: Crown Publishers, 2010), 195.
2 Bush, *Decision Points*, 196.
3 Of course, the supposed universality of objects belies the fact that their human discussants are interested not in the objects' own qualities but in their interlocutors' perceptions and understandings of them – which are anything but universal – so there is a category error in considering an object a straightforward site for interpersonal connection.
4 Bush, *Decision Points*, 196.

https://doi.org/10.1515/9783110742985-007

in their future relationship calls into question whether clear communication was ever a real possibility. In introducing his relationship with Putin this way, Bush erodes the idea that more effective diplomacy could have sustained the comparably warmer relations of the mid-to-late 1990s.

In strikingly similar fashion, the *Ordene de chevalerie*, a short narrative poem composed in northern France in the early thirteenth century (ca. 1220), exploits both the "promise" of objects to facilitate cross-cultural exchange, and the drama of this promise's collapse, in order to argue that only war can bring peace to a multi-faith world.[5] The poem stages an encounter between de facto representatives of two opposing powers: the Latin Christian kingdom of Jerusalem and the Islamic Ayyubid sultanate. Their conversation is focused on chivalry and mediated by concrete, material objects pertaining to knighthood (a sword, spurs, garments, etc.), and for a while it seems as if their object-facilitated interaction might overcome the obvious differences between them. At the end of the poem, however, the interlocutors part ways unchanged, reinforcing the idea that there can be no true dialogue between a Christian and anyone who does not accept Christian orthodoxy. By treating the material objects of chivalry as sensory manifestations of spiritual truth, and by showing the sultan's failure to understand them "correctly," the poem implies that a proper reading of the material world is inaccessible to those outside of the Christian faith.

Although this might seem to concern only the irreconcilability of Christian and Muslim perspectives, the narration of the encounter between the two men serves another aim: to present *all* non-Christians as impossible to convert and thus to validate the continuation of religious war. A reference to Albigensians as enemies of Christianity in the conclusion of the poem suggests that the poet had not only Muslims in his sights but heterodox Christians as well, and was using the experience of one conflict to legitimize another – aligning the struggle for control of the Holy Land with the struggle to suppress heterodoxy in the Languedoc region.[6] I argue that the poet of the *Ordene* uses the chivalric initiation rite to model a single, correct way to "read" material objects, asserting the presence of divine truth in worldly material and dismissing the legitimacy of divergent human responses. In so doing, the poem functions as effective propaganda for the militarization of Christianity in general, and in particular for military action against the Albigensian "heresy," which entailed the rejection of divinity in the material world and was the subject of an ongoing crusade at the time of the poem's composition.

---

5 My quotations from the *Ordene de chevalerie* follow Keith Busby, ed., *Raoul de Hodenc: "Le roman des eles"; The Anonymous "Ordene de chevalerie"*, Utrecht Publications in General and Comparative Literature 17 (Amsterdam: John Benjamins Publishing Company, 1983), 105–119. This edition is cited subsequently as *Ordene*. The poem is cited here by line number, while Busby's editorial commentary is cited by page number. Translations are my own. I am grateful to Dickon Whitewood for his advice on sartorial terminology.
6 See *Ordene*, line 446.

The Construction of an Epistemic Divide

The two historical figures at the center of the narrative are Hugh II of St.-Omer, the titular Prince of Tiberias in the crusader kingdom of Jerusalem, and al-Nasir Salah al-Din Yusuf ibn Ayyub (better known as Saladin), sultan of Egypt and Syria, both of whom had died a generation or so before the poem's composition.[7] They are cast in the roles of teacher and student when Hugh, taken captive by Saladin's forces, is compelled to explain to the sultan "how knights are made."[8] Saladin then undergoes a ritual of induction into chivalry where each step is an interaction with an object, accompanied by an explanatory commentary by Hugh. The sultan is bathed, he is instructed to rest, he is dressed in a series of garments, spurs are attached to his feet, and finally he is girded with a sword. Each step in this process is accorded a significance that intertwines Christian theology with chivalric conduct. The concluding step is the accolade, which Hugh refuses to give on the grounds that he will not strike his captor. The ritual therefore concludes in cordial ambiguity: Saladin offers a gift to the Frankish prince and even helps him raise the money for the ransom Saladin himself had imposed, allowing Hugh to go free. However, Hugh remains with the sultan for more than a week, enjoying his hospitality but nursing resentment over the fact that his men remain in Saladin's prisons. They part, and the narrator offers a fervent defense of militant Christianity which paints knights as embattled protectors of the faith.

Given the conflation of chivalry and Christianity in this text (the obligations spelled out for knights include attending daily Mass and fasting in remembrance of the Crucifixion), it is clear by the end of the poem that Saladin hasn't been made a knight. But the encounter between the two men remains ambivalent. First, Saladin is shown in a position of strength and is generous with wealth that Hugh can barely dream of (the surplus ransom money makes many of Hugh's men rich), yet the validity of the Frank's cause is asserted throughout. Second, although the two men seem at times to enjoy each other's company, and each expresses admiration for the other on at least one occasion, they nonetheless part as enemies.[9] How, then, should we interpret their interaction? Saladin demands that Hugh "make [him] wise" – that is, grant him understanding – but the ritual that follows goes further than that: it seems destined to turn him into a knight. Indeed, Hugh's immediate response ("The holy order of chivalry would be ill-used on you") seems to take for

---

7 Saladin died in 1193, Hugh in 1204.

8 *Ordene*, line 80: "Comment l'en fet les chevaliers."

9 Saladin tells Hugh, "You have a great deal of bravery and are full of chivalry" (*Ordene*, lines 52–53; "Vous estes de grant hardement / Et plains de grant chevalerie"); he also calls him a "worthy man" ("preudom"; line 311). Hugh tells Saladin: "I see no one here as worthy as you are, fair lord king" (lines 332–333; "je ne voi ci si preudom / Com vous estes, biaus sire rois"). This last compliment has ironic potential, as Hugh makes it while surrounded by Saracens; it is also intended to secure Saladin's help, so it ought not to be understood as wholly in earnest.

granted that any lesson he were to give would induct Saladin into the order of knights.[10] By contrast, Saladin's gift to Hugh – the release of *future* captives – indicates that he has not interpreted the lesson in the same way: if they were now part of the same "holy order," they would be on the same side in any interfaith war. While the text stops short of taking an explicit stance on Saladin's (non)transformation, it is clear that he neither adopts the Christian faith nor subscribes to the ultimate purpose of chivalry articulated by the poet: the defense of the church. Yet the validity of Hugh's lesson is not called into question, and the poet goes as far as to state that "one can find in this tale [...] how one makes the knights that everyone must honor."[11] If the lesson itself isn't a failure, the fault must lie with the student.

Indeed, for the poem to dismiss the transmissibility of (Christian) chivalry to non-Christians, the initiation rite must not be accessible to Saladin: he cannot be seen to perform chivalry correctly, or even to understand it. At the same time, an overtly negative portrayal of the sultan would be out of step with the idea of Saladin as an idealized "noble pagan" that was already widespread in the Western imaginary (and is echoed in the *Ordene* with its description of him as a "very honorable Saracen").[12] By contrast, the idea of Saladin as a perfect warrior-king, were he only a Christian, enhances the desirability of Christian knighthood if he is shown to crave it. These factors may explain his ambivalent portrayal: Saladin must appear worthy, yet he must also remain outside of Christianity. Although Saladin might hypothetically be knighted without conversion to Christianity, the spiritualized form of the lesson in the *Ordene* makes it emphatically clear that the two are inseparable, from the bath which is explicitly paralleled with baptism to the insistence on fighting for the church.

The language used by Hugh in his instruction, specifically the term *senefiance* (significance/meaning), plays on associations with scenes of conversion and religious education that would have been familiar to medieval audiences from saints' lives, romances, and heroic epics, if not from catechetical texts and disputations. For example, the popular *Estoire del saint Graal*, also composed around 1220, features a "Saracen" king asking a Christian to explain various points of theology, ultimately resulting in his conversion.[13] Such intertextual resonances point to the necessity of taking the conversion subtext of the *Ordene* seriously. Some readers have even

---

10 *Ordene*, lines 83–84: "Sainte ordre de chevalerie / Seroit en vous mal emploïe."

11 *Ordene*, lines 425–429: "En cest conte puet on trover / [...] / Comment on fet le chevalier / Que toz li mons doit honorer."

12 *Ordene*, line 17: "molt loiaus Sarrasins." As Shirin Khanmohamadi writes, "Perhaps no figure better exemplifies the international code of chivalry than that of Salahadin [...] about whose generosity, wisdom, and romantic prowess Europeans were telling stories in their vernaculars even as he threatened their Levantine coastline." Shirin A. Khanmohamadi, *In Light of Another's Word: European Ethnography in the Middle Ages*, Middle Ages Series (Philadelphia: University of Pennsylvania Press, 2013), 32.

13 Daniel Poirion, Philippe Walter, and Anne Berthelot, eds., *Le Livre du Graal*, 3 vols. (Paris: Gallimard, 2001), 1:82–95.

implied that the *Ordene* shows Saladin converting to Christianity: Keith Busby refers to the episode as "Saladin's conversion by Hue de Tabarie," while Bernard Hamilton writes that "there could be no doubt in the mind of [medieval] readers that Saladin had been truly initiated as a Christian knight."[14] Their confusion may stem, in part, from the fact that many other narratives from this period do portray the conversion of worthy "pagans"; by bringing them into the Christian fold, these narratives enhance the claim of Christian superiority.[15] By contrast, the warmongering stance of the *Ordene* is better served if *even* Saladin, the finest non-Christian known to French audiences, fails to be converted by peaceful evangelism.

To sustain the appearance of Saladin's pagan worthiness while also displaying his lack of receptivity to divine truth, the poet implies that the opposition between Hugh and Saladin is epistemic, resting on how the two men draw knowledge from the world around them. In this way, they can both behold the same things, share the same space, hear the same words, and yet come out of the experience with irreconcilable views (only one of which is legitimate). To see how the *Ordene*'s lesson implies an epistemic divide, we can look at how the steps in the initiation are structured:

> When he [Saladin] had lain in the bed a while,
> He [Hugh] got him up and dressed him
> In white undergarments, made of linen.
> Then he said to King Saladin:
> "Lord, do not treat this as a joke:
> These undergarments, which are close to your flesh,
> And all white, give you to understand
> That a knight must always strive
> To keep his flesh pure
> If he wants to attain God."
> Afterward, he dressed him in a vermilion robe.
> Saladin marveled greatly

---

14 Busby, "Introduction," in *Ordene*, 86; Bernard Hamilton, "Knowing the Enemy: Western Understanding of Islam at the Time of the Crusades," *Journal of the Royal Asiatic Society* 7, no. 3 (November 1997): 373–387, at 383.
15 Notable examples are found both in epics (*La chanson de Roland*, *La prise d'Orange*, *La chanson de Guillaume*) and in romances (*Floire et Blancheflor*, Wolfram von Eschenbach's *Parzival*, the aforementioned *Estoire del saint Graal*). Not all non-Christians are treated in the same way: "pagans" and "Saracens," both of whom are usually portrayed as polytheistic worshippers of idols, are most likely to be converted, whereas Jews and "heretical" Christians are generally excluded from assimilation-through-conversion. The categories of "pagan" and "Saracen" are often applied interchangeably to Muslims in medieval texts; the *Ordene* itself calls Saladin both "Sarrasins" (line 17) and "roi [...] en terre paienie" (line 15). It is worth noting, however, that the *Ordene* does not associate Saladin with polytheism or idol worship, but rather with devotion to Muhammad alone. This makes him somewhat different from the typical converted figure of medieval narrative, and it may support the argument that his example is supposed to be transferable to other groups outside of Christian orthodoxy, notably the Albigensians.

At why the prince did that.
"Hugh," he said immediately,
"What does this robe signify?"
Hugh of Tiberias responded:
"Lord, this robe gives you to understand, in sum,
That you must shed your blood
To defend God and his religion.
That's what's meant by the vermilion."
"Hugh," he said, "I am greatly impressed."[16]

This passage exemplifies several features that recur at each stage of the initiation rite: Hugh directs Saladin's interaction with a concrete object, then offers a verbal elucidation of its significance, sometimes prompted by Saladin. (For the full list of objects, see table 1.) This elucidation frequently has a tripartite progression: (1) the observable qualities of the concrete object recall (2) an absent – and often less concrete – object, which represents (3) a broader principle or value. A fourth element is often added, whereby the value is translated into an ethical obligation. Although not all of the elucidations are rhetorically structured in precisely this way, a similar logical structure can be inferred for each. For example: the bath (1) recalls the baptismal font (2), which represents the casting off of sin (3), which becomes an injunction to maintain honesty and goodness (4); the black stockings (1) recall the grave (2), which represents mortality (3), which becomes the injunction to avoid pride and strive for modesty (4). In the passage above, we may intuit that the white undergarments (1) recall clean flesh (2), which represents bodily purity (3), which the knight is obliged to maintain (4), and that the red robe (1) recalls blood (2), which represents self-sacrifice in the service of God (3), which the knight is obliged to undertake (4). In these last two examples, (3) and (4) are very closely bound together.

In this way, an ultimate ethical obligation is obtained via an absent signifier, which has itself been obtained via a present signifier (frequently drawing on the object's color or form). Often, the objects appear as grammatical subjects with Saladin as their object: "this bed signifies to you," "this robe gives you to understand," etc.[17] This creates the impression that their meanings are latent, or at least that they emerge without any action on the part of the beholder. Saladin expresses his approval in such a way that exactly what he approves of is unclear: whether Hugh's mode of explication or the significance attributed to the object. This repeated structure thus

---

16 *Ordene*, lines 137–158: "Quant el lit ot un poi geü, / Sus le dresce, si l'a vestu / De blans dras qui erent de lin. / Lors dist au roi Salahadin: / 'Sire, nel tenez a eschar: / Cil drap qui sont pres de vos char / Tout blanc vous donent a entendre / Que chevaliers doit adés tendre / A sa char netement tenir / Se il veut a Dieu parvenir.' / Aprés li vest robe vermeille. / Salahadins molt se merveille / Por qoi li princes ce li fait. / 'Hues, fet il, tout entresait, / Ceste robe que senefie?' / Hues respont de Tabarie: / 'Sire, ceste robe vous done / A entendre, ce est la somme, / Que vous devez vo sanc espandre / Por dieu et por sa loi desfendre. / C'est entendu par le vermeil.' / 'Hues, fet il, molt me merveil.'"
17 "Cis lis vous senefie" (*Ordene*, line 131); "Ceste robe vous done / A entendre" (lines 153–154).

constitutes a pattern of object-mediated communication, a cultural exchange between Hugh and Saladin that is predicated on concurrent meditations on material objects. If we take for granted that both characters grasp the objects in the same way, the lesson amounts to an unusually detailed explication of the steps in a chivalric initiation rite. This has certainly been the view of much of the existing scholarship on this work. However, the very presence of the elaborate explanations suggests that an identical interaction with the objects on the part of both Hugh and Saladin cannot be assumed. I argue instead that the text constructs and sustains two perspectives, one of which is spiritually literate, the other illiterate. In the next section, I will discuss how focusing on the manipulation of these perspectives sheds light on an overlooked dimension of the cultural work performed by the text.

Table 1.

Lines	Object	Description	Saladin asks signi-ficance?	Hugh's interpretation (paraphrased)	Saladin responds?
109– 125	Bathtub		Yes	The knight must be cleansed of villainy like the child in the baptismal font; chivalry must bathe in honesty, courtesy, and goodness and be loved by all people	Yes
126– 136	Bed	Fine	Yes	The bed in Paradise that God grants to his friends – the bed of rest; only a fool would not seek it	No
137– 146	(Under) garments	White linen	No	The knight must strive to maintain bodily purity if he is to attain God	No
147– 158	Tunic	Vermilion	Yes	The knight must shed his own blood to defend God and Christianity	Yes
159– 173	Stockings	Finely woven black silk	No	Always remember your death in order to avoid pride; the knight must strive for modesty	Yes
174– 188	Girdle	White, small	No	You must keep your body pure and holy, as in a virginal state; the knight must love his body and keep it pure; God hates lechery	Yes
189– 204	Spurs	Gold(en) all over	No	Just as your horse obeys your spurs, you must serve God your entire life; all knights do this who are truly loved by God	Yes*
205– 221	Sword	Two blades	Yes	A guarantee against the enemy's attack; the knight must combine righteousness and faithfulness, and he must defend the poor and the weak	Yes*

Table 1. *(Continued)*

Lines	Object	Description	Saladin asks signi-ficance?	Hugh's interpretation (paraphrased)	Saladin responds?
222–240	Coif	White, without stain, fine, clean, pure	No	On Judgment Day, you must return your purified soul to God in order to deserve Paradise	No
241–256	Accolade [not given]		Yes	Reminder of the person who gave it	No

* Saladin does not respond verbally, but his emotional response is noted

Chivalric Practice and Crusade Propaganda

The *Ordene* represents one of the oldest surviving vernacular discussions of chivalric ideology.[18] This has long made it enticing to historians, who use it as a source for the historic practices of inducting new knights and/or as an account of the ideology of chivalry.[19] Both uses overlook major features of the poem and risk underestimating the force of the poet's agenda. To consider, for a moment, its value as a source for historical knighthood ceremonies, it is unclear what should be identified as the practice in question: is it the donning of the various accoutrements, the interpretation of their significance, or some combination of the two? Although new clothing was often procured for knighting ceremonies, there is little to suggest that ceremonies ever entailed the verbal articulation of connections between chivalric attire and chivalric ideals.[20] Indeed, men were inducted into knighthood in a range of different circumstances (on the battlefield or at long-planned wedding or coronation celebrations; individually or in large groups), and ceremonies were not standardized until long after

---

18 Busby, in *Ordene*, 88.
19 See, for example, Maurice Keen, *Chivalry* (New Haven: Yale University Press, 1984), esp. 1–17, 64–65; Richard Barber, *The Knight and Chivalry*, rev. ed. (Woodbridge: The Boydell Press, 1995), 33, 46; and David Crouch, *The Birth of Nobility: Constructing Aristocracy in England and France, 900–1300* (London: Routledge, 2015), 36. This approach to the text has been shared by at least two of its editors: see Étienne Barbazan, ed., *L'Ordene de chevalerie, avec une dissertation sur l'origine de la langue française, un essai sur les étimologies, quelques contes anciens, et un glossaire pour en faciliter l'intelligence* (Paris: Chez Chaubert, 1759), esp. xiii–xiv ("Avertissement"); and Roy Temple House, ed., *L'Ordene de Chevalerie: An Old French Poem; Text, with Introduction and Notes*, University of Oklahoma Bulletin, New Series 162, Extension Series 48 (Norman: University of Oklahoma, 1919), esp. 1–7 ("The Historical Basis of the Story") and 8–27 ("The Order of Chivalry").
20 New attire often had a more pragmatic purpose: to demonstrate the wealth and largesse of the lord conducting the ceremony, or to outfit the candidates for their new role.

the act of knighting had become common.[21] This is true even if certain basic elements, such as the attaching of spurs and the girding of a sword, were widely attested. Due to its complexity, specificity, and expense, the process narrated in the *Ordene* would not have been replicable at scale or in contexts where resources or time were anything less than abundant. It is also important to note that even in other texts circulating in the same language at the same time, the meanings attributed to specific chivalric objects are not consistent.[22] Nonetheless, Richard Barber writes that the *Ordene* serves to "explain the symbolism *behind* the ritual" (emphasis mine), implying that the symbolism came first and the ritual followed, and overlooking the poet's agency in the deployment of this symbolic language.[23] More plausible, in my view, is that the poet is actively imposing a symbolic and formal rigidity upon still-fluid practices precisely in order to present a vision of chivalry that essentializes its affinity with Christianity and crusade.

In fact, the most consistent dimension of documented knighting ceremonies is the presence of an audience, since the transformation from squire into knight partly consisted in the recognition of the new status by others. Two transformations simultaneously take place: the transformation of the candidate's self-understanding, serving to regulate future behavior, and the transformation of the observers' understanding of the new knight, shaping future interactions between them. The latter is fully absent from the *Ordene*, as the ceremony is conducted in a private space.[24] Not even Hugh himself is willing to grant the ritual a social dimension, given that he declines to perform the accolade which would forever connect him to Saladin's status as a knight. The absence of the social dimension leaves only the personal transformation – the adoption of a new identity and code of behavior – which Saladin evidently fails to complete. Moreover, a typical candidate would not ask all the questions that Saladin does, nor would the lord performing the ceremony be so reticent. All this undercuts the idea that the narrated exchange between Hugh and

---

21 Richard W. Kaeuper, *Medieval Chivalry*, Cambridge Medieval Textbooks (Cambridge: Cambridge University Press, 2016), 104–107.

22 Thirteenth-century French discussions of the meaning of chivalric objects (including armor, attire, and chargers) can be found in Guiot de Provins's *L'Armëure du chevalier*, Jean de Blois's *Le Conte dou barril*, and Robert de Blois's *L'Enseignement des princes*. See Guiot de Provins, *Les Œuvres de Guiot de Provins, poète lyrique et satirique*, ed. John Orr (Manchester: Manchester University Press, 1915), 94–113; Jean de Blois, *Le Conte dou barril: Poème du XIIIe siècle par Jouham de la Chapele de Blois*, ed. Robert Chapman Bates (New Haven: Yale University Press, 1932), 3–38; Robert de Blois, *Robert von Blois sämmtliche Werke: Zum ersten Male herausgegeben von Jacob Ulrich*, ed. Jakob Ulrich, vol. 3 (Berlin: Mayer und Müller, 1895), 2–54. A visual example of the same phenomenon is British Library, MS Harley 3244, fols. 27v–28r, a large manuscript painting (ca. 1250) of a mounted knight whose armor and charger are annotated with virtues. The image is discussed in Richard W. Kaeuper, *Holy Warriors: The Religious Ideology of Chivalry* (Philadelphia: University of Pennsylvania Press, 2009), 1.

23 R. Barber, *Knight and Chivalry*, 33.

24 See *Ordene*, lines 72–73.

Saladin is either a description of how such ceremonies were conducted or a prescription for how they ought to be conducted.

Yet even scholars who are interested in the construction of chivalric ideology in this work often give short shrift to the interaction between Hugh and Saladin, which Tribit describes as "only a literary device used by the author as pretext" for discussing chivalry.[25] Elsewhere, the *Ordene* has been discussed alongside chivalric manuals or portrayals of knighting and armor in longer narratives, thereby marginalizing the specific dynamic between Hugh and Saladin and, with it, the broader theme of crusade.[26] Though the historical Hugh almost certainly didn't knight the historical Saladin, the episode recounted in the *Ordene* has some basis in fact: Hugh II of St.-Omer was taken captive by Saladin's army in 1179 and released upon payment of a ransom.[27] Indeed, Busby observes that the knighting of Saladin by a Frankish fighter was widely accepted as historical fact by the end of the twelfth century.[28] Linguistic markers in the text suggest that it may have been commissioned by French relatives of Hugh to immortalize their crusader ancestor, in which case the narrative frame is certainly more than a pretext.[29]

That medieval audiences would have been attentive to the crusading theme of the *Ordene* is highly probable; in all likelihood, both the disastrous Fifth Crusade and the Albigensian Crusade were ongoing at the time of the poem's composition. Indeed, it may well have been written at the nadir of crusader fortunes in the latter campaign: by 1220, many of the crusaders' initial conquests had been reversed, their leader had been crushed by a rock, and the certainty of victory had begun to re-

---

25 Anthony Tribit, "Making Knighthood: The Construction of Masculinity in the *Ordene de chevalerie*, the *Livre de chevalerie* de Geoffroi de Charny and the *Espejo de verdadera nobleza*" (PhD diss., University of Oregon, 2018), 42. An exception is Zeynep Kocabiyikoğlu Çeçen, "The Use of 'the Saracen Opinion' on Knighthood in Medieval French Literature: *L'ordene de chevalerie* and *L'apparicion maistre Jehan de Meun*," *The Medieval History Journal* 19, no. 1 (April 2016): 57–92. This essay discusses the role of "Saracen" judgments of chivalry in two different works for Christian audiences. Although insightful, it focuses on how such judgments reflect contemporaneous domestic opinions about knights rather than on their potential mediation of Christian attitudes toward non-Christians.

26 See, for example, Keen, *Chivalry*, introduction; and Busby, in *Ordene*, 88–91.

27 Bernard Hamilton, *The Leper King and His Heirs: Baldwin IV and the Crusader Kingdom of Jerusalem* (Cambridge: Cambridge University Press, 2000), 143.

28 Busby, in *Ordene*, 86. Numerous medieval accounts exist of Saladin and other high-ranking Muslims being knighted by Christians. The likelihood of any of these inductions into knighthood having actually taken place is slight, given that they find no corroboration in Islamic sources. By the mid-thirteenth century, there were also written accounts of Saladin seeking to convert to Christianity on his deathbed. See the discussion in Hamilton, "Knowing the Enemy," 382–386. See also House, "L'Ordene," 3–4.

29 The dialect of the text points to its having been composed in Picardy, which would make sense if it were written to celebrate Hugh as a member of the St.-Omer nobility (although he himself was born in the kingdom of Jerusalem). See the discussion by Busby in *Ordene*, 84–85.

cede.[30] Although the campaign against the Albigensian "heretics" was waged many miles from St.-Omer, the north of France was a strong recruiting ground for crusaders, and it is plausible that the *Ordene* was composed, in part, to reinforce crusading zeal. The poet parallels "Saracens" and "Albigensians" in a telling passage: "Good people could never endure if there were only Saracens, Albigensians, and Barbarians, and people of evil religion who would do us harm."[31] By collapsing these different opponents together, the poet frames them as a single form of threat, to which the long-standing response has been crusade. In this way, the widely accepted rationale for the Levantine crusades might be transferred to crusades in the Languedoc region.

The encounter between Hugh and Saladin is therefore not only important for an understanding of the ways in which Christian and "Saracen" relations were being constructed in thirteenth-century France, but for an understanding of the rhetoric of religious war more generally. Indeed, one way to understand why Saladin's conversion to Christianized chivalry remains unrealized in the *Ordene* is precisely through the political context in which the poem was composed, which was not conducive to toleration or to nonviolent conversion efforts. As previously suggested, Saladin's failure to enter the Christian fold over the course of the poem seems to hinge on his failing to grasp Hugh's object-predicated lesson. It is on this portrayal of attempted learning that the remainder of this chapter will concentrate.

The Status of Objects

Concrete objects take center stage in Hugh's strategy of communication. They seem to grant access to truths beyond their material qualities that are, in turn, validated by these material qualities, instituting a circle of certainty:

> He [Hugh] dressed him [Saladin] in stockings
> Made of finely woven black silk.
> "Lord," he said, "faithfully
> I give you all this in remembrance
> By means of these black stockings:
> That you may always remember
> Death and the earth you will lie in,
> From which you came and to which you will return.
> Your eyes must look upon this
> So that you do not fall into pride,

---

30 As Joseph Strayer puts it in his classic work on the subject, "For a moment, it looked as if the Albigensian Crusades had been a complete failure." Joseph Strayer, *The Albigensian Crusades*, Crosscurrents in World History (New York: The Dial Press, 1971), 122. Malcolm Barber points out that the preaching of dualism started to emerge again in the early 1220s: Malcolm Barber, *The Cathars: Dualist Heretics in Languedoc in the High Middle Ages*, 2nd ed. (Harlow, UK: Pearson, 2013), 122.
31 *Ordene*, lines 444–448: "Ja li bon durer ne porroient, / Si n'estoit fors de Sarrasins, / D'Aubigois et de Barbarins / Et de genz de mauvese loi / Qui nous metroient a belloi."

Because pride may neither reign over
Nor reside in a knight;
He must always strive for modesty."
"All this is very good to hear,"
Said the king. "It does not aggrieve me."[32]

The expression "by means of these black stockings" presents the stockings as a tool for instruction that connects Saladin to something beyond himself. The stockings point to the earth, which points to mortality, the remembrance of which aids in the avoidance of pride. As we have seen, Hugh carries out a multipart unfolding that employs the concrete object as a kind of signpost. At the same time, the form of the tool enhances the plausibility of the lesson, seeming to confirm that the lesson is valid. That is to say, the observable qualities of the stockings are pertinent to this mode of instruction: the color recalls the dark earth of a dug grave and, by extension, the inevitability of death; their shape demands that they be worn on the lower part of the body, allowing them to act as a symbolic and literal conduit between the wearer and the decaying matter beneath his feet. In this way, the repeated form of all the "object readings" implies that the truths they yield are inscribed in the objects themselves, rather than applied to them from without.

At the same time, the material qualities of these objects are not sufficient to generate the semantic unfolding without prior semiotic priming: it is hardly inevitable that one would deduce the ethical imperative of modesty by donning an item of clothing made of a precious material (silk) and dyed in an expensive color (black). Although the stockings offer interpretive clues, Hugh's mediation is essential, otherwise Saladin wouldn't repeatedly demand it (see table 1). By casting Saladin in the role of a curious but uncertain student, the poet positions him outside of the circle of truth: unable to determine directly what the objects signify, Saladin must rely on Hugh as an interpreter.[33] In other words, through Hugh's readings, the poet creates an impression that the meanings of the objects are inherent and decodable, thereby emphasizing the incommensurability of the two characters' faculties of discernment. By rooting the lesson in concrete objects whose quotidian use both Hugh and Saladin recognize – as elite warriors in the Levant, they have both handled swords and presumably both encountered Frankish clothing before – the text plays with the possibility of cross-cultural communication taking place via quasi-universal objects. However, to serve the crusader agenda, the meanings of the objects must be made to

---

32 *Ordene*, lines 159–173: "Aprés li a chauces chauciees / De saie noire delïees. / 'Sire, fet il, tout sanz faillance, / Tout ce vous doing en remembrance / Par ceste chaucëure noire, / Que toz jors aiez en memoire / La mort, la terre ou vous girrez, / Dont venistes et ou irez. / A ce doivent garder vostre oeil, / Si ne charrez pas en orgueil, / Quar orgueus ne doit pas regner / En chevalier ne demorer; / A simplece dois adés tendre.' / 'Tout ce est molt bon a entendre, / Ce dist li rois, pas ne me grieve.'"

33 Of course, the student-in-the-text also facilitates the transmission of the lesson to the extratextual audience, but here I am more interested in this figure's other functions.

appear indubitably discernible to some (Christian audiences) and indiscernible to others (Saladin, the enemies of Christendom). Because of Saladin's "material illiteracy," even when the truth is revealed to him, he is shown to be unable to grasp its status as truth.

Moreover, "reading" each object in this way is no neutral act: the sensory interaction combined with the hermeneutic one yields an ethical-spiritual code that the aspiring knight, now physically dressed in these objects, is induced to embody. Unlike other texts in which chivalric accoutrements are assigned spiritual or ethical meaning, the objects in the *Ordene* are directly implicated in an ethically transformative process whose result can be immediately assessed. For instance, Robert de Blois's mid-thirteenth-century *Enseignement des princes* discusses the spiritual and ethical significance of the following items: sword, shield, lance, helmet, coif, hauberk, surcoat, aketon, chausses, spurs, horse, saddle, stirrups.[34] Although Robert's text likewise aspires to educate its audiences, they receive the lesson from the perspective of an onlooker, examining the items and their chivalric meanings from a safe distance. In the *Ordene*, however, Saladin is literally stripped of his old life and dressed in new values. While both Robert, as didactic first-person narrator, and the *Ordene*'s Hugh, as teacher within the text, privilege chivalric objects as a source for understanding chivalric values, Robert's students – the extratextual audience of the *Enseignement* – encounter these objects only in language and are not drawn into the rhetoric of the lesson in a personal way; the code of chivalry appears as static and impersonal as the decontextualized objects which express it, and the audience may accept (or not) Robert's ethical instruction at their leisure. By contrast, Hugh's student, Saladin, is set up for ethical transformation in the very moment of learning, the process bolstered by the physical transformation that he concurrently undergoes. Heightening the stakes even further, the narration of the scene invites an additional audience (the extratextual one) to judge exactly how well he achieves this. In this way, the scene of learning in the *Ordene* also functions as a test.

More important than Saladin's donning of the special objects is his engagement with their meaning. The distinction between wearing and learning is also present in the aforementioned *Estoire del saint Graal*, which includes a scene in which a character is ritually dressed by Christ himself. In this case, Christ shares with him the ethical-spiritual meaning (*senefiance*) of each of the garments, yet also specifies that "none should wear them except he who seeks the meaning."[35] This implies that

---

34 Robert de Blois, *Sämmtliche Werke*, 3:17–23. Most texts that attribute meanings to the knight's armor attribute them also to his horse, often reflecting its physical form (e. g., in the case of the *Enseignement*, the four feet are four virtues). The intimate association between man and horse in the theory and practice of knighthood is discussed by Jeffrey Cohen, who treats them together as a "chivalric assemblage." Jeffrey Jerome Cohen, *Medieval Identity Machines* (Minneapolis: University of Minnesota Press, 2003), 35–77.
35 Poirion, Walter, and Berthelot, *Le Livre du Graal*, 1:72: "car ne les doit porter se cil non qui la senefiance requiert."

wearing such objects, hearing their meaning, and *seeking* that meaning are separate acts, and that the first two of these are of no value without the third. In both the *Estoire* and the *Ordene*, wearable objects facilitate personal development only in conjunction with intention and commitment. Whatever the objects' inherent qualities (what Graham Harman would call their "real" qualities), their interest lies in the language they offer to the literate "reader," and in the acceptance of that language as true.[36] The objects in the chivalric initiation ritual require activation through both human attention and human understanding.

This is a far cry from the manner in which we tend to think about attire today, and which we often project backward when considering the importance of wearable objects in earlier historical moments: as an expression of personal or collective identity, or (especially when sartorial norms are imposed from above) as a mode of control or surveillance. Yet what is at stake here is quite different. Paradigms for thinking about nonhuman objects are inevitably historically contingent, as seen in Bruno Latour's investigation of "modern" thinking and in Bill Brown's exploration of how historic fluctuations in such paradigms have yielded numerous different readings of Achilles's shield in Homer's *Iliad*.[37] The production and medieval reception of the *Ordene* were subject to a paradigm in which nonhuman things were readily associated with hidden attributes and multiple meanings destined for human interpretation. This can be seen in textual traditions as diverse as bestiaries, exempla, and biblical exegesis. There was widespread belief in the availability of the world's hidden meanings to human "readers," if only they could be correctly decoded; holy scripture, patristic writings, and ancient authorities were all routinely used as tools for this purpose. A particularly famous articulation of this point can be found in Alain de Lille:

> All the creatures of this world
> Are like a book, and a picture,
> And a mirror of our being;
> They are a faithful sign
> Of our life, our death,
> Our state and our destiny.[38]

Situating the *Ordene* within this paradigm is essential if we are to understand the status not only of the objects within it but also of the perspective held by Hugh. For example, we must take seriously the belief that there is no contradiction in a ma-

---

36 See Graham Harman, *Object-Oriented Ontology: A New Theory of Everything* (UK: Pelican, 2017), 157–158.

37 Bruno Latour, *We Have Never Been Modern*, trans. Catherine Porter (Cambridge, MA: Harvard University Press, 1993), esp. 15–32; Bruno Latour, *An Inquiry into Modes of Existence: An Anthropology of the Moderns*, trans. Catherine Porter (Cambridge, MA: Harvard University Press, 2013), 8–10; Bill Brown, *Other Things* (Chicago: University of Chicago Press, 2015), 1–8.

38 PL 210:419: "Omnis mundi creatura / quasi liber & pictura / nobis est & speculum; / nostrae vitae, nostrae mortis, / nostri status, nostrae sortis / fidele signaculum." Translation mine.

terial object pointing to something immaterial through its own materiality. Caroline Walker Bynum has described how medieval devotional images "do more than comment on, refer to, provide signs of, or gesture toward the divine. They lift matter toward God and reveal God through matter. Hence, it is hardly surprising that they call attention to the material through which they achieve their effects."[39] A similar logic seems to be at work in the *Ordene*. The significances attributed to the objects are connected to their materiality but do not sublimate or negate it.

Of course, certain attributes distinguish the objects in the *Ordene* from the devotional images referred to by Bynum. The objects used for Saladin's instruction are valuable items, made of precious materials and dyed in precious colors, yet in contrast to the extensive descriptions of precious fabrics, garments, weaponry, and architecture that we encounter in other medieval works, the poet provides minimal detail about them. Although all the objects are human-made, there is no discussion of their makers or their geographic origins, nor even of their current ownership, creating an ambiguity about their cultural status. Absent other information, the objects are simply present at Saladin's court. Given the significance of gift exchange in medieval culture and its connection to expressions of power, this is a notable omission: if Hugh provided Saladin with these items, it would elevate Hugh's position in the exchange. The uncertain origin of the objects permits a range of impressions that further the *Ordene*'s crusader ideology in different ways. On one hand, Saladin's ready access to exquisite items, together with the enormous ransom that he and his followers pay for Hugh's release, creates the impression that he is exceptionally wealthy. This plays into existing stereotypes about the lavish, dissolute East and reinforces the idea that he is unable to correctly apprehend either meaning or value. As Jacques de Vitry wrote in a sermon for potential crusaders, "there is nothing cheaper to buy than the kingdom of God and nothing dearer to possess."[40] Associating Saladin with the misapprehension of value reinforces the idea that non-Christians lack the aptitude to correctly apprehend theological truth.

On the other hand, divorcing the objects from any stated origin prevents them from becoming too worldly. In this way, the work's resonances with scenes of ordination may paradoxically lend the chivalric objects the appearance of being what Bynum calls "holy matter."[41] Even when an object's significance pertains to phenomena fully beyond the material realm, Hugh's explanation lingers on its materiality:

---

[39] Caroline Walker Bynum, *Christian Materiality: An Essay on Religion in Late Medieval Europe* (New York: Zone Books, 2015), 35.

[40] "Regno quidem Dei nichil vilius cum emitur, nichil carius cum possidetur." Jacques de Vitry, in Christoph T. Maier, ed. and trans., *Crusade Propaganda and Ideology: Model Sermons for the Preaching of the Cross* (Cambridge: Cambridge University Press, 2000), 118 (Latin), 119 (English translation). Vitry also wrote that "Christ is despised by rich and worldly people" ("Christus a divitibus et secularibus hominibus contempnitur"): in Maier, 84–85.

[41] Bynum, *Christian Materiality*, 20.

"Now look:
Just as you see
That this coif is without stain,
Beautiful, white, clean and pure,
And is placed on your head,
So, on the Day of Judgment,
You must strive to free your soul
From the sins that your body will have committed,
Pure and cleansed of the mad acts
That the body has committed without cease,
And return it [the soul] to God, in order to deserve
The Paradise which brings great joy;
Because no tongue can describe,
No ear can hear, no heart can think of
The great beauties of Paradise
That God grants to his friends."[42]

This focus on materiality elevates the objects so that they are not only signs of divine truth but also a validation of the worthiness of God's Creation – of matter itself. In this way, the silence about the origins of the objects allows them to remain subject to different assumptions by the audience, possibly even bolstering conflicting interpretations at once: that the wealth of "Saracens" shows their alienation from God, while at the same time material things manifest God's goodness.

A further important distinction between Bynum's devotional artworks and the chivalric objects of the *Ordene* is the question of "readership." It may be assumed that the audience of devotional artworks would have some familiarity with both their iconographic program and the broader epistemological regime that they partake in, whereas this cannot be assumed of Saladin, who is expected – without any priming – to read familiar objects in a new way. Whereas the evangelist converting the Saracen in the *Estoire* receives guidance directly from God, Hugh is presented simply as an honorable man ("preudom").[43] This characterization trivializes the theological knowledge and hermeneutic training required for him to mediate the objects' messages, suggesting that the objects ought to be legible to anyone. By eliding the fact that beliefs pertaining to the semantic potential of the material world are highly culturally contingent, the poem fosters Christian self-confidence, even self-righteousness: anyone raised in a Christian community would be, by virtue of ideo-

---

42 *Ordene*, lines 225–240: "or esgardez: / Tout autressi com vous veez / Que ceste coiffe est sanz ordure, / Et bele et blanche et nete et pure, / Et est seur vostre chief assise, / Ensement au jor del juïse / Des pechiez qu'avra fet li cors, / Devez l'ame rendre a esfors / Et pure et nete des folies / Que li cors a toz jors basties, / A Dieu, pour avoir le merite / De Paradis que molt delite; / Quar langue ne pourroit conter, / Oreille oïr, ne cuers pensser / Les granz biautez de Paradis / Que Diex otroie a ses amis."
43 *Ordene*, line 484. For the *Estoire*, see Poirion, Walter, and Berthelot, *Le Livre du Graal*, 1:81. For the characterization of Hugh in the *Ordene*, see especially lines 484–490. The message that is drawn from Hugh's life is to try to do well ("pener / De faire bien").

logical osmosis, a quicker study than Saladin. By naturalizing Hugh's "literacy" – the idea that it is *evidently true* that a red robe points to the need to shed blood for Christianity – Saladin's "illiteracy" is made all the more shameful: though he wears the red robe, he does not renounce his war upon the Christians. While the initiation presents itself as a lesson drawn from objects that transcend the cultural boundaries between Saladin and Hugh, in fact only one of them has the cultural priming to apprehend the objects as both material and (Christian) sign – and to value that sign as truth.

Illiteracy and Intention

What does the poet blame for Saladin's misapprehension of the initiation rite? It is not inattentiveness, for the text twice comments on how well he listens to Hugh's explanations.[44] Rather, it is implied that he is listening in the wrong way: carnally, not spiritually, as he lacks the correct intention. His responses emphasize the pleasure he derives from the initiation: "this beginning is very fine"; "all this is very pleasant to hear"; "it pleased Saladin greatly"; "the king listened well […] and found great joy in doing so."[45] This suggests that Saladin has at least a shallow level of access to the truth that is being offered to him, as there is a frequent association in medieval culture between pleasantness, salutariness, and the divine.[46] The implication, however, is that his perceptiveness stalls at the point where it would permit a more thoroughgoing transformation: Saladin displays no commitment to what he has heard once the ritual is over, indicating that he has not understood as true that which was offered to him. By repeatedly reminding the audience of Saladin's presence through his interjections, the poet sustains two perspectives in the didactic scene: that of the Christian, who can read the material world as God's language, and that of the non-Christian, who treats Hugh's readings as artful rhetoric rather than revelation.

In this way, the *Ordene*'s lesson requires a Christian "literacy" which non-Christians are de facto prevented from acquiring by the absence of appropriate priming. Indeed, immediately following the close of the narration, the poet goes one step further in his exclusion of non-Christians from spiritual literacy by associating lack of acculturation in Christian semiosis with a failure of will:

---

44 See *Ordene*, lines 221 and 241.
45 "Molt est biaus cis commencemenz" (*Ordene*, line 124); "Tout ce est molt bon a entendre" (line 172); "Molt plesoit bien Saladin" (line 204); "Li rois a molt bien entendu / […] / Si en a eu joie molt grant" (lines 298–300).
46 See, for example, Rachel Fulton, "'Taste and See That the Lord Is Sweet' (Ps. 33:9): The Flavor of God in the Monastic West," *Journal of Religion* 86, no. 2 (2006): 169–204; and Mary J. Carruthers, *The Experience of Beauty in the Middle Ages*, Oxford-Warburg Studies (Oxford: Oxford University Press, 2013), ch. 3 ("Taking the Bitter with the Sweet").

Lords, this tale should come
Among good people,
Because it isn't worth anything to the others,
Who do not understand any more than sheep do.
By the faith that I owe the God of Paradise,
Whoever would throw his jewels among swine
Would certainly lose them.
May you know that they would trample them
And would never enjoy them
Because they would not know how to
And would misunderstand.
Whoever told them this tale
Would be trampled in exactly the same way
And would be considered vile in their understanding
Unless they wanted to learn something from it.[47]

This passage makes use of a common trope in which poets express their desires for how their works should be received, but here the trope serves a further function by creating space for a commentary on the preceding narrative. The emphatic assertion that certain people are incapable of understanding is juxtaposed with the preceding narrative portrayal of divergent understandings in matters of faith, inevitably coloring its audience's reception of the story. Indeed, the biblical reference to Matthew 7:6 is ascribed a particularly narrow interpretation: swine trample jewels (and would trample future tellers of this tale!) because they lack understanding – which would change if they genuinely wanted to learn. The implication is that hearing the truth, seeing its signs, even trying them on, as Saladin has just done, is insufficient without an act of will (an essential *wanting* to learn the truth qua truth). This makes access to spiritual truth very narrow, because it must be prompted by a pure desire which transcends the learner's own cultural context and yet embraces the specific cultural forms of the medieval Christian catechesis. As a result, we are enticed to believe that Saladin's failure to become Christian squarely derives from a willful persistence in error, which is precisely the definition of heresy. It is easy to imagine how such a text could harden attitudes toward not only "Saracens" but all those who resisted Christian orthodoxy.

In fact, the passage above is not the most inflammatory explanation of Saladin's illiteracy posited by the text. Early on in the poem, Hugh offers his own interpretation of Saladin's suitability for chivalry, likening the requested initiation to the "madness" of "want[ing] to dress and cover a dung-heap in silk cloth in order that it stop

---

47 *Ordene*, lines 410 – 424: "Seignor, bien doit estre venuz / Cis contes entre bone gent, / Quar aus autres ne vaut noient, / Qui n'entendent plus que brebis. / Foi que doi Dieu de Paradis, / Cil perderoit bien ses joiaus / Qui les jetroit entre porciaus. / Sachiez qu'il les defouleroient / Ne ja ne s'en deporteroient, / Quar il ne savroient pas tant, / Si seroient mesentendant. / Qui cest conte lor conteroit / Tout issi defoulez seroit / Et vil tenu par lor entendre, / Mes s'il i voloient aprendre."

smelling."[48] The use of the verb "dress" (*vestir*) is telling, for it will be used several times in the following lesson to refer to what Hugh does to Saladin, as is the reference to silk, which will come up again with the stockings. Such a vivid and prejudicial image, although it occasions no discussion in the narrative, would undoubtedly have stuck in the minds of medieval audiences long after it had first received their laughter. In this way, the text posits a further interpretation of Saladin's limitations as a student: his essential, irreparable corruption.[49] It also exemplifies the poet's exploitation of Hugh as a mouthpiece for a more vitriolic version of his narratorial perspective, thereby lending an appearance of sobriety to his own narration, while at the same time leaving such language unchallenged.

The binary between those who can read God's words and those who are blind to them is conclusively reinforced in the poet's vigorous defense of knights, whom he presents as the guarantors of goodness, for "if bad people did not fear them, good people would never endure."[50] Without the intervention of knights, he reasons, "our chalices would be stolen from before us at God's table."[51] Further statements defend the right to bear arms in church to ensure that Mass can be held and promise that loyal knights will go directly to Paradise. The rhetoric here promotes a siege mentality according to which the church is under constant, violent attack and crusade has no geographic bounds.[52] Intensifying this portrayal of Christian vulnerability is the aforementioned specific naming of enemy groups: "Saracens, Albigensians, and Barbarians, and people of evil religion."[53] The syntactic and semantic parallel between "Saracens" and "Albigensians" invites the audience to imagine another parallel: between the failure of Saladin to grasp Christian teachings and the potential failure of the Albigensian heretics to grasp whatever Christian teachings the crusading armies might offer them. If one enemy is like another, and if Hugh's education of Saladin did nothing to stop the latter's slaughter of Christians at Hattin, then perhaps the violent conquest of the Languedoc region and the policy of no quarter shown to many of its communities can be construed as necessary acts of self-defense.

While it might be imagined that the commonalities between Muslims in the Levant and dualist Christians in Occitania were few, the conflation of their threats to Christians could well have appeared plausible to medieval audiences. Although there continued to be depictions of Saracens worshipping multiple idols, in the

---

48 *Ordene*, lines 87–89: "grant folie entreprendoie / Se un fumier de dras de soie / Voloie vestir et couvrir / Qu'il ne peüst jamés puïr."

49 It is clear that this corruption is premised on his nonadherence to Christianity rather than the specific character of his alternative beliefs (see lines 85–86). The image of a disguised dunghill is deployed elsewhere in medieval writing to express anxiety about how clothing can foster false appearances. See E. Jane Burns, *Courtly Love Undressed: Reading through Clothes in Medieval French Literature* (Philadelphia: University of Pennsylvania Press, 2002), 49–50.

50 *Ordene*, lines 443–444: "Si li mauvés ne les cremoient / Ja li bon durer ne porroient."

51 *Ordene*, lines 438–439: "On nous embleroit nos calices / Devant nous a la table Dé."

52 See *Ordene*, lines 473–475, 456–466.

53 *Ordene*, lines 445–447: "de Sarrasins, / D'Aubigois et de Barbarins / Et de genz de mauvese loi."

twelfth century a different critique of Islam emerged that treated it as a Christian heresy instituted by the prophet Muhammad.[54] This supposed heresy was often characterized in terms of its carnality, including by Alain de Lille in his four-part treatise on Albigensians, Waldensians, Jews, and Muslims, composed in 1200.[55] In the *Ordene*, only one god is attributed to Saladin: "Mahommet," who is mentioned three times.[56] This suggests that the Islam represented here is less the "idolatrous pagan" variant found in the chansons de geste and more the "carnal heretic" variant found in Alain's screed. It is perhaps not so great a leap to see a resemblance between this heresy and one that "misapprehended" the status of matter in an opposite way: instead of embracing carnality, the Occitan dualists rejected it entirely, maintaining that their God had no involvement in the creation of the material world.

Viewed from this perspective, the lesson of the *Ordene* is an antiheretical cure-all, its teachings rooted in material objects precisely in order to refute any suggestion that the fabric of Creation could be the source – or site – of ethical perversion. And yet it is highly doubtful that the poem redeemed anyone from heterodoxy: by essentializing its own perspective at the expense of its accessibility to outsiders, a hermetically sealed system is disingenuously presented as learnable. For "good" humans, the truth is plain to see. The tacit inscription of knighthood's transformative objects into a tradition of Christian hermeneutics allows the poet to preserve spiritual truth for Latin Christians; that he does so while elevating chivalry to a "holy order" and demoting a famous enemy of Christendom to a jewel-trampling swine should make it clear how keenly his work serves the cause of religious war.

Contrary to its own proclamation, the *Ordene* does not simply show how knights are created, it shows *why* they must be: because there are certain humans who cannot perceive truth even when they grasp it in their hands or hear it spelled out to them, and who (barring spontaneous self-reform or divine intervention) will always threaten the lives of their truth-loving fellow humans. Similar claims about the inevitability of a zero-sum clash of civilizations continue to abound in our own time, especially where relations between historically Christian and predominantly Muslim nations are concerned. Paying greater attention to how proponents of such essentializing views often mobilize the purported "neutrality" of objects in their favor may be one strategy for holding them to account.

---

54 John V. Tolan, *Saracens: Islam in the Medieval European Imagination* (New York: Columbia University Press, 2002), 105–169.
55 PL 210:201–278. See the discussion in Tolan, *Saracens*, 165–169.
56 See line 39, line 375, line 380.

Martin Bleisteiner

5 Of Blades and Bodies: Material Objects in the *Alliterative Morte Arthure*

By the late fourteenth century, a streak of skepticism had become evident in English treatments of the Matter of Britain. It appears as if Arthurian heroics were increasingly seen as ripe for critique, even ridicule, with Chaucer's sarcastic japes against Gawain in the "Squire's Tale" being a prominent case in point.[1] And it was not merely the Arthurian subject matter that was cause for misgivings, but also a specific literary vehicle for the martial exploits of King Arthur and his court: epic alliterative poetry. Once again, Chaucer exemplified this sentiment by playfully lampooning the genre in the tournament scene of his "Knight's Tale."[2] Against this backdrop, the roughly contemporary *Alliterative Morte Arthure* can be read as a piece of Arthurian writing whose claim to artistic and ideological relevance is far from self-evident.[3]

The *Morte*'s precarious cultural legitimacy coincides with a penchant for material objects, especially military equipment, which the text depicts in staggering variety

---

1 In reference to the rhetorical prowess and impeccable manners displayed by a mysterious visitor to Cambyuskan's royal court, the Squire quips that even "Gawayn, with his olde curteisye, / Though he were comen ayeyn out of Fairye / Ne koude hym nat amende with a word" ("Gawain, with his old courtesy, / Though he were come again out of Fairyland, / Could not amend one word of his speech"). Geoffrey Chaucer, "The Squire's Tale," in *The Riverside Chaucer*, ed. Larry D. Benson, 3rd ed. (Oxford: Oxford University Press, 2008), frag. 5, lines 95–97. The Modern English translations in this note and the next follow Harvard University's Geoffrey Chaucer Website, accessed February 8, 2021, https://chaucer.fas.harvard.edu/pages/text-and-translations.
2 As the fighting begins, the Knight erupts into an almost comically inept burst of alliteration: "Ther shyveren shaftes upon sheeldes thikke; / He feeleth thurgh the herte-spoon the prikke. / Up spryngen speres twenty foot on highte; / Out goon the swerdes as the silver brighte; / The helmes they tohewen and toshrede; / Out brest the blood with stierne stremes rede; / With myghty maces the bones they tobreste. / He thurgh the thikkeste of the throng gan threste ..." (Chaucer, "The Knight's Tale," frag. 1, lines 2605–2612; "There splinter spears upon thick shields; / He feels the stabbing through the breast-bone. / Up spring spears twenty foot on height; / Out go the swords bright as silver; / The helms they hew to pieces and cut into shreds; / Out burst the blood in strong red streams; / With mighty maces they break the bones to pieces. / He did thrust through the thickest of the throng ..."). The heavy-handed attempt at alliterative versification falters in the bathetic couplet "Ther stomblen steedes stronge, and doun gooth al, / He rolleth under foot as dooth a bal" (frag. 1, lines 2613–2614; "There strong steeds stumble, and down goes all, / He rolls under foot as does a ball"), and peters out altogether just two lines later.
3 The issue of the *Morte*'s date is discussed further below (see notes 5 and 6). All quotations from the poem in this chapter are taken from Larry D. Benson and Edward E. Foster, eds., *King Arthur's Death: The Middle English "Stanzaic Morte Arthur" and "Alliterative Morte Arthure"* (Kalamazoo: Medieval Institute Publications, 1994), with references by line number given in parentheses in the running text. The Modern English translations are taken from Brian Stone, trans., *King Arthur's Death: Alliterative "Morte Arthure" and Stanzaic "Le Morte Arthur"* (Harmondsworth: Penguin, 1988). The line numbers in Stone's translation correspond exactly to those in the Middle English edition cited here.

https://doi.org/10.1515/9783110742985-008

and multitude. In terms of its poetic language, too, the *Morte* revels in materiality: not only does the plethora of narrated artifacts cater to one of the key exigencies of alliterative verse, which thrives on establishing phonetic links between as many words and concepts as possible, but also the onomatopoeic qualities of alliteration are highly conducive to the poem's delight in describing things being resoundingly split, crushed, and scattered in a spectacle of extreme violence. The text's sprawling materiality thus appears to produce a paradoxical effect: the more exuberant the presence of the material in the fictional world, the more pronounced the detrimental consequences of this presence become. In giving free rein to alliterative poetry's tendency to emphasize the sensual aspect of material objects and to make these objects – and the words that describe them – proliferate in number, the *Morte*'s language is complicit in a celebration of materiality that is as lethal as it is excessive. As I will argue in this chapter, the poem's innumerable artifacts are implicated in a vicious cycle leading to the annihilation of almost everyone and, quite literally, everything contained within the narrative world, right down to the very bodies of the protagonists. The *Morte*'s engine of martial destruction grinds to a halt only when nothing is left for it to consume.

I take this paradox as an invitation to read the poem's fascination with material objects against the grain of current scholarship on materiality in medieval literature. Recent research informed by approaches subsumed under capacious categories such as "thing studies" and the "material turn" has tended to focus on outstanding objects, often old, precious, and furnished with unfathomable origins and supernatural powers, objects that lend themselves in a particularly appealing way to Bruno Latour's suggestion to think of things as actants participating in hybrid scenarios that involve human and nonhuman entities.[4] In the *Morte*, however, the vast majority of material artifacts are not special in the sense of being unique or magically predestined for a single purpose. On the contrary: the significance of these items lies in the very fact that they are ubiquitous. Massive quantities of exchangeable objects overwhelm and destroy their human wielders as swords cut, lances pierce, and armor fails to protect – relentlessly, for better or for worse. The basic principle on which this agency operates is not extreme scarcity, but extreme abundance.

The *Morte* is a poem of 4,346 alliterative lines that has survived in a single manuscript (Lincoln, Lincoln Cathedral Library, MS 91) compiled by a certain Robert Thornton. There is broad critical consensus that the manuscript was produced at

---

4 See, for example, Bruno Latour, *Reassembling the Social: An Introduction to Actor-Network-Theory* (Oxford: Oxford University Press, 2005), esp. 1–17 and 63–86. Other seminal contributions to the field include Ian Hodder, *Entangled: An Archaeology of the Relationship between Humans and Things* (Malden, MA: Wiley-Blackwell, 2012); Bill Brown, *Other Things* (Chicago: Chicago University Press, 2015); and Graham Harman, *Object-Oriented Ontology: A New Theory of Everything* (London: Penguin, 2018).

some point in the 1430s or 1440s.[5] The poem's date of composition, on the other hand, is much more difficult to pinpoint, and many uncertainties remain about the social and political environment from which the sole existing copy originated.[6] Even the question of the poem's genre defies straightforward answers: it mixes a variety of influences, combining traits of epic, romance, and chronicle.[7]

These obstacles to precise historical contextualization are, of course, not exclusive to the *Morte*. Given that they apply to much, if not most, of the surviving Middle English alliterative poetry dating from the second half of the fourteenth century onward, it is hardly surprising that the once widespread notion of a homogeneous body of aesthetically and politically conservative texts composed in a return to (or continuation of) Old English poetic traditions has increasingly fallen out of scholarly favor. Indeed, the *Morte* calls into question one of the fundamental premises underpinning the idea of a so-called "alliterative revival": the poem does not simply offer a window onto an oral, rural, traditional, and backward-looking community, preserved as if in a time capsule far to the north and west of the literary, urban, progressive, and innovative cultural environment of the capital.[8] As old-fashioned and "oral" as the *Morte* may at first glance seem, it is in fact the product of a thoroughly literary process based on the compilation, adaptation, and transformation of a multitude of source

---

5 Proposed by Mary Hamel, this terminus ad quem for the manuscript has stood the test of time and remains universally accepted. Mary Hamel, ed., *Morte Arthure: A Critical Edition* (New York: Garland Publishing, 1984), 53–58.

6 Evidence in the form of possible intertextual references and allusions to historical events is tenuous and riddled with inconsistencies, and traces of revisions and dialectal variation complicate the picture even further. The arguments advanced by Larry D. Benson ("The Date of the *Alliterative Morte Arthure*," in *Medieval Studies in Honor of Lillian Herlands Hornstein*, ed. Jess B. Bessinger Jr. and Robert B. Raymo [New York: New York University Press, 1976], 19–40) and Mary Hamel (*Morte Arthure*, 53–58) in support of a date of composition ca. 1400 have long held sway. More recently, however, P.J.C. Field has made an interesting case for the decade from 1375 to 1385 on the strength of highly specific references to the volatile political situation in fourteenth-century Italy and the changing fortunes of the House of Visconti. P.J.C. Field, "*Morte Arthure*, the Montagus, and Milan," *Medium Ævum* 78, no. 1 (2009): 98–117.

7 See Andrew James Johnston, *Performing the Middle Ages from "Beowulf" to "Othello"* (Turnhout: Brepols, 2008), 166–167.

8 In Christine Chism's words, the difficulties associated with "wresting provenances from unique, late, and dialectically transmigrated manuscripts have atomized attempts to read alliterative poems together" along the lines of a unified literary movement. Christine Chism, *Alliterative Revivals* (Philadelphia: University of Pennsylvania Press, 2002), 10. For an even more trenchant critique of the concept of an "alliterative revival" and the concomitant theoretical, methodological, and ideological assumptions, see Ralph Hanna, "Alliterative Poetry," in *The Cambridge History of Medieval English Literature*, ed. David Wallace (Cambridge: Cambridge University Press, 1999), 488–512. In a clean break with a long-standing critical tradition of which Thorlac Turville-Petre is perhaps the most influential and well-known exponent (cf. *The Alliterative Revival* [Cambridge: D. S. Brewer, 1977]), Hanna argues that Old Historicist scholarship has set up Middle English alliterative poetry as "the Other of Chaucerian verse" (508) in "a classic example of abstract principle driving the construction of historical evidence" (488).

texts, many of them English, but some of thcm French or Latin; if the poem appears archaic, then this is a carefully crafted effect produced by self-conscious literary artifice.[9]

In terms of its subject matter, the *Morte* follows a strand of the Arthurian tradition going back to Geoffrey of Monmouth and his *Historia regum Britanniae* (ca. 1136). However, in a significant departure from its sources, the poem focuses exclusively on the events of the last two years of Arthur's reign. Having conquered most of western and northern Europe, the king does not get to rest on his laurels: the Roman emperor, Lucius, sends a diplomatic mission to Arthur's court that repudiates the legitimacy of his imperial conquests and summons him to Rome to swear fealty. After this very public snub, war is inevitable. Even the Roman Empire's most remote regions are drawn into the fray, and Arthur's confrontation with Lucius soon resembles nothing so much as a world war *avant la lettre*, a conflict of enormous proportions between two rival blocs of power.[10] The complex and all-consuming war effort that ensues involves diplomatic machinations, extensive strategic planning, and campaigns against the enemy's supply chains, all of which are described in painstaking detail.[11]

Apart from its concern with imperial politics and the finer technical points of late medieval warfare, the *Morte* also exhibits a profound fascination with physical violence. As Christine Chism has pithily remarked, "The poet delights in verbs of splitting, breaking, thrust, and amputation, a taste for which his unusually inventive alliterative breadth of vocabulary well equips him."[12] In the *Morte*, human bodies are cleaved in two, vertically and horizontally;[13] they are disemboweled, with one rider's intestines getting caught in the legs of his galloping horse;[14] skulls are noisily crushed, limbs severed, and interior organs perforated.[15] While graphic depictions of the

---

9 See Johnston, *Beowulf to Othello*, 168–170. For a synopsis of the numerous textual sources identified so far, see 168n15.
10 The *Morte*'s Roman Empire comprises large parts of "Asia" and "Afrike" (line 573) and has its power base in the vast expanses of the "Orient" (line 570).
11 See Johnston, *Beowulf to Othello*, 196.
12 Chism, *Alliterative Revivals*, 218.
13 "He merkes through the mailes the middes in sonder, / That the middes of the man on the mount falles, / The tother half of the haunch on the horse leved" (lines 2206–2208; "He hewed through his armour and hacked him in two, / So that the man's main part toppled to the turf / While the other half, the haunches, stayed upright on the horse"). In another passage, a body is divided into three parts by two subsequent sword cuts – first Arthur severs the legs of an enemy giant (line 2125), then the head (line 2129).
14 "But Floridas with a sword, as he by glentes, / All the flesh of the flank he flappes in sonder / That all the filth of the freke and fele of his guttes / Followes his fole foot when he forth rides!" (lines 2780–2783; "And suddenly as he slipped by, with his sword Floridas / He flapped free all the flesh on the flank of the other, / Whose intestines tumbled out and trailed with their filth / In the hooves of his horse as onward he rode").
15 See Michele Poellinger, "Violence in Later Middle English Arthurian Romance" (PhD diss., University of Leeds, 2013), 233, for a comprehensive chart of the afflicted body parts and types of injury with corresponding lines.

carnage of battle are fully consonant with the genre conventions of heroic epic, the violence visited on the *Morte*'s characters is remarkable in both its quantity and quality when compared to contemporaneous Middle English treatments of the Arthurian material – especially, though not only, in texts more unequivocally rooted in the domain of romance.

In its rendition of the bloody spectacle of war, the *Morte* relies heavily on the evocative powers of alliterative verse, a barrage of sounds that seemingly acts as a direct and unadulterated conduit for the goings-on on the battlefield, while in fact being the product of a sophisticated literary process. The same holds true for the text's overall relationship to real-life warfare: it simultaneously invites and thwarts the interpretation of its detailed portrayals of combat and military equipment as gritty "realism." Even though the *Morte*'s descriptions can often be aligned with late medieval practices and technological developments (insofar as these can be reconstructed in the first place), the poem is actually highly selective in terms of the aspects it chooses to present – for example, in its complete disregard for diseases such as dysentery that were part and parcel of military campaigns in the Middle Ages, or in its emphasis on decisive strategic victories won in pitched battles, which runs counter to the reality of prolonged and meandering historical conflicts like the Hundred Years' War.[16]

While it is not the *Morte*'s most bone-chilling description of violence nor its most detailed account of tactical and strategic arrangements, a scene set during Arthur's campaign in France exhibits many of the poem's characteristic features in a nutshell. In this passage, a detachment led by Duke Cador of Cornwall encounters a numerically superior Roman force under the command of the kings of Libya and Syria, who are in league with the emperor. Against all odds – and against Arthur's express policy of avoiding engagements in unfavorable conditions[17] – Cador decides to attack:

> And then the Bretons brothely   enbraces their sheldes,
> Braides on bacenettes   and buskes their launces;
> Thus he [Cador] fittes his folk   and to the feld rides,
> Five hundreth on a front   fewtered at ones!
> With trumpes they trine   and trapped steedes,
> With cornettes and clariouns   and clergial notes;
> Shockes in with a shake   and shuntes no longer,
> There shawes were sheen   under the shire eves.
> And then the Romanes rout   removes a little,

---

16 See Johnston, *Beowulf to Othello*, 216–217.
17 When, in the aftermath of the battle, it becomes apparent that victory has been achieved at the cost of several prominent casualties from the king's inner circle of followers, Arthur publicly castigates the independent-minded duke for what he perceives to be his reckless style of leadership (lines 1912–1927). For a discussion of the social and political cost of Arthur's calamitous attempts to impose autocratic governance on the peers of his realm, see Patricia DeMarco, "An Arthur for the Ricardian Age: Crown, Nobility, and the Alliterative *Morte Arthure*," *Speculum* 80, no. 2 (2005): 464–493.

Raikes with a rere-ward   those real knightes;
So raply they ride there   that all the rout ringes
Of rives and rank steel   and rich gold mailes.
Then shot out of the shaw   sheltrones many,
With sharp wepens of war   shootand at ones.
The King of Lyby before   the avauntward he ledes,
And all his lele lege-men   all on loud ascries.
(lines 1753–1768)

(Then the Britons boldly braced their shields,
Put on their helmets and held their lances ready.
So Cador arranged his ranks and they rode to the field,
A front of five hundred, their lances facing forward,
On steeds with trappings, to trumpets' sounds
And calls from cornets and clarions skilfully played.
Shattering was the shock; they shunned nothing
Where the shrubs brightly shone under the shimmering trees.
The Roman ranks retreated a little,
Giving ground in their rearguard's direction.
So rapidly they rode there that the air rang
With the sound of steel and spikes and splendid gold mail.
Then showers of shield-bearers shot out of the woods,
With their weapons of war at once sharply shooting.
The Libyan king led the leading line
And all his loyal liegemen loudly shouted.)

The poem's sustained preoccupation with the matériel required for military operations, be it weapons, cavalry mounts, or signaling equipment, is evident throughout
the passage. It is not that human actors and actions are absent from the narrative:
Cador, the Arthurian commander, arranges his troops in line abreast in preparation
for the charge; the Roman soldiers are initially hidden from view in the brush, reveal-
ing their leaders keen eye for advantageous terrain; the infantry is deployed together
with archers in a tactic of combined arms. Yet from the moment the British men-at-
arms ready their shields, bascinets, and lances (lines 1753–1754), these indicators of
human agency are interspersed with and embedded in a wealth of material objects,
from the horses' caparisons (line 1757) to the vegetation on the battlefield (lines 1760,
1765).

Having provided this panoramic overview, the *Morte* zooms in on the one-on-one
encounter between two individual combatants. As the text proceeds to describe the
adversaries in close-up, its sweeping interest in all types of military accoutrements
gains a sharper focus – namely, Sir Berill's "golet" and "gorger" (line 1772), a detail
to which I shall return farther below:

Then this cruel king castes in fewter,
Caught him a coverd horse,   and his course holdes,
Beres to Sir Berille   and brothely him hittes,
Through the golet and the gorger   he hurtes him even.

The gome and the grete horse   at the ground ligges,
And gretes graithely to God   and gives Him the soul.
(lines 1769 – 1774)

(The cruel king then couched his spear,
And mounted on mailed horse made his charge,
Bearing down on Sir Berill and battering him fiercely,
Gashing him through the gullet and the gorge-piece accurately.
Warrior and warhorse wavered to the ground,
And he called gravely on God and gave up his soul.)

By the time the single combat culminates in Sir Berill's death cry, the scene has acquired a rich acoustic backdrop. The *Morte* describes several different sounds, each with a distinct material basis: the blaring of the trumpets and clarions, coaxed voluntarily and skillfully ("clergial"; line 1758) from purpose-built musical instruments in order to direct and encourage the troops; the "ringing" of the riders' golden (or rather gilded) mail armor (line 1763) as their horses break into a canter; the loud cheering of the king of Libya's army (line 1768); and finally Sir Berill's pained scream (line 1774), a primal, involuntary expression of suffering.[18] In the first two instances, the text establishes an overt connection between the specific materialities of human-made artifacts and the sonic effects they are apt to produce – intentional in the case of the musical instruments, accidental in the case of the armor. The cheering and screaming, on the other hand, do not require the involvement of objects external to the human body, but they do depend on its material fabric, especially the vocal organs. Given that human and animal bodies are equally indispensable for – we might even say instrumental in – the production of the first two sounds, the battle scene's soundscape allows the poem to explore various facets of the interaction and interconnectedness of human and nonhuman materialities. The impact of this "gruesome polyphony" is greatly enhanced by the onomatopoeic cadences of alliterative verse, an effect that reveals itself whenever the text is read or recited.[19]

The *Morte* leaves no doubt as to the cause of these dissonant yet consonant acoustics. They are the audible symptom of deadly violence, of which the king of Libya proves to be a particularly skilled perpetrator: he is portrayed as an expert horseman adept in the art of mounted warfare, resting his couched lance in a state-of-the-art supporting device ("fewter"; line 1769) to direct the combined mo-

---

18 Sir Berill's utterance appears considerably less intense in Stone's translation, partly because "graithely" is rendered as "gravely," and partly because the translator's choice of "called" compromises the original's alliterative impact.

19 For "gruesome polyphony," see Carolin Emcke, *Echoes of Violence: Letters from a War Reporter* (Princeton, NJ: Princeton University Press, 2007), 40, quoted in Kate McLoughlin, *Authoring War: The Literary Representation of War from the "Iliad" to Iraq* (Cambridge: Cambridge University Press, 2011), 23. As Christine Chism points out, the preference of Middle English alliterative poetry for employing identical vowels produces "alliteration for delectation of the reading eye as well as for the listening ear." Chism, *Alliterative Revivals*, 36.

mentum of man and horse against one of his opponent's most vulnerable spots.[20] What the *Morte* stages here is what Jeffrey J. Cohen, drawing on concepts developed by Bruno Latour, has termed an "equine assemblage," in which categories such as "passive vehicle" and "all-controlling driver" collapse – the knight and his mount, human and animal bodies, no longer constitute fully discrete entities.[21] In the passage quoted above, this hybrid chivalric assemblage of human, animal, and technological components projects its full offensive force onto Sir Berill's neck with pinpoint accuracy and fatal effect.[22]

As Sir Berill's demise illustrates, the concept of the assemblage cuts both ways: it applies not only to victorious characters performing feats of prowess in the service of honor and empire, but also to those on the receiving end of such splendid martial performances. And when it comes to the *defensive* capabilities of the chivalric assemblage, the case is radically altered. If, as Elke Brüggen argues, Ither's coat of mail in Wolfram von Eschenbach's *Parzival* (ca. 1200) represents a complex ensemble that operates like a casing, a second skin, this holds even more true for armor coeval with the *Morte*'s timeframe of composition, a period when ever-increasing numbers of steel plates came to be used in more and more sophisticated configurations.[23] The *Morte* seems bent on demonstrating the penetrability of this second skin or exoskeleton, its inability to shelter what lies underneath. No matter how lavish the expenditure, how well-fitting the suit of steel, how ingenious its articulated joints, the level of protection afforded by armor cannot be heightened at will. As the poem makes

---

20 On the severe threat posed to existing forms of neck armor by the technological innovation of the lance rest, see Tobias Capwell, *Armour of the English Knight 1400 – 1450* (London: Thomas Del Mar, 2015), 85 – 87. It is interesting to note that the first known appearances of lance rests in artworks such as effigies and altarpieces date from the 1380s and 1390s (see Capwell, 85n26), a close match with the *Morte*'s likely date of composition. The MED gives only two examples of earlier usage, both from the alliterative romance *William of Palerne* (before 1375, perhaps as early as the mid-1330s). See Robert E. Lewis et al., eds., *Middle English Dictionary*, s.v. "feuter," online in Middle English Compendium, University of Michigan Library, accessed 8 February 2021, https://quod.lib.umich.edu/m/middle-english-dictionary/dictionary/MED15853.

21 Jeffrey J. Cohen, *Medieval Identity Machines* (Minneapolis: University of Minnesota Press, 2003), 49 – 51.

22 Translated as "gullet" in Stone's edition, the term "golet" is ambiguous: according to the MED, it can denote the actual gullet or esophagus, but also "part of a hood covering the throat; armor covering the throat." R. Lewis et al., *Middle English Dictionary*, s.v. "golet," accessed 8 February 2021, https://quod.lib.umich.edu/m/middle-english-dictionary/dictionary/MED19051. Both meanings make sense in this specific context, although the latter option seems slightly more plausible given the sequence in which the two terms "golet" and "gorger" are conjoined; in any case, penetration of the respective piece of clothing or armor is practically tantamount to penetration of the eponymous body part it is meant to protect.

23 On Ither's armor, see Elke Brüggen, "Die Rüstung des Anderen: Zu einem rekurrenten Motiv bei Wolfram von Eschenbach," in *Dingkulturen: Objekte in Literatur, Kunst und Gesellschaft der Vormoderne*, ed. Anna Mühlherr, Heike Sahm, Monika Schausten, and Bruno Quast (Berlin: De Gruyter, 2016), 127–144, at 135–136. Even in death, human contents and metal container may prove hard or even impossible to separate (Brüggen, 142).

unmistakably clear, it is ultimately impossible to shield chivalric bodies from the – literal – impact of the material world. In the *Morte*, there is always a way in, whether because pieces of armor plausibly yield to overwhelming force, because the offensive weapon slips through a convenient opening, or because poetic license modifies the real-life affordances of certain materials to render them more penetrable.

The *Morte* explores all these scenarios with surgical precision and great attention to detail, especially with regard to the specific materialities involved. Arrayed in varying sequences, successive layers of human and animal tissue, textile, and metal become veritable test assemblies inviting evaluation of their resistance to cuts and blows. In the scene where Gawain fights Priamus, the narrative gaze zooms in "with dreamlike slowness" as the enemy's sword finds a gap between the plates on Gawain's arm.[24] It slashes his velvet garments, breaches the skin, and severs a blood vessel that begins to spout blood all over the grievously wounded, fainting knight:

> An alet enameld   he [Priamus] oches in sonder,
> Bristes the rerebrace   with the brand rich,
> Carves off at the coutere   with the clene edge
> Anentis the avambrace   vailed with silver;
> Through a double vesture   of velvet rich
> With the venomous sword   a vein has he touched
> That voides so violently   that all his wit changed;
> The vesar, the aventail,   his vestures rich
> With a valiant blood   was verred all over.
> (lines 2565 – 2573)

> (He sheared through an enamelled shoulder-plate,
> Breaking the rerebrace with his brilliant sword-edge,
> And hacking it off at the elbow-piece,
> By the forearm plate fretted with silver.
> Through the vesture of velvet rich and doubled
> His venomous sword severed a vein
> Which spurted so violently Gawain's senses were dimmed,
> And his visor, lower face-guard and fine vesture
> Were all sprayed with spots of the staunch man's blood.)

A similar description can be found in the context of Arthur's final fight with Mordred. Here, too, the poem follows the latter's blade as it slices through jupon, mail, and flesh, dissecting each layer in turn:

> The felon [Mordred] with the fine sword   freshly he strikes,
> The felettes of the ferrer side   he flashes in sonder,
> Through jupon and gesseraunt   of gentle mailes,
> The freke fiched in the flesh   an half-foot large …
> (lines 4236 – 4239)

---

24 Chism, *Alliterative Revivals*, 220.

> (And the felon struck fiercely with that fine sword,
> Ripping through the rib-plates on Arthur's right side.
> Through surcoat and hauberk of armoured steel
> The hilding hacked off a half-foot of flesh.)

When Arthur's riposte cuts "through [Mordred's] bracer of brown steel and the bright mailes" (line 4247; "through brassard of bright steel and brilliant mail"), taking off his adversary's hand, this is characteristic of the text as a whole. In the *Morte*, material objects employed for offensive purposes almost invariably triumph over those intended to ward them off, and even the one notable exception to this rule ultimately reinforces it: when Gawain attempts to deliver the coup de grâce in his fight with Mordred, his dagger, for once, fails to penetrate, glancing off the latter's armor ("no slit happened"; line 3853); yet the general principle is swiftly reinstated with Mordred's countermove, which sees Gawain stabbed "through the helm and the hed on high on the brain" (line 3857; "through the helmet into the head, and up into the brain").

The ineluctable vulnerability of the poem's defenseless defenders has far-reaching implications. There are human bodies behind the maelstrom of violence, both dealing it out and suffering it – from the Roman emperor and King Arthur through dukes and earls, bannerets and knights bachelor, all the way down to the most humble archers and pikemen, all entangled in a complex network of social, political, and economic relationships. As the narrative progresses, however, these bodies are increasingly in danger of losing their integrity by being pierced or dismembered, through the detachment or spilling out of their various components. The *Morte* pursues the fragmentation and disintegration of its chivalric protagonists in a very concrete, physical sense, to the point where the poem's characters function less as integral human beings than as aggregations of body parts waiting to be undone. At times, the narrative recalls the obliteration of human bodies in the trenches of the First World War as described by Ernst Jünger, Erich Maria Remarque, Siegfried Sassoon, and Wilfred Owen: blood pools on the churned-up battlefield (e. g., lines 1863, 2145) and colors watercourses red (line 2144), soldiers are trampled underfoot by horses (line 2150), and the bodies of the dead and dying are flung into the mud (line 2978).[25]

Especially toward the end of the poem, the characters touch the corpses that begin to pile up in larger and larger numbers. In the aftermath of Gawain's fatal encounter with Mordred, Arthur wanders over the battlefield, turning over the bodies of

---

25 Stone translates "slongen in a slade" (line 2978) as "slung [...] into a swamp," preserving the alliteration. Benson glosses "slade" as "ditch." The MED has "a creek, a stream; a channel": R. Lewis et al., *Middle English Dictionary*, s.v. "slade," accessed 8 February 2021, https://quod.lib.umich.edu/m/middle-english-dictionary/dictionary/MED40756.

his fallen retainers (line 3932).[26] He eventually discovers the lifeless Gawain and cradles him in his arms, drenching his beard in blood as he kisses his dead nephew's face (lines 3969–3971). The king proceeds to scoop up Gawain's "real red blood run upon erthe" (line 3990; "royal red blood running upon the earth") and deposits it in a helmet as if it were a precious relic worthy of being "shrede and shrined in gold" (line 3991; "shrouded and enshrined in gold"). The prominence accorded to blood in this passage is far from exceptional – indeed, the *Morte*'s fascination with the substance is pervasive. As Bettina Bildhauer has noted, issues of bodily coherence, integrity, and control play out with particular urgency when blood is shed in medieval texts, hence their concern with the fluid "in the transitory moment of being neither inside nor outside the body, in the process of 'rushing,' 'spurting,' 'flowing' or 'surging' out of the body and through the armour," or "clinging to bodies and other objects, as something that one can neither incorporate nor get rid of."[27] This uncanny "clinging" that stops just short of an actual merging of materialities is precisely what we encounter on several occasions in the *Morte:* not only is blood spilled in copious quantities, but it attaches itself to items such as Arthur's mail armor (line 2250), Mordred's gleaming greaves (line 3846), and, as quoted above, Gawain's visor, aventail, and luxurious "vestures" (line 2572).

Escalating in the poem's second half, the effusion of blood feeds into the *Morte*'s larger concern with the precarious nature of chivalric identity.[28] In the grander scheme of things, the question of who dispatches whom and how begins to look surprisingly insignificant as the killing becomes ever more universal. In keeping with the mounting death toll, the violence in the *Morte* appears less and less focused on specific bodies encountering specific weapons, or vice versa – it is about countless bodies, and countless weapons that stab and slash away at them. There are passages in the poem where anonymous death comes crashing down from a distance: in one scene, siege engines reduce the city of Metz to a pile of rubble – churches, hospitals, monasteries, and defenders included (lines 3036–3043). But even when it comes to prominent knights engaged in hand-to-hand combat, the *Morte* does a thorough job of dismantling individuality, notwithstanding the fact that the characters are identified by name. In a recurring motif, heraldic devices become unrecognizable, illegible, as a sanguine monochrome takes the place of multicolored coats of

---

26 A similar scene plays out at the very end of the poem, when Arthur picks up the bodies of the slain Knights of the Round Table and arranges them next to each other (lines 4262–4270).

27 Bettina Bildhauer, *Medieval Blood* (Cardiff: University of Wales Press, 2006), 68. The quoted passages are in reference to Wirnt von Grafenberg's *Wigalois*.

28 The increasing frequency with which the motif of shed blood occurs in the text is evident from Poellinger's chart (see Poellinger, "Violence," 233). On the *Morte*'s preoccupation with unstable identities, see Alex Mueller, *Translating Troy: Provincial Politics in Alliterative Romance* (Columbus: Ohio State University Press, 2013), 128. As Mueller points out, important characters in the poem change their heraldic devices over the course of events; consequently, heraldry no longer functions as a reliable marker of identity and aristocratic lineage.

arms – for example, when the poem refers to the dead Gawain's trodden banners with the word "gules" (line 3945), the heraldic term for red, invoking the image of fabric that is both scarlet in color and completely blood-soaked, and describes his shield as "all bloody berunnen" (line 3946; "bloodied all over").

The *Morte*'s growing sense of anonymous detachment encompasses not only the poem's human protagonists but also the equipment they rely on. Only rarely does the *Morte* foreground named weapons such as Arthur's and Gawain's swords, otherwise a staple feature of medieval literature across periods and genres, where they frequently develop a life of their own and turn into veritable comrades-in-arms.[29] This type of personalized, perhaps even humanized, agency is not what we tend to encounter in the *Morte*, where the lion's share of violence is inflicted with anonymous objects that derive their power from sheer force of numbers, a seemingly inexhaustible arsenal of daggers, maces, and crossbow quarrels.[30] Though they are for the most part wielded individually – the crew-served siege engines referred to above are an obvious exception – the fatal potency of the *Morte*'s implements of war resides in their accumulation.

Over time, the mass of mundane weaponry deployed in the poem achieves a depersonalizing effect, not unlike the experience described by participants in more recent armed conflicts: to put it crudely, "if one sword or arrow doesn't get you, the next one will." There may be various levels of personal animosity involved and the text may mark some enemies as particularly outstanding, but the overall picture that emerges is of a death as inevitable as it is impersonal. While there is no denying that the poem continues to devise ever-new vignettes of violence in a struggle to, if not increase, then at least maintain the level of intensity reached by its descriptions of maiming and killing quite early on, it could well be argued that this inventiveness is subject to the law of diminishing returns, as constant repetition dulls the impact of individual representations of suffering and destruction. Yet even if the *Morte* fails to achieve a consistent crescendo of brutality, the poem does create a deeply oppressive sense of attrition as its cast of characters inexorably diminishes.

In light of these observations, the almost clinical and "near-Clausewitzian" way in which the *Morte* so often conceptualizes the conduct of military operations would appear to be infused with a disconcerting dose of Falkenhayn: the ill-conceived attempt to "bleed white" the enemy eventually brings about the ruin of one's own fighting force and imperial ambitions.[31] Some have been tempted to take this as evidence that the poem ultimately deplores the violence it depicts. It has, for example, been argued that the text presents Arthur's appetite for conquest as a form of malicious tyranny that becomes manifest, among other things, in the king's scorched-earth pol-

---

29 See Christine Grieb, *Schlachtenschilderungen in Historiographie und Literatur (1150 – 1230)* (Paderborn: Ferdinand Schöningh, 2015), 209.
30 Benson points out one possible deviation from this rule in his note to line 3709, suggesting that "a good gome" ("a good man") refers to Gawain's sword, Galuth.
31 For "near-Clausewitzian," see Johnston, *Beowulf to Othello*, 209.

icy, which results in the wholesale devastation of Tuscany.[32] On the other hand, however, the narrator has a persistent tendency to slip into the use of first-person pronouns and a tone of gloating commentary when the feats of arms of the Arthurian armies are described.[33] What complicates matters even further is the specific way in which the *Morte* portrays these actions: the fascination with the aesthetic and sensual dimension of violent conflict that the text indulges in reflects back on its ethical and ideological positions, essentially rendering it "unfit for a critique of war."[34]

This fundamental ambivalence toward empire and the chivalric cult of violence permeates the *Morte* through and through. The poem's highly aestheticized perspective on warfare, its pageantry of countless animate and inanimate things presented in what has been termed an "almost cinematic whirl of numbers, speed, and colour," cannot fill or shroud the ideological void at its core.[35] If anything, the *Morte*'s fluttering pennants, sumptuous fabrics, gilded suits of armor, and jewel-studded horse tack only render this void all the more conspicuous. Pervaded by a vast sense of lack – lack of a stable ethical and political purpose – the text resorts to a type of literary world-making heavily reliant on the sheer mass and materiality of its objects. But paradoxically, this reliance on material excess translates into an excess of destruction that ultimately showcases the bankruptcy of the Arthurian ideal so acutely perceived by the likes of Chaucer in the late fourteenth century. Consciously or not, the *Morte* exposes the fragility and vulnerability of all its many beautiful things heaped on top of each other only to be broken and torn apart – a fate that applies to the material artifacts themselves, but also to their human bearers and users, who become engulfed by these artifacts until their bodies, too, are reduced to nothing more than fragmented and dissolving objects.

---

32 See Mueller, *Translating Troy*, esp. 127, where it is argued that the *Morte* rejects the idea of a reversed *translatio imperii* from Britain to Rome, performing instead a veritable "*translatio tyrannidis*" from Emperor Lucius to the Giant of St. Michael's Mount and finally to Arthur.

33 See Johnston, *Beowulf to Othello*, 201.

34 Johnston, *Beowulf to Othello*, 198. In an attempt to iron out these inconsistencies, earlier scholarship tended to read the *Morte* either as a scathing indictment of imperial aggression or an attempt to buttress Arthur's heroic status. More nuanced perspectives have since emerged – see, for example, Lee Patterson, *Negotiating the Past: The Historical Understanding of Medieval History* (Madison: University of Wisconsin Press, 1987); Chism, *Alliterative Revivals*; and Geraldine Heng, *Empire of Magic: Medieval Romance and the Politics of Cultural Fantasy* (New York: Columbia University Press, 2003). For a comprehensive overview of critical positions on this issue, see Mueller, *Translating Troy*, 129–131.

35 Johnston, *Beowulf to Othello*, 197.

Jan-Peer Hartmann

6 Barrow Agency: Reading Landscape in Felix's *Vita Guthlaci*

Introduction

> Landscape is both topography, as it shows traces of water and wind, and history, as it reveals traces of human actions. The human actions may be as local as the daily track of people and animals across a stream between homestead and pasture, or as far ranging as the ancestral migration of tribes and the pilgrimage of believers between home and sacred site. [...] On a site much used for agriculture or defense, the shape of the land can testify vividly to the transformations worked by human occupation.
>
> —Nicholas Howe, 'Writing the Map of Anglo-Saxon England'

One might argue that there is practically no place in Europe where we might find a "natural" landscape. For millennia, Europe's topography, vegetation, and animal populations have been altered by the people living on and with the land. As we find ourselves in the Anthropocene, these human actions are beginning to have alarming effects, from floods caused by land reclamation and the regulation of watercourses to climate change caused by deforestation and the large-scale burning of coal and lignite, along with the mass extinction of animal and plant species. The consequences are becoming serious, not least for the quantity and quality of agricultural produce, and hence our own sustenance. Conversely, people's actions are often influenced and perhaps partly predetermined by natural factors, including topography, vegetation, animal populations, and local climate: certain types of land favor certain types of agriculture or pastoralism, people build structures and transform the topography in response to certain climatic conditions, and so on. Landscape, even in the simple sense of the physical surroundings we encounter, could thus already be described as a hybrid in the sense developed by Bruno Latour: something that is "too social and too narrated to be truly natural," and yet too strongly shaped by forces outside the human grasp to be merely cultural.[1]

With this contribution, I wish to broaden this volume's focus on "things" and "thingness" by concentrating on the concept of the "assemblage," as theorized by

---

Acknowledgements: I would like to thank the participants in the workshops at Stanford University and Freie Universität Berlin that sparked this volume: their comments and discussions helped shape this chapter into its present form. I owe my greatest debt to Andrew James Johnston and Matt Gleeson, whose very sensitive reading and excellent suggestions vastly improved this chapter.

1 Bruno Latour, *We Have Never Been Modern*, trans. Catherine Porter (Cambridge, MA: Harvard University Press, 1993).

https://doi.org/10.1515/9783110742985-009

Latour.[2] I will do so by examining the early eighth-century Anglo-Latin *Vita Guthlaci* and its representation of a particular landscape, the early medieval Fenland – a marshy region in what is now eastern England, covering parts of present-day Cambridgeshire, Lincolnshire, and Norfolk, also known simply as the Fens – as a conglomerate of different material entities, forces, and factors.[3] Specifically, I wish to focus on the literary representation of landscape as one of the factors involved in the construction of the concept "landscape" more generally, and to open up a historical perspective on this construct by examining a text from the early Middle Ages. The *Vita*'s representation of the Fens, I suggest, provides a fruitful starting point for exploring premodern approaches to landscape, not least because the text implicitly challenges the nature–culture binary that, according to Latour, characterizes modern thinking.[4] The *Vita*'s depiction indeed seems to stress the interconnectedness and composite nature of the various "things" landscape is made up of – an aspect perhaps most prominent in Guthlac's *tugurium*, built on what to all appearances are the remains of a barrow – as well as of these things' potential to transform by means of changes in the constellation they are part of. From this perspective, the text provides a test case for the application of this aspect of "thing studies" to early medieval literature, as well as an opportunity to combine Latour's sociological model with recent ecomaterialist approaches.[5] From the latter perspective, the *Vita*

---

2 Bruno Latour, *Reassembling the Social: An Introduction to Actor-Network-Theory* (Oxford: Oxford University Press, 2007). Although thing studies has often tended to focus on individual objects as "things" rather than on their interconnectedness, one might argue that the notion of the assemblage is fundamental to thing theory in general. Bill Brown's introduction to the special issue of *Critical Inquiry* that effectively launched thing studies draws on Heidegger's famous essay "The Thing," which locates the special "thingness" of things in their capacity to interconnect different entities: the jug, as the "thing" used to pour the consecrated libation as an offering to the immortal gods, interconnects "earth and sky, divinities and mortals," which "in the gift of the outpouring [...] are enfolded into a single fourfold." Quotation from Martin Heidegger, "The Thing," in *Poetry, Language, Thought*, by Martin Heidegger, ed. and trans. Albert Hofstadter (New York: Perennial, 2001), 163–184, at 170–171. Bill Brown discusses Heidegger's essay in "Thing Theory," *Critical Inquiry* 28, no. 1 (2001): 1–22, at 5n13, 13, 15n47, 16; and *A Sense of Things: The Object Matter of American Literature* (Chicago: University of Chicago Press, 2003), 7. Brown's discussion of "the thingness of objects" ("Thing Theory," 4) owes more to Heidegger than his references might initially suggest, though he keeps a critical distance from Heidegger's etymological method of argumentation, which traces the essence of things to the Old High German word *thing*, a word Heidegger translates as "a gathering, and specifically a gathering to deliberate on a matter under discussion, a contested matter" (Heidegger, "Thing," 172). On the intersection of thing studies and actor-network theory, see also the introduction to this volume.
3 Quotations from the *Vita Guthlaci* follow Bertram Colgrave, ed. and trans., *Felix's Life of Saint Guthlac: Introduction, Text, Translation and Notes* (Cambridge: Cambridge University Press, 1956), hereafter cited as *VG*. The work is cited in the running text by chapter and page number of the Latin text. The quoted translations are Colgrave's, and they appear on the facing pages of his edition.
4 Latour, *We Have Never Been Modern*, 6.
5 Although it is difficult to draw a clear dividing line between thing studies and the new materialisms more generally, new materialist approaches tend to favor more fluid conceptions of materiality

Guthlaci is especially interesting, since it seems to promote a specifically medieval vision of sustained eco-sensibility, depicting Guthlac as interacting with his environment in an integrative way rather than colonizing it.[6]

Within the assemblage of the Fenland, the saint appears as one element among many that constitute and transform the landscape. In the case of Guthlac, however, the consequences of his presence – the difference he makes – seem to be more semiotic than physical. The spiritual status of the Fens, initially portrayed as a wilderness outside the social and political spheres of the early medieval Christian culture of the time, is radically altered, but the saint's presence appears to have minimal impact on its physical constitution. Given the radical physical transformations that affected the historical Fenland in the centuries following the *Vita*'s composition – described in the final section of this chapter – the work thus provides an alternative vision of human encounters with "landscape," an agential possibility never realized outside the text, testifying to literature's potential for creating alternative worlds and futures.[7] At the same time, the *Vita* shows how depictions of the material world and material culture have a transformative power upon literature: the text's adaptation of early Christian eremitic hagiography to a British environment suffused with material traces of cultural activity suggests that the genre of hagiography itself has been transformed into a specifically "English" (in an early medieval sense) form.[8]

---

than those usually foregrounded in thing studies, stressing the interconnectedness of all matter rather than focusing on seemingly isolated "things" as separate material entities. They are thus, on the whole, less centered on the humanities, seeking rather to bridge the gap between philosophy on the one hand and the social and natural sciences on the other. They promote a middle way between poststructuralist perspectives, which tend to privilege language over materiality in assuming the general constructedness of the world, and approaches that presuppose the existence of a more tangible "reality."

6 Britton Elliott Brooks, in an important study that I became aware of late in the publication process, similarly stresses Guthlac's harmonious relationship with the landscape, which he reads in terms of a restoration of prelapsarian Creation. Despite the difference in approach, Brooks's interpretation is fully compatible with the one proposed here, unlike Heide Estes's recent ecocritical study, which regards the *Vita Guthlaci* as an expression of a Christian ideology of colonization and hence as a direct precursor of modern capitalist environmental exploitation. See Britton Elliott Brooks, *Restoring Creation: The Natural World in the Anglo-Saxon Saints' Lives of Cuthbert and Guthlac*, Nature and Environment in the Middle Ages 3 (Woodbridge: D. S. Brewer, 2019); and Heide Estes, *Anglo-Saxon Literary Landscapes: Ecotheory and the Environmental Imagination*, Environmental Humanities in Pre-modern Cultures (Amsterdam: Amsterdam University Press, 2017), 92.

7 I borrow the phrase "agential possibility" from Karen Barad, *Meeting the Universe Halfway: Quantum Physics and the Entanglement of Matter and Meaning* (Durham, NC: Duke University Press, 2007), 141.

8 It is difficult to ascertain what exactly early medieval writers meant when they used terms such as Latin *Angli* or Old English *Englisc*, and usage must have varied over time and between individuals. It is clear, however, that these terms were used to denote only certain parts of Britain's early medieval population. By placing the word "English" in quotation marks, I am trying to avoid suggesting any form of direct continuity between the early medieval "English" and the population of the modern English nation-state.

Landscape and Literature: Matter and Meaning

The *Vita Guthlaci* presents us with a literary representation of the early medieval Fens that may have some basis in "experiential reality" but is, above all, a literary construct.[9] But then, of course, we never encounter our environment in unmediated form, since our perceptions are always shaped by cultural factors, including literature; conversely, our cultural expectations are partly determined by the limitations and affordances provided by our physical surroundings. As outlined in the opening of this chapter, we cannot separate the notion of landscape from the various factors that shape it, be they human or nonhuman, animate or inanimate, material or immaterial. Landscape, then, can be seen as the result of these forces – or rather, if we take into account the dynamic nature of the constant transformations that characterize landscape, we can see landscape as a process involving a variety of actors engaged in changing their environment even as they are potentially changed by it. As Tim Ingold points out, "The landscape is never complete: neither 'built' nor 'unbuilt,' it is perpetually under construction."[10]

Such a processual notion of landscape has much in common with new materialist notions which view matter as "processes of materialization" or "temporary congealments of a materiality that is a process of becoming."[11] Scientifically speaking, matter is never inert; atoms and molecules are constantly reorganizing in ever-new combinations and arrangements. According to the theoretical physicist and feminist epistemologist Karen Barad, "The world is a dynamic process of intra-activity and materialization in the enactment of determinate causal structures with determinate boundaries, properties, meanings, and patterns of marks on bodies."[12] If we apply this conception of matter as a process of materialization to the idea of landscape, we can conceptualize landscape itself as a process of becoming, shaped by and indeed made up of various agential forces, including human ones. From this perspective, landscape is not a canvas either devoid of human beings or passively altered by them; rather, human beings and their actions are part of the very fabric of the pro-

---

9 Brooks uses the phrase "experiential reality" to challenge Estes's claim that the *Vita*'s Fens "reflect a cultural construction of the area as seen by people who lived elsewhere" (Estes, *Literary Landscapes*, 16). Brooks does regard the *Vita*'s description as a literary construct, but one that is based on "reality" as experienced by people who knew and frequented the area. See Brooks, *Restoring Creation*, 174. As will become apparent farther below, my own reading mediates between the two, suggesting that even an "experiential reality" is ultimately based on cultural constructions.
10 Tim Ingold, "The Temporality of the Landscape," *World Archaeology* 25, no. 2 (1993): 152–174, at 162.
11 The phrase "processes of materialization" is used by Karen Barad, "Posthumanist Performativity: Toward an Understanding of How Matter Comes to Matter," *Signs* 28, no. 3 (2003): 801–831, at 827. The second quotation is from Jane Bennett, *Vibrant Matter: A Political Ecology of Things* (Durham, NC: Duke University Press, 2010), 49.
12 Barad, *Meeting the Universe*, 140.

cess that is landscape. In Ingold's words, "Neither is the landscape identical to nature, nor is it on the side of humanity against nature. [...] Our actions do not transform the world, they are part and parcel of the world's transforming itself. And that is just another way of saying that they belong to time."[13] In recognizing the processual dynamic of becoming, we thus simultaneously recognize landscape's inherent temporality: as a conglomerate or network of different material actors, it is never stable; rather, it is constantly changing and evolving, and hence it is constantly unfolding in time.

Consequently, landscape is not a purely physical entity; it is also constructed, invented, and imagined by human actors.[14] As human beings, we cannot avoid perceiving our environment from a certain perspective, a perspective informed both by our sensory experience and by certain ideas and images of landscape current in our respective cultural environs. According to Simon Schama, "Landscapes are culture before they are nature; constructs of the imagination projected onto wood and water and rock."[15] Yet our cultural perception of landscape is in turn influenced by the various affordances and resistances of the environment. Arguing from an ecocritical perspective, Alfred Kentigern Siewers criticizes "purely materialistic approaches to nature [that] miss the crucial 'immaterial' essence of life as communication and meaning-making."[16] Siewers emphasizes the overlapping nature of human and natural meaningfulness, a phenomenon for which he has coined the term *ecosemiosphere*, "an ecological bubble of meaning."[17]

Siewers's recognition of the overlap of "natural" and "cultural" meaning chimes with Barad's concept of "agential realism," which stresses the interdependency of matter and meaning, or "matter" and "mattering," in the making of the world:

> The world is an open process of mattering through which mattering itself acquires meaning and form through the realization of different agential possibilities. Temporality and spatiality emerge in this processual historicity. Relations of exteriority, connectivity, and exclusion are reconfigured. The changing topologies of the world entail an ongoing reworking of the notion of dynamics itself. Dynamics are a matter not merely of properties changing in time but of what matters in

---

13 Ingold, "Temporality," 154, 164.
14 See Nicholas Howe, "The Landscape of Anglo-Saxon England: Inherited, Invented, Imagined," in *Inventing Medieval Landscapes: Senses of Place in Western Europe*, ed. John Howe and Michael Wolfe (Gainesville: University Press of Florida, 2002), 91–112. In their introduction to the same volume, Howe and Wolfe note that they employ the term "landscape" in preference to "nature" in order to avoid the notion of an untouched, primeval territory; landscape, they suggest, "assumes an environment subject to the human gaze and potentially subject to human modification." J. Howe and Wolfe, introduction to *Inventing Medieval Landscapes*, 1–10, at 2.
15 Simon Schama, *Landscape and Memory* (London: Harper Collins, 1995), 61.
16 Alfred Kentigern Siewers, *Re-imagining Nature: Environmental Humanities and Ecosemiotics* (Lewisburg, PA: Bucknell University Press, 2015), 3.
17 Siewers, *Re-imagining Nature*, 4.

the ongoing materializing of different spacetime topologies. The world is intra-activity in its differential mattering.[18]

Barad sketches material history as an open, nonteleological process where meaning emerges through the realization of different agential possibilities that both are the product of and themselves give rise to the "intra-action" of different material actors. It is in the unfolding of this process that space and time emerge.

Seeking to apply Barad's concept of "agential realism" to literature, Serenella Iovino and Serpil Oppermann argue that the mutual dependency, and simultaneous emergence, of matter and meaning can be understood in terms of a "narrative agency" that emerges in the intra-activity of material formations, a concept they refer to as "material ecocriticism":

> Material ecocriticism argues that there is an implicit textuality in the becoming of material formations, and that this textuality resides in the way the agentic dimension of matter expresses itself, as well as in the way bodies emerge in the combined and simultaneous action of material dynamics and discursive practices. [...] Every being has a story to tell; it is "semiotically active."[19]

Matter's semiotic activity emerges precisely because of the dynamic, and hence temporal, nature of the matter-meaning compound; because matter continually unfolds in space and time, it is "storied."[20] Despite matter's inherent textuality, however, Iovino and Oppermann argue that stories in the human sense are "reciprocal creations" that emerge only through the intra-action of the respective "narrative agencies" of matter and human cognition. As Iovino puts it:

> We do not know whether nonhuman agency – taken in itself – tells a story. But we know that, when it meets our cognitive practices – when it intra-acts with us – this agency produces a story, and this encounter is a way of "bringing forth the world in its specificity, including ourselves."[21]

---

18 Barad, *Meeting the Universe*, 141. My use of the terms "matter" and "mattering" follows that of Serenella Iovino in "The Living Diffractions of Matter and Text: Narrative Agency, Strategic Anthropomorphism, and How Interpretation Works," *Anglia* 133, no. 1 (2015): 69–86, at 72.

19 Serenella Iovino and Serpil Oppermann, "Introduction: Stories Come to Matter," in *Material Ecocriticism*, ed. Serenella Iovino and Serpil Oppermann (Bloomington: Indiana University Press, 2014), 1–17, at 6–7. The expression "semiotically active" is quoted from Donna J. Haraway, *When Species Meet* (Minneapolis: University of Minnesota Press, 2008), 250. A special issue of *postmedieval* on the topic, edited by Jeffrey Jerome Cohen and Lowell Duckert, uses the term "ecomaterialism": "Ecomaterialism," special issue, *postmedieval* 4, no. 1 (2013).

20 Iovino and Oppermann, "Introduction," 6–7. See also Jeffrey Jerome Cohen, "Foreword: Storied Matter," in Iovino and Oppermann, *Material Ecocriticism*, ix–xii; and Serpil Oppermann, "From Ecological Postmodernism to Material Ecocriticism: Creative Materiality and Narrative Agency," in Iovino and Oppermann, *Material Ecocriticism*, 21–36. Ingold similarly notes that "for both the archaeologist and the native dweller, the landscape tells – *or rather is* – a story." Ingold, "Temporality," 152 (emphasis mine).

21 Iovino, "Living Diffractions," 83–84; the quotation at the end is from Barad, *Meeting the Universe*, 353. See also Iovino and Oppermann, "Introduction."

If the world is constituted by the "emerging-together of matter and meaning, of material and discursive practices, of the human and the non-human," as Iovino argues, literary representations do not merely reflect the world but contribute to constituting it.[22] Literature, as Pheng Cheah posits, is "an active power in the making of worlds, [...] both a site of processes of worlding and an agent that participates and intervenes in these processes."[23] Literature not only helps us recognize the multiplicity of worlds we live in, but also participates in bringing forth these worlds, and is itself brought forth in the process.[24]

As Iovino's careful phrasing makes clear, to speak of literature's "agency" does not mean to ascribe to it the capacity to act independently. But then, the same is true of material entities, including human beings: in new materialist terms, all matter can exert its agential potential only by intra-acting with other matter, thereby producing meaning. To put this more succinctly, it would be a misunderstanding to believe that literature is brought forth through the agency of human beings alone, and the same applies to the processes by which meaning is generated: both literature and meaning emerge only through the intra-action of human beings with other material and non-material factors (or "agents"). Latour's version of actor-network theory similarly privileges neither things nor ideas, but rather constantly evolving "chains of associations" whose elements, human and nonhuman, material and immaterial alike, are continually substituted and transformed.[25] Like Barad, Latour is less interested in the various "actors" involved in the configuration of networks than in the "intra-actions" among them that produce meaning. To Latour, "action" is always composite; agency is therefore perceived as a "distributed phenomenon," residing "neither in humans nor in objects but rather in their 'intra-actions.'"[26] Unlike the more static concept of a "network," Latour's notion of the "assemblage" stresses the composite and dynamic nature of the intramaterial actions that lie at the heart of matter in its various configurations.

22 Iovino, "Living Diffractions," 83–84.
23 Pheng Cheah, *What Is a World? On Postcolonial Literature as World Literature* (Durham, NC: Duke University Press, 2016), 2.
24 See also Dana Phillips and Heather Sullivan, "Material Ecocriticism: Dirt, Waste, Bodies, Food, and Other Matter," *Interdisciplinary Studies in Literature and the Environment* 19, no. 3 (2012): 445–447, doi:10.1093/isle/iss064; and Iovino, "Living Diffractions," 74.
25 Bruno Latour, "The Berlin Key or How to Do Words with Things," trans. Lydia Davis, in *Matter, Materiality and Modern Culture*, ed. P. M. Graves-Brown (London: Routledge, 1991), 10–21, at 10–11. For Latour, as for the new materialist thinkers, the social and the material, nature and culture, are never fully separable, except artificially; he refers to such separation as "purification" and sees it as the problematic core of what he terms the "modern constitution." In Latour's terminology, "purification" essentially denotes a gesture of denying the essential hybridity of all things; ironically, this very gesture produces ever-new hybrids. See Latour, *We Have Never Been Modern*, 10–12.
26 Carl Knappett, *Thinking through Material Culture: An Interdisciplinary Perspective* (Philadelphia: University of Pennsylvania Press, 2005), 31.

Latour's concept of the assemblage provides a heuristic that is well-suited to encompass the *Vita*'s representation of the Fens as an entity whose physical characteristics and significance result from the interplay of the various actors of which it is made up. Transferring Latour's concept to the idea of landscape makes it possible for us to imagine landscape both as a conglomerate of various material formations (including inanimate objects, plants, animals, and human beings, as well as topographical features) that are involved in continual processes of reconfiguration, and as something social and cultural, a mental construct perceived, invented, and imagined by a variety of human actors, which also constantly changes, evolves, and is influenced by material factors. In this dual capacity, landscape is itself merely an artificially isolated segment of a larger assemblage – namely, the ongoing intra-activity of the world.[27] As such, it serves as a microcosm where we can observe the interplay of human and nonhuman actors in the constitution of the world.

Guthlac's Fenland as a Physical and Mental Construct

If literature can be attributed an active role, an "agency" in the temporal unfolding of the world, then it makes sense to examine how literary representations themselves imagine an interplay of various material formations in the construction of worlds, and to do so from a historical perspective. The *Vita Guthlaci* records the life of the early medieval 'English' hermit saint Guthlac, centering mainly on the time he spent as an anchorite on the island of Crowland in the Fens, where he stayed until his death in 714.[28] In this section, I will examine how the *Vita* presents literature as an active force in the shaping and manipulating of both the protagonist's and the audience's expectations and initial perception of the Fenland, and how literature – in this case, the genre of hagiography – is transformed in the process.

Scholars have long noted that, over the course of the *Vita*, Crowland – and, by extension, the Fenland – is transformed from a peripheral, little-frequented area into a place of Christian worship, a destination for pilgrimage before and after the saint's

---

27 It is striking to notice how Ingold's article on "landscape" anticipates the new materialists' vocabulary by at least a decade – for instance, when, in rejecting "the division between inner and outer worlds" and of "mind and matter, meaning and substance," he locates the temporality of the landscape in the "process of becoming of the world as a whole." Ingold, "Temporality," 154, 164.
28 The author Felix, who identifies himself as "a servant of the Catholic community" ("catholicae congregationis vernaculus"; *VG*, preface, p. 60), is otherwise unknown. In the prologue he states that he composed the *Vita* at the behest of the East Anglian king Ælfwulf (ca. 713 to 749). Apart from Felix's *Vita*, there are four other early medieval texts on Guthlac: an Old English translation of the *Vita*, which follows its source closely as far as the narrative details are concerned; a sermon now known as *Vercelli Homily 23*, adapted from the former and treated as merely an excerpt by earlier editors; and two Old English poems recorded in the late tenth-century Exeter Book, *Guthlac A* and *B*.

death.[29] But this focus on the *Vita* as a narrative of transformation has tended to obscure the fact that the Fens as portrayed in the text are not a primeval, purely natural landscape to begin with. This is suggested early on in the *Vita*, when Guthlac arrives at Crowland only to find the material traces of former human activity:

> Erat itaque in praedicta insula tumulus agrestibus glaebis coacervatus, quem olim avari solitudinis frequentatores lucri ergo illic adquirendi defodientes scindebant, in cuius latere velut cisterna inesse videbatur; in qua vir beatae memoriae Guthlac desuper inposito tugurio habitare coepit. (*VG*, ch. 28, pp. 92–94)

> (Now there was in the said island a mound built of clods of earth which greedy comers to the waste had dug open, in the hope of finding treasure there; in the side of this there seemed to be a sort of cistern, and in this Guthlac the man of blessed memory began to dwell, after building a hut over it.)

Although the island is currently uninhabited, the fact that the mound is "built of clods of earth" ("agrestibus glaebis coacervatus") and incorporates a "cisterna" – a cistern, or perhaps a stone cist or chamber of the sort that might be found in a barrow, an image invoked by the Latin "tumulus" – shows that Crowland's topography is, to some extent, shaped by human activity, even if that activity lies in the past: this is not a natural hill, formed by geological processes, but a human-made structure.[30] The mention of "avari solitudinis frequentatores," too, suggests human activity. Given the text's use of the word *tumulus*, which is usually (though not exclusively) used to refer to barrows, and the presence of the *cisterna*, the "greedy frequenters of the solitude" (as the phrase could be more literally translated) can well be imagined as grave robbers – the earliest recorded instance in British history, as the text's modern editor Bertram Colgrave notes.[31] Yet the term *frequentatores*, indicative of ongoing or repeated activity, could also be a reference to more regular activities than grave robbing.[32] This is unexpected, because the text's initial description of the Fens suggests a wild, uncultivated area:

> Est in meditullaneis Brittanniae partibus inmensae magnitudinis aterrima palus, quae, a Grontae fluminis ripis incipiens, haud procul a castello quem dicunt nomine Gronte, nunc stagnis, nunc flactris, interdum nigris fusi vaporis laticibus, necnon et crebris insularum nemorumque

29 See, for instance, Justin T. Noetzel, "Monster, Demon, Warrior: St. Guthlac and the Cultural Landscape of the Anglo-Saxon Fens," *Comitatus: A Journal of Medieval and Renaissance Studies* 45 (2014): 105–131, at 129.
30 The usual meaning of *cisterna* is a cistern, a tank or reservoir for water, but in view of the *Vita*'s generally "ornate and bombastic style" (Colgrave, in *VG*, p. 17), it is possible that the word is used imprecisely to denote a stone chamber or cist burial; see *VG*, pp. 182–183.
31 Colgrave, in *VG*, p. 183.
32 See Charlton T. Lewis and Charles Short, *A Latin Dictionary: Founded on Andrews' Edition of Freund's Latin Dictionary* (Oxford: Clarendon Press, 1879), s.v. "frequentator": "a frequent visitor, a frequenter (late Lat.)." Quoted from Perseus Digital Library, Tufts University, accessed 5 April 2021, http://www.perseus.tufts.edu.

intervenientibus flexuosis rivigarum anfractibus, ab austro in aquilonem mare tenus longissimo tractu protenditur. (*VG*, ch. 24, p. 86)

(There is in the midland district of Britain a most dismal fen of immense size, which begins at the banks of the river Granta not far from the camp which is called Cambridge, and stretches from the south as far north as the sea. It is a very long tract, now consisting of marshes, now of bogs, sometimes of black waters overhung by fog, sometimes studded with wooded islands and traversed by the windings of tortuous streams.)

When Guthlac first arrives at the borders of the Fenland and learns about the island of Crowland, it is described as a remote place haunted by demons:

Quidam de illic adstantibus nomine Tatwine se scisse aliam insulam in abditis remotioris heremi partibus confitebatur, quam multi inhabitare temtantes propter incognita heremi monstra et diversarum formarum terrores reprobaverant. Quo audito, vir beatae recordationis Guthlac illum locum monstrari sibi a narrante efflagitabat. [...] Crugland dicitur, insula media in palude posita quae ante paucis propter remotioris heremi solitudinem inculta vix nota habebatur. Nullus hanc ante famulum Christi Guthlacum solus habitare colonus valebat, propter videlicet illic demorantium fantasias demonum. (*VG*, ch. 25, p. 88)

(A certain man among those standing by, whose name was Tatwine, declared that he knew a certain island in the more remote and hidden parts of that desert; many had attempted to dwell there, but had rejected it on account of the unknown portents of the desert and its terrors of various shapes. Guthlac, the man of blessed memory, on hearing this, earnestly besought his informant to show him the place. [...] It is called Crowland, an island in the middle of the marsh which on account of the wildness of this very remote desert had hitherto remained untilled and known to a very few. No settler had been able to dwell alone in this place before Guthlac the servant of Christ, on account of the phantoms of demons which haunted it.)

We see Crowland singled out as having remained untilled and known to very few (although "many had attempted to dwell there"), as well as uninhabited due to demonic visitations. Yet from the *Vita*'s initial description, this is what we would assume any place in the Fens to be like. Characterized as the entire region is by fens (*stagna*), bogs (*flactra*), black waters (*nigri fusi*), fogs (*vapores*), and winding streams (*rivigae*), one wonders why the island is singled out as unknown, unsettled, and untilled. Unless, of course, the *Vita*'s initial description does not correspond to what the text perceives the Fens actually to be like: the fact that Tatwine, the man who takes Guthlac to Crowland, uses a "fisherman's skiff" ("piscatoria scafula"; ch. 25, p. 88), for instance, might indicate that the *Vita*, despite the initial description it gives, imagines the Fens as being habitually exploited for fish.

Until recently, scholars have tended to assume that the *Vita*'s literary representation of the Fens as a wild and sparsely settled region largely corresponds to the actualities of the Fenland during what archaeologists refer to as the Early and Middle Saxon periods. This traditional view of the historical Fens has been challenged, however. Susan Oosthuizen, for instance, has argued that the area was much more densely populated than has hitherto been assumed, although this applies only to the permanently dry upland regions of the Fens.[33] More importantly for the question at hand, however, Oosthuizen provides compelling evidence for the long-term exploitation and management, from the Neolithic onward, of the unsettled lowlands, whose tidal flats afforded good grazing for sheep and cattle, as well as opportunities for fishing, fowling, and harvesting coastal grasses that were used as building materials for low dykes and as stuffing for pillows and mattresses.[34] These are exactly the kinds of seasonal activities that could be aptly described by the term *frequentatores*, as used in the *Vita*: the regular, though periodic, exploitation of the Fens' natural features and resources. Yet even here, the term "natural" creates the wrong impression, because the unsettled, seemingly natural landscape of the Fens is in fact shaped by human activity: according to Oosthuizen, the remarkable stability of the undrained fen basin's ecology over six millennia is in fact a sign of regular human activity, as without human intervention, such as the cropping of reeds, and assuming that sea levels remain relatively stable, "the vegetation of the fen gradually follows the natural succession to evolve into a dryland landscape."[35] In other words, the very "naturalness" of the forbidding fens in the *Vita*'s description is, in the case of the historical Fenland, a sign of human presence.

We should not, of course, conflate the historical realities of the Fens with the literary, and hence imagined, landscape described in the *Vita*, even though we are dealing with a piece of historiographical writing produced in geographic proximity to the place described.[36] It is impossible to say what kinds of action – if any – the *Vita*'s *frequentatores* might be thought of as performing apart from excavating the *cisterna* in Guthlac's hill. Still, it is striking to note how the *Vita* gradually undermines its initial description of the Fens as an area devoid of human beings by introducing a variety of traces of earlier, as well as potentially present and ongoing, cultural activity, thereby also undermining the division between "cultural" and "natural" landscape it initially seems to construct.

---

33 Susan Oosthuizen, *The Anglo-Saxon Fenland* (Oxford: Windgather Press, 2017), 13–28. There is a considerable lack of agreement among archaeologists about the question of the Fenland's settlement during the Early and Middle Saxon periods. For a contrasting opinion, see John Hines, *Voices in the Past* (Cambridge: Cambridge University Press, 2004), 67–69.

34 Oosthuizen, *Anglo-Saxon Fenland*, 1–4. Estes, too, notes that "fenlands, impenetrable to outsiders, may look like wildernesses, but they were exploited for fishing and fowling, salt production, fuel from peat, and for pasturing animals during the growing season, when arable lands needed to be kept free of grazing animals." Estes, *Literary Landscapes*, 15–16.

35 Oosthuizen, *Anglo-Saxon Fenland*, 10.

36 Hagiography is not usually counted as part of historiographical literature, yet in early medieval Britain the two genres are often conflated, starting with Bede's influential *Historia ecclesiastica*, which contains a large amount of hagiographical material. See Michael Hunter, "Germanic and Roman Antiquity and the Sense of the Past in Anglo-Saxon England," *Anglo-Saxon England* 3 (1974): 29–50, at 30.

With the introduction of the human-made hill, the Fens are invested, in Nicholas Howe's terms, not only with a topography but also with a history.[37] Just as the historical Fenland's "natural" landscape was sustained by regular human activity, so Guthlac's hill in the *Vita*'s literary landscape turns out to be a human-built feature that has become part of the topography, a fact that highlights the extent to which cultural activity transforms the landscape and itself can become "natural," almost indistinguishable from non-human-made features.[38] The presence of a human-made hill suggests that the *Vita* imagines Guthlac's Fens as a formerly cultivated landscape in the process of renaturing. Guthlac's decision to settle in the wilderness of the Fens thus might be read less as a foray into hitherto uncharted areas and more as an act of reestablishing human occupation and control over a landscape already formed and shaped by both human and nonhuman forces (whether Guthlac is aware of the fact or not).[39] To the audience, in any case, the mention of Cambridge – whose Latin designation "castello quem dicunt nomine Gronte" immediately evokes Britain's Roman past – does not merely signal a current border between settled and unsettled areas, but also serves as a reminder of past cultural activity that may have extended farther into the region now described as "a most dismal fen," activity whose traces can potentially be perceived in the human-made mound where Guthlac establishes his abode.[40] Similarly, the text's reference to "avari solitudinis frequentatores" (greedy frequenters of the solitude) might be read as a reference to regular human interventions in the Fenland, perhaps precisely the seasonal exploitation of resources below the flood line that was described above. In this case, the adjective *avarus* would have to be interpreted as having a qualifying function with regard to the noun *frequentatores*: not all of the people who regularly frequent the Fens are

---

37 Nicholas Howe, *Writing the Map of Anglo-Saxon England: Essays in Cultural Geography* (New Haven: Yale University Press, 2008), 75; see the epigraph to this chapter.

38 Similarly, Richard Bradley has drawn attention to the fact that natural rock formations such as tors are often difficult to distinguish from megalithic tombs whose stone chambers, originally covered by earth and turf, have been exposed by the weather, so that the two may easily have been conflated. See Richard Bradley, "Ruined Buildings, Ruined Stones: Enclosures, Tombs and Natural Places in the Neolithic of South-West England," *World Archaeology* 30, no. 1 (1998): 13–22.

39 Guthlac is thus perhaps unwittingly acting on Pope Gregory's advice to rededicate rather than destroy older shrines and other places of worship, as quoted in Bede's *Historia ecclesiastica gentis Anglorum* (1.30) – a text the *Vita Guthlaci*'s author Felix seems not to have known, however. For the latter point, see Audrey Meany, "Felix's *Life of Guthlac*: History or Hagiography?," in *Æthelbald and Offa: Two Eighth-Century Kings of Mercia; Papers from a Conference Held in Manchester in 2000*, ed. David Hill, British Archaeological Reports, British Series 383 (Oxford: Archaeopress, 2005), 75–84, at 75.

40 Modern Cambridge stands on the site of the Roman settlement Grantacæstir. The site's Old English name Grantebrycge substitutes *brycge* (bridge) for *cæstir*, while the first element later developed into *cam*. The name of the River Cam is a back-formation. See Bertram Colgrave and R. A. B. Mynors, eds., *Bede's Ecclesiastical History*, Oxford Medieval Texts (Oxford: Clarendon Press, 1969), 394n1.

greedy, only those among them who dug the hole into the hill; potentially there are other nonavaricious *frequentatores* not implicated in the attempted robbery.[41]

By introducing elements suggestive of cultural activity, the *Vita* inverts our expectations after first rousing them: having initially described the Fens as a seemingly primeval landscape, the text suddenly exposes this initial image as a mental construct that reflects Guthlac's (and the reader's) expectations more than the actualities of the landscape later encountered. As Heide Estes notes, "the *Lives* of Guthlac are assumed to 'describe' the wilderness of the fens, but [...] in fact they imagine and construct it, first insisting that the fens *are* untracked and uncultivated despite evidence to the contrary, then imagining the creatures that occupy the area around Guthlac's hermitage as demonic rather than human."[42] Somewhat incongruously, however, Estes later asserts that "Guthlac and his biographers deny the evidence of prior human habitation in their characterization of the fenland island," as if this "evidence" were some historical reality outside the text, when in fact it is part of the text's own literary construction of the Fens.[43] For Estes, the text's characterization of the Fens as a "wilderness" serves to legitimate the territory's future colonization and exploitation by a small class of predominantly male, Christian, "Englisc," upper-class people.[44] However, such a reading necessarily relegates the text's simultaneous insistence on other human activities besides Guthlac's to the status of a mere textual incoherence.

By contrast, I would argue that the Fenland's double characterization is part of the strategy by which the text exposes this landscape as the result of both cultural and natural factors, a fact that the *Vita*'s audience – and apparently Guthlac too – only gradually become aware of. In so doing, the text not only undermines a strict division between nature and culture but also draws attention to the potential of human perceptions of landscape to change, due not only to actual physical transformations of the landscape but also to the selective nature of perception, which may come to incorporate new experiences and insights. The *Vita* does so in a specifically literary manner, by playing on our (and Guthlac's) genre expectations. Immediately prior to the *Vita*'s initial description of the Fens, we learn that Guthlac's monastic readings of the lives of the desert fathers prompted his desire to emulate their example (*VG*, ch. 24). The description of the Fens that follows closes with the information that "when this same man of blessed memory, Guthlac, had learned about the wild

---

41 My argument here differs somewhat from the one I put forth in an earlier article, where I suggested that the *Vita*'s use of the term *frequentatores* might be associated with the clandestine and illicit activities of criminals. Even then, though, my main point was to argue that the text denied the permanency of any human settlement in the region, a point not contradicted here, and perhaps even reinforced. See Jan-Peer Hartmann, "Monument Reuse in Felix's *Vita Sancti Guthlaci*," *Medium Ævum* 88, no. 2 (2019): 230–264, at 236, 244–245.
42 Estes, *Literary Landscapes*, 93.
43 See Estes, 98–99.
44 Estes, 111.

places of this vast desert, he made his way thither with divine assistance by the most direct route" ("igitur cum supradictus vir beatae memoriae Guthlac illius vastissimi heremi inculta loca conperisset, caelestibus auxiliis adiutus, rectissimo callis tramite tenus usque perrexit"; ch. 24, p. 86). The text thus seems to imply that the Fenland is a desert of just the sort that Guthlac had encountered in his readings (the passage even uses the designation *vastissimus heremus,* "a vast desert"), even though we will shortly learn that it is not quite as deserted as it may have initially appeared. In other words, the Fens are initially presented as a desert because this is what Guthlac (and the hagiographically knowledgeable audience) expects to find; as Justin Noetzel notes, "Guthlac needs a vast and remote wilderness that few people traverse and even fewer inhabit, and he finds Crowland to be the perfect representation of his new lifestyle and the location for his ensuing battles."[45] Similarly, when Guthlac hears that Crowland is haunted by demons, he is eager to visit the place precisely because demonic visitations form part of the hagiographical experience of desert saints such as Antony (not to mention Christ's temptation in the desert).

This intertextual interpretation of the *Vita* is supported by the palimpsestic nature of the work itself. The *Vita* is a highly self-conscious literary text, written in an "ornate and bombastic style" with "a flair for inventing new words" that seems to have caused difficulty early on; Colgrave cites Ordericus, who called it "prolixus et aliquantulum obscurus."[46] In addition to scriptural quotations, there are echoes and quotations from Virgil, Aldhelm, and saints' lives, including Jerome's *Vita Pauli* and Evagrius's Latin translation of Athanasius's *Life of Antony*.[47] Joseph Grossi refers to the *Vita Guthlaci*'s use of quotations as

> the textual counterpart of the process whereby early builders of saints' shrines appropriated Roman *spolia* to enhance their structures and of the method apparently used by sixth- and seventh-century Anglo-Saxons to bury members of their communities within prehistoric earthworks. Like a barrow that hints at the deliberate redeployment of resources, a verbal borrowing within exegesis operates within a process of identity building to invest an ancient text or structure with new meaning, thus bolstering the prestige of the person or society staking that claim to the past.[48]

Just as verbal borrowings can invest an ancient text with new meaning, so the cultural repertoire of textual descriptions and definitions can lend meaning to landscape. The *Vita* has Guthlac cast the Fens as a patristic desert in the tradition of Jerome's *Vita Pauli* and Evagrius's *Vita Antonii*. Antony, too, is harassed by demons while spending time in a tomb, so even the introduction of what appears to be a barrow fits into Guthlac's self-fashioning as an early medieval hermit saint. The gradual

45 Noetzel, "Monster, Demon, Warrior," 119.
46 Colgrave, in *VG*, pp. 17–18.
47 Colgrave, in *VG*, pp. 16–17.
48 Joseph Grossi, "Barrow Exegesis: Quotation, Chorography, and Felix's *Life of St. Guthlac*," *Florilegium* 30 (2013): 143–165, at 144–145. The title of this chapter consciously echoes Grossi's.

introduction in the *Vita Guthlaci* of elements that challenge a straightforward reading of the Fens as an eremitic desert even as they become incorporated into Guthlac's reenactment draws attention to this process, suggesting that our perception of landscape is ultimately dependent on cultural preconceptions that may, to a certain extent, be adapted to include new elements. At the same time, the *Vita* self-consciously establishes itself as a specifically "English" hagiographic text that looks back to and is partly shaped by the hagiographical tradition, but which is also prepared to incorporate new elements that adapt the tradition to a different environment, thereby transforming the genre and bringing forth new meaning.

Britton Elliott Brooks has perceptively traced the ways in which the *Vita* changes and develops the traditional model of Antonian progression toward sanctity by tying it to a certain form and perception of the physical landscape.[49] I would go even further by arguing that in introducing elements that appear to contradict the text's initial presentation of the Fens, the *Vita* actually depicts this very process of literary transformation. In exposing the Fenland landscape as the result of both cultural and natural factors, the text undermines a strict division between nature and culture – a binary it initially seems to invoke when it describes the area as "a most dismal fen of immense size," in accordance with customary representations of the "eremitic desert" in early Christian eremitic hagiography. In so doing, it simultaneously draws attention to the ways in which perceptions of landscape are partly shaped by cultural practices, such as the reading of hagiographical literature (which thereby exerts its "agential potential"), and to how these perceptions may change when adapting to a specific environment. To apply Iovino and Oppermann's vocabulary of "storied matter" to the production of literature, the text's specific form is produced by the agency emerging from the intra-action of Guthlac's cultural preconceptions (as presented in the text) and his sensory experience of the landscape: in the *Vita*, Guthlac's Fenland emerges as a "reciprocal creation" produced by the intra-action of matter and cognition. Making sense of landscape, the *Vita* thus suggests, can be interpreted as a process of cultural appropriation determined both by social factors (such as the cultural preconceptions of the perceiver) and by the material affordances and resistances of the various physical entities involved; meaning emerges from the overlap of "natural" and "cultural" meaningfulness via the intra-activity of different human and nonhuman actors, an activity one might call, with Siewers, "ecosemiotic."[50]

---

49 Brooks, *Restoring Creation*, 173–228, esp. 228. Brooks's otherwise compelling reading is somewhat impeded by his repeated insistence that the text closely reflects the "experiential reality" of the *Vita*'s contemporaries upon entering the Fens, which it attempts to emulate through carefully crafted "enargaeic description" (174–175). I would argue that the question is beside the point: it is the changing perception of the Fens as presented in the text that brings about the transformation.
50 Siewers, *Re-imagining Nature*.

Transformation through Integration

If the *Vita* exposes Guthlac's Fenland as both "cultural" and "natural," a hybrid assemblage in the Latourian sense, constituted by the totality of material and social intra-actions that produce meaning, this process of continual reevaluation also perpetuates an ongoing process of transformation. Scholarly discussions have frequently reduced this process to Guthlac's struggle with the demons who inhabit the island when he arrives there, and whose threatening and at times violent assaults are aimed at driving the saint from his newly chosen home. Yet such a reading fails to take into account the extent to which Guthlac interacts with the ecosystem of the Fens in its entirety; in other words, it fails to consider the composite and dynamic nature of the Fenland as an assemblage.

The *Vita* initially presents the whole Fenland as hostile, with the demonic attacks forming only one element, though an admittedly important one. Guthlac's perception of the antagonism of other features of the landscape, I argue, is just as crucial to the *Vita*'s narrative of saintly residence within the Fens: it takes more than the expulsion of the demons to transform Crowland from a place of terror to one of Christian worship. Moreover, if the *Vita Guthlaci* is a narrative of transformation, the transformation is not primarily that of a formerly uninhabited, uncultivated natural landscape into a cultural, inhabited one. Guthlac replaces the demons as the island's inhabitants but leaves the Fens' other features largely intact. To all appearances, the Fenland as a physical place does not change much in the course of the narrative; rather, what changes is its meaning and perception. Guthlac's spiritual transformation of the Fens, I suggest, is accomplished not through an act of colonization but rather by achieving integration into an already existing material-semiotic assemblage. This act nevertheless changes the assemblage as a whole, as it is presented in the *Vita*, from a place hostile to the saint to one attuned to his spirituality.

Demonic visitations are a regular feature in biographies of hermit saints, and they play a major role in the *Vita Guthlaci*'s most direct model, Evagrius's *Life of Antony*.[51] Antony, too, is assaulted by devils when he takes up abode in an ancient

---

51 Intriguingly, there is no item in Helmut Gneuss's list of manuscripts written or owned in England up to 1100 that transmits the *Vita Guthlaci* alongside the *Vita Antonii*, despite the fact that the former is usually found in manuscripts that also feature other lives of hermit saints, including Jerome's *Vita Pauli primi eremitae*, another of the *Vita*'s direct models. See Helmut Gneuss, *Handlist of Anglo-Saxon Manuscripts: A List of Manuscripts and Manuscript Fragments Written or Owned in England up to 1100*, Medieval and Renaissance Texts and Studies 241 (Tempe, AZ: ACMRS, 2001), item 103. Several of these anchorites have ties to particular locations or forms of landscape: Botulf, Tancred, Torthred, and Tova are associated with Thorney in the Fens (item 434.5); Philibert of Jumièges (items 781, 804) and Cuthbert (item 781) retired to islands off the coast. Other lives share further features with the *Vita Guthlaci:* Bavo of Ghent's anchorage in a hollow tree was preceded by a military career (item 804), a profession also envisaged for Aichard of Jumièges (item 781), and one that Guthlac followed before entering the monastery at Repton. Walaric was renowned for his horticultural skills and

tomb. Unlike in the *Vita Guthlaci*, however, Antony experiences these demonic visitations even before moving to the tomb, and they continue after he has left it; there is no sign of an intrinsic relationship between the assaults and the specific site of the tomb. In the *Vita Guthlaci*, by contrast, the haunting of the island is already an established phenomenon when Guthlac arrives there; it does not occur as a consequence of his arrival. Indeed, the visitations are not primarily related to Guthlac's saintly virtue, although the temptation aspect is present too. Rather, the demons' express purpose is to drive Guthlac away from territory they claim as theirs. There is thus a sense of a deeper relationship between the demons and the landscape they inhabit; in the Old English poem *Guthlac A*, which retells this section of the *Vita*, the hill is even said to serve as a temporary place of respite from the tortures of hell for the demons, who are identified as exiled fallen angels.[52]

The two aspects – the territorial conflict and the testing of Guthlac's saintly virtue – are not mutually exclusive, of course. As Katherine O'Brien O'Keeffe has argued, "Felix's *Vita S. Guthlaci* is first and foremost a discourse of contested territory fundamentally altered through acquisition, purgation, and habitation. [...] Guthlac's saintly combat on the island he never leaves opens a space of transformation in which he increases in virtue and the island itself is purged."[53] From this perspective, it is significant that the struggle centers on an ancient human-built monument rather than a purely natural feature: Guthlac's choice of the ancient mound and subsequent physical transformation of it can thus be read as an act of appropriation to reinforce his territorial claim, as well as a gesture signifying his intention to reestablish a permanent human element in the assemblage of the Fens.[54]

Guthlac's act of appropriation, then, has a decidedly material component, which aligns it more closely with more object-oriented approaches within "thing studies."

---

his ability to protect his vegetables from insects (item 804), two forms of engagement with the natural world that stand in marked contrast to Guthlac's near lack of interference with his surroundings. The fact that none of the manuscripts feature Antony, whose *Vita* provides the closest parallels to Guthlac's encounters with demons, is perhaps a sign that the respective compilers perceived other features to be more relevant to Guthlac's particular form of eremitic exile.

52 Brooks notes that *Guthlac A* "exaggerates the role of the landscape to the extent that the central conflict lies in the competition between Guthlac and the demons for Crowland," and links this contest to the doctrine of replacement, which posits that the saved will replace the fallen angels in heaven. Brooks, *Restoring Creation*, 17–18. This same connection is also noted in Stephanie Clark, "A More Permanent Homeland: Land Tenure in *Guthlac A*," *Anglo-Saxon England* 40 (2011): 75–102.

53 Katherine O'Brien O'Keeffe, "Guthlac's Crossings," *Quaestio: Selected Proceedings of the Cambridge Colloquium in Anglo-Saxon, Norse, and Celtic* 2 (2001): 1–26, at 3, 10.

54 As Estella Weiss-Krejci points out, the reuse and modification of ancient monuments – "monument reuse" in archaeological discourse – is widely attested throughout the world and often serves to establish or substantiate political or territorial claims; for instance, through appropriation of ancestors. Estella Weiss-Krejci, "The Plot against the Past: Reuse and Modification of Ancient Mortuary Monuments as Persuasive Efforts of Appropriation," in *The Lives of Prehistoric Monuments in Iron Age, Roman, and Medieval Europe*, ed. Marta Díaz-Guardamino, Leonardo García Sanjuán, and David Wheatley (Oxford: Oxford University Press, 2015), 307–324.

Not only does Guthlac choose the material remains of earlier cultural activity – a human-made mound or barrow, and thus a "thing," or, more properly, an assemblage of different things – as his place of settlement, he also physically transforms these remains by changing or substituting individual components of the assemblage, an element notably absent from Evagrius's *Life of Antony*. When Guthlac establishes his home on or in the mound, he alters it by building a hut (*tugurium*) either on or over the stone chamber or cistern set within the hill; this act of turning the stone chamber into the foundation of his house also transforms the meaning of what was once possibly a burial mound. The human-made hill that had become a topographical feature is thus reappropriated as a human dwelling. Moreover, it is a dwelling whose structural characteristics can potentially be linked to Guthlac's cultural identity as an early medieval "English" saint: a wattle-and-daub construction built over a depression (in this case the stone floor of the chamber), recalling the "sunken-featured buildings" or "Grubenhäuser" widespread throughout the Germanic-speaking areas of northern Europe and archaeologically linked to 'Germanic' rather than '(Romano-)British' settlement within Britain.[55] The *Vita*'s description is not specific enough to definitely establish whether Guthlac's *tugurium* should indeed be identified as a sunken-featured building, but the passage highlights the composite nature of the structure by suggesting different archaeological strata: successive layers of cultural activity interrupted by phases of renaturing.[56] Nevertheless, the different elements – those of the original building and those added by Guthlac – cannot be easily separated; just as the mound has become part of the landscape, so Guthlac's hut is part of an assemblage that comprises old and new, human-made and natural elements.

The interconnection of these elements becomes evident in an episode that describes the demons entering Guthlac's hut, a passage suggesting that the act of intrusion is aided by the components of the dwelling, old and new:

---

[55] According to Helena Hamerow, the "Germanic pedigree" of sunken-featured buildings in Britain "has never been seriously questioned." Helena Hamerow, "Migration Theory and the Anglo-Saxon 'Identity Crisis,'" in *Migrations and Invasions in Archaeological Explanation*, ed. John Chapman and Helena Hamerow, British Archaeological Reports International Series 664 (Oxford: Archaeopress, 1997), 33–44, at 37. The possible identification of Guthlac's *tugurium* with a sunken-featured building has been suggested by Audrey Meaney ("History or Hagiography," 75). Given the sparseness of the description, this claim is difficult to substantiate; moreover, sunken-featured buildings are now recognized to have utilized suspended floors, "the pit forming only one component of a larger ground-level building." Jess Tipper, *The Grubenhaus in Anglo-Saxon England: An Analysis and Interpretation of the Evidence from a Most Distinctive Building Type*, Landscape Research Centre Archaeological Monograph Series 2, no. 1 (Yedingham: The Landscape Research Centre, 2005), 184. On Guthlac's ambiguous cultural identity, see Hartmann, "Monument Reuse."

[56] Estes, too, notes the existence of several layers of cultural activity that characterize the hill. Estes, *Literary Landscapes*, 102, 114.

En subito teterrimis inmundorum spirituum catervis totam cellulam suam inpleri conspexit. Subeuntibus enim ab undique illis porta patebat; nam per criptas et cratulas intrantibus non iuncturae valvarum, non foramina cratium illis ingressum negabant. (*VG*, ch. 31, pp. 100–102)

(He suddenly saw the whole tiny cell filled with horrible troops of foul spirits; for the door was open to them as they approached from every quarter; as they entered through floor-holes and crannies, neither the joints of the doorways nor the openings in the wattle-work denied them entry.)

The text seems to emphasize the demons' corporeality: rather than simply material- izing in the building, they enter through features that characterize the specific type of hut he lives in – the openings in the wattle-work and the gaps between the slabs of the stone floor (see figures 6.1 and 6.2). The mention of "criptas et cratulas" ("floor- holes and crannies") evokes the image of demons entering from *underneath* the an- cient stone chamber, from *within* the hill, as if they were living inside or beneath the human-made mound. Indeed, there is an intriguing sense of complicity between the spirits and the material makeup of Guthlac's dwelling that hints at a deeper relation- ship between the demons and the mound. In most of the phrases describing the spir- its' entry into Guthlac's cell, agency is assigned not merely to the spirits but also to the respective parts of the building: the door is open to them ("illis porta patebat") as they approach, and "neither the joints of the doorways nor the openings in the wat- tle-work *denied them entry*" ("non iuncturae valvarum, non foramina cratium *illis in- gressum negabant*"; my emphasis). This unexpected ascription of agency suggests that it is the building itself – raised as it is on the foundations of what appears to be a former burial mound – and, by extension, the landscape of the Fenland that re- sist Guthlac's presence by granting access to the demons intent on frightening him away. This framing of Guthlac's experience recalls Jane Bennett's contention that matter is never inert but is rather "intrinsically lively" or "vibrant," although she stresses that it is neither "ensouled" nor capable of acting intentionally.[57] Bennett's approach is thus compatible with that of Latour, who similarly rejects the idea of ma- terial intentionality but nevertheless draws attention to matter's agential potential, which it exerts through its capacity to intra-act with other material and nonmaterial configurations. The *Vita*'s intimation of a collaboration between the demons and the building's features, I suggest, promotes a similar notion of composite material agen- cy.

While some of the *Vita*'s demonic visitations are modeled quite closely after sim- ilar attacks in Evagrius's *Life of Antony*, the latter offers no comparable ascription of material agency. When Antony has been shut up in the tomb, he is first tortured by the devil, but it is not mentioned how the latter was able to enter the closed struc- ture. Later, the devil returns with his dogs, who take the shape of various beasts, in a passage closely resembling a later episode in the *Vita Guthlaci* (ch. 36) where the de- mons take the shapes of animals. This time, Antony's attackers enter through holes

---

57 Bennett, *Vibrant Matter*, xvii.

Figure 6.1: Wattle-and-daub technique at Museumsdorf Düppel, Berlin. Photograph by Jan-Peer Hartmann.

Figure 6.2: Wattle-and-daub technique at Museumsdorf Düppel, Berlin. Photograph by Jan-Peer Hartmann.

in the wall, but these are not part of the original makeup of the building; rather, they appear as the result of an earthquake, possibly caused by the attackers themselves: "Sonitus igitur repentinus increuit, ita ut loco funditus agitato, et parietibus patefactis, multifaria dæmonum exinde turba se effunderet." ("Then there was a sudden noise which caused the place to shake violently: holes appeared in the walls and a horde of different kinds of demons poured out.")[58]

Intriguingly, in the *Vita Guthlaci* it is not merely the ancient features, the stone floor of the chamber and the earthen foundation beneath it, that permit the demons to enter, but also the joints of the doorways and the openings in the wattle-work – features added by Guthlac himself when he built his hut. The building is presumably meant to serve as protection against the weather, but also perhaps against animals and other potential invaders, an intention now undermined by its permeability. The lack of differentiation between the old and new elements of the building strengthens the notion of Guthlac's hill as a Latourian assemblage in which agency is a distributed phenomenon: all of the components collaborate with the demons, whose connection to the other elements of the island is clearly still stronger than Guthlac's.

There are other moments in the narrative in which Guthlac experiences the demons' assaults as intimately connected to the material landscape of the Fens, too. Later in the episode in which they enter his hut, the demons drag him to the gates of hell, torturing him and threatening to cast him into the abyss. Yet it is not merely the demons' whips that torture him but also the physical features of the marshland.[59] As the text describes:

> Dicto citius virum Dei praefatum, ligatis membris, extra cellulam suam duxerunt, et adductum in atrae paludis coenosis laticibus inmerserunt. Deinde asportantes illum per paludis asperrima loca inter densissima veprium vimina dilaceratis membrorum conpaginibus trahebant. [...] Dein iterum adsumentes, flagellis velut ferreis eum verberare coeperunt. (*VG*, ch. 31, pp. 102–104)

> (They bound the limbs of the said man of God and took him out of the cell; and leading him away, they plunged him into the muddy waters of the black marsh. Then they carried him through the wildest parts of the fen, and dragged him through the dense thickets of brambles, tearing his limbs and all his body. [...] And once again they took whips like iron and began to beat him.)

The passage emphasizes the corporeality of the encounter: precisely as the chapter title states, Guthlac is dragged to the gates of hell "bodily" ("corporaliter"; ch. 31, p. 100). He is plunged into the muddy waters of the black marsh and dragged through dense thickets of brambles. Yet in spite of the apparent complicity between the demons and certain features of the landscape, that human perception would nor-

---

58 Evagrius of Antioch, *Vita Beati Antonii Abbatis*, ch. 8, in PL 73:126–194, at col. 135; translation from Carolinne White, ed. and trans., *Early Christian Lives* (London: Penguin, 1998), 15.
59 My own reading here differs from that of Brooks, who argues that "the brambles are never inimical towards Guthlac, and only wound him through the agency of the demons." Brooks, *Restoring Creation*, 190.

mally deny any agency, Guthlac's resistance to the demons initiates a gradual process of transformation. Through this process, he inscribes his presence into the hill
and hence into the assemblage, eventually replacing the demons, in a very literal
sense, as the inhabitant of the mound.

In describing this process of transformation, during which Guthlac gains increasing command over the landscape – or rather, as I will argue below, is increasingly
accepted as an element within the assemblage – the *Vita* denies the demons a position of prime importance within Guthlac's struggle of incorporation, just as the episode in which they enter his hut suggests that they could not have done so without
the support of other features of the assemblage. Unlike the Old English *Guthlac A*,
whose account of the saint's struggle with the demons appears to be much more el-
egantly constructed in terms of plot, the *Vita* fails to provide a climactic scene where
the demons are finally dispelled for good.[60] In *Guthlac A*, the visitations become increasingly violent, starting with a verbal encounter and culminating in a scene in
which the demons threaten to throw Guthlac into the mouth of hell. They are
stopped by Saint Bartholomew, who commands them to depart the Fens. In the
Vita, the latter episode is only the second of four direct encounters with the demons.
When the visitations finally come to an end after Guthlac's confrontation with the
beast-shaped spirits (*VG*, ch. 36), we are never told that this is to be their last attack.
Indeed, given that this last encounter with the demons is preceded by an episode in
which Guthlac's servant Beccel, prompted by the devil, attempts to murder him so as
to become his successor and enjoy the veneration of kings and princes, the following
chapter's story of a jackdaw stealing a document and dropping it into a pool could
well be taken as an interlude before the next demonic assault.

Moreover, even though the demons have disappeared for good, this does not
mean that Guthlac's troubles are immediately over. The story of the jackdaw stealing
a document may appear relatively harmless in comparison to the demonic attacks,
but it testifies to the continued resistance of at least some elements of the Fens to
Guthlac's settlement, even as it showcases Guthlac's increasing authority.[61] The
saint consoles the guest whose document was stolen and promises him that it will

---

60 This is also argued in Alaric Hall, "Constructing Anglo-Saxon Sanctity: Tradition, Innovation and
Saint Guthlac," in *Images of Sanctity: Essays in Honour of Gary Dickson*, ed. Debra Higgs Strickland,
Visualising the Middle Ages 1 (Leiden: Brill, 2007), 207–235, at 214. Brooks disagrees, arguing that it
is in the hell's-mouth episode that Guthlac attains "spiritual majority" and that the following episodes serve to illustrate this by showcasing Guthlac's authority (*Restoring Creation*, 186, 215). I
would argue that Brooks's emphasis on a single transforming event is somewhat at variance with
the continued resistance of parts of the landscape, which suggests a more gradual process of transformation, as discussed below.
61 Brooks argues that God allows the ravens to pester Guthlac in order to allow the saint to display
his authority (*Restoring Creation*, 215), but the same could be said of the demonic assaults, which are
also God's means of testing Guthlac's steadfastness. The episodes differ in the adversities' degree of
severity and in the assuredness with which Guthlac dispels them, but this is a gradual process rather
than a sudden shift.

be recovered with God's help; and indeed, when the visitor gets into a boat and makes his way through "dense clumps of reed" ("inter densas harundinum"), a path opens up before him and he finds the stolen pieces of parchment unharmed, balanced on top of a single reed that is "standing with its top bent down and shaken on every side by the moving waters of the pond" ("conspicit non longe in media planitie stagni unam harundinem curvato cacumine stantem, quae stagni tremulis quassabatur undique limphis"; *VG*, ch. 37, p. 118). The miraculous preservation of the parchment signals Guthlac's saintly status as one of God's elect, but it can also be read as a sign of his increasing acceptance by certain features of the landscape, which actively aid the saint's guest in recovering the piece of parchment – in the way, for example, that the path reveals itself ("inter densas harundinum [...] *via sibi monstraret*"; ch. 37, p. 118, emphasis mine). The passage provides a striking parallel to the earlier scene in which parts of Guthlac's *tugurium* showed their complicity with the demons, a sign that some elements of the assemblage have by now shifted their allegiance.

In the next chapter, we are told that Guthlac has authority not only over various beasts but even over water and air: "Not only indeed did the creatures of the earth and sky obey his commands, but also even the very water and the air obeyed the true servant of the true God" ("Non solum vero terrae aerisque animalia illius iussionibus obtemperabant, immo etiam aqua aerque ipsi veri Dei vero famulo oboediebant"; *VG*, ch. 38, p. 120), an almost verbatim quotation from Bede's prose *Vita Cuthberti*.[62] Nevertheless, the jackdaws' mischief continues for another few chapters, and their habit of venturing into the saint's various buildings "with daring familiarity" ("cum familiaribus ausis"; ch. 38, p. 120) and of damaging and stealing objects shows that Guthlac's authority is not to be imagined in absolute terms.

Indeed, Guthlac's relationship with his environment is cast in more symbiotic terms: just as the continued permeability of his buildings indicates the ·lack of a clear demarcation between the human and natural spheres, it is the saint's benevolence that induces various kinds of birds and fishes to feed from his hand, "flying or swimming swiftly to his call as if to a shepherd" ("ad vocem ipsius veluti pastorem ocius natantes volantesque subvenirent"; *VG*, ch. 38, pp. 120), and it is his patient bearing of the jackdaws' mischief that sets an example to other birds and induces them to flock to him, to sit on his breast and shoulder, and to build a nest in a basket he places under the eaves of his dwelling (chs. 38 and 39). Saintly interactions with the "natural" world are by no means uncommon in medieval hagiography.[63] In the *Vita Guthlaci*, however, this aspect is particularly prominent, directing our attention to the assemblage-like character of the Fens. If the image of the shepherd feeding his flock recalls a feudal relationship – wholly compatible in much early medieval "En-

---

62 Brooks, *Restoring Creation*, 216.
63 The *Vita*'s immediate model is probably Bede's prose *Life of St. Cuthbert*, which it paraphrases at several points during the descriptions of Guthlac's interactions with the "natural" world. In the *Vita Guthlaci*, however, this aspect is even more prominent.

glish" literature with the Christian image of the shepherd – Guthlac's authority is not God-given, but rather brought about by his exemplary patience and benevolence in intra-acting with the other elements of the landscape, part of his love of God.[64] This is implied by Guthlac himself when explaining his intimate relationship with the Fenland's birds: "Have you not read how if a man is joined to God in purity of spirit, all things are united to him in God?" ("Nonne legisti, quia, qui Deo puro spiritu co-pulatur, omnia sibi in Deo coniunguntur?"; ch. 39, p. 122.) Guthlac's exemplary love of God and his willingness to accept the sometimes troublesome presence of these other elements cannot be separated; if the text uses the vocabulary of "dominion," it does so without imagining such dominion as either absolute or imposed by divine intervention:

> Nam qui auctori omnium creaturarum fideliter et integro spiritu famulatur, non est mirandum, si eius imperiis ac votis omnis creatura deserviat. At plerumque idcirco subiectae nobis creaturae dominium perdimus, quia Domino universorum creatori servire negligimus. (*VG*, ch. 38, p. 120)

> (For if a man faithfully and wholeheartedly serves the Maker of all created things, it is no wonder though all creation should minister to his commands and wishes. But for the most part we lose dominion over the creation which was made subject to us, because we ourselves neglect to serve the Lord and Creator of all things.)[65]

In terms of the landscape as an assemblage, God is strangely absent, except as its ultimate source. Creation, in the shape of the Fenland's animals and plants, does not obey Guthlac because God forces it to, but out of its own will, in acknowledgment of Guthlac's exceptional virtue.[66] The *Vita* depicts Guthlac not in the role of the feudal lord who has "dominion over the fish of the sea, and over the fowl of the air, and over every other living thing that moveth upon the earth" (Genesis 1:28), but rather as an integrated part of an ecosystem, with his exemplary Christian behavior ensuring that he is accepted by the Fens' other elements, both living and nonliving.[67] In other words, Guthlac's "dominion" is revealed precisely by his decision not to exert it.[68] Again, this is implied by Guthlac himself, when he envisages a similar relationship between himself and the angels (*angeli*) on the one hand, and wild animals (*ferae*) on the other; according to Brooks, the verb *agnoscere*,

---

64 The Old English title *hlaford*, used of both secular lords and God, etymologically means "loaf-giver," with the first element (*hlaf*, "loaf") still recognizable; the image of the lord feeding his followers is thus compatible with both secular and religious interpretations.
65 Again, the *Vita* here quotes almost verbatim Bede's prose *Vita Cuthberti*. See Brooks, *Restoring Creation*, 216–217.
66 Brooks similarly notes that the elements and animals act without direction from God or the saint but are motivated by their implicit understanding of Guthlac's attunement to God's creation. Brooks, *Restoring Creation*, 211–212.
67 The Bible is quoted from the Authorized Version.
68 Thus I do not share Estes's conviction that in the *Vita*, animals, reeds, and even the elements exist only to serve Guthlac. Cf. Estes, *Literary Landscapes*, 104.

used with respect to the latter, indicates not only intimate knowledge but indeed close association or unity.[69] Brooks has convincingly traced the *Vita*'s image of spiritual attunement to patristic interpretations positing that the relationship between human beings and Creation can be restored to prelapsarian harmony by way of saints, whose sanctity is great enough to revoke the effects of the Fall.[70] God may have created the Fens and everything they are made up of, but he does not choose to exert his agential potential – except when his creation threatens to annihilate Guthlac in spite of his proven steadfastness, as occurs in the episode when the demons are stopped from casting Guthlac into hell's mouth by Saint Bartholomew. Otherwise, the land constitutes a field upon which Guthlac can prove his virtue, and he does so precisely by incorporating himself into it.

This reading of Guthlac's transformation of the Fens, a transformation that sees him as an integral part of the landscape and not as a colonizer imposing himself on it, is strengthened by the fact that the physical landscape of the Fens does not, in fact, change much throughout the narrative. Apart from constructing a number of buildings, Guthlac does not alter the physical features of the island, nor does he cultivate or in any other way change the landscape. Adhering to a strict asceticism, Guthlac does not even hunt or fish but only feeds on a daily "scrap of barley bread" and "a small cup of muddy water" ("ordeacei panis particula," "lutulentae aquae poculamento"; *VG*, ch. 28, p. 94). His oratory is consecrated by Bishop Headda, yet his dwelling reverts to its original use when Guthlac is buried in it, according to his own wishes (although his uncorrupted body is later placed in a shrine on the island, gifted by King Æthelbald, in chapter 51). The physical and semiotic continuities implied by the funerary act suggest a narrative of gradual alteration rather than rupture, the transformation of an assemblage or network, some of whose components have been changed or substituted while others remain intact, recalling Latour's "chains of associations." Indeed, the fact that the demons, too, are not the original builders of the monument but rather later arrivals who appropriated the island after it turned into a wilderness suggests that constellations and allegiances can change, and that they may do so again in the future. Guthlac has replaced the demons as the island's inhabitants, and his place is later taken by the priest Cissa (ch. 48).

If the physical makeup of the Fens remains largely (though not completely) unaltered, the Fens' status and definition have nevertheless changed. No longer an isolated wilderness, Crowland has become a sacred site, home to a saint and a pilgrimage destination both during Guthlac's life and after his death, as people flock from all parts of the country to obtain his counsel, benefit from his healing powers (*VG*, chs. 41–49), or, later, visit his shrine (chs. 52–53). But these pilgrims are not perma-

---

69 Brooks, *Restoring Creation*, 219–220.
70 Brooks specifically mentions Ambrose, Augustine, and Bede as proponents of this belief who were particularly influential in early medieval Britain. See Brooks, 4–15; with regard to the *Vita Guthlaci*, see esp. 207–221.

nent settlers or colonizers. They remain fleeting presences, "frequentatores" not much different from the shadowy figures alluded to in the description of Guthlac's mound (ch. 30). As Siewers notes, Guthlac's victory over the demons signifies "not the restoration of people to the landscape" but rather the expulsion of some of its inhabitants – namely, the demons – who are replaced by Guthlac himself in a process resembling Latour's notion of transformation through substitution.[71]

Conclusion

Reading the *Vita Guthlaci*'s Fenland in terms of an assemblage allows us to examine the mechanisms by which the *Vita* imagines its physical and semiotic transformation from a peripheral border region into an integrated part of an imagined early-medieval British religious landscape. It also allows us to examine various forms of collaboration between different sets of actors, human and nonhuman, animate and inanimate. These actors exhibit a surprising degree of hybridity in terms of their resistance to clear categorization, suggesting that agency, as imagined by the *Vita*, is to some degree composite in nature. Even more intriguingly, the *Vita*'s narrative of the Fens' transformation turns out to be much less anthropocentric than has usually been acknowledged.

   Throughout the narrative, the Fens are hardly altered physically; they are neither drained nor cultivated. Yet neither are they a "natural" area to begin with: they show signs of human activity, past and present. The human presence is felt throughout their history as recorded in the *Vita*, but it forms only one element among others. Guthlac is not presented as an external colonizer who shapes a hitherto stable land at will; rather, the saint appears to constitute a new element that is being integrated into an existing network, in a process of substitution that transforms the assemblage but does not replace it. This does not mean that Guthlac's integration into the network leaves the Fens unchanged; indeed, the perceived image of the landscape is altered radically from that of a dismal borderland to a place of Christian worship. But the *Vita* does not provide us with a triumphant narrative of human colonization and cultivation of wild, untamed nature; rather, it presents us with a narrative of gradual transformation brought about by a process of substitution of what Latour has referred to as elements in a chain of associations. Guthlac's hill, constructed in the past by now-forgotten human builders, has become the site of demonic visitations; over the course of the narrative, it becomes associated with Guthlac. This process of substitution is enacted not only through Guthlac's struggle with the demons but also through the material allegiances that become visible when Guthlac's house

---

71 Alfred K. Siewers, "Landscapes of Conversion," *Viator* 34 (2003): 1–39, at 25. Siewers's further contention that the barrow "is virtually an empty tomb, a literary cenotaph" (18) would seem to fit better with the Old English *Guthlac A* than with the *Vita*, however.

permits the demons to enter, in a surprising bid for material independence and agency. The permeability of Guthlac's buildings, their failure to clearly demarcate a border between inside and outside, between the human and the natural spheres, continues after the departure of the demons, as shown by the familiarity with which birds are seen to enter them, from jackdaws wreaking havoc to swallows nesting in a basket under the house's eaves.

The *Vita* presents Guthlac as achieving integration with the landscape, in life as in death. In the later part of the narrative, he is shown in near-symbiosis with the animate and inanimate elements of the landscape; after his death, while his soul goes to heaven, his body remains inscribed into the island, cementing its semiotic transformation into a sacred place. Yet if the *Vita* seems to promote a vision of sustained eco-sensibility, this is because it does not provide a narrative of colonization; Guthlac's influence over the landscape's elements is based not on establishing power over them but rather on accepting the equilibrium that seems to characterize the Fens. Guthlac replaces the demons, but the act of substitution is presented as having no physical consequences for the environment. The Fens' various *frequentatores* – whether exploiters of its resources, pilgrims, or others – are merely that, *frequentatores*, and through their repeated activities they maintain the landscape's fragile equilibrium.

The *Vita Guthlaci*, then, portrays Guthlac as a saint who is particularly attentive to the fragile equilibrium of the ecosystem, even as the work acknowledges processes of adaptation and substitution that transform the material composition and, even more importantly, the meaning and perception of the landscape. In providing an alternative agential possibility that involves interacting with landscape beyond the paradigm of colonization, the text invites ecomaterialist readings that move beyond purely object-oriented "thing studies" by stressing the interdependence of material processes, as well as their inherently temporal character.

Outside the narrative frame of the *Vita*, however, this eco-friendly vision has not proved to be sustainable: with the establishing of a monastic community at Crowland and the growth of a town around it, human actions altered the landscape beyond recognition. The draining of the Fens had effects not only on the landscape's physical appearance but also on its vegetation and its animal population, which formed the basis of the people's sustenance. Oosthuizen gives some idea of the extent to which drainage changed the face of the landscape. Whittlesey Mere (Cambridgeshire), once southern England's largest freshwater lake, extended over an area of around 4,653 hectares in 1610, before drainage began, as deduced from information provided by William Camden. In 1786, its size was about 635 hectares, and today it has vanished completely. Of Ramsey Mere, whose location is preserved in the name of the settlement Ramseymereside (Huntingdonshire), late medieval sources claimed that "fishers and fowlers cease neither by day nor by night to frequent it, yet there is always no little store of fish."[72] Today the lake has disappeared, together with its animal population. The people of the area adapted to these changes, yet as we witness ecological challenges grow in the present day, adaptation to environmental change may come at an increasingly high price. In the light of the Fens' modern development, Guthlac's experience, as described in the *Vita*, assumes the character of an alternative future, an "agential possibility" that never materialized outside the literary frame of the text, a religiously inspired vision of ecological integration that conceives of sainthood not as a form of colonizing the environment but as one of integration into it. In this light, the *Vita Guthlaci* not only testifies to literature's potential to create alternative (literary) worlds, it also demonstrates how, by transforming genre expectations, a literary text may be capable of shaping its own readers' responses to landscape.

---

72 Oosthuizen, *Anglo-Saxon Fenland*, 5.

Falk Quenstedt

7 The Things Narrative Is Made Of: A Latourian Reading of the Description of Enite's Horse in Hartmann of Aue's *Erec*

In the final sections of the Arthurian romance *Erec*, a Middle High German adaptation of Chrétien de Troyes's *Erec et Enide* written by Hartmann of Aue around 1180–1190, a wondrous horse appears, equipped with a full set of incredibly precious, artfully crafted tack.[1] The horse is presented to the heroine Enite as a gift, signaling her rehabilitation as an ideal courtly lady – after a period spent in somewhat less ladylike fashion. Before this, Enite was forced to accompany her husband Erec on a series of knightly adventures in order to restore their reputations, which were damaged when the newlyweds neglected their royal duties, spending all their time in bed.[2] Wasting time and sensual pleasure seem to be serious matters in *Erec*.

Marvelous gifts like Enite's horse are hardly remarkable in courtly narratives. More curious in this case, however, is the fact that the text dedicates almost five hundred lines to describing this sensually appealing animal-material artifact.[3] Taking up theoretical impulses from actor-network theory (ANT) and Bruno Latour, I want to show that this description can be qualified as an *inventory* of courtly narrative: in pointing out different entities that form part of this art or craft, the description seeks to account for the specific "actors" and "associations" peculiar to it. Furthermore, this inventory, in presenting courtly narrative as a form of art or craft requiring certain materials and skills for its accomplishment, also points to the peculiar forms of sensory experience it provokes and its peculiar "mode of existence."[4] By account-

---

1 I quote from Hartmann von Aue, *Erec: Text und Kommentar*, ed. Manfred Günter Scholz, trans. Susanne Held (Frankfurt: Deutscher Klassiker-Verlag, 2004). The work is cited by line number in the running text. The English translation is quoted from Hartmann von Aue, *Erec*, ed. and trans. Cyril Edwards, vol. 5 of *German Romance* (Rochester, NY: D. S. Brewer, 2014). As the line numbers in the German edition and the edition by Edwards deviate from each other, the respective passages in Edwards's edition can be found referenced by page number, also directly in the text. Any glosses and translations not cited from Edwards's edition are my own.
2 For a concise English summary of the plot, see Francis G. Gentry, "The Two-Fold Path: Erec and Enite on the Road to Wisdom," in *A Companion to the Works of Hartmann von Aue*, ed. Francis G. Gentry (Rochester, NY: Camden House, 2005), 93–104, at 94.
3 This is more than ten times the length of text devoted to it in the Old French source. See Alois Wolf, "Hartmann von Aue and Chrétien de Troyes: Respective Approaches to the Matter of Britain," in Gentry, *Companion*, 43–70, at 58.
4 Latour uses the term "modes of existence" in his more recent work (see the discussion below) to distinguish between different procedures that associate entities following different "paths of veridiction." See Bruno Latour, *An Inquiry into Modes of Existence: An Anthropology of the Moderns* (Cambridge, MA: Harvard University Press, 2013), 56: "All [modes of existence] depend on a certain amount of equipment, a certain number of regroupings, expert opinions, instruments, judgments

https://doi.org/10.1515/9783110742985-010

ing for the many "things" that courtly narrative is made of (with "thing" understood not as an isolated object but as a material/immaterial site of intertwining, of assembling, of quarreling, that only comes to the fore because it takes part in an actor network), the text tries to specify and develop a set of criteria by which courtly narrative should be judged.[5] In so doing, it stresses the experience of time in particular as one aspect of the sensual experience of narrative.

Hartmann's description of the horse demonstrates many characteristics of the classical and medieval tradition of ekphrasis, but departs from it in unusual directions too.[6] Parts of the passage are concerned with the (imagined) creation or manufacturing of the artifact, which includes not only the saddlery but the horse itself as well: both are intertwined with each other, forming an artwork as a whole, an assemblage of different entities. Furthermore, the description noticeably focuses on the various materials used in this artifact. At one point, a debate flares up between the narrator and a fictional listener as to what exact materials make up the saddle and how they are combined. These disturbances of the narrative, time and again postponing Erec's departure and the advancement of the plot, are all the more puzzling in the light of the romance's apparent reservations about wasting time. What, then, is the function of these overlong digressions?

The passage has been extensively studied, resulting in many different readings.[7] Most influential are interpretations that see the description primarily as a self-reflexive comment on the poetics of the text itself, or as an early reflection or expression of

---

whose arrangement and use make it possible to identify in each order of truth what it means to 'speak truths' and to 'speak untruths.' [...] On each path of veridiction, we will be able to ask that the conditions that must be met for someone to speak truths or untruths be specified according to its mode." As the book forms only one part of a broader project, see also the website http://modesofexistence.org/.

5 The term *things* is considered by Latour in "From Realpolitik to Dingpolitik or How to Make Things Public," in *Making Things Public: Atmospheres of Democracy*, ed. Bruno Latour and Peter Weibel (Cambridge, MA: MIT Press; Karlsruhe: Center for Art and Media, 2005), 14–41, at 22–23. Here Latour conceives of "things" as assemblies, as "matters of concern" constituted by complex interplays between different actors. Although this understanding is reminiscent of Heidegger's etymology-based concept of the thing, it is not to be misunderstood as "Heideggerian." As Latour clarifies: "*Gatherings* is the translation that Heidegger used, to talk about those Things, those sites able to assemble mortals and gods, humans and non-humans. There is more than a little irony in extending this meaning to what Heidegger and his followers loved to hate, namely science, technology, commerce, industry and popular culture" ("From Realpolitik to Dingpolitik," 23).

6 Kathryn Starkey, "Time Travel: Ekphrasis and Narrative in Medieval German Literature," in *Anschauung und Anschaulichkeit: Visualisierung im Wahrnehmen, Lesen und Denken*, ed. Hans Adler and Sabine Gross (Paderborn: Wilhelm Fink, 2016), 181–184; Haiko Wandhoff, *Ekphrasis: Kunstbeschreibungen und virtuelle Räume in der Literatur des Mittelalters* (Berlin: De Gruyter, 2003), 157–180.

7 For a general overview, see the extensive commentary in Hartmann von Aue, *Erec*, ed. Scholz, 898–932.

fiction or fictionality.[8] Recent research has treated the description as a staging of the specific mastery ("meisterschaft") of the poet, who shows his skills as narrator in negotiation with those employed in other arts and media.[9] The tendency to adhere to the above readings means, however, that other aspects of the description have not been sufficiently considered: namely, first, its interest in the multiplicity and diversity of entities that take part in the process of narration and the art of storytelling in general; and second, the description's links to other digressive passages in the same work that deal with marvels and the question of their credibility.

In my view, these two aspects – the text's self-reflexive notion of courtly narrative and of the corresponding forms of material interplay, and the various discussions of the marvelous – are interconnected. While other narratives of the time, particularly when dealing with marvels, try to legitimize themselves by claiming their veracity, Hartmann's description of the horse seems to suggest that such attempts at authentication are completely beside the point, precisely because they ignore what narrative actually is – or rather, what it is *made of*. Therefore, I argue that the connection between portrayals of materiality and discussions of the marvelous in the description of Enite's horse is of utter importance for an understanding of the passage and has to be scrutinized in more detail.[10]

One may object that this coherence could also be described – and probably more effectively – as a historically and culturally specific instance of fictionality.[11] However, I take a Latourian approach here, because it aids in concentrating on the things

8 For a survey of recent literature, see Joachim Hamm, "'Meister Umbrîz': Zu Beschreibungskunst und Selbstreflexion in Hartmanns 'Erec,'" in *Vom Verstehen deutscher Texte des Mittelalters aus der europäischen Kultur*, ed. Dorothea Klein and Elisabeth Schmid (Würzburg: Königshausen & Neumann, 2011), 191–218, at 192–195. Studies on *Erec* and fictionality include Ingrid Strasser, "Fiktion und ihre Vermittlung in Hartmanns Erec-Roman," in *Fiktionalität im Artusroman*, ed. Volker Mertens and Friedrich Wolfzettel (Tübingen: Niemeyer, 1993), 63–83; and Walter Haug, "Die Entdeckung der Fiktionalität," in *Die Wahrheit der Fiktion: Studien zur weltlichen und geistlichen Literatur des Mittelalters und der frühen Neuzeit* (Tübingen: Niemeyer, 2003), 128–144.
9 See Susanne Bürkle, "'Kunst'-Reflexion aus dem Geiste der 'descriptio': Enites Pferd und der Diskurs artistischer 'meisterschaft,'" in *Das fremde Schöne*, ed. Manuel Braun and Christopher John Young (Berlin: De Gruyter, 2007), 143–170; J. Hamm, "Meister Umbrîz"; Mireille Schnyder, "Der unfeste Text: Mittelalterliche 'Audiovisualität'?," in *Der unfeste Text: Perspektiven auf einen literatur- und kulturwissenschaftlichen Leitbegriff*, ed. Barbara Sabel and André Bucher (Würzburg: Königshausen & Neumann, 2001), 132–153; Gerhard Wolf, "'bildes rehte brechen': Überlegungen zu Wahrnehmung und Beschreibungen in Hartmanns 'Erec,'" in *Beschreibend wahrnehmen – wahrnehmend beschreiben: Sprachliche und ästhetische Aspekte kognitiver Prozesse*, ed. Peter Klotz and Christine Lubkoll (Freiburg: Rombach, 2005), 167–188; Wandhoff, *Ekphrasis*, 170.
10 Volker Mertens suggests that the passage can be read as "ein poetologischer Metatext über die Möglichkeiten des Erzählens" (a poetological metatext dealing with the capabilities of narrative). Hartmann von Aue, *Erec: Mittelhochdeutsch – Neuhochdeutsch*, ed. and trans. Volker Mertens (Stuttgart: Reclam, 2008), 681.
11 For a discussion of historically and culturally different premodern fictionalities, see the essays recently collected in Bruce Holsinger, ed., "Medieval Fictionalities: An NHL Forum," special issue, *New Literary History* 51, no. 1 (2020).

and the interrelations between them that the description itself draws attention to, before bringing established concepts like fiction or fictionality into play. The latter concepts – even when thoroughly historicized – stem from contexts of modern literature and prescribe certain paths of scrutiny that center primarily on notions of credibility and probability, leaving questions of materiality and sensual experience aside. Since the description of Enite's horse draws together so many different things and themes in apparently inexplicable ways, a reading that "follows the actors" first – as ANT demands – seems eminently useful to me.

Controversies: Latourian Preliminaries

Two aspects of Latourian theory are especially important for my reading: Latour's understanding of action as fundamentally composite, with "controversies" recognized as sites for the identification of participating "actors"; and his differentiation between different "modes of existence."

As far as the first aspect is concerned, Latour understands action as being made possible by a multiplicity of associations among different entities. To describe such an actor network adequately, as many as possible of the entities that make a difference in it have to be accounted for.[12] Yet, given that many of these entities act behind the scenes – since social practices are stabilized by protocols of social etiquette, political institutions, scientific routines, logistical operations, juridical procedures, or computerized techniques – how can they be made visible? Latour describes various situations in which such silent "intermediaries" can become "full-blown mediators." Such situations tend to be different types of "accidents, breakdowns, and strikes."[13] Latour calls them "controversies" and gives a rather insensitive example: "Those who watched the *Columbia* shuttle instantly transformed from the most complicated human instrument ever assembled to a rain of debris falling over Texas will realize how quickly objects flip-flop their mode of existence."[14] I argue that Hartmann's description is just such a controversy, or – as I would call it instead – a staged disturbance, one that is itself full of further disturbances. By adding more and more entities to the inventory, this disturbance in the unfolding of the narrative renders visible the things that make a difference in the actor network of courtly narrative.

---

12 Latour thereby avoids questions of intentionality: "agency" can be attributed not only to humans but also to things. This is not to say that they act by themselves. What Latour stresses is that nothing acts completely autonomously, that action is always distributed among a network of different actors attached to each other. Bruno Latour, *Reassembling the Social: An Introduction to Actor-Network-Theory* (Oxford: Oxford University Press, 2007), 47.

13 Latour, *Reassembling the Social*, 81.

14 Latour, 81.

The second aspect of Latourian theory I am concerned with is the notion of "modes of existence," which leads me to his more recent work.[15] With this term Latour addresses certain limitations that he perceives in ANT, especially its tendency to level out dissimilarities. As he remarks in an interview: "[ANT] was very good at giving freedom of movement but very bad at defining differences."[16] Modes of existence can be understood as different types of connecting that are at the same time procedures of veridiction.[17] In order to observe different modes of existence at work, Latour again considers the question of controversies. In this case he is interested in "category mistakes," a term he borrows from Gilbert Ryle.[18] If different modes of existence are mixed up with each other – which is not an exception but rather the rule – category mistakes happen and give rise to controversies or disturbances.[19]

For Latour, the best way of finding out about different modes of existence is to scrutinize such "crossings" between them and the category mistakes these crossings produce.[20] Furthermore, Latour (re)connects the analysis of different modes of veracity with the material actor networks that are necessary to create, sustain, and stabilize them. Rita Felski lays out why the concept of modes of existence can be helpful for literary studies:

> In contrast to cartographic metaphors such as field or domain, with their connotations of discrete and bounded spaces, mode of existence identifies differences without delineating borders. We can agree, for example, that literary texts are connected to countless things that are not literature, while also acknowledging that there cluster around literature certain ways of talking,

---

15 See Latour, *Modes of Existence*.

16 John Tresch and Bruno Latour, "Another Turn after ANT: An Interview with Bruno Latour," *Social Studies of Science* 43, no. 2 (1 April 2013): 302–313, at 304. See also Lars Gertenbach and Henning Laux, *Zur Aktualität von Bruno Latour: Einführung in sein Werk* (Wiesbaden: Springer VS, 2019), 157.

17 "Modes of existence" can designate different social fields like religion, jurisdiction, or politics, but also types of reference and connections like "reproduction," "attachment," "network," or "double click." See the table of fifteen modes of existence at the end of Latour, *Modes of Existence*, 488–489.

18 Latour, *Modes of Existence*, 17.

19 A case in point from recent German literary history would be the banning of Maxim Biller's novel *Esra* (2003). The German Federal Constitutional Court banned the novel from being published in 2007 because of an invasion of privacy. Many authors, publishers, and critics saw this juridical prohibition as a case of censorship of a literary work. The example shows how jurisprudence and values of modern literature are two different but interconnected modes of existence, and in the controversy at hand, their differing values and paths of veridiction come to the fore. See Ralf Grüttemeier, "Literature Losing Legal Ground in Germany? The Case of Maxim Biller's 'Esra' (2003–2009)," in *Literary Trials: "Exceptio Artis" and Theories of Literature in Court*, ed. Ralf Grüttemeier (New York: Bloomsbury Academic, 2016), 141–158.

20 Sociological theories of difference (connected to names such as Luhmann, Bourdieu, and Boltanski/Thévenot) have extensively dealt with such epistemic differences between different social spheres, but always rather abstractly and in disconnection from material realms. See Gertenbach and Laux, *Aktualität*, 150.

experiencing, acting, interpreting, and evaluating. It is crucial, Latour remarks, to speak about a mode of existence in its own language: to engage its criteria of verification and value, its conditions of felicity and unfelicity.[21]

Latour's concept of modes of existence helps us understand what the description of Enite's horse does: in order to uncover how courtly narrative works, not only does the description repeatedly stage disturbances to account for associated actors, it also orchestrates category mistakes, especially regarding representations of the marvelous.

That is why the treatment of the marvelous in *Erec* is so relevant in this regard. Other vernacular texts of the time frequently dramatize the problem of the veracity of marvels and use particular rhetorical and narrative techniques to claim their truth-value, not least to legitimize themselves. Hartmann's description – that is, his inventory of narrative – polemicizes against that type of poetics of the marvelous: in the process of pointing to the many things narrative is made of, the description causes courtly narrative itself to become visible as a mode of existence with specific procedures of veridiction and felicity conditions, and in doing so, it also insinuates that the question of the veracity of marvels is simply a category mistake.

Moreover, the description repeatedly stresses that courtly narrative engenders peculiar sensory experiences in its audience, which are shaped by narrative's various constituents. This is again crucial for the question of its felicity conditions: it is not the veracity of the story and the marvels presented in it that are important; rather, it is the way the story unfolds. One of the most fundamental constituents of narrative is time, for narrative events must unfold in some temporal relation to each other. The passage describing Enite's horse repeatedly stresses temporality. In fact, the entire story unfolds because its protagonists have been wasting time. Seen from the perspective of plot progression, the ekphrasis and its digressive disturbances are themselves a waste of time, since they interrupt the temporal unfolding of narrative events.[22] Thus, the performative contradiction that appears repeatedly when the narrator proclaims that he will cut the description short, only to prolong it further, is not just a stock rhetorical flourish. It aims to make the sensual experience of time palpable. And I do mean palpable: Hartmann's description doesn't just point to narrative's peculiar capabilities to shorten or prolong the (experience of the) passing of time, it lets the audience actually feel this. The disturbances the text deploys even seem to aim at having a frustrating effect.[23] They create a tension between a state of impatience – an urgent desire to move on – and a situation in which one is forced to endure delay after delay. This tension is mirrored on the level of plot: right before the overlong description, Erec wishes to leave the castle, where the horse is present-

---

21 Rita Felski, "Latour and Literary Studies," *PMLA* 130, no. 3 (2015): 737–743, at 738–739.
22 See Starkey, "Time Travel," 184.
23 Geoffrey See, "'Wes möhten si langer bîten?': Narrative Digressions in Hartmann von Aue's 'Erec,'" *Neuphilologische Mitteilungen* 96, no. 4 (1995): 335–349, at 341.

ed to Enite, as soon as possible.[24] Thus the text not only tries the patience of its recipients, but also of its protagonist.

Category Mistakes: Negotiating the Marvelous

How exactly, then, is the description connected to negotiations of the marvelous? A first connection can be seen on the level of plot. Before Enite receives the gift of the horse and the description is set in motion, the protagonist couple spends fourteen days in Penefrec, the castle of the dwarf king Guivreiz. Erec is wounded, and the king's two sisters treat him with the help of a marvelous bandage or plaster ("phlaster"; line 5132). This same bandage was used earlier in the narrative at Arthur's court, but with limited success. This time, however, it works. After recovering, Erec – who throughout the entire narrative vehemently rejects any kind of comfort – insists that they leave as soon as possible (lines 7260–7264). As Enite earlier lost her own horse, Guivreiz's two sisters present her with the wondrous horse (lines 7274–7280). From the beginning of the description, the text signals that the horse is a being that is generated by narrative discourse. This is indicated already by its status as a gift given by the two sisters of the dwarf king Guivreiz, which associates the horse with an imaginary realm.

How does the description of the horse itself signal its imaginary status? The passage begins with the assertion that this horse is unlike any other, especially in its beauty (lines 7342–7346). The horse's coat is white on one side and black on the other, with the two sides separated by a finger-thick green line (line 7313) that is compared to a brushstroke ("penselstrich"; line 7317). The line encircles the eyes of the horse and runs along its entire body, bisecting it. It proceeds from the horse's muzzle up to the gap between its ears, over its mane, down to its buttocks, and up again to chest and forehead (lines 7318–7323). The comparison with a brushstroke and the animal's overall unlikely appearance together mark the horse as a work of art, a "Kunst-Tier."[25] This impression is further reinforced by the statements that it is "soft-haired" (line 7383) and that riding it feels like floating ("sweben"; line 7795). In the description of its white left flank (lines 7294–7299), the intensity of the horse's beauty is emphasized and linked to temporality: it dazzles the eyes (line 7296) and can be looked at only for a short amount of time (line 7298). In the description of the opposite, black flank, Hartmann uses formulations that invoke visual sensations of contrast and reflection ("ze widerstrîte / gekêret"; line 7300). Thus, an ephemeral visual experience of the horse is created, and at the same time mediated as such, foregrounding its illusionary status.

---

24 See Scholz's commentary in Hartmann von Aue, *Erec*, ed. Scholz, 898.
25 Christoph Huber, "Wilde Rede bei Hartmann von Aue? Beobachtungen zum 'Erec,'" in *"wildekeit": Spielräume literarischer obscuritas im Mittelalter; Zürcher Kolloquium 2016*, ed. Susanne Köbele et al. (Berlin: Erich Schmidt, 2018), 119–134, at 123.

The imaginary production of a marvelous horse whose beauty has dazzling, blinding effects can even at this stage be understood as a playful demonstration of what narrative is capable of.[26] Because the text says that the account given of the horse is based on the telling of a "master" (line 7299), the whole scene is marked as being mediated through storytelling. Further support for this assumption comes from reflections on the part of the narrator. He posits two juxtaposed realms of origin for the horse: on the one hand, the mind of a scholar, and on the other, a mountainous world where dwarfs dwell.[27]

After having described these features, the narrator announces that he will say more about the horse, thus drawing attention to his own discourse (lines 7336–7337). He calls the horse desirable ("erwünschet"; line 7340) and gives a long description of its perfect proportions (lines 7340–7365), culminating in the comment that even if a groom were never to brush its coat, the coat would still remain fair and smooth ("schœne und sleht"; line 7365). Overall, the horse has been made to delight the audience ("daz es iuch wol mohte lüsten"; line 7354) "there" as well as "here" ("geschaffen dort unde hie"; line 7354) – meaning in the diegesis as well as in the moment of narration.

The narrator also makes an extended playful comparison describing how the horse might have been constructed: If a "werltwîser man" (world-wise man) with knowledge of all things – presumably a scholar – sat and reflected for eight whole years on the question of how a beautiful and perfect horse might look, examining ("erpruofte") it meticulously in his mind, he would create exactly the same horse as this one (lines 7366–7376).[28] Moreover, if this master had the power ("gewalt"; lines 7377, 7383) to permanently place the envisioned horse ("daz ez belibe stæte"; line 7379) right before himself ("daz er vür sich stalte"; line 7382), he would not change a single hair. This description of a creation *in potentia*, a mental invention of the horse, underlines the perfection of the animal and also insinuates its imagina-

---

26 On the connection between imagination and wonder in medieval philosophy, see Michelle Karnes, "Marvels in the Medieval Imagination," *Speculum* 90, no. 2 (2015): 327–365. For an examination of a literary treatment of this connection (which bears some resemblance to Hartmann's playful account of the marvelous horse), see also Michelle Karnes, "Wonder, Marvels, and Metaphor in the *Squire's Tale*," *ELH* 82, no. 2 (11 June 2015): 461–490.

27 See Huber, "Wilde Rede," 123–124.

28 For the identification with a scholar, see Starkey, "Time Travel," 184. Worstbrock suggests that the passage depicts the typical process of manufacturing an artwork as contemporaneous poetical treatises (like Geoffrey of Vinsauf's *Poetria nova*) conceive it. According to these treatises, there is always a planning phase followed by a period of execution. See Franz Josef Worstbrock, "Wiedererzählen und Übersetzen," in *Mittelalter und frühe Neuzeit: Übergänge, Umbrüche und Neuansätze*, ed. Walter Haug (Tübingen: Niemeyer, 1999), 128–142, at 137. The same argument is already present in Franz Josef Worstbrock, "Dilatatio Materiae: Zur Poetik des 'Erec' Hartmanns von Aue," *Frühmittelalterliche Studien* 19, no. 1 (1985): 1–30, at 10.

ry status.[29] Nevertheless, the horse is there – be it in the mind of the scholar or the mind of the audience. It is existent as an imagined being, formed by the narrative.

After this, a second origin is established. This origin is preceded by an anticipated objection by a potential recipient who does not believe what is being presented by the text:

> giht ieman: "er enhât niht wâr",
> dem bescheide ich die rede baz,
> daz er rehte erkenne daz
> diu rede wese ungelogen.
> ez [the horse] enwas dâ heime niht erzogen.
> (lines 7389 – 7393)

> (If anyone says: "He's not telling the truth,"
> I will so improve on my wording
> that he must rightly recognise
> that what I say is no lie.
> That horse was not reared back home.)
> (trans. Edwards, 389)

Similar reactions to anticipated objections can be frequently found in other contemporaneous texts when they deal with wondrous phenomena. Hartmann's narrator goes on to tell an origin story about the horse in order to prove that his account is true. Already at this point, in light of the preceding passages, one wonders what the term "wâr" (true) can possibly signify here. The story goes as follows: Guivreiz has taken the horse from another dwarf, though not a cultivated one like himself, but rather a "wild dwarf before a hollow hill" ("wilden getwerge / vor einem holen berge") (trans. Edwards, 398; lines 7396 – 7397) who left the horse unattended, tied to a branch. When he becomes aware of the theft, the wild dwarf starts to scream and cry (line 7412), and even offers Guivreiz three thousand gold marks (line 7417). But the king remains unpersuaded and takes the horse with him. When he leaves, the dwarf's cries of grief reverberate for a long time throughout the mountains (lines 7423 – 7425).

This story does not convincingly confirm the real existence of the horse. Furthermore, the motif of a wild dwarf in a hollow mountain who is the keeper of a marvelous treasure – found, for example, in the *Nibelungenlied* – would have been recognizable to Hartmann's contemporaries.[30] In its prosaic manner, however, this telling is not apt to establish the kind of mythical truth associated with heroic epic, even if the narrator claims it does. Rather, it has a comical effect.[31] Thus, a story that is claimed to function as a device of authentication accomplishes just

---

29 Huber, "Wilde Rede," 123.
30 See Mertens's commentary in Hartmann von Aue, *Erec*, ed. Mertens, 682.
31 See also Bürkle, "'Kunst'-Reflexion," 168. Likewise, Kathryn Starkey points out that "any claim to historical veracity in the story must be interpreted as tongue in cheek" ("Time Travel," 187).

the opposite. It reveals that the horse is not only imagined but also informed by earlier narrations. Like the description itself, it points back to the realm of the manifold stuff of storytelling.[32] Moreover, it shows that the question of whether the horse is real or a lie is simply the wrong one to ask about a narrative being – in other words, a category mistake. In courtly narrative, Hartmann seems to say, it makes no sense to insist on the veracity of such wonders.

However, medieval discourses on the marvelous, including those in other courtly narratives, do exactly that. They regularly include discussions of the veracity of wonders and develop complex rhetorical and narrative techniques to claim the truth-value of the marvels they recount. Frequently, such claims respond to anticipated, sometimes openly dramatized, accusations of lying, just as in the description of Enite's horse.[33] This holds true not only for narratives in the vernacular of the time (such as the Middle High German *Herzog Ernst*, the *Straßburger Alexander*, or the version of the *Brandan* narrative known as the *Reise-Fassung*) but also for Latin courtly texts like the *Otia imperialia* by Gervase of Tilbury.[34] In one of the *Otia*'s prefaces, Gervase distinguishes between the marvelous phenomena that he reports having either seen with his own eyes or heard from reliable sources – including, for instance, werewolves and advice-giving horses – and the "crude falsehoods of idle tales" ("importunis fabularum mendaciis") or "lying fictions of players" ("mimorum mendaciis").[35] Gervase's reflections on wonders suggest that verifying marvels is of such great concern because only authentic *mirabilia* were thought to be capable, or worthy, of triggering astonishment.[36]

The poem *Erec*, in my opinion, satirizes such techniques. This can also be seen in the passage about the wondrous bandage (lines 5132–5245): in this earlier digression, the narrator, in a tongue-in-cheek manner, talks about the qualities of the bandage and the fact that it was originally in the possession of a diabolical fairy

---

32 Wandhoff, *Ekphrasis*, 170, suggests that the description indicates that the stuff or material that the horse is made of ("[der eigentliche] Stoff aus dem das Pferd gemacht ist") is "imagination produced by words" ("durch Worte erzeugte Imagination"). I would argue that not just words are at stake here, but also their configuration as narrative.

33 Such accusations are a rhetorical commonplace in the clerical discourse on *fabula*: see Dennis Howard Green, *The Beginnings of Medieval Romance: Fact and Fiction, 1150–1220* (Cambridge: Cambridge University Press, 2002), 31–34.

34 The latter book was dedicated to Emperor Otto IV in 1214 but used materials that Gervase had already begun to gather during his time as a courtier at the Anglo-Norman court in the 1180s. See Gervase of Tilbury, *Otia imperialia: Recreation for an Emperor*, ed. S. E. Banks and J. W. Binns, Oxford Medieval Texts (Oxford: Clarendon Press, 2002), xxxix.

35 Gervase of Tilbury, *Otia imperialia*, 558–559, 562–563. For werewolves and advice-giving horses, see Gervase of Tilbury, chs. 120 ("De hominibus qui fiunt lupi") and 107 ("De equo Girardi de Cabreria").

36 See Caroline Walker Bynum, "Wonder: Presidential Address Delivered at the American Historical Association Annual Meeting in New York on January 3, 1997," *American Historical Review* 102, no. 1 (1997): 1–26, at 24.

with wondrous skills named Fâmurgân.[37] That passage makes the text's concern with the theme of the marvelous very explicit, mentioning "wonder" multiple times (lines 5153, 5162, 5198).[38]

The horse's description begins with an explicit mention of this magical plaster (lines 7225–7228), connecting both passages to each other. Furthermore, many thematic and motific analogies show that the same problems are at stake in the digressions about Fâmurgân's plaster and Enite's horse. Both of these marvels are connected to female figures and sisters of kings. A discourse related to mastery is present, since Fâmurgân is called a "meisterinne" (line 5229) and hypothetical scholars are introduced using analogous wording ("wîser man" and "werltwîser man"). Dubious stories are told in order to claim the truth of the wondrous objects. It is playfully insinuated that both Fâmurgân's and the horse's existences are only momentary and dependent on perception: the horse's flank dazzles the eyes and can be looked at only briefly, while it is said about Fâmurgân that she could circumnavigate the world in an instant: "ê ich die hant umb kêrte / oder zuo geslüege die brâ, / sô vuor si hin und schein doch sâ" ("Before I could turn over my hand / or might close my eyes / she had departed and yet was back at once") (lines 5173–5175; trans. Edwards, 279). What is more, both figures are connected to the verb "sweben" (to hover, to float): Fâmurgân could hover on and beneath the waves (lines 5177–5179), while riding the horse feels like "floating on smooth waters" (trans. Edwards, 411) (line 7791; see also lines 7446–7449). Hence, as discussions of the marvelous that point to its unreal status, and as playful disturbances of the narration that point to the different constituents that make up narrative (particularly temporal aspects), both passages form a cohesive unit.

Hartmann's discussion of the marvelous is continued with the description of the wondrous horse's tack – namely, the treatment of the saddlecloth (lines 7545–7581). The saddlecloth is part of a complex pictorial program that spans different parts of the horse's furnishings. Ivory relief carvings on the saddle tell "the long song of Troy" (line 7546; "daz lange liet von Troiâ"). On the front "stands" ("stount," as if speaking of letters forming a text) the story of the destruction of Troy; on the back is engraved ("ergraben"; line 7564) the tale of how Aeneas left Dido, married Lavinia, and became the sovereign.[39] Pictures on the saddle pillow illustrate the story of Pyramus and Thisbe (lines 7709–7713). Since the pictures are referred to as though they

---

37 The excursus has been read in the context of the marvelous in Manuela Niesner, "Das Wunderbare in der 'Conjointure': Zur poetologischen Aussage des Feimurgan-Exkurses in Hartmanns 'Erec,'" *Zeitschrift für deutsches Altertum und deutsche Literatur* 137, no. 2 (2008): 137–157.

38 At the beginning of the horse's description, such lexical markers of the marvelous are not as obvious, but they are present. For example, the horse is designated as a "seltsæniu dinc" (line 7324), and at the end of the description the narrator remarks that there are many more "wunder" (line 7434) he might report about this horse.

39 Middle High German *stuont*, like Modern German *stehen* (Eng. "to stand"), can refer to something that is written in a text.

are inscriptions, and because all of them tell stories, the attention is turned to Hartmann's story itself. Furthermore, all of these pictorial elements found on the saddlery connect Erec and Enite to other couples in the realm of storytelling.[40] The saddlecloth depicts a cosmological program, structured by the classical elements of
earth, water, wind, and fire (line 7650). To begin with, the blanket is introduced
with markers of the marvelous: "dâ stuonden an besunder / aller werlde wunder"
("On it were embroidered / all the world's wonders") (lines 7588–7589; trans. Edwards, 399). The description goes on to draw special attention to the lifelike quality
and apparent vitality of its depiction of the animals that inhabit the sea ("rehte sam
si lebeten"; line 7648), and especially to a human figure so lifelike that it appears as
if it might start to speak and, in so doing, "break the law of image" ("sam si wolde
sprechen / und bildes reht brechen"; line 7607–7608). A depiction of a human so
animated that it even speaks is not within the abilities of pictorial crafts, at least
not in the twelfth century. Yet a story has the force to form a mental image of
such a speaking artificial figure. This figure's connection to language points to linguistic crafts and foregrounds its status as something narrated. Thus, in analogy
to (and competition with) other crafts or arts, the description of the saddlery points
to different aspects of narrative: First, narrative is formed of a story that must be written down and is informed by a tradition of earlier narratives. Second, it is capable of
evoking vivid images.

In the passage describing the sea creatures so vividly depicted on the blanket, an
excursus on "merwunder" (wonders of the sea) occurs which again picks up the comical tone of earlier digressions on marvels in the text. Here the narrator, as in the case
of his discussion of Fâmurgân's plaster, starts referring to himself and his knowledge, and he evokes a knowledge seeker striving for certainty. In the earlier excursus,
he states that if someone were to look for the fairy's wondrous powers in medical
books ("arzâtbuochen"; line 5239), his search would be to no avail. This time,
though, the narrator directly addresses the recipients of his text: If "you" ("ir")
want to know all the wonders of the sea, he says, you should go to the sea yourself
and search for them; go and stand by the shore and ask the sea's wonders to come
out. And if these wonders don't comply, as will probably be the case, then you
should go to the bottom of the sea, although this is not advisable, because it engenders great harm and little profit (lines 7610–7638). Finally, he advises the recipients
to give up such curiosity and stay at home ("nû rate ich mînen vriunden sumen, / daz
si die niugerne lân / unde hie heime bestân"; lines 7635–7637).

In both cases, the audience is playfully advised that a quest for such wondrous
knowledge and an effort to verify it would be entirely in vain. Barbara Haupt suggests
that the digression within the description of the saddlecloth alludes to the well-

---

40 On the intermedial or "interartistic" implications of the representation of pictures that tell a story
used within a larger story, see Bürkle, "'Kunst'-Reflexion," 160; and M. Schnyder, "Der unfeste Text,"
148.

known legend of Alexander's journey under the sea in a glass diving bell, and also to the German version of the *Brandan* legend from the second half of the twelfth century, in which Brandan, because he does not believe the marvels he reads in books, has to go on a journey to experience them for himself.[41] The advice to stay at home brings to mind the prologue of *Herzog Ernst*, a text that narrates the travels (presented as historical) of a Bavarian duke in the Far East, where he interacts with monstrous people. That prologue tries to establish its ideal readers by distinguishing between those who have traveled to far and foreign lands and those who stay at home, noting that only the former will be able to properly understand and believe the story.[42] One could read *Erec*'s excursus on "merwunder" as a polemical reply to this performative strategy of claiming the veracity of the narrative: it points out that narrative affords the advantage of allowing you to stay at home and still satisfy your curiosity – as long as you are not seeking mistaken criteria of truth.

By invoking this other textual tradition, Hartmann's excursuses on Fâmurgân and the wonders of the sea polemically point out that those texts are caught in a category mistake.[43] The imaginary creations of narrative are not found in the real world, and hence they cannot be true. Nonetheless, they are valid, albeit on the basis of other criteria. They dwell in their own mode of existence, which can't be addressed by questions of truth or falsehood. This raises the question, then, of what kind of associations their mode of existence is constructed through.

Disturbances: An Inventory of Narrative

Hartmann's text indicates and renders sensually palpable the diverse material and immaterial entities that collectively form courtly narrative. And it does so by using a range of deliberate interruptions or disturbances that seek to irritate the audience. The disturbances, in Latourian terms, provide "figurations" of actions, making the anonymous forces of the process of narrative perceptible, giving them a tangible

---

41 Barbara Haupt, "Literaturgeschichtsschreibung im höfischen Roman: Die Beschreibung von Enites Pferd und Sattelzeug im 'Erec' Hartmanns von Aue," in *Festschrift für Herbert Kolb zu seinem 65. Geburtstag*, ed. Klaus Matzel and Hans-Gert Roloff (Bern: Lang, 1989), 202–220, at 214. Although the motif is missing in the earliest complete German version of the Alexander romance, the so-called *Straßburger Alexander*, it could have been known from other early German texts, such as the *Annolied* or the *Kaiserchronik*, or from Latin sources. For the reference to Brandan, see *Brandan*, lines 17–84, cited from Reinhard Hahn and Christoph Fasbender, eds., *Brandan: Die mitteldeutsche "Reise"-Fassung* (Heidelberg: Winter, 2002).
42 *Herzog Ernst B*, lines 1–30, cited from Cornelia Weber, ed., *Untersuchung und überlieferungskritische Edition des Herzog Ernst B* (Göppingen: Kümmerle, 1994).
43 By stating this, I am not necessarily saying that Hartmann directly responds to the exact texts about wonders that I have mentioned, but rather that they all act within the same discourse, which closely connects the presentation of wonders, the accusation that these are merely lies, and rhetorical and narrative strategies of claiming their truth.

shape, transforming "actants" into "actors."[44] In so doing, the text brings into view a network of associations between different entities peculiar to courtly narrative, which can be understood as a particular mode of existence.

One segment of the description of the horse's tack that recounts the saddle's process of creation shows deliberate interest in the work of yet another "master" and, in addition, the interplay of different materials. Its way of presenting artistic handiwork shows many parallels to the reflections on the creation of the horse:

> ez hete geworht vil manegen tac
> der wercwîseste man
> der satelwerkes ie began,
> ein meister, hiez Umbrîz,
> der doch allen sînen vlîz
> dar leite vür wâr
> wol vierdehalbez jâr,
> unz er in vollebrâhte
> dar nâch als er gedâhte.
> (lines 7467–7475)

> (It [the saddle] had been wrought full many a day
> by the most skilled man
> who ever took to saddle-work,
> a master called Umbriz,
> who invested all his skill
> in it, truly,
> for some three and a half years,
> until he had perfected it
> as he had intended.)
> (trans. Edwards, 393)

The passage resumes the discourse of mastery: the "werltwîse man" (world-wise man) who couldn't think of a more perfect horse is now joined by a "wercwîster man" (work-wise man) named Umbrîz.[45] The mention of a concrete period of time necessary to complete the artwork is a further commonality between the descriptions of the horse and the saddle. The name Umbrîz – if not a (deliberate?) misunderstanding of Chrétien's "uns brez taillierres" (a Breton sculptor) – seems to emphasize an act of planning or designing (as in Ger. *Umriss* or *umreißen*: Eng. "outline," "to outline").[46] This is reminiscent of Geoffrey of Vinsauf's advice (in his *Poetria nova*) to "mentally outline" a work of poetry before starting to write it down, and to "first cir-

---

44 On "figuration" and the distinction between "actors" and "actants," see Latour, *Reassembling the Social*, 54–55. In this passage Latour indicates his theoretical indebtedness to the study of literature and art – namely, to the work of the semioticians Algirdas Julien Greimas and Louis Marin. He also points out the significance of narrative for his work, quoting from a novel by Richard Powers: see Latour, 56.

45 On the imagery of the poet as a "homo faber," see J. Hamm, "Meister Umbrîz," 210–214.

46 For the possible source in Chrétien's phrase, see Hartmann von Aue, *Erec*, ed. Edwards, 393n1.

cle the whole extent of the material."[47] It has been read in this regard as an intertextual reference to Heinrich von Veldeke's *Eneas*, like *Erec* a founding text of Middle High German courtly literature. In that romance – during its long description of the marvelous tomb of Camilla – a master figure named Geometras appears. "Umbrîz" would be a possible Middle High German translation of that name.[48] Furthermore, because the term also connotes circularity (as in Ger. *umkreisen*: Eng. "to circle"), the name can also be seen as having cosmological associations.[49] Finally, the name could refer to the Latin *umbra* (shadow, darkness), as some of this word's plural forms (dat., abl., loc. *umbris*: "from, in, into the shadows") are homonymous with Umbrîz, which thus might denote "the one (speaking) from, out of, or into the shadows."[50] This interpretation would be congruent not only with the *gestus* of the whole description, playing with forms of veiling and unveiling, but also with recent readings of the passage as an application of a poetics of *obscuritas*.[51]

I want to show that the description of the saddle – like that of the horse – repeatedly signals that the artifact and its creation can be read as an analogy to narrative. Since exact translatability between the elements that form part of the saddle and the elements of the art of narrative is, in my view, not intended, the comparison does not qualify as allegory. Rather, the passage draws a somewhat loose comparison between the creative processes of the different crafts or arts – a comparison, however, that emphasizes the interplay of different material and immaterial entities in all of these processes:

> er [the saddle] was von helfenbeine
> und von edelem gesteine
> und ouch von dem besten golde
> daz ie werden solde
> geliutert in dem viure:
> valsch was im tiure.
> von disen mâterjen drin
> sô hâte des meisters sin
> geprüevet diz gereite
> mit grôzer wîsheite.
> er gap dem helfenbeine
> und dâ bî dem gesteine
> sîn gevellige stat,
> als in diu gevuoge bat.
> er muosete dar under

47 Geoffrey of Vinsauf, *Poetria nova of Geoffrey of Vinsauf*, trans. Margaret F. Nims (Toronto: Pontifical Institute of Mediaeval Studies, 1967), 17.
48 J. Hamm, "Meister Umbrîz," 214–217.
49 J. Hamm, 214.
50 I owe this suggestion, which was made during the workshop at Stanford University, to Björn Buschbeck. To my knowledge, the connection of the name Umbrîz to Lat. *umbra* has not been considered before this.
51 See Huber, "Wilde Rede."

den goltlîm besunder,
daz muoste daz werc zesamene haben.
(lines 7528–7544)

(It [the saddle] was of ivory
and of precious stones
and of the best gold
that was ever to be
purified in fire –
it lacked any impurity.
The master's cunning
with great wisdom
had perfected that saddle
from those materials.
He gave both the ivory
and the jewels
their due place,
as fitness required of him.
He put in a separate inlay
of gold solder
to hold the work together.)
(trans. Edwards, 395–396)

Tellingly, the text uses the Latin loanword "mâterjen" in describing the process of creation, pointing to contexts of medieval poetic theory in which the term *materia* was crucial, since medieval poetry was considered for the most part to be a process of reconfiguring preexisting material.[52] Thereby, it suggests that the work of the craftsman who forms the saddlery out of different materials is analogous to the work of the author of a text.[53] If the latter can be understood as a practice that likewise brings different "materiae" together in order to form a new whole, the description could be read as a comment on intertextuality (which, as the many references to other texts and stories show, plays a significant role in *Erec*). But the analogy of artisanal and poetical "mâterjen" could also be read in a broader sense – namely, as identifying different entities interacting in the creation of these arts.

Moreover, in this passage it is not solely the "creative subject," the master craftsman, who determines the process of the saddle's creation. Rather, the master is guided (and lets himself be guided) in the process of combining the materials by both theoretical and practical knowledge, and by the "gevellige stat" and the "gevuoge"

---

52 See poetic treatises such as the *Ars versificatoria* of Matthew of Vendôme (ca. 1175) or the *Poetria nova* of Geoffrey of Vinsauf (ca. 1210), pointed out in Worstbrock, "Dilatatio Materiae," 4, 9, 21–27. Both treatises were influenced by the anonymous so-called "materia" commentary (between 1125 and 1175): see Rita Copeland and Ineke Sluiter, eds., *Medieval Grammar and Rhetoric: Language Arts and Literary Theory, AD 300–1475* (Oxford: Oxford University Press, 2009), 551–556.
53 See Sonja Glauch, "Inszenierungen der Unsagbarkeit: Rhetorik und Reflexion im höfischen Roman," *Zeitschrift für deutsches Altertum und deutsche Literatur* 132, no. 2 (2003): 148–176, at 154.

– that is, by "guidelines" emanating from the materials themselves.[54] Thus, although the passage might foreground the mastery of the saddle's creator, it ends up accounting for the interaction of various different entities in the process of manufacturing the artifact. Furthermore, other segments of the description of the whole set of tack stress the interaction between different objects, materials, and humans, too. (Not to mention that the saddlery as a whole is essentially depicted as a multifaceted assemblage of different elements: numnah and pillion, bridle, surcingle, horse blanket, and so on.) For example, the clasps that form part of the golden surcingle and stirrups are made from silver with the deliberate intent of creating a contrast with the dark golden cloth (lines 7690 – 7694), while the concrete materiality of the fabric itself can be revealed only by touching it (lines 7680 – 7689). Seen in the light of the self-reflexivity of the whole passage, these accounts of different interacting materials suggest an interrelation of different entities in narrative, too.

The actual description of the process of creation in Hartmann's passage about the horse is repeatedly delayed. This happens at one point when the narrator interrupts himself to disparage – drawing on a range of topoi of modesty – his own ability to give the description; subsequently it happens again through another interruption by a listener.[55] The first of these disturbances highlights temporal aspects of narrative and its mediated character in particular. Moreover, material entities involved in narrative are brought to the fore:

daz ich iu rehte seite
von diseme gereite,
wie daz erziuget wære,
daz würde ze swære
einem alsô tumben knehte:
und ob ich'z aber rehte
iu nû gesagen kunde,
sô wære'z mit einem munde
iu ze sagenne al ze lanc.
ouch tuot daz mînem sinne kranc,
daz ich den satel nie gesach:
wan als mir dâ von bejach,
von dem ich die rede hân,
sô wil ich iuch wizzen lân
ein teil, wie er geprüevet was,
als ich an sînem buoche las,

54 On "gevuoge" as an aesthetic principle, also with reference to *Erec*, see Annette Gerok-Reiter, "Die 'Kunst der vuoge': Stil als relationale Kategorie; Überlegungen zum Minnesang," in *Literarischer Stil: Mittelalterliche Dichtung zwischen Konvention und Innovation*, ed. Elizabeth Andersen, Ricarda Bauschke-Hartung, and Silvia Reuvekamp (Berlin: De Gruyter, 2015), 97–118, at 105–106.
55 See Hartmann von Aue, *Erec*, ed. Scholz, 911. Scholz sees this as a "Fiktionssignal." On the function of topoi of modesty or inexpressibility in the description as a means of self-reflexivity, see Glauch, "Inszenierungen der Unsagbarkeit."

sô ich kurzlîchest kan.
(lines 7476 – 7492)

(If I were to give you a true account
of this saddle
and how it was fashioned,
that would be too hard
for such a foolish squire as myself –
even if I were to give you
a correct account of it now,
it would be too long a tale
to tell you for one mouth.
Moreover, my wit is rendered weak
by never having seen the saddle,
except in the words of that man
from whom I have this tale.
Therefore I will let you know
something of how it had been fashioned,
as I read in his book,
and as briefly as I possibly can.)
(trans. Edwards, 393)

How should we understand the statement that an adequate description would be too long for a single mouth to tell? This connection between the speech's duration and only one mouth is confusing.[56] But this comment identifies a characteristic of narrative, here in the sense of its courtly performance – namely, that one person speaks while all others are silent. It also indicates time, because the words have to come out of that single mouth one after another in time. Furthermore, it highlights the physical organ of speech, thus foregrounding situational and bodily conditions of narrative. The narrator also stresses the limitations of his "sinne" – his perception and/or imagination – because he never actually saw the saddle, whose account was already mediated for him by storytelling. He claims that the same unidentified source that he got the "rede" from told him ("bejach") about it (which connects to his earlier statement that he derives his description of the horse from the telling of an unnamed master). The sense of telling and listening implies orality. But then the narrator also states that he wants to describe the saddle just the way he read it in "sînem buoche" (his – the master's – book), which implies writing.[57] Throughout the whole passage the narrator never clearly identifies what or who this source is, leaving its identity, and also its materiality, deliberately unclear.

---

56 Since such topoi of inexpressibility accumulate to an unusual amount in the description and are also acted out on the level of narrative, they take on a self-reflexive quality. See Glauch, "Inszenierungen der Unsagbarkeit," 151.

57 Also, Scholz sees a contradiction between acoustic reception and written source, which he tries to resolve with the suggestion that verbs of speech could also be used for written transfer. See Hartmann von Aue, *Erec*, ed. Scholz, 912.

Scholarship has interpreted these puzzling references to the conditions of narrative primarily as "signals of fiction."[58] I perfectly agree with that. Yet the question remains whether this is their sole purpose. Why should the text make such huge efforts to identify so many *diverse* entities that play a role in narrative if it were only concerned with calling certain demands about its truth-value invalid? I suggest that it does so because the necessary "suspension of disbelief" – which is a lot to ask for – can only be upheld through a well-connected actor network, a specific web of associations that not only calls for certain behaviors and attitudes but also makes very specific sensory experiences possible.[59] Important immaterial/material entities in such an actor network might include temporal relations on many levels; preexisting stories, sources, books, and oral traditions, as well as the relations between them; the body of the speaker; the relation between speaker and listener; and the relation to different arts and crafts. In inventorying different constituents of courtly narrative, the text responds – as I tried to show earlier – to a particular poetics of the marvelous that vainly tries to legitimize narrative by claiming its truth-value. Thus, the polemic and the inventorying disruptions are closely interrelated.

But what are the criteria for well-connectedness? One further disturbance of the narration deals with this exact question: a metaleptic scene in which an anonymous fictitious listener (who is part of the audience) suddenly interrupts the narrative discourse.[60] The listener addresses the narrator directly as "Hartmann," asking if he himself can continue with the description of the saddle:

"Nû swîc, lieber Hartman:
ob ich ez errâte?"
ich tuon: nû sprechet drâte.
"ich muoz gedenken ê dar nâch."
nû vil drâte: mir ist gâch.
"dunke ich dich danne ein wîser man?"
jâ ir. durch got, nû saget an.
(lines 7493–7499)

("Be silent, now, Hartmann –
perhaps I can guess [how the saddle was made]."
I will – tell me quickly, now.
"I must think about it first."
Be quick about it now – I am in a hurry!
"Do I strike you as a wise man?"

---

58 Glauch, "Inszenierungen der Unsagbarkeit," 152–153; Hartmann von Aue, *Erec*, ed. Scholz, 910–911.
59 Latour often speaks about the difference between well-made and badly made networks as a criterion by which to judge modes of association. For instance, see Latour, *Modes of Existence*, 246.
60 Most scholars read the dialogue in this way: see Hartmann von Aue, *Erec*, ed. Scholz, 912–915. Bürkle, "'Kunst'-Reflexion," 166, interprets the scene differently as a dialogue between author-figure and narrator.

Yes, you do. Pray tell me now!)
(trans. Edwards, 395)

This interruption foregrounds more of the entities and relations to be found in narrative: a connection between intradiegetic and extradiegetic worlds is made, and we see the presence of the entities of author, narrator, and individual recipient. This recipient is part of an audience – here in the context of a performance in which the author appears as speaker and the recipient as listener – and he breaks with the "protocol" of courtly narrative by interrupting the discourse of the narrator. The listener also claims the position of master. His question as to whether he himself is a "wîser man" refers back to the master figures who planned and created horse and saddle.[61] But now the planning period ("ich muoz gedenken ê dar nâch") overlaps with the period of telling ("nû vil drâte: mir ist gâch"). This alone disqualifies the fictional listener: he speaks in an unprepared manner. With this, again, the planning phase is stressed as a part of narrative.

The intruding listener suggests that the saddle has certain material properties, proposing that it is made of beechwood ("guot hagenbüechîn"; line 7502) and covered with gold ("mit liehtem golde übertragen"; line 7504). The narrator responds derisively to this idea. Interestingly, his mockery only becomes apparent to the reader of Hartmann's text because the listener refers to his facial expression: "ja stât dir spotlîch der munt" ("Your mouth has taken a mocking turn") (line 7514; trans. Edwards, 395; see also line 7512). This adds the body of the speaker (of narrative in general) to the inventory and also marks that the listener is proposing something ludicrous in the eyes of "Hartmann." The listener's suggestion that the saddle is composed of gilded wood implies the practice of feigning: one material (wood) is treated in order to make it appear to be another material (gold).[62] The narrator counters this suggestion with the lines about the master Umbrîz quoted above – that is, the passage about combining the "mâterjen drin" of gold, precious stones, and ivory. In Umbrîz's assembly of different materials, as described by the narrator, every material retains its own properties and appearance.[63] The narrator, in characterizing this attitude toward dealing with different materials in the production process, uses the sententious phrase "valsch was im tiure" (line 7533) – Edwards translates this as "it/he [the saddle or the master] lacked any impurity" (trans. Edwards, 395), but it might also be taken to mean "falsehood was held in high esteem by it/him." The theme of veracity and forgery is also alluded to when the listener asks (using a word not quite applicable to the situation) if he *lied* when he made his suggestion

---

61 In a later remark, the narrator also calls the interrupter a "weterwîser man" (line 7511).
62 For a differentiation between different forms of material interplay or "intermateriality" that informed my discussion here, see Thomas Strässle, "Pluralis materialitatis," in *Das Zusammenspiel der Materialien in den Künsten: Theorien, Praktiken, Perspektiven*, ed. Thomas Strässle, Christoph Kleinschmidt, and Johanne Mohs (Bielefeld: transcript, 2013), 7–23, at 14–15.
63 Strässle, "Pluralis materialitatis," 14.

about the materials (line 7522) – to which the narrator (or Hartmann) answers: "No, your childish thinking has led you astray" ("Niht, iuch hât sus betrogen / iuwer kintlîcher wân") (trans. Edwards, 395; lines 7579–7580). I would argue that this rejection of the feigning of materials, and the signaling of such an act as a result of ignorance and associated with lying, implies a poetological polemic against a certain treatment of literary material, a treatment that can be connected to practices of faking and even forgery.

The Well-Made Truth of Falsehood

In conclusion, *Erec* stages a number of disturbances that make transparent the process of narration itself, foregrounding the material and immaterial entities that interact within it. By particularly calling attention to and rendering palpable temporal aspects that can have a frustrating effect, the description points to temporality as one of the elements that narrative is made of, next to other elements such as preexisting stories, texts as sources, the phase of planning, the author, and the different elements involved in the performance situation (the audience, the body of the narrator). The inventorying of narrative that the description performs is connected to a polemic against (and maybe triggered by) a contemporaneous poetics of the marvelous that insists on the truth-value of wonders. During the description of the saddle, a listener speaks up, suggesting that precious materials are feigned in its creation, a suggestion that is ridiculed by the narrator, himself identified as the author Hartmann. The polemic suggests that the poetics of the marvelous should be judged as something similar to "gilded wood": their proclaimed truths are nothing but rhetorical effects with the purpose of provoking wonder. The text seems to say that to claim the validity of narrative, it is not necessary to render one thing (wood, for example, or *fabula*) as something else (gold, or *historia*). Instead, it suggests that there is an intrinsic value in narrative and that narrative is a particular mode of existence with its own proper mode of veracity, upheld by a dense and rich network of associations, a network that affords peculiar sensory experiences.

The *sententia* of "valsch was im tiure" (line 7533) can be interpreted in this sense. If it is understood as saying – somewhat paradoxically – that "valsch" (falsehood or forgery) is greatly valued and at the same time rare, this could signify an elevation of the worth of a "forged" text, performed by reclaiming the definition of "forgery": only when the narrative is not trying to conceal "valsch" can it become a real and precious asset, foregrounding its sumptuous materiality. And on a second level, when "valsch" is not concealed, the way it is in so many other texts, it is a rarity too – making it an even more precious, or even marvelous, artifact. When wonders are given a "faked" truth, by contrast, it diminishes the preciousness of the text. Such texts fall victim to a category mistake, for the source of narrative's validity is not some kind of extraneous truth, but rather the complex body and craft of courtly narrative itself. The outcome of these negotiations is the characterization of narrative as a temporal, processual, and interactive fabric consisting of different material and immaterial elements: the things narrative is made of. To describe this characterization with the term "fictionality" is certainly not invalid, yet it would fail to do justice to the attention Hartmann's text pays to the interaction of various "mâterjen" in its account of what narrative does. And that indeed makes a difference.

Tilo Renz

8 Community of Things: On the Constitution of the Ideal Kingdom of Crisa in Heinrich von Neustadt's *Apollonius von Tyrland*

Introduction: Objects and Community Building

This chapter addresses the central importance of objects in the formation and reten-tion of ideal communities in medieval literature. In recent years, so-called actor-net-work theory has drawn attention to the contribution of nonhuman actors to the co-herence and permanence of human communities. Bruno Latour, one of the major exponents of this field of theory, has in particular given careful consideration to the crucial function of objects in group building in his reflections on social theory. One of the central purposes of Latour's 2005 book *Reassembling the Social* is to in-vestigate the ways in which things promote the creation of social alliances and work to stabilize them.[1] Focusing on the role of nonhuman actors in the course of group formation is very productive for medievalists, since objects were essential for community building in the Middle Ages. Religious communities, for example, would gather at a particular holy site or around a specific object of devotion, be it the sepulchral monument of a saint, a relic, or a devotional object less closely con-nected to a sacred body.[2]

Object-related communities are also prevalent in the literary tradition. Quintes-sential to the Arthurian community, as Bruno Quast recently reminded us, is the Round Table.[3] This object both produces a practical effect and has a symbolic mean-ing: with its unusual circular shape, it affords a specific way of positioning people at the table and is also symbolic of a particular group structure. Both aspects of the ob-ject aim at leveling hierarchies and minimizing the potential for conflict between members of the group.[4] To take one example of its treatment in literature, the table's

---

1 Latour claims to "follow the actors in their weaving through things they have added to social skills so as to render more durable the constantly shifting interactions." Bruno Latour, *Reassembling the Social: An Introduction to Actor-Network-Theory* (Oxford: Oxford University Press, 2005), 68.
2 See Arnold Angenendt, *Heilige und Reliquien: Die Geschichte ihres Kultes vom frühen Christentum bis zur Gegenwart* (Munich: Beck, 1997), 123–137, 182–189. Bruno Quast goes so far as to state that in medieval societies, the creation of community in general is effected through relationships to ob-jects. See Bruno Quast, "Dingpolitik: Gesellschaftstheoretische Überlegungen zu Rundtafel und Gral in Wolframs von Eschenbach *Parzival*," in *Dingkulturen: Objekte in Literatur, Kunst und Gesell-schaft der Vormoderne*, ed. Anna Mühlherr, Heike Sahm, Monika Schausten, and Bruno Quast (Berlin: De Gruyter, 2016), 171–184, at 171.
3 See Quast, "Dingpolitik," 171–181.
4 See Quast, 172–173.

https://doi.org/10.1515/9783110742985-011

egalitarian implications are explicated in Wolfram von Eschenbach's *Parzival*, in the two sequences in which the protagonist and his brother Feirefiz respectively become members of the community of the Round Table (*P*, 309,3–310,7; 775,1–26).[5] Both of these passages describe the king's initiative in making the Round Table (309,12–25; 775,2–11). Arthur has taken care to ensure that all seats at the table are alike, allowing no one to be distinguished by where they sit: "nâch gegenstuol dâ niemen sprach, / diu gesitz warn al gelîche hêr" ("no-one should claim the seat of honor, facing the host. All the seats were equal in rank") (309,24–25; trans. Edwards, 131).

In *Parzival* there is a second community centered around an object as well: the society of the Grail. Like the Round Table, the Grail, which in *Parzival* is imagined as a stone (see, e. g., *P*, 469,3), exerts power over the community. Whereas the description of the Round Table emphasizes how the making and use of this object binds the community together, in the society of the Grail the physical effects of immaterial and spiritual forces are brought to the fore. Solely on festive occasions, the Grail is carried around the castle of Munsalvaesche so that its followers can gaze upon it: "den truoc man zallem mâle / der diet niht durch schouwen für, / niht wan ze hôchgezîte kür" ("On every occasion it was brought forth, it was not a spectacle for the company, but only when a festivity required it") (807,16–18; trans. Edwards, 338; see also 235,15–236,11). The power of the stone guarantees the survival of the society: "der rîterlîchen bruoderschaft, / die pfrüende in gît des grâles kraft" ("To that knightly brotherhood the Grail's power gives such provender") (470,19–20; trans. Edwards, 198). This giving of provender can be understood in the concrete sense of providing nourishment.[6] In addition, merely seeing the Grail has a physical effect, delaying both aging and death (469,14–27). The stone's power is transmitted to it through a wafer that is carried down by a dove from heaven every Good Friday (470,1–15). Given this connection to transcendent powers, it follows that the members of the society of the Grail are chosen and called by God himself (471,26–28; 468,12–14).

In the analysis that follows, I will further pursue the question of how objects contribute to building and stabilizing community by taking a closer look at a German vernacular text written about a century after Wolfram's *Parzival*, one that takes up

---

5 Wolfram von Eschenbach's *Parzival* is quoted here from Wolfram von Eschenbach, *Parzival: Studienausgabe*, ed. Karl Lachmann (Berlin: De Gruyter, 2003). Passages from *Parzival* are cited in the running text by *Dreißiger* (section) and line, and identified with the abbreviation *P*. The English translations of *Parzival* are quoted from Wolfram von Eschenbach, *Parzival and Titurel*, trans. Cyril Edwards (Oxford: Oxford University Press, 2006), and are cited separately by page number.

6 Further passages support this reading: "Man sagte mir [...] / daz vorem grâle wære bereit / [...] / swâ nâch jener bôt die hand, / daz er al bereite vant / spîse warm, spîse kalt, / spîse niwe unt dar zuo alt, / daz zam unt daz wilde" ("They told me [...] that before the Grail there was in good supply [...] whatever anyone stretched out his hand for, he found it all in readiness – hot food, cold food, new food and old too, tame and wild") (*P*, 238,8–17; trans. Edwards, 101); "ich wil iu künden umb ir nar. / si lebent von einem steine: / des geslähte ist vil reine" ("I will tell you of their food: they live by a stone whose nature is most pure") (*P*, 469,2–4; trans. Edwards, 198).

elements of courtly literature from around 1200 and combines them with other influences. My argument focuses on the Viennese author and physician Heinrich von Neustadt's *Apollonius von Tyrland* (*Apollonius of Tyre*, ca. 1310), the first German translation of, and a significant expansion on, the late antique *Historia Apollonii regis Tyri*.[7] Heinrich's text is influenced by the urban social and cultural context it derives from.[8] It bears witness to the contemporary Viennese elite's interest in courtly ideals and the privileges of nobility.[9] The text suggests other concerns as well that are distinctive to the social milieu of its origin, such as material assets and money, government, social hierarchy, and interaction within an urban community.[10] In an extended passage that Heinrich adds to his textual source, he describes several ideal communities. Of these, I will focus on the so-called golden land of Crisa. Crisa is also known through encyclopedic texts of the time and found on *mappae mundi*, although Heinrich fleshes the place out in an elaborate way that is beyond comparison.[11]

Crisa shares features with the societies of the Round Table and the Grail, and it too can be addressed as an ideal community: similar to the community of the Round Table, Crisa's hierarchical structure displays some peculiarities, and in keeping with the community of the Grail, foodstuffs are abundant for the populace of the golden land. Nevertheless, some important differences between Crisa and the societies of the Round Table and the Grail run counter to these similarities. To begin with, in the imagined world of Heinrich's *Apollonius*, Crisa is geographically situated far from Europe and separated from surrounding lands by defined borders.[12] As such, it is dis-

---

7 Heinrich's *Apollonius* is quoted here from the following edition: Heinrich von Neustadt, *Apollonius von Tyrland*, ed. Samuel Singer (Berlin: Weidmannsche Buchhandlung, 1906). Passages from *Apollonius* are cited in the running text by line number and identified with the abbreviation *AvT*. All translations of the text are my own.

8 On the historically specific notion of the term *bourgeois*, see Alfred Ebenbauer, "Der 'Apollonius von Tyrlant' des Heinrich von Neustadt und die bürgerliche Literatur im spätmittelalterlichen Wien," in *1050–1750: Die österreichische Literatur; Ihr Profil von den Anfängen im Mittelalter bis ins 18. Jahrhundert*, vol. 1, ed. Herbert Zeman, Jahrbuch für österreichische Kulturgeschichte vol. 14–15 (Graz: Akademische Druck- und Verlagsanstalt, 1986), 311–347, at 340–343.

9 See Ebenbauer, "Apollonius von Tyrlant," 341.

10 Heinrich's *Apollonius*, for example, elaborates on the decision-making process of the citizens ("di purger"; *AvT*, 11063) of Crisa with respect to how to welcome the protagonist. On the importance of material assets and money in *Apollonius*, see Fritz Peter Knapp, "Heinrich von Neustadt," in *Die Literatur des Spätmittelalters in den Ländern Österreich, Steiermark, Kärnten, Salzburg und Tirol von 1273 bis 1439*, vol. 2, bk. 1, of *Geschichte der Literatur in Österreich: Von den Anfängen bis zur Gegenwart*, ed. Herbert Zeman (Graz: Akademische Druck- und Verlagsanstalt, 1999), 280–297, at 291. The following analyses give further evidence of the tendency to address specifically urban concerns.

11 See, for example, *De imagine mundi* by Honorius Augustodunensis, the German *Lucidarius*, the *Weltchronik* of Rudolf von Ems, and the *Ebstorf Map*.

12 Crisa is a three-day journey away from the castle of Gabilot (*AvT*, 8836–8837), which probably refers to Gabala in modern Syria, and the land extends far to the north (to the Caspian Mountains: 10950–10952) and to the east (to India: 10940, 10962–10964). In addition, Crisa is demarcated ("peslossen"; 8848) from its surroundings.

tant from any places that most of the text's historical recipients probably knew. Additionally, there is an abundance of material resources – not only foodstuffs – that are accessible to everyone who is part of the community: "The riches are uncountable there" (*AvT*, 8847; "Da ist reichait ane zal"). In particular, "there is so much gold that nobody is tempted to take from it for himself" (8898 – 8899; "Goldes ist da also vil / Das es niemand nemen wil"). The bountifulness of goods has a strong impact on the living conditions and behavior of people in Crisa. Moreover, the availability of these goods to everyone makes the land less hierarchical, since when it comes to access to nourishment all members of the community have equal opportunities.[13] As I have mentioned above, the community of the Grail also provides enough nourishment for its members. Nevertheless, the castle Munsalvaesche shows a close relation to transcendent powers, is fundamentally characterized by mystery, and is distinctly marked by illness and suffering.[14] In stark contrast, Heinrich's description of Crisa emphasizes the exhilarating effects of the society's material basics on members of the community and combines this with accounts of several marvelous phenomena, to which I will turn below.

The aforementioned features that differentiate Crisa from the two other societies allow it to be seen as an ideal community of a specific kind: Crisa shows similarities with early modern utopias, the ideal communities that were conceived some two hundred years later. Thomas More coined the term *utopia* in 1516, using it as the title of the fictional narrative ascribed to world traveler Raphael Hythlodaeus. In this narrative, Utopia is the name of a community with ideal living conditions, situated on the margins of the known world – specifically, it is located on a faraway island and can thus conceivably be reached on a long-distance journey.[15] The ideal living conditions on the island stem from the general availability of material resources,

---

13 With reference to foodstuffs, the text says: "Da enleydet nieman hungers not" (*AvT*, 8873; Nobody has to go hungry there).

14 Munsalvaesche is distinctly marked by a lack of joy (*P*, 227,9 – 16; 242,4 – 6) and by the suffering of its ruler (231,1 – 5; 240,7 – 8; 472,21 – 26). On the narrative formation of the mystery of the Grail, see Arthur Groos, *Romancing the Grail: Genre, Science, and Quest in Wolfram's "Parzival"* (Ithaca, NY: Cornell University Press, 1995), 121 (with further references); and Jutta Eming, "Aus den *swarzen buochen*: Zur Ästhetik der Verrätselung von Erkenntnis und Wissenstransfer im *Parzival*," in *Magia daemoniaca, magia naturalis, zouber: Schreibweisen von Magie und Alchemie in Mittelalter und Früher Neuzeit*, ed. Peter-André Alt, Jutta Eming, Tilo Renz, and Volkhard Wels (Wiesbaden: Harrassowitz, 2015), 75 – 99. On the mysteries of the Grail, see also William C. McDonald, "Wolfram's Grail," *Arthuriana* 8 (1998): 22 – 34. One can pointedly say that while *Parzival* time and again evokes mystery, Heinrich's *Apollonius*, in contrast, is a text of riddles that have to be and can be solved. On riddles in *Apollonius*, see Tomas Tomasek, *Das deutsche Rätsel im Mittelalter* (Tübingen: Max Niemeyer Verlag, 1994), 184 – 199.

15 See Thomas More, *Utopia*, vol. 4 of *The Complete Works of St. Thomas More*, ed. Edward Surtz and Jack H. Hexter, 2nd ed. (New Haven: Yale University Press, 1993), 50 – 52.

which influences the social order of the community as a whole.[16] In a slightly different way, we see the same characteristic in Crisa, where material riches and foodstuffs – without the help of divine powers – are so abundant as to be available to everyone.[17] Furthermore, the virtuous behavior of the members of the community is a central characteristic in Utopia and Crisa alike.

What specifically distinguishes Crisa from early modern utopias as well as from other ideal communities of the Middle Ages is its objects. Objects are more prevalent in Crisa than they are in the ideal societies of the Round Table and the Grail. For this reason, the objects of the utopian community of Crisa hold great promise for analysis. To begin with, there are not just one but several objects involved in the process of group formation in Crisa's ideal community. This large number of objects allows us to scrutinize and differentiate the ways in which they work, including how they interact with one another and with other actors. In addition, the objects populating this specific ideal community are remarkably active. They outperform even the Grail and its ability to physically sustain its followers.[18]

Given these features, Heinrich's description of the land of Crisa shows various roles that objects can play in the process of building and retaining an ideal community. In particular, the objects in Crisa guide the incorporation of strangers into the community: interaction with the community's nonhuman objects makes the integration of human characters from elsewhere possible.

The Objects of Medieval Utopias from a Latourian Perspective

Bruno Latour, whether one accepts or rejects his ideas, has greatly influenced the study of objects in the humanities in recent years with the thesis that things are equipped with a certain kind of agency. In his introduction to actor-network theory,

16 In More's *Utopia*, property held in common is the basis for just organization of the community: "omnia sunt communia" (More, *Utopia*, 100; "all things are common"). For further detail, see More, 102–106. This characteristic is too strict, though, to apply to utopian concepts of the Middle Ages.
17 In her recent book on medieval utopias, Karma Lochrie has made it clear that we have to go beyond the characteristics of More's *Utopia* if we want to give an account of the specificities of utopian thinking in the Middle Ages: Karma Lochrie, *Nowhere in the Middle Ages* (Philadelphia: University of Pennsylvania Press, 2016). Nevertheless, we have to keep on relating medieval utopias to the so-called classical utopias of early modern times in some way – and even Lochrie clings to what she calls the "productive dialogue with More's 'Utopia'" (Lochrie, *Nowhere*, 6). For a careful estimation of the features of classical utopias that can be found in concepts of ideal communities of the late Middle Ages as well, see Tilo Renz, "Utopische Elemente der Reiseliteratur des späten Mittelalters," *Das Mittelalter* 18, no. 2 (2013): 129–152, at 130–138.
18 See Quast, "Dingpolitik," 181. The Round Table, in contrast, is not itself active. Quast has underlined that the table has to be set up by members of the group every time they want to gather ("Dingpolitik," 178, 180–181).

Reassembling the Social, to which I have already referred, Latour has made it clear that speaking of an "agency of things" is meant to establish a heuristic tool, and to this end he conceives the term in the broadest possible sense. What Latour understands by "agency of things" he expresses concisely in his definition of an actor: "*any thing* that does modify a state of affairs by making a difference is an actor" (emphasis in the original).[19] Based on this determination, actor-network theory aims at investigating whether or not a given object contributes to a modification of status, and if so, in what way it facilitates change. As Latour puts it: "There might exist many metaphysical shades between full causality and sheer inexistence. In addition to 'determining' and serving as a 'backdrop for human action,' things might authorize, allow, afford, encourage, permit, suggest, influence, block, render possible, forbid, and so on."[20] An investigation that takes up these considerations will make a differentiated analysis of the various contributions of objects to processes of change – in our case, processes that lead to the building and sustaining of an ideal community – and will also scrutinize the objects' relations and interactions with other actors.

In medieval literature, utopian communities often include marvelous objects. For example, according to the fictitious letter claimed to be by Prester John, that ruler's Far Eastern kingdom features, among other things, a fountain of youth and a mirror mounted on a pillar that allows one to take a look at every place in the kingdom, however distant.[21] The presence of these objects is not in the least surprising if the motifs and topoi that medieval depictions of ideal communities draw on are taken into account. All too often, these communities are situated in a beautiful and pleasant landscape (a *locus amoenus*), and their portrayals borrow from the Garden of Eden as described in the Book of Genesis, as well as from the medieval topos of the earthly paradise derived from this same passage of the Bible.[22] Among other things, descriptions of these communities can include plants that possess remarkable abilities and also a lot of water, in particular the four rivers of paradise.

Despite these borrowings, however, there is a decisive difference between the Garden of Eden and the earthly paradise, on one hand, and the communities that I understand as being utopian on the other: utopian communities in the Middle Ages, as well as in early modernity, are worldly communities. They depict groups that have the privilege of experiencing ideal living conditions on Earth at a time preceding the day of the Last Judgment. The earthly paradise, according to medieval encyclopedias, cartography, and literature, is – as its name suggests – also situated on

---

19 Latour, *Reassembling the Social*, 71.

20 Latour, 72.

21 See Friedrich Zarncke, *Der Priester Johannes: Erste Abhandlung* (Leipzig: Hirzel, 1879), 94–95, secs. 71–72 and 79–84.

22 See Reinhold R. Grimm, *Paradisus coelestis, paradisus terrestris: Zur Auslegungsgeschichte des Paradieses im Abendland bis um 1200* (Munich: Wilhelm Fink Verlag, 1977); Alessandro Scafi, *Mapping Paradise: A History of Heaven on Earth* (London: University of Chicago Press, 2006).

Earth. And yet, as the Book of Genesis tells us, it is not accessible to us. As an example, in medieval romances that narrate the life and conquests of Alexander the Great, the inaccessibility of this paradise becomes manifest in a wall – the hero of antiquity, in his hubris, attempts to enter this secluded paradise but fails.[23]

This fundamental difference in accessibility of ideal places corresponds to a difference in the types of objects found in them. Things that populate utopian communities are not divine or spiritual (in the strict sense of the word – e.g., the tree of knowledge), but in general belong to the tradition of the marvelous that can be traced back to antique *mirabilia*. According to several authors writing at the turn of the thirteenth century, the marvelous is not a result of God's direct intervention – phenomena of that sort are called *miracula* – but a more or less spontaneous deviation from the usual course of natural processes.[24] The historical classification provides a starting point for analysis, though in particular instances – especially in literary texts – it may be undermined. A wide range of phenomena can be affiliated to this concept of the marvelous.[25] Probably the most prominent is what modern scholarship has called the "marvels of the East" – that is, types of creatures with unusual physical features whose tradition goes back to antiquity and whose connection to mankind was extensively discussed in the Middle Ages.[26] There are also inanimate objects that have special abilities; for example, stones, gems, or rings, often imbued with magical powers.[27] Finally, there are objects that have particular mechanical or artistic features. In medieval texts, the ways in which these objects work are often not fully explained, and thus can be attributed to magic.[28] What all these phenomena

---

23 See, for example, an early version of the Alexander romance in German vernacular, the so-called *Straßburger Alexander*. Pfaffe Lambrecht, *Alexanderroman: Mittelhochdeutsch/Neuhochdeutsch*, ed. Elisabeth Lienert (Stuttgart: Philipp Reclam, 2007), lines 6166–6572.

24 On the differentiation between *miracula* and *mirabilia*, see Caroline Walker Bynum, "Miracles and Marvels: The Limits of Alterity," in *Vita religiosa im Mittelalter: Festschrift für Kaspar Elm zum 70. Geburtstag*, eds. Franz J. Felten and Nikolaus Jaspert (Berlin: Duncker & Humblot, 1999), 799–817, at 803–804. Works that differentiate between the two terms are: *Otia imperialia*, by Gervase of Tilbury (1214); *Topographia Hibernica*, by Gerald of Wales (1180s); *Dialogus miraculorum*, by Caesarius of Heisterbach (1220s); and *Summa theologiae* (1.105.6–7), by Thomas Aquinas (ca. 1270). On the notion of nature that corresponds to this differentiation, see Lorraine Daston and Katharine Park, *Wonders and the Order of Nature 1150–1750* (New York: Zone Books, 1998), 48–49.

25 For a broad notion of the marvelous in premodern times as designating phenomena that are not limited to a geographical region but generally mark "nature's farthest reaches," see Daston and Park, *Wonders*, 14.

26 See Daston and Park, *Wonders*, 25–39; cf. the seminal study on the tradition: Rudolf Wittkower, "Marvels of the East: A Study in the History of Monsters," *Journal of the Warburg and Courtauld Institutes* 5 (1942): 159–197.

27 See Daston and Park, *Wonders*, 41 (on lapidaries); see also Ulrich Engelen, *Die Edelsteine in der deutschen Dichtung des 12. und 13. Jahrhunderts* (Munich: Wilhelm Fink Verlag, 1978).

28 On insufficient explanations, see Daston and Park, *Wonders*, 88–94. On the attribution to magic, see Udo Friedrich, "*Contra naturam:* Mittelalterliche Automatisierung im Spannungsfeld politischer, theologischer und technologischer Naturkonzepte," in *Automaten in Kunst und Literatur des Mittelal-*

have in common is that they engender wonder and amazement, reactions that are at once cognitive and emotional.[29] These reactions are caused by something that recipients are unfamiliar with, and which they are unable, at least at the moment, to connect to what they already know. Among the aforementioned phenomena, even those that at first glance seem to be inanimate (stones, automata), on closer inspection, actually turn out to be engaged in activities and thus seem to be endowed with some kind of agency.

When we consider the importance of wondrous objects to medieval ideal communities, it comes to the fore that the specificities of these objects are bound to a certain historical context. Thus, if one applies Latour's recent considerations to medieval phenomena, one has to account for the historical specificities of the objects in question, and especially their epistemological context. While Latour deals with inanimate objects in his studies (e.g., a gun, a key, or an experimental setup in a laboratory), the marvelous things of medieval utopias can be living creatures, or they can give the impression of being alive. In addition, as I pointed out, monstrous races and marvelous objects are considered to be part of nature in the medieval episteme. When the objects in question are undeniably active and already part of the animate world, this makes it even easier to take a Latourian perspective on their assembling force.[30] Additionally, and quite aside from reflections on how and whether we are to speak about medieval objects in a Latourian manner, Latour's considerations on the relation and interaction of different actors inspire fundamental analytical questions: What exactly is the relationship between things and humans in a medieval community with utopian qualities? And how important is the objects' contribution to building and maintaining such a community?

---

ters und der Frühen Neuzeit, ed. Klaus Grubmüller and Markus Stock (Wiesbaden: Harrassowitz Verlag, 2003), 91–114, at 96–97; and Ulrich Ernst, "Mirabilia mechanica: Technische Phantasmen im Antiken- und Artusroman des Mittelalters," in Das Wunderbare in der arthurischen Literatur: Probleme und Perspektiven, ed. Friedrich Wolfzettel (Tübingen: Max Niemeyer Verlag, 2003), 45–77, at 72–73.

29 Daston and Park characterize wonder as "cognitive passion" (Wonders, 14). In addition to this epistemic and emotional connection with the marvelous experienced by recipients, Michelle Karnes has shown that some medieval thinkers make marvelous phenomena dependent on contemporaneous concepts of imagination. By focusing on this facet of the medieval marvelous, she has emphasized anew the importance of accounting for the recipients' involvement when theorizing and analyzing mirabilia. See Michelle Karnes, "Marvels in the Medieval Imagination," Speculum 90, no. 2 (2015): 327–365.

30 According to Latour, a discursive strategy of those who identify themselves as modern is to strictly differentiate between things and humans; according to this strategy – and probably also according to Latour's own estimation – in premodern times this distinction was not made. Instead there was a "mishmash of things and humans." Bruno Latour, We Have Never Been Modern, trans. Catherine Porter (Cambridge, MA: Harvard University Press, 1993), 39.

Transformation and Integration through Objects in the Golden Land of Crisa

Things That Discipline Characters and Change Their Behavior

The journey to Crisa is one of the adventures Apollonius has during his extensive travels in the eastern parts of the Mediterranean. Inspired by an account given by the Babylonian king Nemrot, Apollonius develops a desire to visit this land, to which he is only able to gain access by first overcoming the dangerous *monstra* Serpanta and Ydrogant (*AvT*, 10686–10863). After defeating them, Apollonius encounters several objects of different sizes, which exhibit sculptural or architectural elements. These objects control access to certain places within Crisa by testing the moral fiber of those wishing to enter.

In order to enter Walsamit, the first city that Apollonius reaches in the golden land, he must ride over a wheel that is studded with gold and precious stones and forms part of an architectural ensemble that is described vaguely (*AvT*, 11205–11333).[31] The wheel decides if knights who want to cross over it are free of vice: "an alle missetat" (11214; without any misconduct). Apollonius and the majority of his companions succeed in passing the test (11321–11322). Only a handful of them are found guilty of being cowardly, unfaithful, or villainous (11313, 11354–11355, 11377). The wheel throws them into a river and they are forbidden to travel farther inland.

Soon thereafter, Apollonius and his companions enter a city that bears the name of Crisa, where King Candor, the ruler of the land, resides. Candor invites the guests to a garden which is protected by a fountain (*AvT*, 11755) and a colossus (11749–11751; see also 11980–11984) that are both incorporated in its entranceway.[32] The visitors must place their hands in the fountain's water, and they are only allowed to enter if their hands do not change color (11728–11993). The fountain marks people who have lewd behavior or thoughts (11808). Characters who do not pass the test are forced to remain outside the gate with stained hands, visibly distinguished from those who are allowed to pass. This is not the final judgment passed on those rejected, though, as we find out when Apollonius and all the others fail the test. Rather, they have an audience with the goddess Venus. At her temple a priest explains to them what their misdeed was (11803–11809) and then sends them to Venus to ab-

---

31 The wheel follows the thematic tradition of the wheel of fortune: cf. Alfred Doren, "Fortuna im Mittelalter und in der Renaissance," *Vorträge der Bibliothek Warburg* 1 (1924): 71–144; Howard R. Patch, *The Goddess Fortuna in Mediaeval Literature* (Cambridge, MA: Harvard University Press, 1927), 147–177.
32 For a description of the precious materials the gate is made of, see *AvT*, 11985–11989. For the golden pipes and emerald basin of the fountain, see 11752–11753, 11755.

solve themselves by confessing their misdeed to the goddess (11810 – 11813).[33] There is thus a functional connection between the fountain, Venus, and the priest: together they convey what counts as virtuous behavior in Crisa, and they also convey that lewd behavior can be overcome by confession and penance. Once all the guests have acknowledged their guilt, they are permitted to enter the garden (11991– 11993).

The travelers soon find themselves standing at the foot of a staircase leading up to an artfully designed pillar. On its surface, observers are able to see anything they wish, anywhere in the world (*AvT*, 11994 – 11999). The image is familiar from the *Letter of Prester John*, mentioned above.[34] As they climb the staircase, Apollonius and his men are thrown off it one by one. This is revealed to be another test of virtue, with each step representing a different vice – mockery, malice, laziness, cowardice, dishonesty, vanity, thirst for glory, gluttony, and drunkenness (12046 – 12062). Apollonius is thrown down from the fourth step, an accusation of cowardice. He turns once again to the goddess Venus. She first explains what he did to earn this accusation – among other things, he stabbed Kolkan, the monstrous ruler of the land of Galacides, in the back (12129 – 12145) – and then she gives the Tyrian the opportunity to purify himself through a challenge that pits him against ten knights and a lion (12202– 12204, 12217– 12221).

The guests must then repeat the challenges of the fountain (*AvT*, 12635 – 12638) and staircase (12640 – 12648) once again. The second attempt at the fountain test demonstrates that the purification was a success. On the fifth step of the staircase, however, Apollonius finds himself now accused of lying, for having presented himself to King Nemrot under the false name Lonius, a diminutive form of his actual name (12655, 12691– 12698). Once again, Venus exonerates him following his confession (12721), after which the protagonist is finally able to ascend the staircase (12741– 12744).

The function of the first three objects that Apollonius encounters in Crisa – the wheel, the fountain, and the staircase – is to put the protagonists' virtuous behavior and moral judgment to the test. The objects do this by way of interactions with the characters. Members of the Crisian nobility show the visitors around, and sometimes they explain or even demonstrate how these objects are to be used (*AvT*, 12008, 11212– 11230, 11758 – 11764). Often, though, what the visitors must do to use the objects can be at least partially deduced from their form.[35]

---

33 For the term "confession," see *AvT*, 11837; for the respective process, see 11819 – 11833.

34 See Zarncke, *Priester Johannes*, 94, secs. 71– 72. For its use in literary texts, see, for example, the mirror brought by the wizard Clinschor to the Chastel Marveille in *Parzival*, which Gawan uses to watch over the landscape around the castle (*P*, 589,1– 594,20, in particular 592,1– 19).

35 The process shows parallels to the concept of affordance, which James Gibson has coined to describe the possibilities offered by materials – in particular their surfaces – to potential users. See James J. Gibson, "The Theory of Affordances," in *Perceiving, Acting, and Knowing: Towards an Ecological Psychology*, ed. Robert Shaw and John Bransford (New York: The Halsted Press, 1977), 67– 82.

Yet there is more to it than this: the objects themselves intervene in the process of their use, and in so doing they act according to their own sensibility. They perceive the qualities of the characters they encounter – in particular, those qualities that are imperceptible to the human protagonists – and react to them. The details of where the objects' sensibility comes from and how their unique abilities function are neither explained nor explicitly ascribed to magic.[36] The objects' reactions are repeated, following regular parameters. The fact that the objects can manipulate their response to their users becomes particularly clear in the case of the wheel and staircase: whoever steps upon one of these objects and is not in compliance with the Crisian idea of virtuous behavior is thrown off.

By intervening in this way, the objects reveal wrongdoing and penalize the travelers for it.[37] They mark characters (as when the water from the fountain stains their fingers or hands black) and also punish them physically by forcing them into humiliating and even painful positions (as when characters are thrown by the wheel into a river or from the staircase to the ground).[38] Furthermore, these objects grant or refuse access to certain places or to further objects.

After the objects' intervention, our travelers are sent to an audience with the goddess Venus. She explains what they have been accused of and gives them the possibility of confessing their wrongdoings, thus purifying themselves, and finally repeating the test. These interactions with Venus ultimately change the characters' morality. Thus, the confessions and tests of behavior that follow the objects' interventions bring about cognitive and behavioral changes in the characters. Above all, the tests of virtue create an awareness of wrongdoing (through the explanation of the offense and its acknowledgment via confession) and give the wrongdoers the opportunity to change it through practical action (further challenges).

A Thing to Transform Mind and Body

In the garden where the aforementioned marvelous pillar stands, the travelers subsequently come across another object: a fountain of youth (*AvT*, 12951), adorned with

---

36 A "tugent" (virtue; *AvT*, 11212) is ascribed to the wheel; the material that the staircase is made of is explained as being "edel" (noble, illustrious) and "lawter und raine" (bright and pure) (12043–12044).

37 We can find parallels here to the disciplinary power of the object as described by Latour in the case of the so-called Berlin key. See Bruno Latour, "The Berlin Key or How to Do Words with Things," in *Matter, Materiality and Modern Culture*, ed. Paul Graves-Brown (London: Routledge, 1991), 10–21, at 19.

38 These acts of physical punishment by the objects go beyond the disciplinary measures described by Latour in the case of the Berlin key. The effects of the sanctions are suggestive of Foucault's remarks about prison practices, which Latour mentions as a reference in his essay. See Latour, "Berlin Key," 17; and Michel Foucault, *Discipline and Punish: The Birth of the Prison*, trans. Alan Sheridan (New York: Vintage Books, 1995).

large architectural elements that are decorated with precious materials. This fountain functions in a different way from the tests of virtue outlined above, and it has different properties. The only people ultimately allowed to bathe in the fountain, after having undergone the aforementioned series of tests, are Apollonius and two of his companions: Printzel, the ruler of a land called Warcilon, and Palmer, the king of Syria. The fountain imbues them with several distinguishing qualities: they receive knowledge that makes them particularly adept at politics (12090 – 12093), and they attain an idealized version of the physical condition of early youth (around twenty years of age) (12089, 13006), along with beauty (12088), the ability to overcome any form of disease (12084), and a supernatural sheen (13010).[39] They achieve this physical and cognitive transformation by submerging their entire bodies in the fountain, including their heads and limbs (13008 – 13009).

Following his bath in the fountain of youth, Apollonius is presented to Diomena, the daughter of the ruler of the land, in an artistically designed part of the garden; soon afterward, religious dignitaries, who are not Christians, give her to him as a bride.[40] Once married (*AvT*, 13407– 13413), after enjoying an incomparably ostentatious and lavish feast (13415 – 13468), Apollonius is "kunig nu genant / In dem guldin tal" (13472– 13473; now named king in the golden valley). As such, the physical and mental condition conferred upon the protagonist by the fountain of youth proves to be the prerequisite for him to marry the daughter of the ruler of Crisa and attain the highest position in the land.

Apollonius's interactions with various objects in Crisa thus, first, enable him to gain access to the land (and certain particularly well-protected areas) and, second, ensure that he is qualified to take on the position of ruler. The wheel, the fountain, and the staircase require one to have inner virtue, and thus they characterize Crisa as a community based on shared values and corresponding behaviors. An additional object, the fountain of youth, adds physical qualities to the list of required characteristics: it grants the characters' appearance a transcendent quality that implies permanence. The impression of permanence is conveyed through the fountain's enduring effect on the bodies of the protagonists in general, and in particular through its promise of eternal youth. Since the characters stay young after having bathed, they seem to have established a durable connection to the fountain. We thus are left with the impression that the act of connecting nonhuman objects and human characters leads to a stable association with the Crisian community. Clearly, these objects – in particular the fountain of youth – are an important part of the process of integration into the group.

---

39 On Heinrich's specific combination of the worldly and transcendent aspects of the fountain of youth motif, see Lea Braun, *Transformationen von Herrschaft und Raum in Heinrichs von Neustadt "Apollonius von Tyrland"* (Berlin: Walter de Gruyter, 2018), 275 – 278.
40 Diomena herself tells Apollonius that the land, including all its riches, is at his disposal (*AvT*, 13372– 13374). The high patriarch and numerous bishops of the local religion hand Diomena over to Apollonius to be his wife shortly thereafter (13397– 13398).

Objects That Do Not Act Alone

The episode of the fountain of youth in particular gives the impression that the paradigmatic process of integration into the community of Crisa is an interaction of visitors with marvelous objects, and that this interaction leads to a stable – and in this case physical – connection. According to such an understanding of what happens to Heinrich's protagonist and his companions in the Crisa episode, the series of narrative events appears to straightforwardly connect human visitors with objects. Upon closer inspection, though, a coupling of objects and different characters – human as well as divine, Crisian as well as non-Crisian – can already be observed from the first moment the visitors encounter objects in Crisa.

As I have already mentioned, the objects that examine inner virtue (i.e., the wheel, fountain, and staircase) succeed in implementing the necessary norms in conjunction with the nobles of the land, the goddess Venus, and her priest. King Candor and others accompany Apollonius and his followers to the objects and at times also tell them what to do once in front of them. After interacting with fountain and staircase and failing their tests, the visitors are led to the goddess Venus and her priest. As such, the objects are not solely responsible for keeping up Crisa's ethical standards but rather are accompanied in this process by further actors. They all work together to achieve their goal, and Heinrich von Neustadt does not make clear which of the divine, human, and nonhuman actors are primarily responsible for securing Crisa's norms of conduct.[41] Crisa's marvelous objects don't determine the process of integrating new members into the community, but at the same time, neither are they simply King Candor and the Crisian nobles' means for achieving this aim. They are instead an essential part of a network of different actors that all contribute to this process.

Since the fountain and staircase do no more than detect in what respect Apollonius and his companions fail to attain Crisian norms, and since King Candor subsequently directs the visitors to the goddess Venus (*AvT*, 11788 – 11799, 12110 – 12115, 12685 – 12689), it seems to be she who has the last word. As a result, among Crisa's different actors, it is Venus who appears to occupy the most powerful position when it comes to securing moral standards. What undercuts this, however, is the fact that Venus does not sternly enforce Crisa's morals, and that she is amenable to suggestions made by both the character on trial and others.[42]

---

41 See Burghart Wachinger, "Heinrich von Neustadt, 'Apollonius von Tyrland,'" in *Positionen des Romans im späten Mittelalter*, ed. Walter Haug and Burghart Wachinger (Tübingen: Max Niemeyer Verlag, 1991), 97–115, at 108.

42 For an overestimation of Venus's power in the supposed "Venusreich" (Venus empire) of Crisa, cf. Braun, *Transformationen*, 283–284 (the term itself on 277). Similarly, Achnitz is of the opinion that the "rules" of Venus determine "communal life in Crisa": cf. Wolfgang Achnitz, *Babylon und Jerusalem: Sinnkonstituierung im "Reinfried von Braunschweig" und im "Apollonius von Tyrland" Heinrichs von Neustadt* (Tübingen: Max Niemeyer Verlag, 2002), 320.

When Apollonius explains his indecent glances at Candor's daughter Diomena as being driven by virtuous love, Venus immediately responds by turning his finger-nail white once again (*AvT*, 11833). When he later begs Venus to describe why he has been charged with cowardice (12120–12124), she points out to him precisely what his "weak-spirited misdeed" (12144; "zaglichen missetat") was and reproaches him for it. Apollonius subsequently gives his version of what happened (12147–12182) and begs the goddess to help him absolve the guilt detected by the staircase (12183–12184, 12192–12194). With that, Venus assures him that she will look after him (12198–12201) and advises him about the further test of virtue he will have to pass (12210–12224).

These examples show that Venus reacts to explanations given by the visitor who has been found guilty by the objects that examine his virtue; Apollonius's interventions even lead Venus to revise the judgment that she presented as her own in the first place. Thus, within certain limits, the behavior of those she judges is up for negotiation.[43] Venus does not, however, allow the protagonist to avoid taking further tests to prove his virtue (*AvT*, 12202–12204).

When the staircase detects that Apollonius lied by calling himself Lonius, another actor becomes involved once again: after the protagonist explains what happened (*AvT*, 12699–12716), King Candor personally takes Apollonius's side and states that he should not be found guilty (12717–12720). Venus subsequently pardons him (12721). In this case, the process of negotiation with Venus is joined by an intercessor.

Members of the Crisian community seem to have an equivocal relationship with the objects' tests of virtue. They not only let the objects examine visitors but appear to also take the tests themselves from time to time. As an example, a prince named Arfaxat who resides in the borderlands of Crisa reports that he has been thrown off by the wheel and as a result is forbidden from advancing farther into the land (*AvT*, 11301, 11316). It seems apparent that the restrictions of access to Crisa also apply to him. Another example is King Candor himself: he shows Apollonius by example how to successfully climb the staircase (12008). All of these incidents suggest that members of the Crisian community submit themselves to the judgment of the objects, while on other occasions they try to influence or even manipulate those very same objects. When Apollonius is thrown from the staircase for a second time, this time accused of lying, the princess Diomena wants to ensure his entrance into the garden no matter what. She gives Apollonius a ring with the power to let him pass every ensuing test (12668–12676). Since Apollonius is later exonerated by Venus (12721), the ring turns out to be no more than a precautionary measure (12737–12738). Nevertheless, Diomena's gift shows that members of the Crisian community at times are will-

---

43 See Almut Schneider, *Chiffren des Selbst: Narrative Spiegelungen der Identitätsproblematik in Johanns von Würzburg "Wilhelm von Österreich" und in Heinrichs von Neustadt "Apollonius von Tyrland"* (Göttingen: Vandenhoeck & Ruprecht, 2004), 67; and Britta Maria Wittchow, *Erzählte mediale Prozesse: Medientheoretische Perspektiven auf den "Reinfried von Braunschweig" und den "Apollonius von Tyrland"* (Berlin: De Gruyter, 2020), 362–363.

ing and capable when it comes to acting against one of Crisa's virtue-enforcing objects.

The whole episode in Crisa shows that while characters can negotiate the consequences of their behavior with the goddess Venus, in the case of the Crisian objects that watch over the community's virtues, their judgment can only be influenced by fooling them. Their rigor becomes clear when Candor warns Apollonius that the artificial giant, part of the architectural ensemble of the fountain, will immediately kill him if it sees his black fingernail (*AvT*, 11765–11766, 11791), without hesitating or giving any warning. This brief episode shows paradigmatically that Crisa's objects interpret the community's standards of behavior in the strictest of ways. Machinelike, they follow their program of testing virtues and controlling boundaries.

The tests of virtue that visitors to Crisa must undergo at the wheel, the fountain, and the staircase encompass interactions with three groups of actors: the objects themselves, the Crisian nobles, and the goddess Venus (including her priest). Human members of the Crisian community seem to support and even utilize the objects and the goddess Venus in probing and guaranteeing the visitors' virtues. These members of the community also have to conform to Venus's and the object's judgments themselves, but they can likewise influence or manipulate them. As such, none of the actors seems to have final control over the country's standards of ideal behavior. Instead, they are all capable of affecting one another. The mutual influences are accompanied by standards of behavior and moral concepts that are not entirely consistent. As a result, the ideals of behavior in Crisa's utopian community are somewhat mutable.

An Object of Detachment from Crisa

Although the interactions of Apollonius and his companions with Crisa's various objects convey the impression that they become firmly integrated into the community, Heinrich continues his narration by describing how Apollonius leaves the country about a year and twelve weeks after his arrival (*AvT*, 13513). Apollonius initially intends to leave Crisa temporarily, but it turns out that he will never return. In terms of the topic I am investigating here, it is of great interest that Apollonius's decision to leave Crisa also has something to do with an object. As such, objects not only support the integration of new members into the community but can also initiate their detachment from that very same community. It is part of the complexity of Heinrich's take on the role of objects in the process of building a utopian community that he also accounts for their importance in processes of emigration from Crisa.

Here is what happens in detail: In Crisa, Apollonius has the opportunity to inform himself about Tarsia, his daughter from his first marriage. By successfully completing the staircase's test of virtue, he gains access to the pillar mentioned above, through which beholders can see any corner of the world they desire. In the larger narrative tradition, such a pillar is connected to use by a ruler controlling a huge country (e.g., in the Letter of Prester John).[44] In Heinrich's *Apollonius*, it is endowed with abilities that go far beyond this. The wondrous pillar allows Apollonius to see the city of Tarsis and shows him that his daughter Tarsia is still alive (*AvT*, 12877– 12879, 13536). It awakens the desire in him to travel there and bring her to the golden land (13526–13529).

Thus we can see that the objects in Crisa with which Apollonius interacts not only integrate him into the Crisian community but also exceed this, enabling him to resume other ties outside of Crisa. These ties are responsible for him leaving Crisa once again. The pillar admittedly belongs to Crisa and is only accessible there. However, in Apollonius's case, it does not stabilize the Crisian community but rather enables the protagonist to reengage with a contact that predates his involvement with Crisa. When Apollonius makes use of it, the wondrous pillar proves to be an object that indeed supports a broader sense of community.

From this episode, we can infer that not every marvelous object in Crisa durably ensures integration into the ideal community. Despite this medieval utopia's appearance of stability, Heinrich's narration hints that Crisa allows both immigration and emigration – and, at least in this respect, that the community is in constant flux.

Heinrich further shows that the migration of characters in and out of Crisa, in which objects play an important role, affects the ideal community's living conditions. To begin with, when Apollonius enters the country, he frees it from Serpanta and Ydrogant's influence (*AvT*, 10859–10863, 11030–11039). These monsters had gained control over Crisa's borders (8840–8844, 10625–10628), rendering it almost impossible to enter the country. This dominion ends when Apollonius succeeds in overcoming them.

Later, Apollonius himself becomes a member of the community and rises to the position of ruler of the land. As king of Crisa he acts in harmony with his father-in-law King Candor, who seems to retain his power. As an example, they give away gifts together at Diomena and Apollonius's wedding (*AvT*, 13419–13421). An uncertainty about the hierarchical structure of the land results from their double reign. Since Candor stays in power when Apollonius is named king of the land, the relationship between the two remains unresolved. This dual leadership – once again – reveals Crisa's hierarchy as a peculiar one. As already mentioned above, the ubiquity of riches also undermines Crisa's hierarchical structure and can be considered one of the land's utopian traits. Thus, as a result of Apollonius becoming a member of the community, the nonrigidity of its hierarchy, which is one of the place's utopian features, is further emphasized.

Nevertheless, the influence of migratory processes on the utopian community is limited. What happens when Apollonius enters Crisa paradigmatically shows that migratory processes do not change the utopian community's most basic features. Crisa's abundance of material goods and foodstuffs remains, for example, untouched.

---

44 See footnote 34.

The analysis of Apollonius's migration to and from Crisa has shown, however, that through their important role in migratory processes, objects participate in the mutability of the utopian community and even contribute to the evolution of the community and the underscoring of its central characteristics.

Conclusion

In contrast to the society of the Grail in Wolfram's *Parzival*, whose prospective members God elects, the Crisa episode in Heinrich von Neustadt's *Apollonius* reveals a range of concrete procedures and interactions that control access to the utopian community and – where possible – lead to the integration of strangers into this ideal land. The criteria for access are laid out over the course of a process occurring in various steps: the visitors' repeated tests demonstrate the elaborate set of virtues that members of the Crisian community conform to and show the ways in which prospective members must behave, or morally and physically change, in order to gain access. As such, objects play a significant part here in the processes of integrating human characters into the utopian community. Several objects are able to detect even the slightest violation of the Crisian norms of virtuous behavior and, by doing so, establish a basis for those being tested to acknowledge their wrongdoings and change their behavior. Moreover, a specific object, the fountain of youth, can change certain carefully selected visitors cognitively and physically. As such, the objects' special abilities lead to and bring about changes that are prerequisites for becoming a member of the Crisian community.

Nevertheless, this analysis has shown that objects in Crisa don't interact alone with visitors to the land; rather, they are always already involved with a number of further actors. These actors participate in the process of integrating new members into the community, especially by taking part in the decision about whether or not to grant an outsider access to Crisa: in addition to the various objects, the goddess Venus (and her priest), the nobles of the land (especially King Candor), and the visitors themselves are involved. Thus, behavioral norms in Crisa are established and maintained by a network of actors within which the role of objects is not to be neglected. Conversely, the analysis has shown that objects in Crisa gain agency only in combination with other actors. This is part of the text's complexity in representing the agency of objects. The complexity goes even further: when Apollonius once again leaves the country, an object also contributes to the process of his detachment. In sum, in the Crisa episode, Heinrich describes intricate processes of immigration and emigration, of integration and detachment, all involving objects. The unresolved situation of double kingship following Apollonius's coronation shows that the Crisian objects, by way of fostering processes of integration, even contribute to the production of fundamental characteristics of the utopian community. When Apollonius becomes king of Crisa, the hierarchy of the land is shifted, but the shift itself can be seen as according with Crisa's utopian traits.

Ultimately, this exploration of a medieval utopian community has led to some notable findings with respect to its relation to early modern utopias. Similar to the way that Thomas More, in *Utopia*, describes a society based on common property, in Crisa certain material objects – such as foodstuffs and riches – are ubiquitous and generally accessible, and they play an important role in the formation and preservation of the community. In addition, we have seen that things of a particular kind are especially active in the medieval utopian community of Crisa. Marvelous objects that have special abilities and even act, as described here, to establish and maintain the ideal community seem to be specific to utopian lands of the Middle Ages. What is furthermore specific to Crisa is that its objects not only interact with one another, but also with those who visit the community. In contrast to the so-called classical utopias of the sixteenth and early seventeenth centuries, visitors to Crisa are not detached observers but rather become involved with and subsequently integrated into the community.[45] As we have seen, this is essentially realized through their interaction with things. The visitors' integration goes hand in hand with their contributions to the organization of the ideal community. The fact that the integration and participation of visitors brings change to Crisa leads to the hypothesis that interaction with visitors and the change that results from this might play a more important part in medieval utopian communities than is generally acknowledged in the case of early modern utopias.[46]

---

[45] Although in More's *Utopia* Raphael Hythlodaeus claims to have lived for more than five years in the ideal community (see More, *Utopia*, 106, 116), his description is – though sometimes explicitly focalized ("conspicitur"; More, 120) – detached and analytic throughout. Recourse to sensual experience in this text seems only to be relevant on a conceptual level: by seeing Utopia with one's own eyes, one can overcome the unfamiliarity of this society's organization (see More, 106). To be precise, More's take on sensual perception may exhibit a tendency of classical utopias (another example is Tommaso Campanella's *La città del sole* / *City of the Sun* [1623]), but it is not without counterexamples: cf. Anton Francesco Doni's *Il mondo savio e pazzo* (1552, *Wise and Crazy World*). I have further elaborated the comparison of medieval utopias with so-called classical utopias, like Thomas More's, in my postdoctoral dissertation (*Habilitation*) (Freie Universität Berlin, 2020).

[46] For a recent example of characterizing More's utopian community as stable, see Otfried Höffe, "Thomas Morus' *Utopia*: Eine Einführung," in *Über Thomas Morus' "Utopia"*, ed. Joachim Starbatty (Hildesheim: Olms-Weidmann, 2016), 11–35, at 31–32. In contrast, William T. Cotton has taken the widely recorded absence of history in More's utopian community as a starting point from which to look for hints about changes in the community over time: cf. William T. Cotton, "Five-Fold Crisis in Utopia: A Foreshadow of Major Modern Utopian Narrative Strategies," *Utopian Studies: Journal of the Society for Utopian Studies* 14, no. 2 (2003): 41–67.

Christopher Hutchinson

9 Printing Things: Materiality and Immateriality in Hieronymus Brunschwig's *Liber de arte distillandi de simplicibus*

What is the difference between a thing and an image of a thing? Hieronymus Brunschwig's 1500 distillation handbook, the *Liber de arte distillandi de simplicibus* (typically referred to as his *Small Book of Distillation*), contains a woodcut depicting a mold for making bricks that invites the reader to reflect on this question. The illustration in question (see figure 9.1) also contains a twenty-line poem that instructs the reader to cut the image of the mold out of the book: "the part here in the middle should be cut out completely."[1] The reader can then fill the mold with clay to make bricks for a distillation furnace: "the space around which the roses are shown is where the bricks are made."[2] This presents a problem, however. The mold is printed on double-sided pages that have text and images on the reverse of both leaves. If the reader follows the instructions in the poem and cuts out the mold, they will destroy this text and these images. Moreover, it is precisely the text on the other sides of these leaves that provides the most detailed instructions on how to make the bricks. This is unlikely to have been a simple printer's error, as subsequent editions maintain this arrangement of text and image. There is a paradox here. Why does this work contain a mold to be cut out, when the act of cutting it out would threaten not only to damage the book itself but also to destroy Brunschwig's instructions for use?

This mold is deeply unusual in the corpus of printed artisanal manuals from the start of the sixteenth century. It is common for such manuals to include woodcut or copperplate images of objects, or diagrams that illustrate mathematical phenomena or aspects of the human body, but there are to my knowledge no other examples of images from the turn of the sixteenth century that invite the reader to physically incorporate the image into their artisanal practice. Brunschwig's mold has mostly been cited by scholars as an example of the innovative ways in which writers and printers sought to convey practical information to their readers.[3] It is life-size and printed on

---

1 Hieronymus Brunschwig, *Liber de arte distillandi de simplicibus* [Small Book of Distillation] (Strasbourg: Johannes Grüninger, 1500) (GW 05595), C4v: "Das teyl als hye ist in der mitten. / Soll gantz vnd gar syn vß geschnytten." All translations are my own unless otherwise noted. Diacritical abbreviations have been resolved using italics.

2 Brunschwig, *Small Book*, C4v: "Dar ynnen die rosen stond gezeicht. / So dar ynn die steyn sint gemacht."

3 Michael Giesecke, *Sinnenwandel, Sprachwandel, Kulturwandel: Studien zur Vorgeschichte der Informationsgesellschaft* (Frankfurt: Suhrkamp, 1992), 538; Tillmann Taape, "Distilling Reliable Remedies:

https://doi.org/10.1515/9783110742985-012

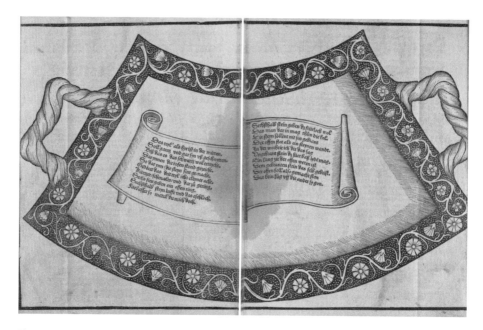

Figure 9.1: Woodcut of a brick mold with instructions to cut it out of the book, from Hieronymus Brunschwig, Liber de arte distillandi de simplicibus [Small Book of Distillation] (Strasbourg: Johannes Grüninger, 1500) (GW 05595), C4v–C5r. Courtesy of the Universitäts- und Landesbibliothek Darmstadt (Inc. IV 206).

the innermost double-page spread of a signature, so it could in theory be cut out, as the instructions demand, or even traced and used as a template to form a mold to produce bricks for building a distillation furnace. The mold in the woodcut even includes handles on either side, suggestive of Brunschwig's intention that the illustration be used in practice.

But does this illustrated brick mold really have a practical purpose? I know of no surviving copies of the book in which the illustration has been cut out and the pages are missing or heavily damaged. Furthermore, the floral pattern on the lip of the mold in the illustration, together with other features like the shading inside the mold and the detail on the rope handles, suggest that we read the image as an aesthetic object rather than one designed primarily for practical use as a brick mold. Although the poem in the center of the mold instructs the reader to treat the illustration as a real thing, the formal integration of the image into the larger work calls its utility into question, standing in the way of its transition out of the book and into the real world of things.

Hieronymus Brunschwig's *Liber de arte distillandi* (1500) between Alchemical Learning and Craft Practice," *Ambix* 61, no. 3 (2014): 236–256, at 252.

In this chapter, I argue that the paradox presented by this brick mold stems from a peculiar tension in Brunschwig's conception of materiality. Brunschwig casts his larger work – a handbook on the materials and practices of medicinal distilling – as a practical manual that should allow the reader to re-create his techniques of distilling. The book is informed by a trend in printing at the start of the sixteenth century in which information about artisanal practice was communicated in a manner that stimulated the reader's material engagement with its tools, things, and techniques. Despite its concern with communicating a physical experience involving matter, however, Brunschwig's work is also concerned with transcending this materiality. The field of medicinal distilling, according to the alchemical theories that supported it, aimed to remove the material qualities of matter, refining it into immaterial elixirs whose incorruptibility could be transferred to the human body, curing it of its ailments. How can a printed book – a material object – adequately represent the physical matter of craft practice when the particular craft at hand is ultimately concerned less with matter itself than with the immaterial qualities and potentialities that inhabit it?

This tension between the book's focus on replicable craft practice involving physical matter and its implicit concern with distilling the immaterial qualities of matter also raises questions about the arcane quality of the latter form of knowledge. Texts on alchemy and distillation in Europe throughout this period are generally replete with the language of secrecy, and new issues arise when this knowledge is presented in printed books with a relatively large distribution. The questions of materiality/immateriality and secrecy evident in Brunschwig's handbook are reflective of a broader concern in the genre of the printed artisanal manual that developed at the turn of the sixteenth century: How to represent matter in a way that is meant to be reproducible by a broad readership when this matter is inhabited by immaterial and arcane components? The tension between the material focus of craft practice and the immaterial ideas and theories of distillation, I argue, necessitates a form of representation that gives voice to both the practical material qualities of matter and the immaterial qualities that also inhabit it.

Scholars have traditionally identified the primary function of these printed artisan's handbooks as that of conveying practical competencies in the relevant craft by encouraging the reader's bodily encounter with matter. Rather than simply learning why bees produce honey, for instance, readers should learn how to build hives and keep bees themselves. That is, they should physically engage with the craft processes that these books elucidate. Pamela Smith has proposed the term "artisanal epistemology" to describe this bodily engagement with craft knowledge. Smith argues that "[artisans] articulated in their writings and in their works of art a view that certainty is located in matter and nature and that knowledge can be gained by observing and experiencing – often by bodily struggle – the particularity of nature."[4] Arti-

---

4 Pamela H. Smith, *The Body of the Artisan: Art and Experience in the Scientific Revolution* (Chicago: University of Chicago Press, 2004), 6.

sans were less concerned with the communication of theoretical knowledge than with a corporeal encounter with matter. Smith goes on to link this sixteenth-century artisanal focus on matter to alchemical practices and discourses, highlighting the two fields' common purpose of "ennobling matter through manual work."[5] I would argue, though, that in works like Brunschwig's *Small Book of Distillation*, this artisanal emphasis on a bodily encounter with matter is undercut rather than supported by the alchemical theories of immateriality that inform the particular artisanal practices depicted.

The few scholarly works that have discussed Brunschwig's text view it as a work whose primary goal is the communication of practical competence. Alisha Rankin has argued that Brunschwig's *Small Book* broke new ground in its focus on "the *labor* of making medicines as an important path to medical knowledge."[6] For Rankin, Brunschwig's text provides a central example of artisanal literature focused on the communication of practical skills and the physical encounter with things. Its purpose is to allow the reader to translate the techniques it contains into a real-world praxis. While the *Small Book of Distillation* is replete with detailed instructions and illustrations meant to allow the reader to enact the techniques the book describes, it also contains a number of woodcuts, like that of the brick mold, whose direct practical value is limited. This diversity of illustrations is reflective of the tension between the material engagement with the practice of distilling that the book purports to grant the reader and the immaterial associations, ideas, and goals that underlie this practice. This inconsistency in the representation of matter in the printed book constitutes a working-through of these concerns about the immaterial and arcane qualities of matter. As I demonstrate in this chapter, the book's function is less to allow the reader to directly imitate the techniques of distillation described within it than to offer the reader an insight into the material and immaterial components that inhabit things.

The turn of the sixteenth century is a fruitful time period in which to examine this shifting landscape of materiality. Many of the social, economic, and cultural changes impacting Europe at this time brought with them a growing appreciation of the role of material things in everyday life.[7] Lisa Jardine has shown how the fifteenth and sixteenth centuries formed a period characterized by the ownership of

---

5 Smith, *Body of the Artisan*, 144. See also Tara Nummedal, *Alchemy and Authority in the Holy Roman Empire* (Chicago: University of Chicago Press, 2007). Taape has also linked the material focus of artisanal practice with alchemical theory in his discussion of Brunschwig's *Small Book*. See Taape, "Reliable Remedies."

6 Alisha Rankin, "How to Cure the Golden Vein: Medical Remedies as *Wissenschaft* in Early Modern Germany," in *Ways of Making and Knowing: The Material Culture of Empirical Knowledge*, ed. Pamela H. Smith, Amy R. W. Meyers, and Harold J. Cook (Ann Arbor: University of Michigan Press, 2014), 113–135, at 121.

7 See Pamela O. Long, *Artisan/Practitioners and the Rise of the New Sciences, 1400–1600* (Corvallis: Oregon State University Press, 2011), 3. See also Paula Findlen, ed., *Early Modern Things: Objects and Their Histories, 1500–1800* (New York: Routledge, 2013).

things, by "a celebration of the urge to own, the curiosity to possess the treasures of other cultures, and pride in a new craftsmanship which can make the most humdrum commodities desirable."[8] The expansion of global trade networks, the development of urban middle classes in many parts of Europe, and innovations in diverse fields such as mining, bookkeeping, and navigation all contributed to a growing culture of commodities and consumption in Europe. Material things proliferated, as did writing about things.[9]

Printed manuals form part of this growing appreciation of material things, as they are explicitly concerned with how best to communicate information about things and how to create and manipulate things.[10] Whereas previously craft knowledge could only be learned through observation and imitation of the techniques in question, these handbooks strove to make aspects of artisanal practice accessible to people outside of the networks engaged in these processes of making and doing. In theory at least, any literate person with sufficient financial resources could pick up a book on shipbuilding, follow the instructions contained within, and construct their own ship, without ever being instructed by a master shipbuilder in person. Over the course of the sixteenth century, hundreds of practical manuals were published, primarily but not exclusively in vernacular languages, on a variety of craft techniques ranging from surgery to cannon foundry to beehive construction, as printers and booksellers sought to capitalize on a growing market for them.

This chapter is concerned with how printed books represent the materiality of things. By looking at how artisan's handbooks depict material things through both text and image, and how they encourage engagement with matter, we get a clearer sense of the growing role that printed books played in the burgeoning marketplace of ideas at the turn of the sixteenth century, as well as the ways in which artisanal practice engaged with this new medium in order to communicate, and reflect on, the knowledge it involved. As Smith points out, "Craft is productive knowledge and its products are records of practices as well as repositories of knowledge."[11] When investigating the history of craft practice, a focus on the things themselves that are central to this practice and on the ways in which books engage with, depict, and communi-

---

8 Lisa Jardine, *Worldly Goods: A New History of the Renaissance* (New York: Doubleday, 1996), 34.
9 On the link between globalization and early modern commodity culture, see, in particular, Timothy Brook, *Vermeer's Hat: The Seventeenth Century and the Dawn of the Global World* (New York: Bloomsbury, 2008); and Christine Johnson, *The German Discovery of the World: Renaissance Encounters with the Strange and Marvelous* (Charlottesville: University of Virginia Press, 2008).
10 For an overview of artisan's manuals of the period, see Pamela O. Long, *Openness, Secrecy, Authorship: Technical Arts and the Culture of Knowledge from Antiquity to the Renaissance* (Baltimore: Johns Hopkins University Press, 2001); and Pamela H. Smith, "Making Things: Techniques and Books in Early Modern Europe," in Findlen, *Early Modern Things*, 173–204.
11 Pamela H. Smith, "Making as Knowing: Craft as Natural Philosophy," in Smith, Meyers, and Cook, *Making and Knowing*, 17–47, at 20. See also Pamela H. Smith and Benjamin Schmidt, eds., introduction to *Making Knowledge in Early Modern Europe: Practices, Objects, and Texts, 1400–1800* (Chicago: University of Chicago Press, 2007), 1–16.

cate information about things is especially necessary. Such an approach can provide insight into the multifaceted ways in which writers, printers, and consumers conceived of the role of the book, the ways in which artisans at the turn of the sixteenth century reflected on the materiality of the things they utilized, and the ways in which print changed understandings of things.

Craft Manuals as Handbooks for Engaging with Matter

Craft manuals formed a significant part of the landscape of print culture at the start of the sixteenth century, and many enjoyed multiple reprints and were translated into Europe's major languages. While the texts were mostly written by active practitioners of the crafts they describe, the boom in the printing of handbooks prompted some writers to copy, compile, and rebrand existing texts from the genre, often combining them or interspersing them with translations from the theoretical works of scholarly authorities like Hippocrates, Galen, Rhazes, or Avicenna. At issue is a set of texts that draw on a wide range of sources, learned and lay, and that target a wide readership, again learned and lay. These texts, with their claim to practical utility, coexisted with and were influenced by more theoretical writings, and many authors penned books that offered both practical instruction in a craft and an exposition of its theoretical underpinnings. For my definition of artisanal writing, I follow Long, who defines artisans as "all skilled workers and practitioners who learned through formal or informal apprenticeships and oral instruction."[12] This definition includes individuals active in diverse fields, from surgeons and builders to weavers and farmers, but emphasizes that what they have in common is the practical, hands-on nature of the knowledge they possess. While university-educated thinkers and practitioners are not included in this category of artisans, knowledge – especially in medical fields – was frequently exchanged between the two groups: artisanal writers drew on many of the canonical sources of knowledge that dominated university curricula, and learned writers in turn read artisan's manuals.[13] What differentiates artisanal writing from texts by artisans' learned colleagues is a focus on conveying practical competencies as opposed to theoretical knowledge, although this is not a binary distinction.

Hieronymus Brunschwig was one of the most influential artisanal writers of the turn of the sixteenth century and a pioneer in the genre, though he has received relatively little scholarly attention. Born in Strasbourg around 1450, Brunschwig spent a

---

12 Long, *Artisan/Practitioners*, 1n1.

13 Brunschwig's use of Latin in the title of his *Liber de arte distillandi de simplicibus*, even though the rest of the book is in the vernacular, attests to the broad readership he targets with his work. Whereas all literate readers could understand the main body of the text – written in German – the Latin title signals that the work also has value to learned readers.

large period of his life as a military doctor in Alsace, Swabia, and Bavaria before returning to settle in Strasbourg, where he obtained the post of city surgeon.[14] In collaboration with his regular printer, Johannes Grüninger, he produced a series of medical textbooks on surgery, plague treatment, medical botany, and distillation at the turn of the sixteenth century, many of which became defining works in their fields and were reprinted a number of times in the following decades.[15] His *Buch der Cirurgia* was reprinted five times in the half century following its first publication in 1497. The *Small Book of Distillation* was the first printed book to convey the techniques of distillation, and most sixteenth-century German writings on distillation drew heavily from Brunschwig's work.[16] It was reprinted nineteen times in German alone during the sixteenth century and was one of the earliest printed works in the natural sciences to be translated into English. Highly popular and situated at the beginning of the sixteenth-century boom in printed compendia of practical knowledge, Brunschwig's oeuvre, and especially his *Small Book*, makes for a useful object of study for anyone hoping to consider the ways in which artisanal writing conceives of and depicts things.

The *Small Book* is a work designed with practical use in mind. In the text's introduction, Brunschwig explains that he wrote the book for three main reasons. First, he claims his initial motivation was to satisfy repeated requests by friends and colleagues: "I have often been asked what I have done in my practice; namely, how one should boil, distill, use, and keep waters."[17] Second, he intends the work to serve as a memory aid for distillers, again emphasizing the practical goals of the text. Third, Brunschwig contends that he has written the book for the sake of "those who desire to learn the measures and craft of distilling, and the means of beginning this labor as well as its ends."[18] In other words, this work should not just inform readers abstractly about the craft of distilling: it should support their own material labor,

---

14 Henry E. Sigerist, "Hieronymus Brunschwig and His Work," in *The Book of Cirurgia*, by Hieronymus Brunschwig, ed. Henry E. Sigerist (Milan: R. Lier, 1923), v.

15 Grüninger was a prolific and well-regarded printer in Strasbourg who worked alongside prominent humanists like Sebastian Brant and Jakob Wimpfeling and printed a number of richly illustrated volumes of classical works, Bible editions, and works on natural history. On Grüninger's oeuvre, see Catarina Zimmermann-Homeyer, *Illustrierte Frühdrucke lateinischer Klassiker um 1500: Innovative Illustrationskonzepte aus der Straßburger Offizin Johannes Grüningers und ihre Wirkung* (Wiesbaden: Harrassowitz, 2018). On the printing scene in Strasbourg, see Miriam Usher Chrisman, *Lay Culture, Learned Culture: Books and Social Change in Strasbourg, 1480–1599* (New Haven: Yale University Press, 1982).

16 The first known printed work on distillation is a 1476 pamphlet by the Viennese physician Michael Puff: Michael Puff, *Von den ausgebrannten Wassern* (Augsburg: Johann Bämler, 1476) (GW M36472). In later sixteenth- and seventeenth-century editions, Puff's work was often bound together with sections of Brunschwig's 1512 *Large Book of Distillation*.

17 Brunschwig, *Small Book*, A2v: "Ich offt vnd vil gefragt byn / so ich gehandelt hab in myner practica wie man die wasser brennen / distillieren / bruchen vnd behalten soll."

18 Brunschwig, *Small Book*, A2v: "Zum dritten die do begeren zů leren die maß vnd kunst der distillierung diß wercks an zefahen mittel vnd das end."

providing them with the knowledge necessary to start distilling on their own. Brunschwig demonstrates that he is concerned with providing his readers with functional competencies.

The form and structure of the book itself also support its practical usability. It contains an extensive list of headings as well as alphabetized indexes of the contents of each chapter. These strategies of information organization respond to Brunschwig's and Grüninger's concern that their volume function as a useful reference book. If the reader wants to distill a certain plant, or create a distillate to treat a certain malady, they can easily locate the relevant passage in the book.[19] The work as a whole is divided into three sections. In the first section, Brunschwig provides an introduction to the art of distillation and educates his audience in the necessary practical processes of the craft. The second section is an illustrated catalogue that alphabetically lists various herbs and other substances that can be distilled, alongside their medical uses. The third section contains a register of diseases organized in anatomical order from head to toe, accompanied by page references to the relevant distillates. The work is substantial: a comprehensive handbook meant to guide readers' material engagement with the methods, applications, and things of distillation.

Alchemy, Distilling, and Making the Material Immaterial

Distillation was a discipline whose central concern was the mutability of matter. The practice of distilling substances for medicinal purposes goes back to at least the thirteenth century, as works by the Franciscan friars Roger Bacon and John of Rupescissa attest, and it developed out of an alchemical tradition concerned with transmuting metals whose roots lay in the medieval Islamic world and, ultimately, Ptolemaic Egypt.[20] It is this interest in manipulating metals that colors our contemporary image of alchemy: we think primarily of the alchemist's desire to turn base metals into gold. However, European alchemy in the late Middle Ages was a diverse branch of knowledge, embracing theories and practices that might seem to us more at home in the fields of medicine or natural philosophy.[21] In particular, the strand of alchemy developed by medieval writers like Bacon and John of Rupescissa set as its goal the distillation of matter into elixirs that could maintain human health and prolong life.

---

19 On the development of indexes and lists of headings in printed books, see Ann M. Blair, *Too Much to Know: Managing Scholarly Information before the Modern Age* (New Haven: Yale University Press, 2010).

20 For the influence of the historical tradition of alchemy on medieval and early modern European practices, see Lawrence M. Principe, *The Secrets of Alchemy* (Chicago: University of Chicago Press, 2013).

21 See Leah DeVun, *Prophecy, Alchemy, and the End of Time: John of Rupescissa in the Late Middle Ages* (New York: Columbia University Press, 2009), esp. 54.

Thus, alchemy was not only concerned with transmuting metals; it was concerned more broadly with the study and manipulation of matter – in particular, its refinement and perfection.[22]

Thirteenth- and fourteenth-century debates on alchemy had revolved around the question of the relationship between nature and products of human artifice. A number of thinkers, Thomas Aquinas foremost among them, argued that all artificial products, whether transmuted metals or distilled waters, are weak versions of natural things that lack these things' fundamental qualities.[23] The arguments contrary to Thomas's position, espoused by Bacon and others, held that since the techniques of alchemy are natural, their outcomes are just as natural as matter not produced by human labor. Many even argued that things produced by alchemy were better or more potent than the natural substances they originated as.[24]

This belief that the products of alchemical practice could be purer than their natural bases coincided with an interest among alchemical writers in overcoming the constraints of earthly matter. The fourteenth-century alchemist and friar John of Rupescissa was especially influential in this regard. John, whose ideas formed the basis of medicinal distillation, argued that by distilling earthly matter multiple times one could create a substance impervious to decay. This substance, which John termed the "quintessence" (or "fifth essence") of the distilled matter, was greater than, and free from all traces of, the four elements – that is, the earthly matter that had constituted the thing distilled. As he wrote, "And the thing we seek is [incorruptible and immutable] in respect to the four qualities of our body: the fifth essence has been made in itself incorruptible, not hot and dry like fire, nor wet and cold like water, nor hot and wet like air, nor cold and dry like earth."[25] It is this transcendence of the four elements that compose earthly matter that gives John's quintessence the power to

---

22 While later writers like Brunschwig do distinguish between medicinal distilling and alchemical practices concerned with transmuting metals, these two fields share the same theoretical interest in perfecting or transcending matter, and this is reflected in sixteenth-century works on distilling like Brunschwig's. On the links between medicinal distilling and alchemy, see Bruce T. Moran, *Distilling Knowledge: Alchemy, Chemistry, and the Scientific Revolution* (Cambridge, MA: Harvard University Press, 2005), 11–25. On the tension between these disciplines, see Nummedal, *Alchemy and Authority*, esp. 33–39; and Lauren Kassell, "Reading for the Philosopher's Stone," in *Books and the Sciences in History*, ed. Marina Frasca-Spada and Nick Jardine (Cambridge: Cambridge University Press, 2000), 132–150.

23 For Thomas's anti-alchemical writings, see William R. Newman, *Promethean Ambitions: Alchemy and the Quest to Perfect Nature* (Chicago: University of Chicago Press, 2004), 93–97. For the wider controversy surrounding alchemy, see Principe, *Secrets of Alchemy*, 58–62.

24 Bacon, for instance, argued that alchemy could produce gold purer than twenty-four karats, the purest natural gold. See W. Newman, *Promethean Ambitions*, 88.

25 Johannes de Rupescissa, *De consideratione quintae essentie rerum omnium* (Basel: Heinrich Petri and Peter Perna, 1561) (VD16 J 691), 19: "Sic [incorrupilis et immutabilis] et res quam quærimus est respectu quatuor qualitatum corporis nostri: quinta Essentia, in se incorruptibilis sic facta, non calida sicca cum igne, nec humida frigida cum aqua, nec calida humida cum aere, nec frigida sicca cum terra." The English translation is adapted from DeVun, *Prophesy*, 66, with modifications of my own.

heal. It is a fifth element that is immutable and incorruptible – and thus immaterial – and it can convey this incorruptibility to the human body. John's attempts to distill the quintessence belong to a tradition of striving to make the material immaterial. Whereas alchemical theory and practice, at its inception, was principally concerned with transmuting matter – with turning one metal into another – John writes instead of transcending it.

Brunschwig, who was greatly influenced by John's writings, as Tillmann Taape has shown, stands firmly in this tradition.[26] In the introduction to his *Small Book*, he offers the reader some theoretical background on distilling:

> It is worth knowing that distilling is nothing other than separating the subtle from the coarse, and the coarse from the subtle; making that which is fragile or destructible indestructible; making the material more immaterial; making the physical more spiritual; tending to that which is unpleasant in a more pleasant way, so that the spirit can lovingly, as well as more easily and more quickly, through its subtlety permeate and penetrate the physical with the virtue and power that are hidden and sunken into it, so that the human body may feel its healing effect.[27]

The notion of distilling that Brunschwig elucidates here aims at removing the earthly qualities of matter in order to make it "more immaterial," so that the resulting distilled water can heal the human body – a notion that borrows from John's idea of "quintessence."

However, one crucial difference between Brunschwig's depiction of distillation and earlier writers' presentation of alchemical knowledge in their texts is the level of secrecy with which they treat this knowledge. Alchemical writers had, since the discipline's beginnings, cast their techniques as arcane knowledge, obfuscating them with a series of code words – or *Decknamen* – that were designed to ensure this knowledge stayed out of the hands of undesired readers.[28] Medieval writings on distilling, and alchemy more broadly, are deliberately recondite and contain warnings that emphasize the arcane nature of the works.[29] In his work on the quintessence, John of Rupescissa highlighted the danger that a wide reception of his work

---

26 Taape, "Reliable Remedies." For the wider reception of John's ideas in Germany, see Udo Benzenhöfer, *Johannes' de Rupescissa "Liber de consideratione quintae essentiae omnium rerum" deutsch: Studien zur Alchemia medica des 15. bis 17. Jahrhunderts mit kritischer Edition des Textes* (Stuttgart: Franz Steiner, 1989).

27 Brunschwig, *Small Book*, C1r–v: "Darumb so ist zů wissen das distillieren nichtz anders ist dan das subtyl von dem groben / vnd das grob von dem subtilen zů scheiden / das gebrechlich oder zerstörlich vnzerstörlicher zů machen das materialisch vnmaterialischer zů machen / das lyplich geistlicher zemachen / das vnlieplich lieplicher zů behalten / vff dz lyplich der geist dz lyplich durch sin subtilithet dester lichter darzů behender dringen vnd penetrieren mag mit siner tugende vnd krafft die dar in verborgen vnd gesencket ist vmb entpfintlichheit syner heylsamen würckung in dem menschlichen lyb."

28 Principe, *Secrets of Alchemy*, esp. 62–71.

29 On these "secrecy clauses," see Robert Halleux, *Les textes alchimiques* (Turnhout: Brepols, 1979), 79–83.

might present: "Know and be attentive to the fact that many masters, to whom this mystery has been revealed through revelations, invoked harm and cursed with horrible maledictions, fearing that these secrets might come into the hands of the unworthy."[30] The knowledge of how to transcend matter was something to be closely guarded and not spread widely.

William Eamon has shown how the sixteenth century saw a rapid increase in the production and distribution of what he terms "books of secrets": vernacular books containing usually short recipes and formulas used in everyday techniques from cookery to medicine making, or even general household hints.[31] These books, which, like artisanal manuals, focus on communicating practical competencies to the reader, often strike a revelatory tone.[32] They promise to reveal the secrets of nature to their readers and often actively describe them in terms that demonstrate that these secrets – and the practices that derive from them – are occult; that is, that their natural causes are hidden from human knowledge.[33]

The language of secrecy is notably absent in Brunschwig's *Small Book*. He makes no attempt to highlight the occult or arcane qualities of alchemical practice or flaunt his revelation of nature's secrets. However, there is a contradiction inherent in his work. It takes as its topic a subject – distillation – laden with secrecy due to its ability to create substances whose power transcends that of earthly matter, yet it presents this subject in an artisanal manual whose publication and distribution should allow the harnessing of this immaterial power by all those with the means to buy the book and the necessary equipment, even if they are, as John had feared, "unworthy." This is the problem that print presents in general. The arcane quality that infused medieval alchemy, predicated on the idea of transcending earthly matter, is undercut by the advent of print, which offers to make this arcane knowledge commonplace.

We can read this tension between secret knowledge and its public distribution in printed books the way Elizabeth Eisenstein does: as a demystification of the medieval world by print, which laid the groundwork for the public empiricism of the Sci-

---

30 Quoted in DeVun, *Prophecy*, 59: "Scito autem et animadverte quod multi Magistri, quibus revelatum fuit hunc misterium a revelantibus, imprecati fuerunt et maledicti horrendas maledictiones, timentes ne hec arcana venirent in manus indignorum." Translation DeVun's.

31 William Eamon, *Science and the Secrets of Nature: Books of Secrets in Medieval and Early Modern Culture* (Princeton, NJ: Princeton University Press, 1994), esp. 93 – 133.

32 On printed books of secrets, see Eamon, *Secrets of Nature*, 234 – 259. For strategies printers took to generate this revelatory tone, see also Allison Kavey, *Books of Secrets: Natural Philosophy in England, 1550 – 1600* (Urbana: University of Illinois Press, 2007), 66 – 72.

33 Volkhard Wels has demonstrated that the word *occult* only gained its modern meaning, describing practices with supernatural causes, in the mid-sixteenth century, with the writings of Paracelsus and his followers. See Volkhard Wels, "Die Alchemie der Frühen Neuzeit als Gegenstand der Wissensgeschichte," in *Magia daemoniaca, magia naturalis, zouber: Schreibweisen von Magie und Alchemie in Mittelalter und Früher Neuzeit*, ed. Peter-André Alt, Jutta Eming, Tilo Renz, and Volkhard Wels (Wiesbaden: Harrassowitz, 2015), 233 – 265, at 248.

entific Revolution.[34] But it also raises concomitant questions about materiality. If anyone can make the material immaterial, then doesn't the immaterial become mundane? Isn't the immaterial elixir produced by distillation then just another material? It is this tension between the alchemical quest for immateriality and the artisanal focus on matter that informs both the paradox of the brick mold (see figure 9.1) and the broader repertoire of images that Brunschwig and Grüninger employ to illustrate the *Small Book*.

Materiality and Immateriality in Brunschwig's Images

When we look at Brunschwig and Grüninger's *Small Book*, we find a number of images that seem designed to support the reader's material engagement with the practices of distillation outlined in the book. However, like the brick mold, many of these images also appear to resist the practical usefulness they aspire to. The depictions of the tools and materials of distillation they offer are oftentimes stylized versions of the things they illustrate, in which certain immaterial characteristics of the things in question come to the fore as much as the material aspects that would be most pertinent in helping the reader re-create the practices of distilling. The images betray an awareness that the matter they represent is inhabited by immaterial components: by knowledge, aims, and practices that cannot be explained solely by manifest causes.

The book's title page contains an image of a garden in which various figures tend plants and distill waters from them (figure 9.2). On the one hand, this image shows an engagement with the material objects of distilling. Many of the figures are actively laboring: one figure hoes a small plot, another stokes a furnace, and a further group of figures is harvesting plants to be distilled. At the same time, though, this scene takes place in a utopic space: a perfect garden with the requisite plants, animals, and equipment for promoting human health, separated from the real, material world by the gated fence at the bottom of the image. This garden is not a real garden, but rather an allegory for the book itself: both contain the materials and knowledge necessary to promote human health. Although this image provides vignettes depicting the material engagement with distillation that the book is meant to allow the reader, the setting of these scenes of physical labor is, because of its allegorical nature, ultimately immaterial. As such, this image perfectly reflects the larger tension between the material work offered to the reader and the immaterial qualities that distilling aspires to.

The book contains an uncommonly large number of images, and I do not intend to suggest that this discrepancy between the materiality of artisanal labor and the

---

34 Elizabeth Eisenstein, *The Printing Press as an Agent of Change: Communications and Cultural Transformations in Early-Modern Europe* (Cambridge: Cambridge University Press, 1979), 520–575.

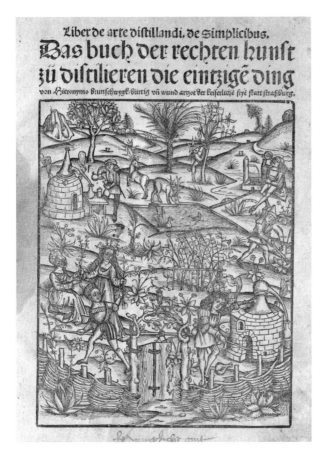

Figure 9.2: Title page, including woodcut of a garden with figures laboring, from Brunschwig, Small Book, A1r. Courtesy of the Universitäts- und Landesbibliothek Darmstadt (Inc. IV 206).

alchemical search for immateriality is equally present in every single one.[35] Images in this genre of book had a variety of possible functions: they could serve as mnemonics, reinforcing the text they accompanied; they could convey a sense of the author's or printer's scholarly authority; they could allow illiterate or less literate readers to access some facet of the work, even though they might struggle to read the surrounding text; they could clarify technical aspects of the text; or they could perform some combination of any of the above. As Sachiko Kusukawa has pointed out, "There was no established consensus as to what illustrations represented and how they might be used in gaining knowledge about nature, and indeed [this was] a time when people

---

35 In all, the book contains 294 woodcuts. Of these, 264 depict various plants, animals, or other substances used in distillation; 25 depict the pieces of equipment – stills, furnaces – necessary to distill; and the remaining 5 are stock woodcuts of general scenes of teaching and learning that Brunschwig and Grüninger also employ in a number of their other collaborations.

experimented with different ways to represent nature on two-dimensional paper and devised rules of representation."[36] This experimentation with the uses of representation attests to writers' and printers' interest in working through questions of materiality at the turn of the sixteenth century. Images served a variety of functions and could inhabit diverse relationships to the things they depicted. This diversity in strategies of representation of material things and techniques is richly present in the *Small Book*.

The genre of the printed artisanal manual, with its stated focus on the practical usability of the information it contains, makes images play the role of usable things – that is, things that shape the reader's physical labor, rather than ones that solely contribute to the reader's theoretical understanding of a subject. In the case of Brunschwig's brick mold, the physical image itself claims to be directly usable. More often, though, it is not the material page that is directly usable; rather, it is the cognitive information the image contains that helps the reader visualize necessary techniques or materials. In the case of Brunschwig's *Small Book*, the stills, furnaces, and plants the book illustrates correspond to detailed textual instructions regarding how the thing depicted is to be used in the reader's craft practice. As such, the images lay an implicit claim to being usable things. The image of a still should show the reader what kind of still to use for a given function, and the image of a dandelion should help the reader identify the plant itself. In fact, most of these images have little practical value as usable things, as they do not accurately represent the things they lay an implicit claim to representing.

This inaccuracy is especially prevalent in certain images of the plants and animals to be used in distilling: these are oftentimes stylized representations of the things in question, laden with immaterial meanings and associations. Figure 9.3 depicts one such image. It shows two mandrakes, the root of plants from the genus *Mandragora*. The image depicts the mandrakes in the shape of homunculi – one male, the other female. Many myths surrounded this plant, most notably the belief that the mandrake-homunculus, when uprooted, would let out a blood-curdling screech with the power to kill those within earshot.[37] Another myth held that the mandrake first grew out of the same soil from which God had made Adam, and this gave the root particular potency as an aphrodisiac. These mythical aspects of the mandrake come to the fore in this image. The image depicts not the real mandrake but a stylized representation that reflects the "signature" of the plant: the configuration of qualities, uses, and associations that surround the plant and are made

---

36 Sachiko Kusukawa, "Illustrating Nature," in Frasca-Spada and Jardine, *Books and the Sciences*, 90–113, at 108.

37 Helmut Birkhan, *Magie im Mittelalter* (Munich: C. H. Beck, 2010), 65–69. See also Heinrich Marzell, "Alraun," in *Handwörterbuch des deutschen Aberglaubens*, 10 vols., ed. Hanns Bächtold-Stäubli and Eduard Hoffmann-Krayer (Berlin: De Gruyter, 1927–1942), 1:312–324.

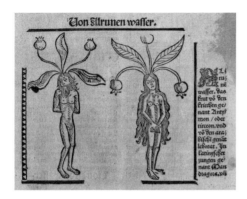

Figure 9.3: Woodcut of a mandrake root, from Brunschwig, Small Book, E5v. Courtesy of the Universitäts- und Landesbibliothek Darmstadt (Inc. IV 206).

materially manifest in its physical appearance in this image.[38] These mandrake roots are overlain with mythical meanings and associations: they evoke the myth of the mandrake-homunculus, and they also seem to reference Adam and Eve.

The text accompanying the image describes the plant and outlines the medicinal uses of the waters distilled from the plant: they can promote sleep and alleviate headaches. The practical information given in the surrounding text, as well as the practical aspirations of the entire book, gives this image an implicit claim to being usable in craft practice; that is, it should help the reader identify the mandrake. At the same time, the image doesn't depict the plant's real form; rather, it depicts a signature – the roots in the form of homunculi – that expresses the plant's mythical, immaterial associations. The stylized quality of this woodcut resists an interpretation of the image as a usable thing, for it resists the reader's practical engagement with the mandrake as a real plant. The image is informed by an awareness that this matter is inhabited by immaterial components.

The inclusion in printed books of stylized images of natural things more reflective of these things' signatures than of their material reality is by no means exclusive to this text. The 1485 *Gart der Gesundheit* – an encyclopedia of natural knowledge – even includes images of mythical creatures such as phoenixes, harpies, and dragons alongside more familiar natural flora and fauna.[39] Indeed, many of the woodcuts that Brunschwig and Grüninger employ in the *Small Book*, including that of the mandrakes, are borrowed from the two editions of the *Gart der Gesundheit* that Grüninger himself printed in the late 1480s or early 1490s.[40] However, by combining these im-

---

38 On the doctrine of signatures, see Scott Buchanan, *The Doctrine of Signatures: A Defense of Theory in Medicine*, 2nd ed., ed. Peter P. Mayock Jr. (Chicago: University of Chicago Press, 1991); and Will-Erich Peuckert, "Signatur," in Bächtold-Stäubli and Hoffmann-Krayer, *Handwörterbuch des deutschen Aberglaubens*, 7:1710–1712.
39 Johannes de Cuba, *Gart der Gesundheit* (Augsburg: Johann Schönsperger, 1485) (GW M09751).
40 Johannes de Cuba, *Gart der Gesundheit* (Strasbourg: Johann Grüninger, [ca. 1488/1494]) (GW M09739); Johannes de Cuba, *Gart der Gesundheit* (Strasbourg: Johann Grüninger, [after 1487]) (GW M09741).

ages with the form of the artisanal manual – whose aim is to allow the reader to re-create material techniques – and with the alchemical quest to transcend matter, Brunschwig and Grüninger throw the immaterial qualities of the things they depict into relief and highlight a tension between the arcane nature of alchemical and pharmacological knowledge and the market-driven ability of print to spread knowledge and encourage its translation into the reader's material practice.

A number of the book's images of the tools to be used in distilling can also be read in light of this discrepancy between the practical materiality the work aspires to and the alchemical focus on immateriality that pervades it. Figure 9.4 depicts a large distillation furnace in action, with steam emerging from three of its chimneys and a figure on the left collecting the distillates as they pour out of it. The surrounding text describes how to build a furnace like the one depicted in the image, listing the materials needed and the dimensions of the constituent parts. The role that the image itself should play in the reader's practical engagement with the text's instructions is unclear, however. The text makes explicit reference to the image, instructing the reader that "you may make an oven like this with as many helmets [the conical metal stills on top of the furnace] as you like or desire, according to your fancies, as the image here shows."[41] The image's purpose, according to Brunschwig, is simply to illustrate his point that the reader can decide how many helmets to include. The image is not necessarily an accurate depiction of a real furnace, nor does Brunschwig intend the reader to re-create the furnace as depicted in the image.

The image's aesthetic aspirations also detract from its ability to represent a real-world furnace, or to offer an image translatable by the reader into a real-world furnace. The image depicts the furnace as a completed, functioning piece of equipment, and not as a thing to be constructed. Although this image may, in a general sense, show a reader what a completed furnace could look like, it does not communicate to the reader any useful information concerning the steps required to actually repli-

Figure 9.4: Woodcut of a furnace, from Brunschwig, Small Book, C6v. Courtesy of the Universitäts- und Landesbibliothek Darmstadt (Inc. IV 206).

---

41 Brunschwig, *Small Book*, C6v: "Sollichen offen magstu machen mit wie vil helmen du wilt oder begeren du bist nach dinem gefallen. vnd die figur hie zeigen ist."

cate the furnace it depicts. Moreover, the fumaroles of steam rising from its chimneys and the distillates pouring out of its stills are details tangential to the practical labor of building a furnace; these are suggestive instead of an interpretation of the wood-cut as an image whose aesthetic qualities are more important than its claims to practical usability. This image's main function is to help the reader conceive of the idea of a furnace as a material object that could be used to distill waters, rather than to assist them in actually constructing the furnace.

In her work on late sixteenth-century English books of secrets, Allison Kavey argues that these books – on topics from alchemy to cookery – were designed to give readers across the social spectrum the sense that they too could perceive and manipulate the natural world, even though the books do not require them to actually practice the given discipline themselves.[42] Brunschwig's images play the very same role. Even those readers who cannot understand the written instructions the book contains, or those who lack the means, time, or even interest to do their own distilling, can still have some stake in the engagement with matter that distilling entails. They can imagine building a furnace, boiling the waters, and collecting the distillate when they regard and enjoy the visual depictions of things that the book contains. This does not necessarily mean, however, that they will be able to materially re-create the techniques and practices the book offers.

Even though Brunschwig casts his work as one that should allow the reader to re-create his craft practice and produce their own medicinal elixirs, the images he and Grüninger include to support the reader's practical engagement with matter undermine this do-it-yourself impulse. This engagement with matter is not a straightforward process that can be replicated exactly by following the instructions in a printed book. Matter is not solely material; it is also inflected by immaterial qualities, beliefs, and practices. However material the activities it presents, the printed book cannot fully communicate the arcane knowledge of the immaterial.

Brunschwig's Brick Mold

At the beginning of this chapter, I asked why the brick mold in Brunschwig's *Small Book of Distillation* (see figure 9.1) contains directions to the reader to cut it out of the book and use it to make bricks, when doing so would destroy the very instructions that describe how to use it. This paradox has implications for the book's ability to represent real-world things. By instructing the reader to cut out the image and use it as a real-world mold, the poem invites the reader to treat the image as the very thing it depicts. At the same time, however, the mold resists its own transition from a representation of the thing to the thing itself by its inclusion in a printed book. The evident improbability of this illustration's actual excision and direct use

---

42 Kavey, *Books of Secrets*, 3.

in material practice is suggestive of a reflective, perhaps even playful, attitude on the part of Brunschwig and Grüninger toward the materiality of the things their book depicts. Is the brick mold a thing to be used in craft practice or is it just a representation of a thing?

What invites this question is a particular tension in Brunschwig's notion of the materiality and immateriality of things. The *Small Book* is a practical handbook that claims the reader can replicate the techniques of distilling that it outlines. As such, it is concerned with allowing the reader a physical engagement with matter. At the same time, though, the work casts doubt on the ability of printed books to fully communicate such information to the reader: its way of representing matter emphasizes the immaterial ideas, associations, and practices that the things used in distilling are imbued with. The image of the brick mold displays this problem. It explicitly encourages the reader's material engagement with the larger book as a manual for building a distillation furnace, yet it also resists this use of the book through its stylization as an aesthetic object and its incorporation into the book itself. As such, it simultaneously gives voice to both an artisanal understanding of matter as something that can be manipulated by applying the correct techniques, and an alchemical understanding of matter as something that must be transcended through arcane practices and that cannot be communicated fully through the medium of a printed book.

The genre of the printed artisan's manual that gained in popularity over the course of the sixteenth century takes as its stated aim the communication of a material engagement with craft practice. The writers, printers, and artists involved in their production experimented with new techniques in illustration and *mise-en-page* to address this problem and communicate a material experience of things through the pages of the book. There is a tension at work in these texts, however. Despite these innovations, and their claims to allow the reader to replicate the crafts they discuss, they cannot fully represent the arcane, immaterial qualities of these crafts. However much Brunschwig's *Small Book* may laud the practical usability of the text, these immaterial components of his things, tools, and practices stand in the way of its practical value. Texts like Brunschwig's do not so much facilitate the reader's direct imitation of the physical techniques they present as offer the reader an insight into the overlapping relationship between the material and immaterial facets of things.

Leonardo Velloso-Lyons

10 Seeing Like God: Envisioning History in Sixteenth-Century Iberia

> There are only as many realities as you care to imagine.
> —Lawrence Durrell, *Balthazar*

In this chapter, I examine a new mode of seeing that emerged in sixteenth-century Europe. I do so by analyzing two objects, one physical and another imaginary. The first is Abraham Ortelius's atlas *Theatrum orbis terrarum* (1570), and the second is the "machine of the world" described in canto 10 of Luís de Camões's *Os Lusíadas* (1572).[1] This chapter is an invitation to read Camões's machine as a poetic staging of how readers reacted to books like Ortelius's, which *materially* presented readers with a God-like perspective on the world. Whether or not Camões was familiar with Ortelius's volume and was therefore consciously staging a reading of the *Theatrum* in the *Lusíadas* matters very little to the argument presented here. Rather, the purpose of this chapter is to show how the machine imagined by Camões crystallizes a new mode of seeing that emerged in the second half of the sixteenth century and lay at the intersection of several important changes to European material culture – namely, the advent of printed books, developments in Renaissance cartography, and the expansion of the Spanish and Portuguese colonial empires.

Behind both the *Theatrum* and *Os Lusíadas*, and behind said changes to European material culture, lies a common predecessor: Johannes de Sacrobosco's influential book *Tractatus de sphaera* (ca. 1230).[2] The early modern reception of this treatise in Spain and Portugal laid the ground for an understanding of the universe, and particularly Earth, as a chartable object. Nevertheless, the key difference between the way that early modern editions of Sacrobosco's work present a chartable Earth and what Ortelius had to say about his own volume in its prologue is precisely the

Acknowledgements: In addition to thanking all my colleagues who were part of the workshop and have authored chapters in this volume, I wish to thank Kathryn Starkey and Jutta Eming for their participation at the inception stage of this piece. I also want to extend my thanks to Vincent Barletta, Roland Greene, Andrea Nightingale, Luis Rodríguez-Rincón, Serge Gruzinski, and Mae Velloso-Lyons, the most careful readers of this piece at various stages.

1 Textual passages from Ortelius's atlas are cited in this chapter from Abraham Ortelius, *Theatrum orbis terrarum* (Antwerp: Apud Aegid. Coppenium Diesth, 1570). The work is cited in the running text by leaf number according to the printer's original signatures, identified with the abbreviation *T*. Passages from *Os Lusíadas* are cited from the following edition: Luís de Camões, *Os Lusíadas*, ed. Emanuel Paulo Ramos (Porto: Porto Editora, 2006). The work is cited in the running text by canto and stanza number, with line number added when relevant, identified with the abbreviation *L*. All translations in this chapter are mine, except when otherwise indicated.
2 I wish to thank Serge Gruzinski for having urged me to look more closely into Sacrobosco's book when writing this chapter.

https://doi.org/10.1515/9783110742985-013

latter's desire to make a book that embodied a distinctively sixteenth-century way of seeing. Largely dependent upon the material aspects of the book, this novel way of seeing, on the one hand, trained readers to navigate different levels of observation (from the most general to the most specific) and, on the other, taught them a selective gaze that would underpin the production of maps and texts depicting places in which European countries had their colonial interests.

It is precisely with this move in mind – that is, from a more diagrammatic way of seeing the world, as depicted in fifteenth- and sixteenth-century editions of Sacrobosco, to the more embodied, novel way of seeing in Ortelius's *Theatrum* – that I discuss Camões's machine of the world. I argue that Camões recontextualizes the experience of reading volumes like Ortelius's by creating a machine – an object that exists only in the semantic field of the poem – that incorporates the materiality of books that provided readers with a visualization of the world.[3] Instead of simply conveying concepts, respectively, about Earth and the universe, Ortelius's atlas and Camões's machine aim to relay *some* immediate experience of that which they purport to represent. In other words, both objects reconfigure the divine view of the world and the universe that was already familiar to their European audiences through Sacrobosco's diagrams by adding a dynamism that hinges on an understanding of the book as a material object which appeals to both the senses and the minds of the readers who interact with it.

I conclude by reasserting the importance of more closely looking into the reading experiences that were emerging in the second half of the sixteenth century, paying special attention to Iberia's role in shaping European readership during this period.[4] The *material* dissemination of this new way of seeing the world – first within the different parts of the Spanish and Portuguese empires, and then among the other European colonial powers – cannot be understood without the historical backdrop of early modern European colonialism. After all, both Ortelius and Camões served the Spanish and Portuguese colonial maritime empires throughout their lives, the former as a geographer and the latter as a soldier/poet. In this sense, one can fairly de-

---

3 By "materiality of books" I mean not only the book's physical aspects, such as size and weight, but also editorial qualities like page layout and the ordering of contents. While the former are more immediately impactful on the reader's sensory experience of the object, a reader can only *materially* experience the latter in the process of leafing through the pages of the volume. For discussions of books as material objects that inspired this chapter, see Leah Price, "Introduction: Reading Matter," *PMLA* 121, no. 1 (2006): 9–16; Fernando Bouza, *Hétérographies: Formes de l'écrit au siècle d'or espagnol* (Madrid: Casa de Velázquez, 2010), accessed May 16, 2020, https://www.digitaliapublishing.com/visor/30288; and Albert Lloret and Miguel Martínez, "Introducción: Poesía y materialidad / Introduction: Poetry and Materiality," *Calíope: Journal of the Society for Renaissance and Baroque Hispanic Poetry* 23, no. 2 (11 December 2018): 7–19.

4 For monographs in the field of early modern Iberian studies that take a similar approach to books as material objects, see Albert Lloret, *Printing Ausiàs March: Material Culture and Renaissance Poetics* (Madrid: CECE, 2013); and Mary E. Barnard, *Garcilaso de la Vega and the Material Culture of Renaissance Europe* (Toronto: University of Toronto Press, 2014).

scribe this chapter as an attempt to show that the atlas and the machine tell a story of how books *embodied* a new way of seeing the world that was intimately connected to the ambiguous status of books as both conceptual and material objects, and to the Spanish and Portuguese colonial endeavors.

From Illustration to Immersion: Johannes de Sacrobosco's *De sphaera*

As Malcolm Walsby and Andrew Pettegree attest, the sixteenth-century European book market was quite integrated.[5] Because early modern books circulated between Europe's various countries and kingdoms, a book's place of printing was not necessarily an impediment to its procurement by readers from other places. As the work of Alexander S. Wilkinson attests, such integration of book markets was even more relevant in the Iberian context, where volumes circulated both among the different kingdoms of the Iberian Peninsula and between their European and overseas territories.[6]

Historians of early modern print culture such as Fernando Bouza have increasingly considered the various different types of reading and writing practice to be all part of the same realm of experience. For Bouza, the distinctions between different types of writing (political, administrative, religious, private, literary, etc.) are all but artificial constructs that fail to capture the complexity of reading and writing practices that took place in the early modern Iberian Peninsula.[7] Because such distinctions would have hardly made any sense to early modern readers in the same way that they do to modern ones, he goes so far as to propose the concept of "graphic culture" to remind scholars that reading words on a page is but one way of interacting with early modern print culture. Moreover, Bouza also suggests that early modern readers did not make hierarchical distinctions between the multiple objects that were part of what he calls early modern graphic culture – books, manuscripts, illustrations on a page, etc.[8] That is, for the early modern audience, a commentary on Sacrobosco's *De sphaera* would be of a (graphic) piece with Ortelius's *Theatrum* or Camões's *Os Lusíadas*.

---

5 Andrew Pettegree and Malcolm Walsby, *Netherlandish Books: Books Published in the Low Countries and Dutch Books Printed Abroad before 1601*, 2 vols. (Leiden: Brill, 2010), 1:7.

6 Alexander S. Wilkinson, *Iberian Books / Libros ibéricos: Books Published in Spanish or Portuguese or on the Iberian Peninsula before 1601 / Libros publicados en español o portugués o en la Península Ibérica antes de 1601* (Leiden: Brill, 2010), xvi–xviii.

7 For more on Bouza's approach, see Fernando Bouza, *Comunicación, conocimiento y memoria en la España de los siglos XVI y XVII*, Publicaciones del SEMYR 2 (Salamanca: Seminario de Estudios Medievales y Renacentistas, 1999).

8 Bouza, *Hétérographies*.

Although Bouza's work mostly focuses on Castile, his findings about early modern graphic culture nonetheless implicate other kingdoms and territories.[9] That is, the relevance of these books to their Iberian readers was profoundly conditioned by the sprawling reach of the Spanish and Portuguese empires.[10] I propose that we think of the atlas called the *Theatrum* and the machine of the world as Iberian objects that present a seemingly divine perspective – a "God's-eye view" – of the world to their readers. Particularly relevant for the rise of this presentation was Sacrobosco's thirteenth-century treatise known as *De sphaera*, which, though written in Paris, became particularly important in the Iberian Peninsula as overseas expansion became a central concern for the Habsburg and Aviz dynasties. Hundreds of manuscripts and many of the over 320 early modern print editions of Sacrobosco's treatise have survived; in many respects, the story of the circulation of this work, both in manuscript and print, coincides with the development of the early modern European imaginary of the world and with the Habsburg and Aviz dynasties' maritime imperial ambitions.

Although Sacrobosco's treatise first came out in print in Italy (Venice, 1472), early commentaries in Latin and the vernacular by scholars from the Iberian Peninsula contributed substantially to its spread all over Europe.[11] While the text itself certainly shaped early modern ideas about the universe, this textual dimension is outside the scope of my argument. Rather, what is important here is the extent to which two crucial diagrams of Earth and the universe that Sacrobosco used to illustrate his work may be considered predecessors of Ortelius's *Theatrum* and Camões's machine.[12]

One of the earliest surviving manuscript copies in the vernacular of Sacrobosco's treatise belonged to Íñigo López de Mendoza (1438–1500), the third Marquis of Santillana, grandson of Iberia's most prominent fifteenth-century poet and humanist. Translated from Latin into Spanish, this manuscript helps illustrate how learned, nonscholarly readers in the Iberian Peninsula might have engaged with Sacrobosco's treatise (see figures 10.1 and 10.2). First, we can note that the two diagrams – of Earth and the universe – appear right after the prologue on folio 3. At first glance, the choice to front-load the diagrams may seem odd, given that, placed where they

---

9 Fernando Bouza, *Imagen y propaganda: Capítulos de historia cultural del reinado de Felipe II* (Mexico City: Ediciones AKAL, 1998).

10 Serge Gruzinski, *Les Quatre parties du monde: Histoire d'une mondialisation* (Paris: Martinière, 2006), 58.

11 For how Sacrobosco's treatise was read in early modernity, see Richard J. Oosterhoff, "A Book, a Pen, and the *Sphere:* Reading Sacrobosco in the Renaissance," *History of Universities* 28, no. 2 (2015): https://doi.org/10.1093/acprof:oso/9780198743651.001.0001.

12 For a discussion of how Sacrobosco's diagrams were supposed to trigger the "mind's eye" of late medieval and early modern readers, see Kathleen M. Crowther and Peter Barker, "Training the Intelligent Eye: Understanding Illustrations in Early Modern Astronomy Texts," *Isis* 104, no. 3 (1 September 2013): 429–470, https://doi.org/10.1086/673269. Crowther and Barker argue that the images trained the readers' "intelligent eye," serving as pedagogical tools that prompted them to imagine a moving structure of the cosmos when looking at the diagrams.

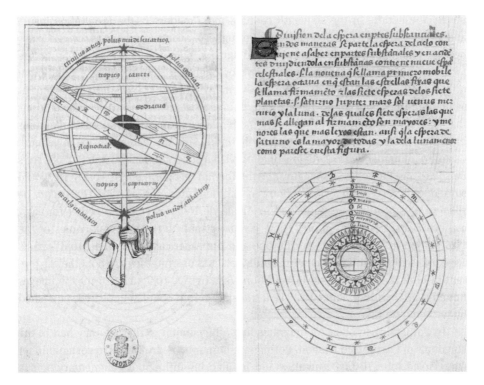

Figures 10.1 and 10.2: Diagram of Earth, from a 1493 Spanish manuscript of Johannes de Sacrobosco, *Tratado de la esfera*. Madrid, BNE, RES 151, fol. 3r. Image from the collection of the Biblioteca Nacional de España.

are, they do not accompany the parts of the text that seem to require such illustrations, as in other manuscripts and editions. This is symptomatic of such diagrams taking precedence over the text. The translator begins with a citation of Ecclesiastes, saying that "all things that man cannot express in words are difficult" ("todas las cosas son dificiles las quales no puede el hombre manifestar por la palabra").[13] It is as if the translator implicitly recognized that without diagrams one cannot learn about "the secrets of natural things, especially those that are most distant from men, which are the celestial bodies" ("los secretos de las cosas naturales en especial de aquellas que mas lexos stan de los hombres que son los celestiales cuerpos"). These observations allude to the purpose that the diagrams meant to serve: that is, making ideas about the universe and Earth visible to human sight as a means to aid the reader.

---

13 Both quotations in this paragraph are from Johannes de Sacrobosco, *Tratado de la esfera*, manuscript copy, 1493 (Madrid, BNE, RES 151), fol. 1r. Available online at http://bdh-rd.bne.es/viewer.vm?id=0000051089&page=1 (accessed 23 April 2021).

By the middle of the sixteenth century, most readers in the Iberian Peninsula and other parts of the Spanish and Portuguese overseas territories would have been acquainted with Sacrobosco's two diagrams. They would not have had access to ornate manuscript copies like the one belonging to the Marquis of Santillana; rather, they would have seen them in the many printed books and commentaries available to humanists and the growing bourgeoisie. It was via early print editions that scholars contributed to the early modern reception of Sacrobosco's diagrams in the Iberian Peninsula, the Spanish Netherlands, and ultimately Europe in general. Castilian humanist Pedro Ciruelo would publish a short commentary on Sacrobosco's *De sphaera* in Paris (1515), inaugurating the Iberian reception of the work.[14] He would subsequently expand his commentary in another Latin edition titled *Opusculum de sphaera mundi*, this time published in Alcalá de Henares (1526), a center for early modern Hispanic book culture. There are more than thirty surviving copies of the 1526 edition in libraries all over Europe and the Americas. While the two diagrams appear in a different order than in Santillana's manuscript, they are nonetheless present in both the 1515 and the 1526 editions (see figures 10.3 and 10.4 for the images from the 1515 edition). Later, in 1545, a translation into Spanish appeared, published by Jerónimo de Chaves.

In Portugal, Sacrobosco's diagrams had a life similar to the one they had in the kingdoms of Castile and Aragon. Portuguese humanist Pedro Nunes, a cosmographer who served John III of Portugal, would publish his influential commentary on the treatise in 1537.[15] Like its predecessors, Nunes's edition also contains a diagram of Earth and one of the universe, but there are some differences between Nunes's version and the others. First, Nunes's diagrams appear in a different order than that of Santillana's manuscript and Ciruelo's commentaries. Instead of first showing the diagram of Earth, as the translator of Santillana's manuscript and Ciruelo had both done, Nunes chooses to introduce the diagram of the universe first. Second, Nunes's diagram of Earth is markedly simpler than the other two (see figures 10.5 and 10.6), a plain circle with its roundness outlined by the equator and the two poles. It is worth noting that it was Pedro Nunes's edition that would later become available in Antwerp (1566), accompanied by the commentaries of prominent humanists such as Élie Vinet and Francesco Giuntini.

Despite their differences, these editions all participated in the same double movement. They were simultaneously updating Sacrobosco's influential treatise to better conform to the imperial maritime mandates of the sixteenth century and shaping how people in the Iberian kingdoms imagined the world. Circulating widely through a web of copyists, translators, publishers, and commentators, Sacrobosco's diagrams of Earth and the universe are integral in helping us recover not only the

---

14 Pedro Ciruelo, *Habes lector Johannis de Sacro Busto sphere textum [...]* (Paris: Apud Johannes Parvo, 1515).

15 Pedro Nunes, *Tratado da sphera com a theorica do sol e da lua* (Lisbon: Per Germão Galharde, 1537).

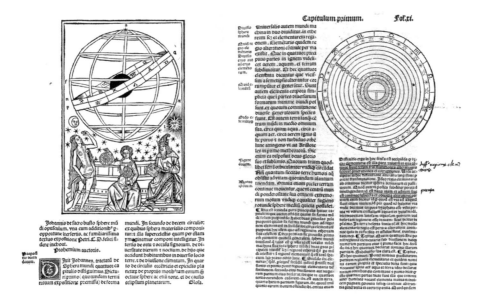

Figure 10.3: Diagram of Earth, from Pedro Ciruelo's *Habes lector Johannis de Sacro Busto sphere textum* (1515), a commentary on Sacrobosco's *De sphaera*. Diagram of the universe, from Pedro Ciruelo's *Habes lector Johannis de Sacro Busto sphere textum* (1515). Seville, Biblioteca de la Universidad de Sevilla, A. Res. 54/3/05, fol. 5v. Courtesy of the Biblioteca de la Universidad de Sevilla.
Figure 10.4: Diagram of the universe, from Pedro Ciruelo's *Habes lector Johannis de Sacro Busto sphere textum* (1515). Seville, Biblioteca de la Universidad de Sevilla, A. Res. 54/3/05, fol. 11r. Courtesy of the Biblioteca de la Universidad de Sevilla.

context to which Ortelius and Camões responded, but also how their learned readers understood objects that purported to represent the whole world.

It is worth pointing out that there is one key difference between the way in which Sacrobosco's diagrams represent the world and what Ortelius and Camões intended their objects to do. The former are diagrams; that is, they are visual representations of abstract ideas that cannot ultimately be seen or experienced firsthand. What Santillana's manuscript and Pedro Ciruelo's and Pedro Nunes's print editions all have in common is the assumption that the images in them will help their readers visualize what is otherwise impossible to see. They illustrate the fact that reading about the universe and seeing diagrams of it go hand in hand, even if text and diagrams resort to fundamentally different strategies to communicate the same concepts. In sum, such diagrams are static representations of ideas about the Earth and the universe, and not of the Earth and the universe themselves.

Ortelius's atlas and Camões's machine are, on the other hand, dynamic representations. By dynamism I mean that they cannot be reduced to a single concept that they purport to relay to their readers. Precisely because they depart from the tradition of representing ideas, the two objects signal a shift in reading experiences in the sixteenth century, a shift that first occurs, I argue, in the Spanish and Portuguese em-

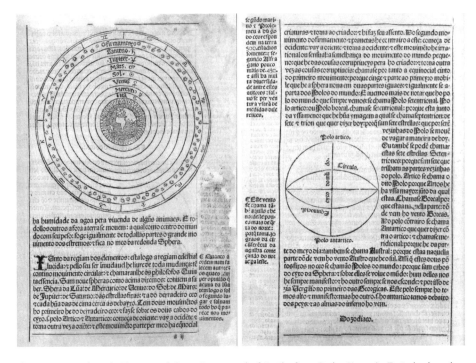

Figures 10.5 and 10.6: Diagram of the universe and of Earth, from Pedro Nunes's *Tratado da sphera com theoria do sol e da lua* (1537), a commentary on Sacrobosco's *De sphaera*. Lisbon, Biblioteca Nacional de Portugal, Res. 410 V, fol. 7r. Courtesy of the Biblioteca Nacional Digital, Biblioteca Nacional de Portugal.

pires. It depends upon an understanding of books as material objects, which means that they move their readers not only intellectually, as a diagram might, but also physically.[16] The awareness of the physical and editorial aspects of books – their size, how one sifts through their pages, the order in which the content is organized – is a main distinguishing factor between how Ortelius and Camões on the one hand and Sacrobosco's translators and commentators on the other understood their representations of the world. With this distinction in mind, when we read Ortelius's ideas

---

16 What I describe here is not so different from what Hans Ulrich Gumbrecht calls the presence effect. This type of more bodily interaction with the world and its objects, he argues, gives way to another type of interaction that focuses almost exclusively on the meaning of things. Instead of focusing solely on presence effects, however, I propose that we think of early modern books as objects that trigger both meaning and presence effects simultaneously. In other words, reading such books is not just an intellectual and pedagogical experience, but also inherently a sensory one. For more details on meaning and presence, see Hans Ulrich Gumbrecht, *Production of Presence: What Meaning Cannot Convey* (Stanford, CA: Stanford University Press, 2004), ch. 1 ("Materialities / The Nonhermeneutic / Presence"). For a discussion of sensory experience in learning about past societies, see Fiona Griffiths and Kathryn Starkey, eds., *Sensory Reflections: Traces of Experience in Medieval Artifacts* (Berlin: De Gruyter, 2019), 1–21.

about his book's physical aspects in the prologue to the *Theatrum* alongside Camõ-es's poetic rendering of the machine of the world as a dynamic atlas that opens itself up to Vasco da Gama, we see how both objects are a break from Sacrobosco's graphic representation of concepts. Instead of mainly conveying concepts about the Earth and the universe, respectively, Ortelius's atlas and Camões's machine are objects that embody what they purport to represent in order to relay *some* immediate experience, in a way that Sacrobosco's diagrams could not. In other words, the atlas and the machine add a dynamism to the divine view of the world and the universe depicted in diagrams precisely by mobilizing the ambiguous status of books as material objects that appeal both to the senses and the minds of their readers.

The Book as a Machine: Material Dynamism in Ortelius's *Theatrum*

Abraham Ortelius's *Theatrum orbis terrarum* (1570) is an atlas that was published in Antwerp, in the Netherlands. Credited by many as the first of its kind, the *Theatrum* found rapid success in late sixteenth-century Europe.[17] It was dedicated to the Habsburg king, Philip II, whom Ortelius would later serve as royal geographer. In 1580, when Philip II became the king of Portugal as well, Ortelius's position granted him access to maps and accounts from even more regions of the world. The first edition of the *Theatrum* has seventy maps on fifty-three sheets, with a short text preceding each map (see figures 10.7 and 10.8). The work went through many subsequent editions, translations, revisions, and expansions over the course of four decades, carried out by Ortelius himself while he was alive and continued by others after he died in 1598. The revisions and expansions of the *Theatrum* aimed to accommodate the influx of novel information about the world's regions, especially those that the first edition did not cover.

According to Peter H. Meurer, the uniform style in which the maps were drawn and the presence of texts in the *Theatrum* were its two most groundbreaking features. By presenting maps all drawn in a single style, Ortelius moved away from the predominant Italian cartographic tradition of binding different maps together in a volume made to suit the desires of a particular customer.[18] This uniformity of style creates a sense of aesthetic unity. Also, the texts accompanying every map ensured that the volume fulfilled the purpose Ortelius expected it to serve for its readers: to teach them how to use maps to improve their way of seeing the world.

17 Marcel van den Broecke, Peter van der Krogt, and Peter Meurer, eds., *Abraham Ortelius and the First Atlas: Essays Commemorating the Quadricentennial of His Death, 1598–1998* ('t Goy-Houten, Netherlands: HES, 1999).
18 Peter H. Meurer, *Fontes cartographici Orteliani: Das "Theatrum orbis terrarum" von Abraham Ortelius und seine Kartenquellen* (Weinheim: VCH, 1991), 10–12.

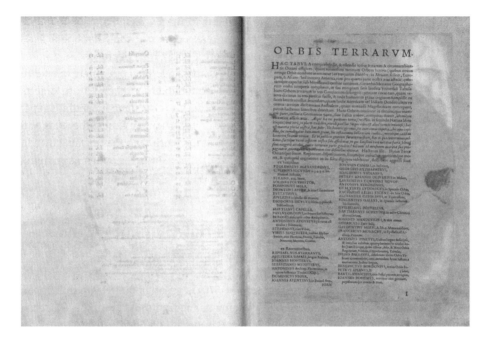

Figure 10.7: Text introducing the map of the planisphere, from Abraham Ortelius's *Theatrum orbis terrarum* (Antwerp: Apud Aegid. Coppenium Diesth, 1570), folio 1. Courtesy of the Library of Congress, Washington, D.C., Geography and Map Division (MSS. G1008). LOC Control Number: 2003683482.

Figure 10.8: Planisphere, from Ortelius's *Theatrum*, folio 1. Courtesy of the Library of Congress, Washington, D.C., Geography and Map Division (MSS. G1008). LOC Control Number: 2003683482.

Ortelius begins the prologue by claiming that the science of geography expands the utility of history. For him, because "nobody disputes the need for geography in order to better understand history," it is "rightfully called by some the eye of history" (*T*, B2r).[19] He continues:

> Certainly, this very necessary knowledge of geography [*Geographiae cognitio*] you can learn and obtain from the maps [*ex Tabulis Geographicis*] with great ease and over some time, as many distinguished and learned men have attested. And once we have gotten used to those maps, and from them have attained some knowledge of geography [*Geographiae cognitionem*], anything we read will adhere to our memory for longer, because we have those maps before our eyes [*ante oculos collocates*] as if they were mirrors of the things themselves; that is how it is, when we see that which we read, we learn it more fruitfully. I leave aside that it seems and in fact is much more pleasant to read histories if we are permitted to have such maps placed right before our eyes [*ob oculis*], as if we were present to see [*intueri*] the events [*res gestas*], or rather the places [*loca*] where the events took place. (*T*, B2r)[20]

The complementary relationship between seeing and reading presented above is at the center of Ortelius's project. It is also indicative of what I call the new mode of seeing that both the atlas and the machine share. For Ortelius, having maps before one's eyes serves the purpose of creating a multifaceted experience of reading history. By imparting geographic knowledge, maps change how histories are read: they enable a reader to imagine events coming to life as if the reader were witnessing them, or the places where they happened.

Although diagrams may seem to animate scientific readings just as Ortelius wishes his maps to animate historical ones, there are four aspects to his *tabulae geographicae* that distinguish them from the diagrams previously discussed. First, Ortelius's maps are more than illustrations of abstract ideas; they play a markedly pedagogical role in their own right. He explicitly writes that his maps would teach his audience the "very necessary knowledge of geography." The Latin word for "knowledge" that Ortelius uses is *cognitio*, which stresses the active role of one's mental faculties in the process of learning. In fact, his choice of word resonates with what he has to say about how one acquires the "knowledge of geography" – that is, from observing maps. Describing how this process of acquisition happens, Ortelius employs the adverbs "facilime" (with great ease) and "longe" (over some time). These adverbs

---

19 The full quote reads: "equidem mihi persuadeo, neminem poenè esse, modò historias primis (quod aiunt) labris gustarit, qui nesciat, quàm necessaria sit ad eas rectè intelligendas, Geographiae (quae meritò à quibusdam historiae oculus appellata est,) cognitio."

20 "Haec verò tam necessaria Geographiae cognitio, ut multi egregij & docti viri testati sunt, ex Tabulis Geographicis longè facilimè peti addiscique potest. Atque vbi aliquantulum harum Tabularum vsui adsueuerimus, vel mediocrem etiam Geographiae inde cognitionem adepti, quecunque leguntur, Tabulis his quasi rerum quibusdam speculis nobis ante oculos collocatis, memoriae multò diutius inhaerent. Quò sit, ut tum demum cum fructu aliquo, quae legimus, percipere videamur. Omitto iam, multò iucundiorem videri & esse, historiarum lectionem, si Tabulis ob oculos propositis leceat quase praesentem, res gestas, aut loca in quibus gestae sunt, intueri."

suggest that, though the process of learning is easier because of the maps them-selves, such pedagogical engagement with them would still take some time.[21] Instead of being illustrations of abstract ideas that could be quickly glanced at like diagrams, these maps required a longer and more immersive type of interaction from Ortelius's early modern readers.

Second, according to Ortelius, maps fulfill another role on top of teaching their observers the "knowledge of geography." They fundamentally change the experience of reading by making the learning of histories more effective and pleasant. Maps ren-der histories easier to learn, because they provide their readers with an image that will create the sensation that one is seeing the events oneself, as if in a mirror.[22] What Ortelius describes here is that maps are more than visual aids for learning about the past. Because they make both the places depicted in them and the events narrated in a history book come alive to the reader, maps generate a pleasure that is connected to, but cannot be subsumed within, their pedagogical role. This multilay-ered reading experience is what I call dynamic, as opposed to the more static expe-rience of diagrams in scientific writings.

Third, Ortelius is quite explicit in his prologue about the importance of the ma-terial aspects of maps: these include manageable dimensions, meaning that maps should be able to be manipulated by an individual, and affordable price, meaning that they should not be too expensive to make or buy. As he specifically composed the *Theatrum* to be read alongside works of history, Ortelius saw the need to generate maps that were smaller than other maps circulating during his time. He writes:

---

21 This issue of how long one has to interact with a book is central to the distinction I am proposing here between diagrams – that is, conceptual illustrations with little impact on the senses – and books as complex pedagogical machines – that is, objects that activate an individual's senses while simul-taneously fulfilling the conceptual function. Considering the book as a material object means paying attention to the content that it relays (conceptual) while also acknowledging what the experience of physically interacting with such an item means for the senses and for the process of learning some-thing from it. Another important distinction is between immediate and delayed sensory experiences. On the one hand, we have qualities such as size, texture, and smell, which are material aspects that appeal more immediately to the reader's senses, usually by virtue of just being in the presence of the book. On the other hand, there are material aspects that are less immediately processed but no less material, such as the order of the content, page layout, and others. These require an individual to become familiar with the book's materiality much more slowly – that is, by leafing through the book's pages, carefully observing what the content is and how it is displayed, absorbing the way this content develops over the course of the book, etc. By considering editorial aspects to be impactful on the senses, I do not mean to deny that they are also conceptual; therein lies the point I wish to highlight in this chapter about the particular materiality of early print books such as Ortelius's.
22 Perhaps there is a resonance between Ortelius's idea of a mirror and influential theories about sight in medieval Iberia, which depart from a Platonic paradigm to arrive at an Aristotelian approach to sight. For Ibn Sina (Avicenna), sight was a product of light beams that came into the eye from out-side. For a review of Ibn Sina's and Albert the Great's recuperation of Aristotle's theory of vision (in-tromission), in contrast to Plato and Platonist philosophy, see Cemil Akdogan, "Avicenna and Al-bert's Refutation of the Extramission Theory of Vision," *Islamic Studies* 23, no. 3 (1984): 151–157.

Given that it is such [i.e., that everyone learns more when geographical images accompany their study of histories], it is rather easy to see how hindered, constricted, and even wrong those who study histories may be, either because they cannot find descriptions of all regions, or because, even when they can procure them, they cannot afford them because of high prices, because those historians have little financial means. For there are many who really enjoy Geography and Chorography, and even more so the various images with description and delineations of the regions that one can find in them [treatises on Chorography and Geography]; but because they do not have the means to purchase them, or if they do, they have just enough to purchase them, they do not want to spend it on them. They leave them aside, and are not pleased by them. Likewise, there are those who have the substantial means to procure them, and so they would if they had a place where they could comfortably unfold and look at those very big and broad maps [*Chartae*]. They do not procure them because, in fact, those big and broad unfolded geographic maps are not as easy or comfortable to look at as something one can read, and for he who would want to unfold them all, and then display them on a wall, he would need not only an enormous house, but very likely a royal theater. Having gone through these feelings many a time, I began to think how I could remedy these inconveniences, either to reduce or eliminate them completely. And finally, it seems that, according to this way of reasoning, our goal could be achieved in our book, about which we hope and wish that everyone will be easily able to find a space for it among their books. (*T*, B2r)[23]

The passage above shows that providing maps of a more manageable size was a major motivation for Ortelius to produce the *Theatrum*. His thoughts on the volume's physical aspects show that he was keenly aware of the book as a material object. To impart geographical knowledge and change the way sixteenth-century people read histories, these readers had to be provided with maps that were both physically manageable and accurate. Each map and each text in Ortelius's *Theatrum* works like a piece of a much larger "machine" that aims to mobilize the images in the hands and the minds of readers, while diagrams simply illustrate the arguments presented in the text.[24] Furthermore, maps like Ortelius's provided readers with an all-encom-

---

23 "Quae cum ita sint, quantopere impediantur retineanturque, immo retrahantur etiam saepè in ipso cursu, historiarum studiosi, facilè est videre: cum vel omnes Regionum descriptiones non possint haberi; vel si haberi quidem possint, cariores sint, quàm ut quiuis possit, praesertim cùm plurimi sint tenuioris fortune, coemere. Multi enim sunt, qui delectantur quidem Geographia vel Chorographia, imprimis verò Tabulis, quae de Regionum descriptionibus, delineationib. Que variae extant: sed, quoniam aut non habent, quod iis comparandis impendant; aut, si quidem habeant, tantum, quanti illae valere solent, impendere nolunt, ab iss abstinent; nec sibi ipsis satisfaciunt. Sunt etiam, qui cùm habeant quo emant, emere quàm lubentissimè vellent, nisi locorum angustia obstaret, quò minus latae Chartae explicari & inspici commodè possint. Nam, ut verum fatear, magnae illae & amplae Geographicae Chartae conuolutae, non ita commodae sunt; nec, cùm aliquid fortè legitus, inspectu faciles. Omnes verò ordine parieti expansas adsigere volenti, opus esset, non modò amplissima, latissimaque domo, verùm etiam Regio quodam Theatro. Haec ego saepenumero expertus, cogitare coepi, quase ratio inueniri posset, hisce, quae iam dixi incommodis, medendi, vel vt diminuerentur aliquo modo; vel, si sieri posset, ut omninò e medio tollerentur. Ac tandem visum est, hac ratione, quam in hob libro nostro (cui (vti speramus singulisque optamus) quiuis facilè locum inter suos libros dare poterit) obseruauimus; fieri posse."

24 I wish to thank Vincent Barletta for a productive dialogue about the multiple implications and applications of the concept of a "machine" to late medieval and early modern Iberian cultures.

passing experience that was supposed to inflect their reading not only of the *Theatrum* but of other books too. Readers were expected to look at maps actively, feeling the wonder they provided when they were read alongside histories, unfolding the pages, and not just using a diagram as a visual aid that illustrates an otherwise ungraspable concept like the structure of Earth and the universe. To make maps that instruct, delight, and change the experience of readers simultaneously, Ortelius had to consider the material affordances of books.

Fourth and last, there is the question of the order in which Ortelius presents the regions of the world – which, as we will see, is likewise important for Camões's machine. Ortelius deals with this question in his prologue:

> First of all, we display the image that encompasses the whole orb of Earth; then, its main parts, just as they are, America, Africa, Asia, and Europe, following the natural order, which states that before parts can exist, there must exist a whole to which those parts belong. From there, we laid out the particular regions belonging to each part, beginning with the westernmost part of the Orb, following Ptolemy, prince of Geographers, and followed by all the rest. (*T*, B2v)[25]

Beyond its relevance in teaching geography to sixteenth-century readers, helping them visualize the histories they read in books, and presenting manageable, uniform maps, the *Theatrum* is also a philosophical lesson on the natural order of things. By leafing through the *Theatrum*'s pages, one also learns about how parts belong to a whole, with Earth as the principal object (see figure 10.8). Starting with the opening view of the whole globe, Ortelius's famous "Typus orbis terrarum," the reader would then turn pages to view the four parts of the world, with each plate displaying a map dedicated to each continent (see figures 10.9 – 10.12). Subsequently, the reader would zoom in on the parts of each continent, rendering details visible that were initially invisible in the first map of the whole world (see figures 10.13 – 10.15). The dynamism of the *Theatrum* lies in how the book as an object imparts a variety of lessons to its readers that depend upon a reading experience that is intellectual and sensory at once. Leafing through its pages would teach readers the knowledge of geography, stimulate their historical imagination, invite them to touch and manipulate the maps while interacting with other books, and, finally, physically demonstrate the relation of Earth to its parts through a progression from the most general to more specific levels of observation. It is this whole reading experience, I will argue in the next section, that Camões recontextualizes with the machine of the world.

---

25 "Primò, omnium Tabulam vniuersum terrarum Orbem complexam exhibemus; deinde eius praecipuas partes, veluti sunt; America, Africa, Asia & Europa; naturam secuti, qua semper ante, quàm partes sint; totum aliquod, ciuus illae sint, necesse est esse. His subiecimus harum partium singulas regiones ab Occidentaliore Europae parte exorsi, Ptolemaerum Geographorum Principem, & cereros poenè omnes imitati."

Figure 10.9: Map of the Americas, from Ortelius's *Theatrum*, folio 2. Courtesy of the Library of Congress, Washington, D.C., Geography and Map Division (MSS. G1008). LOC Control Number: 2003683482.

Vasco da Gama as the Early Modern Reader: Camões's Machine as a Recontextualization of Reading

Camões's *Os Lusíadas* (1572) is an epic poem written in Portuguese that recounts the discovery of the maritime route from Portugal to India in 1497–1499, the first expedition to connect Europe and South Asia by sea. The poem earned Camões (1524?–1580) a modest stipend from the Portuguese crown and increased his fame among the learned circles of the Iberian Peninsula. It was only after his death, however, that Camões's reputation attained clearer continental proportions. The poem was published in Castilian in 1580, the same year Portugal underwent a dynastic crisis that led to the union between the Spanish and Portuguese crowns, and a few months before Camões died. There were three subsequent Portuguese editions published be-

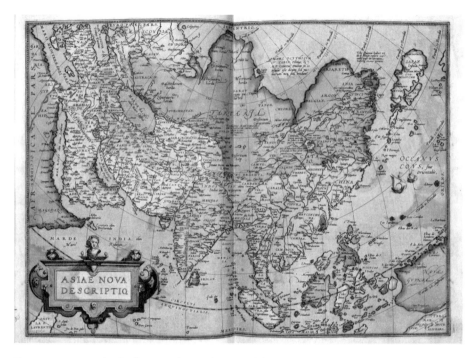

Figure 10.10: Map of Asia, from Ortelius's *Theatrum*, folio 3. Courtesy of the Library of Congress, Washington, D.C., Geography and Map Division (MSS. G1008). LOC Control Number: 2003683482.

tween 1584 and 1597, and the poem later appeared in Latin (1622), English (1655), and Italian (1658).[26]

In the poem, before Vasco da Gama and his crew head back to Portugal from India, the object called the "máquina do mundo" appears in order to expose the mysteries of the universe and deliver a final prophecy about Portuguese colonial endeavors. The name "máquina do mundo" (machine of the world) carries echoes of the work of many medieval and early modern scholars, including the expression famously used by Lucretius to explain the workings of the world: "moles et machina mundi" ("the mighty and complex system of the world").[27] Besides lying at the intersection of

---

26 For a study of the Portuguese editions, see Isabel Almeida, "Edições dos séculos XVII e XVIII," in *A biblioteca camoniana de D. Manuel II: Camões nos prelos de Portugal e da Europa, 1563–2000*, ed. Maria de Fátima Bogalho et al. (Coimbra: Imprensa da Universidade / Fundação da Casa de Bragança, 2015). For a study of Spanish and English editions, see Miguel Martínez, "A Poet of Our Own: The Struggle for 'Os Lusíadas' in the Afterlife of Camões," *Journal for Early Modern Cultural Studies* 10, no. 1 (2010): 71–94.

27 Titus Lucretius Carus, *De rerum natura*, trans. William H. D. Rouse, rev. Martin Ferguson Smith (Cambridge, MA: Harvard University Press, 2006), 386–387. For more on the multiple ideas around the concept *machina mundi*, see Jürgen Mittelstrass, "Nature and Science in the Renaissance," in *Metaphysics and Philosophy of Science in the Seventeenth and Eighteenth Centuries: Essays in Honour of Gerd Buchdahl*, ed. R. S. Woolhouse (Heidelberg: Springer Science & Business Media, 2012), 17–40.

Figure 10.11: Map of Africa, from Ortelius's *Theatrum*, folio 4. Courtesy of the Library of Congress, Washington, D.C., Geography and Map Division (MSS. G1008). LOC Control Number: 2003683482.

fifteenth- and sixteenth-century scientific and philosophical discourses, Camões's machine became an influential literary motif, impacting the work of poets from the sixteenth century to the twentieth.[28] Alonso de Ercilla's *La araucana* (the second part, published in 1578) and Bento Teixeira's *Prosopopeia* (1601) are but two examples that show the resonance of Camões's machine in other works from early modern Ibero-American literatures.[29]

Mittelstrass traces the multiple ideas around the concept of *machina mundi* in his study of the concept of nature during the Renaissance. *Machina mundi* was an important conceptual development of the "so called mechanization of the world-picture," mostly carried out in the work of astronomers and Neoplatonist commentators. The early modern idea of *machina mundi* implied a specific relationship between the physical world and its maker, whereby the maker of the machine wanted humans to see the universe from a privileged perspective. This resonates well with the multiple meanings of *machina* in Latin in the early modern period, which included the sense of craftsmanship, skill in using a certain tool, and the tool as a physical object itself. For an account of Lucretius's larger impact on Renaissance culture, see Gerard Passannante, *The Lucretian Renaissance: Philology and the Afterlife of Tradition* (Chicago: University of Chicago Press, 2011).

28 Hélio J. S. Alves, "Máquina do Mundo n'Os Lusíadas (A)," in *Dicionário Luís de Camões*, ed. Vítor Aguiar e Silva (Alfragide: Caminho, 2011).

29 For more resonances between Camões's machine of the world and other poems, see Aude Plagnard, "A descrição da máquina do mundo: Francisco Garrido de Villena e Luís de Camões," *Criticón*,

Figure 10.12: Map of Europe, from Ortelius's *Theatrum*, folio 5. Courtesy of the Library of Congress, Washington, D.C., Geography and Map Division (MSS. G1008). LOC Control Number: 2003683482.

The scene takes place on a mythical island in the Indian Ocean, a place that Venus, the goddess who champions Portuguese interests, has prepared for da Gama and his men as a reward for their successful trip to India.[30] There, after each sailor has pursued and captured his designated nymph in the troubling canto 9, Tethys and da Gama, together with the other "couples," convene to enjoy delicious food, precious ornaments, and prophetic songs in canto 10.[31] Once the ban-

no. 134 (10 December 2018): 115–140, https://doi.org/10.4000/criticon.5056. See also Antônio Soares Amora, *A prosopopéia, de Bento Teixeira, à luz da moderna camonologia* (Lisbon: Universidade de Lisboa, 1957).

30 For a reading of this episode as part of the tradition of Lusotropicalism, see Anna Klobucka, "Lusotropical Romance: Camões, Gilberto Freyre, and the Isle of Love," *Portuguese Literary and Cultural Studies* 9 (2003): 121–138. Ayesha Ramachandran stresses how Camões's treatment of Venus and the nymphs speaks to the Portuguese ability to mingle with other peoples as a way of colonizing, as well as their mastery of the natural world, which Venus and the nymphs stood for metaphorically in the Renaissance, following Lucretius's *De rerum natura*. See Ayesha Ramachandran, *The Worldmakers: Global Imagining in Early Modern Europe* (Chicago: University of Chicago Press, 2015), 120–121.

31 This scene was not solely allegorical for readers throughout the centuries. In fact, canto 9's very sexual tone warranted the poem a strong reproach in the nineteenth century, not to mention the veiled violent pursuit that da Gama's men carry out in the form of a "game" that much resembles

Figure 10.13: Map of Great Britain and Ireland, from Ortelius's *Theatrum*, folio 6. Courtesy of the Library of Congress, Washington, D.C., Geography and Map Division (MSS. G1008). LOC Control Number: 2003683482.

quet is over, Tethys invites da Gama and his men to accompany her up a hill, saying that she wishes "to double, with more glory, / The rewards in this joyful and beautiful day" (*L*, 10.75.6 – 7).[32] Right before their encounter with the machine, Tethys hints at the opportunity she is about to offer him:

> "The Supreme Wisdom favors you, baron,
> To see with bodily eyes
> That which the vain science of the
> Wandering and wretched mortals cannot.
> Follow me, steadfastly and strongly, with prudence,
> Through this mountain path, you and the others."

---

a hunt, with the subsequent subjugation of female bodies that allows for canto 10's peaceful gathering. Poet and critic José Agostinho de Macedo (1761–1831) objected to the scene's "indecent" imagery. According to this critic, if the objective of the scene was da Gama's lesson in astronomy taught by Tethys, the sexual prelude to it that takes place in canto 9 was utterly unnecessary. See José Agostinho de Macedo, *Censura das Lusíadas* (Lisbon: Impressão Regia, 1820).

32 "Pera que com mais alta glória dobre / As festas deste alegre e claro dia." The question of whether all of da Gama's men accompany him to see the machine is an open one. The poem indicates that all of the Portuguese sailors are invited with him (*L*, 10.76.6). However, the language that Tethys uses when commenting on the machine and commanding da Gama to look at its different parts is often in the singular, suggesting that only da Gama is seeing the machine with her.

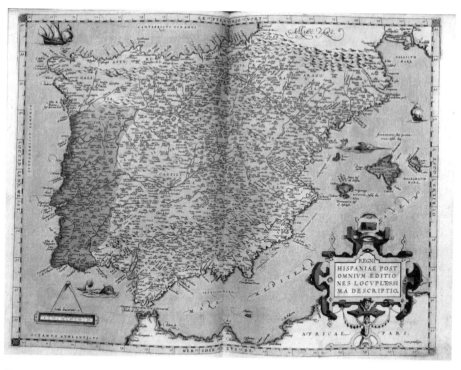

Figure 10.14: Map of the Iberian Peninsula, with focus on Spain, from Ortelius's Theatrum, folio 7. Courtesy of the Library of Congress, Washington, D.C., Geography and Map Division (MSS. G1008). LOC Control Number: 2003683482.

So she says, and guides him through a thick
And difficult forest path, unwelcoming for humans.

Little they walked to find themselves on a summit
Where a meadow was so thickly sown
With emeralds and rubies; with this sight,
He assumed that he treaded on holy ground.
Here, suspended in the air, they see a globe, so
Translucent that the light passes through it,
Making its center just as clear
As its bright surface [i.e., the outer sphere].

Its substance one could not see [*enxerga*],
But one sees plainly it is composed
Of different orbs, which the divine rod
Had shaped, giving them a single fixed center.
(*L*, 10.76 – 78)[33]

---

33 "'Faz-te mercê, barão, a Sapiência / Suprema de, cos olhos corporais, / Veres o que não pode a vã ciência / Dos errados e míseros mortais. / Sigue-me firme e forte, com prudência, / Por este monte espesso, tu cos mais.' / Assi lhe diz e o guia por um mato / Árduo, difícil, duro a humano trato. //

Figure 10.15: Map of the Iberian Peninsula, with focus on Portugal, from Ortelius's Theatrum, folio 8. Courtesy of the Library of Congress, Washington, D.C., Geography and Map Division (MSS. G1008). LOC Control Number: 2003683482.

Tethys emphasizes here that he will see with his "bodily eyes" that which the "vain science" of mortals cannot. At first glance, she uses a chiasmus to establish a simple contrast between da Gama, who sees the machine, and human knowledge, which cannot see the universe at all. But by eliding the verb *to see* in line 4 of stanza 76, Camões creates an ambiguity in this opposition. The elision can imply the verb *see* alone, which would emphasize the antagonism of sight and blindness. However, I suggest that this contrast could also imply the ablative – that is, "That which the vain science of the / Wandering and wretched mortals cannot see *with bodily eyes*," which would highlight a contrast between two kinds of sight, one that is bodily and one that is only conceptual. What if Tethys means that both da Gama and human knowledge *can see* the workings of the universe? I interpret her contrast not as an opposition between blindness and sight, but between two ways of seeing, between da Gama's bodily experience and human knowledge's diagrammatic representations, themselves a form of seeing. While inner sight, in the context of Sacrobo-

---

Não andam muito que no erguido cume / Se acharam, onde um campo se esmaltava / De esmeraldas, rubis, tais que presume / A vista que divino chão pisava. / Aqui um globo vêm no ar, que o lume / Claríssimo por ele penetrava, / De modo que o seu centro está evidente / Como a sua superfície, claramente. // Qual a matéria seja não se enxerga, / Mas enxerga-se bem que está composto / De vários orbes, que a Divina verga / Compôs, e um centro a todos só tem posto."

sco's work, expands the possibilities beyond the limitations of bodily sight by rendering on a page what human eyes cannot see, in Camões's poem we observe the opposite move – that is, bodily sight is expanding the possibilities beyond the limitations of conceptual visualization.

The latter contrast underscores a difference between corporeal and intellectual ways of seeing. While diagrams in scientific books like Sacrobosco's were considered a way of seeing, late medieval and early modern scholars would not have necessarily described this kind of sight as bodily or corporeal. Rather, these diagrams worked as visual aids, illustrating that which only the mind can see.[34] While the combination of inner and outer sight was what granted mortals their capacity to fully see the world they lived in, it was the mind's eye alone that permitted humans to visualize what was only immediately available to God, such as the structure of the universe.

The planetary structure that da Gama sees follows Ptolemy's description of the universe, the same one that we find in Sacrobosco's work (see figures 10.2, 10.4, and 10.5). But what if the main point of this scene is not to indicate to Camões's early modern reader that he was educated in the geography and astronomy of the time and the relevant diagrams, but rather to imply the idea that books as objects can deliver an immersive experience of the world in more dynamic ways than a static diagram on a single page can? Although the machine may simply seem to be a poetic rendering of the Ptolemaic diagram, I argue that Camões's choice to create a physical, dynamic object like the machine rests on an understanding of books like Ortelius's as multifaceted machines. Both the *Theatrum* and the machine of the world go beyond illustrating a concept by creating a multifaceted sensory experience that requires a longer, more somatic, but simultaneously intellectual engagement from readers.

Tethys's initial comment announces the tension between the bodily and the conceptual (or diagrammatic) ways of seeing embodied in the machine. The same tension also pervades the poet's description of the machine:

> With its spheres spinning, first falling, then rising,
> The whole never rose nor fell,
> But looked the same in each of its parts; and each part
> Reflects the whole [*começa e acaba*], for it is the work of divine art,
>
> Uniform, perfect, and self-sustained
> Just as the very Pattern [*Arquétipo*] who fashioned it.
> Da Gama, seeing the globe, stood there affected

---

34 The distinction between the body's sight and the mind's echoes the long-standing Christian idea that humans have both physical and spiritual senses, most notably Augustine's distinction between the two ways of seeing in his *De Trinitate*. For more on this, see Augustine, *On the Trinity*, bk. 3, in *Nicene and Post-Nicene Fathers, First Series*, vol. 3, ed. Philip Schaff, trans. Arthur West Haddan (Buffalo, NY: Christian Literature, 1887); and Margaret Miles, "Vision: The Eye of the Body and the Eye of the Mind in Saint Augustine's 'De trinitate' and 'Confessions,'" *Journal of Religion* 63, no. 2 (1983): 125–142, accessed 23 April 2021, http://www.jstor.org/stable/1202858.

By astonishment and desire.
Then the goddess says: "This model [*trasunto*] of the World,
I lay before your eyes,
Reduced to a small volume, so you may see
Where you have been, and are, and wish to be.

"Here you see the great machine of the world
Ethereal and elemental, just as it was made
By the highest and deepest Wisdom,
Who is without beginning and end.
He, who encircles this round globe
All round, and its polished surface,
Is God; but what God, no one understands,
For human wit [*engenho*] cannot extend itself thus."
(*L*, 10.78–80)[35]

Camões employs vivid language to describe the machine as something that simultaneously moves and stands still, with its spheres that rise and fall without compromising the stability of the whole. Though inspired by the Ptolemaic model, Camões's machine is nonetheless more dynamic than the diagram of the universe a reader could have found in any early modern copy of Sacrobosco's treatise.

By highlighting just how different the machine is from the diagram that translated the same Ptolemaic structure of the universe, I do not mean that the machine does not play a diagrammatic function. Rather, I believe that it does more than just this, precisely because of the complex sensory experience it triggers in da Gama, which transcends a diagram's purpose of facilitating the learning of an idea. The machine resembles, I argue, an atlas like Ortelius's: it delivers to da Gama a privileged perspective of the world that is experienced bodily and also imparts a certain kind of complex knowledge that combines astronomy, history, and geography. While a single

---

35 "Volvendo, ora se abaxe, agora se erga, / Nunca se ergue ou se abaxa, e um mesmo rosto / Por toda a parte tem; e em toda a parte / Começa e acaba, enfim, por divina arte. // Uniforme, perfeito, em si sustido, / Qual, enfim, o Arquetipo que o criou. / Vendo o Gama este globo, comovido / De espanto e de desejo ali ficou. / Diz-lhe a Deusa: "O trasunto, reduzido / Em pequeno volume, aqui te dou / Do Mundo aos olhos teus, pera que vejas / Por onde vás e irás e o que desejas. // 'Vês aqui a grande máquina do Mundo: / Etérea e elemental, que fabricada / Assi foi do Saber, alto e profundo, / Que é sem princípio e meta limitada. / Quem cerca o derredor este rotundo / Globo e sua superfícia tão limada, / É Deus: mas o que é Deus, ninguém o entende, / Que a tanto o engenho humano não se estende.'"

"Trasunto," in stanza 79, is also a word that scholars have interpreted in various ways. The consensus has been to understand it as referring to a miniature scale model. However, the word *trasunto* may also have the inferred meaning of something that has been written down, because of its proximity to the word *traslado*. Jerónimo Cardoso records the Latin word *antigraphu* as "O Trasunto. Ou traslado," indicating that, at least in this case, *trasunto* and *traslado* are synonyms. See Jerónimo Cardoso, *Dictionarium latino lusitanicum & vice versa lusitanico latinum* (Coimbra: Joan Barrerius, 1570), fol. 15v.

diagram is unable to produce an immersive experience like the machine does, a book may actually do so, since it requires the reader to actively leaf through its pages.

In fact, the four crucial aspects of the *Theatrum* discussed in the section above resonate with Camões's description of the machine and what it does in the poem. First, there is the machine's pedagogical function. Instead of conceiving Camões's machine as just a poetic move that responds to the well-established tradition of ekphrasis and prophecy in classical epic poems, I propose that we interpret it as Camões's response to the interactive pedagogical experience that early modern books like Ortelius's provided their readers.[36] The process of learning through interacting with an immersive object is at the center of da Gama's encounter with the machine in *Os Lusíadas*, as it materially provides him with important knowledge about the universe, the nature of God, and the planetary order, as well as the histories of the regions upon which he concentrates, such as Africa and India. Though this knowledge seems to come to da Gama with relative ease, it is only when he overcomes the machine's initial impact on him that he is able to acquire knowledge about the many things conveyed by the machine with Tethys's help.

Second, da Gama's experience of the machine would have changed his experience of reading books of history, just like with Ortelius's reader. By integrating the histories of Portugal's colonial endeavors in Africa and Asia into da Gama's experience of the machine, Camões recontextualizes the same dynamic reading experience described by Ortelius, one that invites the reader into an immersive mode of reading that is as active as it is pleasant. On the one hand, Camões's choice of word to describe the machine ("volume") evokes the image not just of something that takes up space but also of something that da Gama reads like a book. In fact, in Jerónimo Cardoso's contemporaneous Portuguese–Latin dictionary, *volume* was said to correspond to the Latin word meaning "book."[37]

On the other hand, the machine solicits from da Gama an active use of the two types of sight (visualizing immaterial concepts that the machine embodies and seeing the machine as an actual object). By calling the machine "ethereal and elemental," Tethys implies that not *everything* that composes the machine is physically observable. The combination of the conceptual and the material types of sight in Tethys's description of the machine constitutes the very essence of what I identified

---

36 There are many analyses of the relevance of ekphrasis for Camões, especially with regard to the machine of the world. For some of the most important examples, see António José Saraiva, *Luís de Camões: Estudo e antologia* (Amadora: Bertrand, 1980). See also João Adolfo Hansen, "Máquina do Mundo," *Teresa*, no. 19 (13 December 2018): 295–314, https://doi.org/10.11606/issn.2447–8997.teresa.2018.149115.

37 While the first edition of Cardoso's dictionary (1562) simply matches the Portuguese word *volume* with its Latin cognate "volumen, inis," the second edition (1570) is very direct, translating "volumen, inis" as "ho libro" (the book). See Jerónimo Cardoso, *Hieronymi Cardosi Lamacensis Dictionarium ex Lusitanico in latinum sermonem* (Lisbon: Ioannis Aluari, 1562), fol. 105r; and Cardoso, *Dictionarium latino lusitanicum*, fol. 269r.

as the *Theatrum*'s third aspect – that is, its material composition and affordances. Considering books as objects means that their material aspects (such as their size and what they are made of) are as important to the process of learning as the immaterial ideas that they convey. Da Gama's reading experience is an immersive one; it resembles the kind that Ortelius imagined for the readers of the *Theatrum*, which was in turn very different from the learning experience that diagrams conveyed, as described in the foreword written by the translator of Santillana's manuscript copy of *De sphaera*.

Finally, I wish to address the final aspect of Ortelius's book, which also finds a correlate in Camões's machine – that is, the copresence of texts and images and the ordering of the content presented. Once Tethys has shown da Gama the structure of the whole universe, his gaze slowly travels from the outermost layers of the machine (the planets, the moon, etc.) to its center – that is, Earth. It is Tethys who directs his focus with commands in the imperative ("Behold!" or "You see"), glossing every region with a commentary on its important events, its present (and future) condition, etc. She calls attention to each place and tells its story, leading herself and da Gama through an inspection of kingdoms and regions in Europe, Africa, Asia, and (briefly) America.

Because Tethys narrates the past and future events that illuminate what da Gama sees in the machine of the world, I argue that she plays the role of a metatext to this machine. In other words, the function she fulfills is similar to that of the texts Ortelius provided in his atlas as an introduction to each of the maps. This is what the goddess herself has to say about her role and that of other pagan gods:

> This outer sphere, which encircles
> The other smaller orbs which it contains,
> Which radiates with such bright light,
> Blinding mortal sight and wretched mind,
> Is named the Empyrean, where the pure souls
> Who attained that Immense Good dwell,
> An Immense Good that only God comprehends and reaches;
> Nothing in the world resembles it.
>
> Here, only the true, glorious
> Gods dwell, because I, Saturn and Janus,
> Jupiter and Juno, were fabulous,
> Dreamed by human and blind mistake.
> We serve only for making delightful
> Verses, and, if humans entreat us
> With more, it is only because your wit
> Has named these stars with our names.
> (*L*, 10.81–82)[38]

---

[38] "Este orbe que, primeiro, vai cercando / Os outros mais pequenos que em si tem, / Que está com luz tão clara radiando / Que a vista cega e a mente vil também, / Empírio se nomeia, onde logrando / Puras almas estão daquele Bem / Tamanho, que ele só se entende e alcança, / De quem não há no

First, Tethys belittles all pagan gods, herself included, with respect to the Christian one, the machine's artisan. Second, she says humans created the pagan gods, dreaming them because of their blindness. Third, there is the word she deploys to explain how humans created the pagan gods, whom she calls "fabulous." Tethys's first and second points suffice to establish an order whereby the machine, as a divine artifact, is vested with more agency than a human-wrought goddess like herself. The third point requires more careful examination. After all, *fabula* was an important concept in sixteenth-century romance and Latin vocabulary, one that expressed the same basic idea of narrative as its Greek counterpart *mythos*. Tethys's interpretation of the pagan gods as "fables" also resembles the manner in which scholars such as Juan Pérez de Moya read myths as a way to interpret other cultures.[39] Tethys's role is a contradictory one: on one hand, she mediates da Gama's experience of the machine, while at the same time the experience he undergoes allows him to see her true nature as *fabula*. Moreover, as *fabula*, Tethys embodies the act of storytelling itself. She is the text that is part of the machine's process of producing a novel way of seeing that combines sensory and intellectual stimuli, one very similar to that produced by Ortelius's *Theatrum*. In other words, if Tethys were not the mediator of da Gama's experience, as he could have presumably looked at the machine without listening to her comments, da Gama's experience of the machine would be more akin to that of a viewer who looks at a single map or diagram, or a reader who leafs through Ortelius's atlas without reading the texts that precede each map. By playing the role of text that enhances one's reading experience of maps, her presence is crucial for the machine to teach da Gama a way of seeing that combines the cartographic vision of the world with an equal attention to historical texts.

Finally, da Gama's gaze travels from the most general level of observation to the specific, just like Ortelius's reader would have done when leafing through the pages of the *Theatrum*. The difference between the machine and the *Theatrum* lies in which parts of the world they show to their readers. While the first edition of Ortelius's atlas mainly scrutinizes Europe and some parts of Asia, because of his familiarity with the work of cartographers who had previously charted those spaces and his lack of access to others, Camões's machine reveals the past and present of the Asian and African regions where the Portuguese would pursue their colonial endeavors. Both the atlas and the machine combine scientific knowledge, narratives, and maps, condens-

---

mundo semelhança. // Aqui, só verdadeiros, gloriosos / Divos estão, porque eu, Saturno e Jano, / Júpiter, Juno, fomos fabulosos, / Fingidos de mortal e cego engano. / Só pera fazer versos deleitosos / Servimos; e, se mais o trato humano / Nos pode dar, é só que o nome nosso / Nestas estrelas pôs o engenho vosso."

39 Pérez de Moya's popular treatise *Philosophia secreta* (1585) examines the historical and literary value of a particular kind of *fabula*, that which concerned the genealogy of the pagan gods. These fables about the origin of the pagan gods were, according to Moya, a tool that poets and historians used to impart true knowledge about the world in a more palatable way. For Pérez de Moya, the knowledge of those stories was essential for historians and poets alike.

ing all of this in a manageable object that triggers an interactive reading experience, establishing a perspective that would begin to shape the early modern Iberian imagination of the world.

Conclusion

I hope to have shown not only how the *Theatrum* and the machine partook in a broader conversation with elements of the European scientific and literary discourses, but also how they developed those discourses by materially embodying a novel way of seeing the world. This way of seeing depended on both the abstract ideas with which Ortelius and Camões were familiar and their particular understanding of books as material objects that were capable of conveying a visual, immersive, and somatic experience of the world that had been previously understood as impossible. Ortelius and Camões created objects that represented the world while simultaneously appealing to both types of sight that humans were understood to possess: the intellectual capacity to visualize an idea by means of illustration (diagram) and the somatic ability to see an object that is laid in front of them and be physically moved by it. Because they were able to trigger a multifaceted and immersive reading experience, Ortelius's *Theatrum* and Camões's machine conveyed more than the abstract ideas that informed the creation of these objects. They could teach – intellectually and somatically – their European audience the ability to move between different levels of observation (from general to specific, and vice versa) based on one's various interests in the different parts of the world.

Moreover, it is the ability to navigate multiple levels of observation, which I have called "God-like sight," hinted at in this chapter's title, that was equally central to the development of Western scientific discourse and to the upscaling of early modern European colonial endeavors. Although the story told here mainly concerns itself with two European objects, the *Theatrum* and the machine, which were respectively produced and imagined in the Spanish and Portuguese empires, I understand both of them as encapsulating a broader cultural, literary, and ultimately material history of European colonialism that was consequential not only for Europeans, but first and foremost for people in other parts of the world. In other words, this novel "God-like" way of seeing the world that emerged in the Spanish and Portuguese territories later became instrumental in other European colonial powers' expansion of their maritime empires, most notably the English, the French, and the Dutch. Despite their focus on different parts of the world and the different strategies each of these powers deployed in each place they colonized, early modern European colonialism more broadly relied on this God-like way of seeing which was propagated through advancements in the sciences, changes in print culture, and its staging in literary works.

There are many other objects produced in Europe and elsewhere that could tell alternative histories of early modern European colonialism. By offering a new perspective on two well-known European objects, I hope this chapter will contribute to emphasizing how important it is that literary scholars turn their attention to issues of historical and material culture in their efforts to uncover the many ways in which objects – both physical and imagined – embody the dark and challenging history of early modern European colonialism. Furthermore, the novel way of seeing that I have traced in Ortelius's *Theatrum* and Camões's machine did not remain unchanged. Rather, it was adapted, reified, and even subverted when exported to the Spanish and Portuguese colonial territories – but that is a subject for another piece.

List of Abbreviations

Archives

BNE   Biblioteca Nacional de España
BnF   Bibliothèque nationale de France
BSB   Bayerische Staatsbibliothek (Munich)
SB   Staatsbibliothek
StiftsB Stiftsbibliothek
UB   Universitätsbibliothek

Catalogues

GW   Gesamtkatalog der Wiegendrucke
VD16 Verzeichnis der im deutschen Sprachbereich erschienenen Drucke des 16. Jarhunderts

Books

PL   Migne, J.-P., ed. *Patrologia cursus completus: Series latina.* 221 vols. Paris: Migne, 1844–1865.
[2]VL Keil, Gundolf, Kurt Ruh, Werner Schröder, Burghart Wachinger, and Franz Josef Worstbrock, eds. *Die deutsche Literatur des Mittelalters: Verfasserlexikon.* 2nd ed. Berlin: De Gruyter, 1978–2008.

https://doi.org/10.1515/9783110742985-014

Bibliography

Manuscripts

Berlin, SB, ms. germ. qu. 762.
Colmar, Les Dominicains, Ms. 267bis.
Cologne, Historisches Archiv, Ms. GBf 129.
Cologne, Historisches Archiv, Ms. Wkf 119.
Florence, Biblioteca Medicea Laurenziana, Cod. Cor. 3.
Freiburg, UB, HS 1500,30.
Heidelberg, UB, cod. pal. germ. 108.
Karlsruhe, Badische Landesbibliothek, Cod. Lichtenthal 87.
Lincoln, Lincoln Cathedral Library, MS 91.
London, British Library, MS Harley 3244.
Madrid, BNE, RES 151.
Munich, BSB, cgm 783.
Munich, BSB, cgm 856.
Nuremberg, Stadtarchive Nürnberg, Rep. F 10 (FA Ebner).
Paris, BnF, Rés. 4° O^{2}f. 13.
St. Gallen, StiftsB, Cod. 591.

Other Primary Sources

Augustine. *On the Trinity*. Translated by Arthur West Haddan. Vol. 3 of *Nicene and Post-Nicene Fathers, First Series*, ed. Philip Schaff. Buffalo, NY: Christian Literature, 1887.
Barbazan, Étienne, ed. *L'Ordene de chevalerie, avec une dissertation sur l'origine de la langue française, un essai sur les étimologies, quelques contes anciens, et un glossaire pour en faciliter l'intelligence*. Paris: Chez Chaubert, 1759.
Benson, Larry D., and Edward E. Foster, eds. *King Arthur's Death: The Middle English "Stanzaic Morte Arthur" and "Alliterative Morte Arthure"*. Kalamazoo: Medieval Institute Publications, 1994.
Brunschwig, Hieronymus. *Liber de arte distillandi de simplicibus* [Small Book of Distillation]. Strasbourg: Johannes Grüninger, 1500. GW 05595.
Busby, Keith, ed. *Raoul de Hodenc: "Le roman des eles"; The Anonymous "Ordene de chevalerie"*. Utrecht Publications in General and Comparative Literature 17. Amsterdam: John Benjamins Publishing Company, 1983.
Caesarius of Heisterbach. *The Dialogue on Miracles*. Translated by E. Scott and C. C. Swinton Bland. Introduction by G. G. Coulton. 2 vols. London: G. Routledge & Sons, 1929.
Camões, Luís de. *Os Lusíadas*. Edited by Emanuel Paulo Ramos. Porto: Porto Editora, 2006.
Cennini, Cennino d'Andrea. *Cennino Cennini's Il libro dell'arte: A New English Translation and Commentary with Italian Transcription*. Translated by Lara Broecke. London: Archetype, 2015.
Cennini, Cennino. *The Craftman's Handbook: The Italian "Il libro dell'arte"*. Translated by Daniel V. Thompson Jr. 1933. Reprint, New York: Dover, 1960.
Cennini, Cennino. *Il libro dell'arte*. Edited by Fabio Frezzato. 2nd ed. Vicenza: Pozza, 2004.

https://doi.org/10.1515/9783110742985-015

Chaucer, Geoffrey. *The Riverside Chaucer*. Edited by Larry D. Benson. 3rd ed. Oxford: Oxford University Press, 2008.

Ciruelo, Pedro. *Habes lector Johannis de Sacro Busto sphere textum [...]*. Paris: Apud Johannes Parvo, 1515.

[Clûsenêre, Heinrich]. "Marienlegende." In *Mitteldeutsche Gedichte*, edited by Karl Bartsch, 1–39. Stuttgart: Litterarischer Verein, 1860.

Colgrave, Bertram, ed. and trans. *Felix's Life of Saint Guthlac: Introduction, Text, Translation and Notes*. Cambridge: Cambridge University Press, 1956.

Colgrave, Bertram, and R. A. B. Mynors, eds. *Bede's Ecclesiastical History*. Oxford Medieval Texts. Oxford: Clarendon Press, 1969.

Dominicus de Prussia. *Liber experientiae II*. Edited by James Hogg, Alain Girard, and Daniel Le Blévec. Salzburg: s.n., 2013.

Fabri, Felix. *Felix Fabri, Die Sionpilger*. Edited by Wieland Carls. Texte des späten Mittelalters und der Frühen Neuzeit 39. Berlin: Erich Schmidt Verlag, 1999.

Geoffrey of Vinsauf. *Poetria nova of Geoffrey of Vinsauf*. Translated by Margaret F. Nims. Toronto: Pontifical Institute of Mediaeval Studies, 1967.

Gertrude d'Helfta. *Le héraut: Livre 4*. Vol. 4 of *Œuvres spirituelles*. Edited and translated by Jean-Marie Clément and Bernard de Vregille. Paris: Éditions du Cerf, 1978.

Gervase of Tilbury. *Otia imperialia: Recreation for an Emperor*. Edited by S. E. Banks and J. W. Binns. Oxford Medieval Texts. Oxford: Clarendon Press, 2002.

Gottfried von Straßburg. *Tristan und Isold*. Edited by Walter Haug and Manfred Günter Scholz. Berlin: Insel Verlag, 2012.

Guiot de Provins. *Les oeuvres de Guiot de Provins, poète lyrique et satirique*. Edited by John Orr. Manchester: Manchester University Press, 1915.

Hahn, Reinhard, and Christoph Fasbender, eds. *Brandan: Die mitteldeutsche "Reise"-Fassung*. Heidelberg: Winter, 2002.

Hamburger, Jeffrey F., and Nigel F. Palmer, eds. *The Prayer Book of Ursula Begerin*. 2 vols. Dietikon: Urs-Graf Verlag, 2015.

Hamel, Mary, ed. *Morte Arthure: A Critical Edition*. New York: Garland Publishing, 1984.

Hartmann von Aue. *Erec*. Edited and translated by Cyril Edwards. Vol. 5 of *German Romance*. Rochester, NY: D. S. Brewer, 2014.

Hartmann von Aue. *Erec: Mittelhochdeutsch – Neuhochdeutsch*. Edited, translated, and with commentary by Volker Mertens. Stuttgart: Reclam, 2008.

Hartmann von Aue. *Erec: Text und Kommentar*. Edited by Manfred Günter Scholz. Translated by Susanne Held. Frankfurt: Deutscher Klassiker-Verlag, 2004.

Heinrich von Neustadt. *Apollonius von Tyrland*. Edited by Samuel Singer. Berlin: Weidmannsche Buchhandlung, 1906.

Herz, Randall Eugene. "Briefe Hans Tuchers aus dem Heiligen Land und andere Aufzeichnungen." *Mitteilungen des Vereins für Geschichte der Stadt Nürnberg* 84 (1997): 61–92.

House, Roy Temple, ed. *L'Ordene de Chevalerie: An Old French Poem; Text, with Introduction and Notes*. University of Oklahoma Bulletin, New Series 162, Extension Series 48. Norman: University of Oklahoma, 1919.

Jean de Blois. *Le conte dou barril: Poème du XIIIe siècle par Jouham de la Chapele de Blois*. Edited by Robert Chapman Bates. New Haven: Yale University Press, 1932.

Johannes de Cuba. *Gart der Gesundheit*. Augsburg: Johann Schönsperger, 1485. GW M09751.

Johannes de Cuba. *Gart der Gesundheit*. Strasbourg: Johann Grüninger, [ca. 1488/1494]. GW M09739.

Johannes de Cuba. *Gart der Gesundheit*. Strasbourg: Johann Grüninger, [after 1487]. GW M09741.

Johannes de Rupescissa. *De consideratione quintae essentie rerum omnium*. Basel: Heinrich Petri and Peter Perna, 1561. VD16 J 691.

Lucretius Carus, Titus. *De rerum natura*. Translated by William H. D. Rouse. Revised by Martin Ferguson Smith. Cambridge, MA: Harvard University Press, 2006.

Maier, Christoph T., ed. and trans. *Crusade Propaganda and Ideology: Model Sermons for the Preaching of the Cross*. Cambridge: Cambridge University Press, 2000.

[Mechthild of Hackeborn]. *Sanctae Mechtildis virginis ordinis Sancti Benedicti Liber specialis gratiae [...]*. In *Revelationes Gertrudianae ac Mechtildianae*, edited by Solesmensium O.S.B. monachorum, vol. 2, 1–421. Paris: H. Oudin, 1877.

More, Thomas. *Utopia*. Vol. 4 of *The Complete Works of St. Thomas More*. Edited by Edward Surtz and Jack H. Hexter. 2nd ed. New Haven: Yale University Press, 1993.

Nunes, Pedro. *Tratado da sphera com a theorica do sol e da lua*. Lisbon: Per Germão Galharde, 1537.

Ortelius, Abraham. *Theatrum orbis terrarum*. Antwerp: Apud Aegid. Coppenium Diesth, 1570.

Pfaffe Lambrecht. *Alexanderroman: Mittelhochdeutsch/Neuhochdeutsch*. Edited by Elisabeth Lienert. Stuttgart: Philipp Reclam, 2007.

Poirion, Daniel, Philippe Walter, and Anne Berthelot, eds. *Le livre du Graal*. 3 vols. Paris: Gallimard, 2001.

Puff, Michael. *Von den ausgebrannten Wassern*. Augsburg: Johann Bämler, 1476. GW M36472.

Robert de Blois. *Robert von Blois sämmtliche Werke: Zum ersten Male herausgegeben von Jacob Ulrich*. Edited by Jakob Ulrich. 3 vols. Berlin: Mayer und Müller, 1895.

Sacrobosco, Johannes de. *Tratado de la esfera*. Manuscript, 1493. Madrid, BNE, RES 151.

Stone, Brian, trans. *King Arthur's Death: Alliterative "Morte Arthure" and Stanzaic "Le Morte Arthur"*. Harmondsworth: Penguin, 1988.

Tucher, Hans. *Die "Reise ins Gelobte Land" Hans Tuchers des Älteren (1479–1480): Untersuchungen zur Überlieferung und kritische Edition eines spätmittelalterlichen Reiseberichts*. Edited by Randall Herz. Wissensliteratur im Mittelalter 38. Wiesbaden: Dr. Ludwig Reichert Verlag, 2002.

Ulrich von Zatzikhoven. *Lanzelet: Text – Übersetzung – Kommentar*. Edited by Florian Kragl. Berlin: De Gruyter, 2013.

Unserer Frauen Mantel. Ulm: Johann Zainer the Younger, [ca. 1500]. GW M20668.

Vasari, Giorgio. *Le vite de' più eccellenti pittori, scultori ed architettori*. Edited by Gaetano Milanesi. Le opere di Giorgio Vasari 2. Florence: G. C. Sansoni, 1878.

Weber, Cornelia, ed. *Untersuchung und überlieferungskritische Edition des Herzog Ernst B*. Göppingen: Kümmerle, 1994.

Wernher der Gärtner. *Helmbrecht*. Edited by Fritz Tschirch. Stuttgart: Reclam, 1986.

White, Carolinne, ed. and trans. *Early Christian Lives*. London: Penguin, 1998.

Wolfram von Eschenbach. *Parzival*. Edited by Karl Lachmann, Peter Knecht, and Bernd Schirok. Berlin: De Gruyter, 1998.

Wolfram von Eschenbach. *Parzival: Studienausgabe*. Edited by Karl Lachmann. Berlin: De Gruyter, 2003.

Wolfram von Eschenbach. *Parzival and Titurel*. Translated by Cyril Edwards. Oxford: Oxford University Press, 2006.

Dictionaries

Cardoso, Jerónimo. *Dictionarium latino lusitanicum & vice versa lusitanico latinum*. Coimbra: Joan Barrerius, 1570.

Cardoso, Jerónimo. *Hieronymi Cardosi Lamacensis Dictionarium ex Lusitanico in latinum sermonem*. Lisbon: Ioannis Aluari, 1562.

Glare, P. G. W., ed. *Oxford Latin Dictionary*. Oxford: Clarendon Press, 1982.

Lewis, Charlton T., and Charles Short. *A Latin Dictionary: Founded on Andrews' Edition of Freund's Latin Dictionary*. Oxford: Clarendon Press, 1879. Available online in Perseus Digital Library, Tufts University, http://www.perseus.tufts.edu.

Lewis, Robert E., et al., eds. *Middle English Dictionary*. Accessed online in Middle English Compendium, University of Michigan Library, https://quod.lib.umich.edu/m/middle-english-dictionary/dictionary.

Secondary Sources

Achnitz, Wolfgang. *Babylon und Jerusalem: Sinnkonstituierung im "Reinfried von Braunschweig" und im "Apollonius von Tyrland" Heinrichs von Neustadt*. Tübingen: Max Niemeyer Verlag, 2002.

Akdogan, Cemil. "Avicenna and Albert's Refutation of the Extramission Theory of Vision." *Islamic Studies* 23, no. 3 (1984): 151–157.

Almeida, Isabel. "Edições dos séculos XVII e XVIII." In *A biblioteca camoniana de D. Manuel II: Camões nos prelos de Portugal e da Europa, 1563–2000*, edited by Maria de Fátima Bogalho et al. Coimbra: Imprensa da Universidade / Fundação da Casa de Bragança, 2015.

Alt, Peter-André, Jutta Eming, Tilo Renz, and Volkhard Wels, eds. *Magia daemoniaca, magia naturalis, zouber: Schreibweisen von Magie und Alchemie in Mittelalter und Früher Neuzeit*. Wiesbaden: Harrassowitz, 2015.

Altman, Janet Gurkin. *Epistolarity: Approaches to a Form*. Columbus: Ohio State University Press, 1982.

Alves, Hélio J. S. "Máquina do Mundo n'Os Lusíadas (A)." In *Dicionário Luís de Camões*, edited by Vítor Aguiar e Silva. Alfragide: Caminho, 2011.

Anderson, Christy, Anne Dunlop, and Pamela H. Smith, eds. *The Matter of Art: Materials, Practices, Cultural Logics, c. 1250–1750*. Manchester: Manchester University Press, 2015.

Angenendt, Arnold. *Geschichte der Religiosität im Mittelalter*. 4th ed. Darmstadt: Primus Verlag, 2009.

Angenendt, Arnold. *Heilige und Reliquien: Die Geschichte ihres Kultes vom frühen Christentum bis zur Gegenwart*. Munich: Beck, 1997.

Angenendt, Arnold, Thomas Braucks, Rolf Busch, Thomas Lentes, and Hubertus Lutterbach. "Gezählte Frömmigkeit." *Frühmittelalterliche Studien* 29 (1995): 1–71.

Armitage, Natalie, and Ceri Houlbrook, eds. *The Materiality of Magic: An Artifactual Investigation into Ritual Practices and Popular Beliefs*. Oxford: Oxbow Books, 2015.

As-Vijvers, Anne Margreet W. "Weaving Mary's Chaplet: The Representation of the Rosary in Late Medieval Flemish Manuscript Illumination." In Rudy and Baert, *Weaving, Veiling, and Dressing*, 41–79.

Auerbach, Erich. *Dante als Dichter der irdischen Welt*. 2nd ed. Berlin: De Gruyter, 2001.

Auerbach, Erich. "Figura." Translated by Ralph Manheim. In *Scenes from the Drama of European Literature*, 1–79. Minneapolis: University of Minnesota Press.

Aurenhammer, Hans, and Daniela Bohde, eds. *Räume der Passion: Raumvisionen, Erinnerungsorte und Topographien des Leidens Christi in Mittelalter und Früher Neuzeit*. Vestigia bibliae 32/33. Bern: Peter Lang, 2015.

Bächtold-Stäubli, Hanns, and Eduard Hoffmann-Krayer, eds. *Handwörterbuch des deutschen Aberglaubens*. 10 vols. Berlin: De Gruyter, 1927–1942.

Barad, Karen. *Meeting the Universe Halfway: Quantum Physics and the Entanglement of Matter and Meaning*. Durham, NC: Duke University Press, 2007.

Barad, Karen. "Posthumanist Performativity: Toward an Understanding of How Matter Comes to Matter." *Signs* 28, no. 3 (2003): 801–831.

Barber, Malcolm. *The Cathars: Dualist Heretics in Languedoc in the High Middle Ages.* 2nd ed. Harlow, UK: Pearson, 2013.

Barber, Richard. *The Knight and Chivalry.* Rev. ed. Woodbridge: The Boydell Press, 1995.

Barnard, Mary E. *Garcilaso de la Vega and the Material Culture of Renaissance Europe.* Toronto: University of Toronto Press, 2014.

Bartal, Renana, Neta Bodner, and Bianca Kühnel. "Natural Materials, Place, and Representation." In *Natural Materials of the Holy Land and the Visual Translation of Place, 500–1500*, edited by Renana Bartal, Neta Bodner, and Bianca Kühnel, xxiii-xxxiii. London: Routledge, 2017.

Baxandall, Michael. *The Limewood Sculptors of Renaissance Germany.* New Haven: Yale University Press, 1980.

Beebe, Kathryne. "The Jerusalem of the Mind's Eye: Imagined Pilgrimage in the Late Fifteenth Century." In *Visual Constructs of Jerusalem*, edited by Bianca Kühnel, Galit Noga-Banai, and Hanna Vorholt, 409–420. Cultural Encounters in Late Antiquity and the Middle Ages 18. Turnhout: Brepols, 2014.

Beebe, Kathryne. *Pilgrim and Preacher: The Audiences and Observant Spirituality of Friar Felix Fabri (1437/8–1502).* Oxford Historical Monographs. Oxford: Oxford University Press, 2014.

Beer, Ellen J. "Marginalien zum Thema Goldgrund." *Zeitschrift für Kunstgeschichte* 46 (1983): 271–286.

Belting-Ihm, Christa. *"Sub matris tutela": Untersuchungen zur Vorgeschichte der Schutzmantelmadonna.* Heidelberg: Carl Winter, 1976.

Benjamin, Walter. "The Work of Art in the Age of Its Technological Reproducibility: Second Version." In *The Work of Art in the Age of Its Technological Reproducibility, and Other Writings on Media*, by Walter Benjamin, edited by Michael W. Jennings, Brigid Doherty, and Thomas Y. Levin, 19–55. Cambridge, MA: The Belknap Press of Harvard University Press, 2008.

Bennett, Jane. *Vibrant Matter: A Political Ecology of Things.* Durham, NC: Duke University Press, 2010.

Benson, Larry D. "The Date of the *Alliterative Morte Arthure*." In *Medieval Studies in Honor of Lillian Herlands Hornstein*, edited by Jess B. Bessinger Jr. and Robert B. Raymo, 19–40. New York: New York University Press, 1976.

Bent, George R. *Monastic Art in Lorenzo Monaco's Florence: Painting and Patronage in Santa Maria degli Angeli, 1300–1415.* Lewiston: Edwin Mellen Press, 2006.

Benzenhöfer, Udo. *Johannes' de Rupescissa "Liber de consideratione quintae essentiae omnium rerum" deutsch: Studien zur Alchemia medica des 15. bis 17. Jahrhunderts mit kritischer Edition des Textes.* Stuttgart: Franz Steiner, 1989.

Biedermann, Johann Gottfried. *Geschlechtsregister des hochadelichen Patriciats zu Nürnberg [...].* Bayreuth: Dietzel, 1748.

Bildhauer, Bettina. *Medieval Blood.* Cardiff: University of Wales Press, 2006.

Bildhauer, Bettina. *Medieval Things: Agency, Materiality, and Narratives of Objects in Medieval German Literature and Beyond.* Columbus: Ohio State University Press, 2020.

Birkhan, Helmut. *Magie im Mittelalter.* Munich: C. H. Beck, 2010.

Blair, Ann M. *Too Much to Know: Managing Scholarly Information before the Modern Age.* New Haven: Yale University Press, 2010.

Boschung, Dietrich, and Jan N. Bremmer, eds. *The Materiality of Magic.* Paderborn: Wilhelm Fink, 2015.

Boskovits, Miklós. "Immagine e preghiera nel tardo Medioevo: Osservazioni preliminari." In *Immagini da meditare: Ricerche su dipinti di tema religioso nei secoli XII–XV*, 73–106. Arti e scritture 5. Milan: Vita e Pensiero, 1994.

Boskovits, Miklós. "Su Don Lorenzo, pittore camaldolese." *Arte Cristiana* 82, no. 764–65 (1994): 351–364.

Boskovits, Miklós, and Daniela Parenti, eds. *Da Bernardo Daddi al Beato Angelico a Botticelli: Dipinti fiorentini del Lindenau-Museum di Altenburg.* Florence: Giunti, 2005. Exhibition catalogue.

Bouza, Fernando. *Comunicación, conocimiento y memoria en la España de los siglos XVI y XVII.* Publicaciones del SEMYR 2. Salamanca: Seminario de Estudios Medievales y Renacentistas, 1999.

Bouza, Fernando. *Hétérographies: Formes de l'écrit au siècle d'or espagnol.* Madrid: Casa de Velázquez, 2010. Accessed May 16, 2020. http://www.digitaliapublishing.com/a/30288/heterographies— formes-de-l-ecrit-au-si-cle-d-or-espagnol.

Bouza, Fernando. *Imagen y propaganda: Capítulos de historia cultural del reinado de Felipe II.* Mexico City: Ediciones AKAL, 1998.

Bradley, Richard. "Ruined Buildings, Ruined Stones: Enclosures, Tombs and Natural Places in the Neolithic of South-West England." *World Archaeology* 30, no. 1 (1998): 13–22.

Brahms, Iris, and Klaus Krüger, eds. *Gezeichnete Evidenz auf kolorierten Papieren in Süd und Nord von 1400 bis 1650.* Berlin: Walter de Gruyter, forthcoming.

Braun, Lea. *Transformationen von Herrschaft und Raum in Heinrichs von Neustadt "Apollonius von Tyrland".* Berlin: Walter de Gruyter, 2018.

Breitenstein, Mirko. "Das 'Haus des Gewissens': Zur Konstruktion und Bedeutung innerer Räume im Religiosentum des hohen Mittelalters." In *Geist und Gestalt: Monastische Raumkonzepte als Ausdrucksformen religiöser Leitideen im Mittelalter,* edited by Jörg Sonntag, 19–55. Berlin: LIT Verlag, 2016.

Brinkmann, Hennig. *Mittelalterliche Hermeneutik.* Tübingen: Max Niemeyer, 1980.

Brook, Timothy. *Vermeer's Hat: The Seventeenth Century and the Dawn of the Global World.* New York: Bloomsbury, 2008.

Brooks, Britton Elliott. *Restoring Creation: The Natural World in the Anglo-Saxon Saints' Lives of Cuthbert and Guthlac.* Nature and Environment in the Middle Ages 3. Woodbridge, Suffolk: D. S. Brewer, 2019.

Brown, Bill. *Other Things.* Chicago: University of Chicago Press, 2015.

Brown, Bill. *A Sense of Things: The Object Matter of American Literature.* Chicago: University of Chicago Press, 2004.

Brown, Bill. "Thing Theory." *Critical Inquiry* 28 (2001): 1–22.

Brüggen, Elke. "Die Rüstung des Anderen: Zu einem rekurrenten Motiv bei Wolfram von Eschenbach." In Mühlherr et al., *Dingkulturen,* 127–144.

Buchanan, Scott. *The Doctrine of Signatures: A Defense of Theory in Medicine.* 2nd ed. Edited by Peter P. Mayock Jr. Chicago: University of Chicago Press, 1991.

Bürkle, Susanne. "'Kunst'-Reflexion aus dem Geiste der 'descriptio': Enites Pferd und der Diskurs artistischer 'meisterschaft.'" In *Das fremde Schöne,* edited by Manuel Braun and Christopher John Young, 143–170. Berlin: De Gruyter, 2007.

Burns, E. Jane. *Courtly Love Undressed: Reading through Clothes in Medieval French Literature.* Philadelphia: University of Pennsylvania Press, 2002.

Burns, E. Jane. *Sea of Silk: A Textile Geography of Women's Work in Medieval French Literature.* Philadelphia: University of Pennsylvania Press, 2009.

Buschbeck, Björn Klaus. "Sprechen mit dem Heiligen und Eintauchen in den Text: Zur Wirkungsästhetik eines Passionsgebets aus dem 'Engelberger Gebetbuch.'" *Das Mittelalter* 24, no. 2 (2019): 390–408.

Buschbeck, Björn Klaus. "Ein vollkommenes Handwerk des Geistes? Gebet und Andacht als produktive Tätigkeiten im Alemannischen Marienmantel und bei Dominikus von Preußen." In

Vita perfecta? Zum Umgang mit divergierenden Ansprüchen an religiöse Lebensformen in der Vormoderne, edited by Henrike Manuwald, Daniel Eder, and Christian Schmidt, 245–278. Tübingen: Mohr Siebeck, 2021.

Bush, George W. *Decision Points*. New York: Crown Publishers, 2010.

Bußmann, Astrid. "Versehrte Briefe, unversehrte Siegel – zur Materialität des Briefes in der Brieffälschungs-Episode von Philippes de Remi *Roman de la Manekine*." In *Der Brief – Ereignis & Objekt: Frankfurter Tagung*, edited by Waltraud Wiethölter and Anne Bohnenkamp, 72–91. Frankfurt: Stroemfeld, 2010.

Büttner, Frank O. *Imitatio pietatis: Motive der christlichen Ikonographie als Modelle zur Verähnlichung*. Berlin: Mann, 1983.

Bynum, Caroline Walker. "The Blood of Christ in the Later Middle Ages." *Studies in Christianity and Culture* 71 (2002): 685–714.

Bynum, Caroline Walker. *Christian Materiality: An Essay on Religion in Late Medieval Europe*. New York: Zone Books, 2011.

Bynum, Caroline Walker. "Miracles and Marvels: The Limits of Alterity." In *Vita religiosa im Mittelalter: Festschrift für Kaspar Elm zum 70. Geburtstag*, edited by Franz J. Felten and Nikolaus Jaspert, 799–817. Berlin: Duncker & Humblot, 1999.

Bynum, Caroline Walker. "Wonder: Presidential Address Delivered at the American Historical Association Annual Meeting in New York on January 3, 1997." *American Historical Review* 102, no. 1 (1997): 1–26.

Capwell, Tobias. *Armour of the English Knight 1400–1450*. London: Thomas Del Mar, 2015.

Carruthers, Mary J. *The Book of Memory: A Study of Memory in Medieval Culture*. Cambridge: Cambridge University Press, 1990.

Carruthers, Mary J. *The Experience of Beauty in the Middle Ages*. Oxford-Warburg Studies. Oxford: Oxford University Press, 2013.

Caseau, Béatrice. "The Senses in Religion: Liturgy, Devotion, and Deprivation." In *A Cultural History of the Senses in the Middle Ages*, edited by Richard Newhauser, 89–110. A Cultural History of the Senses 2. London: Bloomsbury Academic, 2014.

Çeçen, Zeynep Kocabiyikoğlu. "The Use of 'the Saracen Opinion' on Knighthood in Medieval French Literature: *L'Ordene de chevalerie* and *L'apparicion maistre Jehan de Meun*." *The Medieval History Journal* 19, no. 1 (April 2016): 57–92.

Cheah, Pheng. *What Is a World? On Postcolonial Literature as World Literature*. Durham, NC: Duke University Press, 2016.

Chism, Christine. *Alliterative Revivals*. Philadelphia: University of Pennsylvania Press, 2002.

Chrisman, Miriam Usher. *Lay Culture, Learned Culture: Books and Social Change in Strasbourg, 1480–1599*. New Haven: Yale University Press, 1982.

Clark, Stephanie. "A More Permanent Homeland: Land Tenure in *Guthlac A*." *Anglo-Saxon England* 40 (2011): 75–102.

Clarke, Georgia. "Diverse, Synoptic, and Synchronous Descriptions of the Church of the Holy Sepulchre in Jerusalem in Fifteenth-Century Accounts." *Città e Storia* 7, no. 1 (2012): 43–75.

Cohen, Jeffrey Jerome. "Foreword: Storied Matter." In Iovino and Oppermann, *Material Ecocriticism*, ix–xii.

Cohen, Jeffrey Jerome. *Medieval Identity Machines*. Minneapolis: University of Minnesota Press, 2003.

Cohen, Jeffrey Jerome, and Lowell Duckert, eds. "Ecomaterialism." Special issue, *postmedieval* 4, no. 1 (2013).

Coleridge, Samuel Taylor. *Biographia Literaria, or Biographical Sketches of My Literary Life and Opinions II*. Edited by James Engell and Jackson Bate. Vol. 7 of *The Collected Works*. New York: Princeton University Press, 1983.

Collareta, Marco. "Il primato del disegno: Un percorso attraverso le arti minori." In *L'eredità di Giotto: Arte a Firenze 1340–1375*, edited by Angelo Tartuferi, 57–65. Florence: Giunti, 2008. Exhibition catalogue.

Copeland, Rita, and Ineke Sluiter, eds. *Medieval Grammar and Rhetoric: Language Arts and Literary Theory, AD 300–1475*. Oxford: Oxford University Press, 2009.

Cordez, Philippe. *Treasure, Memory, Nature: Church Objects in the Middle Ages*. London: Turnhout, 2020.

Cotton, William T. "Five-Fold Crisis in Utopia: A Foreshadow of Major Modern Utopian Narrative Strategies." *Utopian Studies: Journal of the Society for Utopian Studies* 14, no. 2 (2003): 41–67.

Crouch, David. *The Birth of Nobility: Constructing Aristocracy in England and France, 900–1300*. London: Routledge, 2015.

Crowther, Kathleen M., and Peter Barker. "Training the Intelligent Eye: Understanding Illustrations in Early Modern Astronomy Texts." *Isis* 104, no. 3 (1 September 2013): 429–470. https://doi.org/10.1086/673269.

Daston, Lorraine, and Katharine Park. *Wonders and the Order of Nature 1150–1750*. New York: Zone Books, 2001.

Dauven-van Knippenberg, Carla, Cornelia Herberichs, and Christian Kiening, eds. *Medialität des Heils im späten Mittelalter*. Medienwandel – Medienwechsel – Medienwissen 10. Zurich: Chronos, 2009.

De Benedictis, Cristina. *Devozione e produzione artistica in Umbria: Vetri dorati dipinti e graffiti del XIV e XV secolo*. Florence: Edizioni Firenze, 2010.

Degler, Anna, and Iris Wenderholm, eds. "Der Wert des Goldes – der Wert der Golde." Special issue, *Zeitschrift für Kunstgeschichte* 79, no. 4 (2016).

DeLanda, Manuel. "The New Materiality." *Architectural Design* 85, no. 5 (2015): 16–21.

Deleuze, Gilles, and Félix Guattari. *A Thousand Plateaus: Capitalism and Schizophrenia*. Translated by Brian Massumi. Minneapolis: University of Minnesota Press, 1987.

Deleuze, Gilles, and Claire Parnet. *Dialogues*. New York: Columbia University Press, 1987.

De Marchi, Andrea. "Angels Stippled in Gold: The Perugia Madonna." In *Gentile da Fabriano and the Other Renaissance*, edited by Laura Laureati and Lorenza Mochi Onori, 94–95. Milan: Electa, 2006. Exhibition catalogue.

De Marchi, Andrea. "Oggetti da maneggiare tra sacro e profano." In *Da Jacopo della Quercia a Donatello: Le arti a Siena nel primo Rinascimento*, edited by Max Seidel, 356–361. Milan: F. Motta, 2010. Exhibition catalogue.

De Marchi, Andrea. "Oro come luce, luce come oro: L'operazione delle lamine metalliche da Simone Martini a Pisanello, fra mimesi e anagogia." In *Medioevo: Natura e figura; La raffigurazione dell'uomo e della natura nell'arte medievale*, edited by Arturo Carlo Quintavalle, 701–715. Milan: Skira Editore, 2015.

DeMarco, Patricia. "An Arthur for the Ricardian Age: Crown, Nobility, and the Alliterative *Morte Arthure*." *Speculum* 80, no. 2 (2005): 464–493.

DeVun, Leah. *Prophecy, Alchemy, and the End of Time: John of Rupescissa in the Late Middle Ages*. New York: Columbia University Press, 2009.

Dinzelbacher, Peter. "Das Blut Christi in der Religiosität des Mittelalters." In *900 Jahre Heilig-Blut-Verehrung in Weingarten, 1094–1994*, edited by Norbert Kruse and Hans U. Rudolf, 1:415–434. Sigmaringen: Jan Thorbecke Verlag, 1994.

Dinzelbacher, Peter. "Religiöses Erleben von bildender Kunst in autobiographischen und biographischen Zeugnissen des Hoch- und Spätmittelalters." In *Images of Cult and Devotion: Function and Reception of Christian Images in Medieval and Post-Medieval Europe*, edited by Søren Kaspersen and Ulla Haastrup, 61–88. Copenhagen: Museum Tusculanum Press, 2004.

Dlabačová, Anna. "Spinning with Passion: The Distaff as an Object for Contemplative Meditation in Netherlandish Religious Culture." *The Medieval Low Countries: History, Archaeology, Art and Literature* 4 (2018): 177–209.

Doren, Alfred. "Fortuna im Mittelalter und in der Renaissance." *Vorträge der Bibliothek Warburg* 1 (1924): 71–144.

Dümpelmann, Britta. "Presence as Display: Carved Altarpieces on the Threshold to Eternity." In *Temporality and Mediality in Late Medieval and Early Modern Culture*, edited by Christian Kiening and Martina Stercken, 75–113. Cursor Mundi 32. Turnhout: Brepols, 2018.

Dümpelmann, Britta. *Veit Stoß und das Krakauer Marienretabel: Mediale Zugänge, mediale Perspektiven*. Medienwandel – Medienwechsel – Medienwissen 24. Zurich: Chronos, 2012.

Eamon, William. *Science and the Secrets of Nature: Books of Secrets in Medieval and Early Modern Culture*. Princeton, NJ: Princeton University Press, 1994.

Ebenbauer, Alfred. "Der 'Apollonius von Tyrlant' des Heinrich von Neustadt und die bürgerliche Literatur im spätmittelalterlichen Wien." In *1050–1750: Die österreichische Literatur; Ihr Profil von den Anfängen im Mittelalter bis ins 18. Jahrhundert*, vol. 1, edited by Herbert Zeman, 311–347. Jahrbuch für österreichische Kulturgeschichte, vol. 14–15. Graz: Akademische Druck- und Verlagsanstalt, 1986.

Ecker, Gisela. "Gabe." In *Handbuch Literatur & materielle Kultur*, edited by Susanne Scholz and Ulrike Vedder, 403–405. Berlin: De Gruyter, 2018.

Ecker, Gisela. *Giftige Gaben: Über Tauschprozesse in der Literatur*. Munich: Wilhelm Fink, 2008.

Eclercy, Bastian. "'Granare': Zur historischen Terminologie des Goldgrunddekors im Traktat des Cennino Cennini." *Mitteilungen des Kunsthistorischen Institutes in Florenz* 51, no. 3/4 (2007): 539–554.

Egidi, Margreth. "Gabe, Tausch und *êre* in der Alexiuslegende." In *Anerkennung und Gabe: Literaturwissenschaftliche Beiträge*, edited by Martin Baisch, 353–370. Frankfurt: Peter Lang, 2017.

Eisenbichler, Konrad, ed. *A Companion to Medieval and Early Modern Confraternities*. Leiden: Brill, 2019.

Eisenstein, Elizabeth. *The Printing Press as an Agent of Change: Communications and Cultural Transformations in Early-Modern Europe*. Cambridge: Cambridge University Press, 1979.

Emcke, Carolin. *Echoes of Violence: Letters from a War Reporter*. Princeton, NJ: Princeton University Press, 2007.

Eming, Jutta. "Aus den *swarzen buochen*: Zur Ästhetik der Verrätselung von Erkenntnis und Wissenstransfer im *Parzival*." In Alt et al., *Magia daemoniaca*, 75–99.

Eming, Jutta. *Emotionen im "Tristan": Untersuchungen zu ihrer Paradigmatik*. Göttingen: V&R Unipress, 2015.

Engelen, Ulrich. *Die Edelsteine in der deutschen Dichtung des 12. und 13. Jahrhunderts*. Munich: Wilhelm Fink, 1978.

Erler, Adalbert. "Mantelkinder." In *Handwörterbuch zur deutschen Rechtsgeschichte*, edited by Adalbert Erler and Ekkehard Kauffman, vol. 3, 255–258. Berlin: Schmidt Verlag, 1984.

Ernst, Ulrich. "Mirabilia mechanica: Technische Phantasmen im Antiken- und Artusroman des Mittelalters." In *Das Wunderbare in der arthurischen Literatur: Probleme und Perspektiven*, edited by Friedrich Wolfzettel, 45–77. Tübingen: Max Niemeyer Verlag, 2003.

Esch, Arnold. "Anschauung und Begriff: Die Bewältigung fremder Wirklichkeit durch den Vergleich in Reiseberichten des späten Mittelalters." *Historische Zeitschrift* 253, no. 2 (1991): 281–312.

Estes, Heide. *Anglo-Saxon Literary Landscapes: Ecotheory and the Environmental Imagination*. Environmental Humanities in Pre-modern Cultures. Amsterdam: Amsterdam University Press, 2017.

Eswarin, Rudy. "Terminology of *Verre Eglomisé*." *Journal of Glass Studies* 21 (1979): 98–101.

Fehrenbach, Frank. "'Eine Zartheit am Horizont unseres Sehvermögens': Bildwissenschaft und Lebendigkeit." *kritische berichte* 38, no. 3 (2010): 33–44.

Fehring, Günther, and Anton Ress. *Die Stadt Nürnberg: Kurzinventar.* 2nd ed. Bayerische Kunstdenkmale 10. Munich: Deutscher Kunstverlag, 1977.

Felski, Rita. "Latour and Literary Studies." *PMLA* 130, no. 3 (2015): 737–743.

Field, P. J. C. "*Morte Arthure*, the Montagus, and Milan." *Medium Ævum* 78, no. 1 (2009): 98–117.

Findlen, Paula, ed. *Early Modern Things: Objects and Their Histories, 1500–1800.* New York: Routledge, 2013.

Fletcher, Angus. *Allegory: The Theory of a Symbolic Mode.* Foreword by Harold Bloom. Princeton, NJ: Princeton University Press, 2012.

Foucault, Michel. *Discipline and Punish: The Birth of the Prison.* Translated by Alan Sheridan. New York: Vintage Books, 1995.

Foucault, Michel. *The Order of Things: An Archaeology of the Human Sciences.* New York: Vintage Books, 1994.

Fox, Richard, Diamantis Panagiotopoulos, and Christina Tsouparapolou. "Affordanz." In *Materiale Textkulturen: Konzepte – Materialien – Praktiken*, edited by Thomas Meier, Michael R. Ott, and Rebecca Sauer, 63–70. Berlin: De Gruyter, 2015.

Frasca-Spada, Marina, and Nick Jardine, eds. *Books and the Sciences in History.* Cambridge: Cambridge University Press, 2000.

Freuler, Gaudenz. "Don Silvestro dei Gherarducci." In Kanter, *Painting and Illumination*, 124–176.

Fricke, Beate. "A Liquid History: Blood and Animation in Late Medieval Art." *RES: Anthropology and Aesthetics* 63/64 (2013): 53–69.

Fricke, Beate. "Matter and Meaning of Mother-of-Pearl: The Origins of Allegory in the Spheres of Things." *Gesta* 51, no. 1 (2012): 35–53.

Friedrich, Udo. "*Contra naturam:* Mittelalterliche Automatisierung im Spannungsfeld politischer, theologischer und technologischer Naturkonzepte." In *Automaten in Kunst und Literatur des Mittelalters und der Frühen Neuzeit*, edited by Klaus Grubmüller and Markus Stock, 91–114. Wiesbaden: Harrassowitz Verlag, 2003.

Fulton, Rachel. "'Taste and See That the Lord Is Sweet' (Ps. 33:9): The Flavor of God in the Monastic West." *Journal of Religion* 86, no. 2 (2006): 169–204.

Fulton Brown, Rachel. *Mary and the Art of Prayer: The Hours of the Virgin in Medieval Christian Life and Thought.* New York: Columbia University Press, 2018.

Fulton Brown, Rachel. *See also* Rachel Fulton.

Ganz, David. *Medien der Offenbarung: Visionsdarstellungen im Mittelalter.* Berlin: Reimer, 2008.

Gardner, Julian. "The Back of the Panel of Christ Discovered in the Temple by Simone Martini." *Arte Cristiana*, n.s., 78, no. 741 (1990): 389–398.

Gentry, Francis G., ed. *A Companion to the Works of Hartmann von Aue.* Rochester, NY: Camden House, 2005.

Gentry, Francis G. "The Two-Fold Path: Erec and Enite on the Road to Wisdom." In Gentry, *Companion*, 93–104.

Gerok-Reiter, Annette. "Die 'Kunst der vuoge': Stil als relationale Kategorie; Überlegungen zum Minnesang." In *Literarischer Stil: Mittelalterliche Dichtung zwischen Konvention und Innovation*, edited by Elizabeth Andersen, Ricarda Bauschke-Hartung, and Silvia Reuvekamp, 97–118. Berlin: De Gruyter, 2015.

Gertenbach, Lars, and Henning Laux. *Zur Aktualität von Bruno Latour: Einführung in sein Werk.* Wiesbaden: Springer VS, 2019.

Gibson, James J. *The Ecological Approach to Visual Perception.* Boston: Houghton Mifflin, 1979.

Gibson, James J. "The Theory of Affordances." In *Perceiving, Acting, and Knowing: Towards an Ecological Psychology*, edited by Robert Shaw and John Bransford, 67–82. New York: The Halsted Press, 1977.

Giesecke, Michael. *Sinnenwandel, Sprachwandel, Kulturwandel: Studien zur Vorgeschichte der Informationsgesellschaft*. Frankfurt: Suhrkamp, 1992.

Glasner, Peter, Sebastian Winkelsträter, and Birgit Zacke. "Einführendes in das *Abecedarium* mittelalterlicher Dingkultur." In *Abecedarium: Erzählte Dinge im Mittelalter*, edited by Peter Glasner, Sebastian Winkelsträter, and Birgit Zacke, 9–25. Berlin: Schwabe, 2019.

Glauch, Sonja. "Inszenierungen der Unsagbarkeit: Rhetorik und Reflexion im höfischen Roman." *Zeitschrift für deutsches Altertum und deutsche Literatur* 132, no. 2 (2003): 148–176.

Gneuss, Helmut. *Handlist of Anglo-Saxon Manuscripts: A List of Manuscripts and Manuscript Fragments Written or Owned in England up to 1100*. Medieval and Renaissance Texts and Studies 241. Tempe, AZ: ACMRS, 2001.

Gordon, Dillian. "The Mass Production of Franciscan Piety: Another Look at Some Umbrian *verres églomisés*." *Apollo* 140, no. 394 (1994): 33–42.

Green, Dennis Howard. *The Beginnings of Medieval Romance: Fact and Fiction, 1150–1220*. Cambridge: Cambridge University Press, 2002.

Grieb, Christine. *Schlachtenschilderungen in Historiographie und Literatur (1150–1230)*. Paderborn: Ferdinand Schöningh, 2015.

Griffiths, Fiona, and Kathryn Starkey. "Sensing through Objects." In Griffiths and Starkey, *Sensory Reflections*, 1–21.

Griffiths, Fiona, and Kathryn Starkey, eds. *Sensory Reflections: Traces of Experience in Medieval Artifacts*. Sense, Matter, and Medium: New Approaches to Medieval Literary and Material Culture 1. Berlin: De Gruyter, 2018.

Grillmeier, A. "Jesus Christus. II. Die nachbiblische Christologie. A: Dogmengeschichte der kirchl. Christologie." In *Lexikon für Theologie und Kirche*, 2nd ed., edited by Josef Höfer and Karl Rahner, vol. 5, 941–953. Freiburg: Herder, 1960.

Grimm, Reinhold R. *Paradisus coelestis, paradisus terrestris: Zur Auslegungsgeschichte des Paradieses im Abendland bis um 1200*. Munich: Wilhelm Fink Verlag, 1977.

Groos, Arthur. *Romancing the Grail: Genre, Science, and Quest in Wolfram's Parzival*. Ithaca, NY: Cornell University Press, 1995.

Grossi, Joseph. "Barrow Exegesis: Quotation, Chorography, and Felix's *Life of St. Guthlac*." *Florilegium* 30 (2013): 143–165.

Grüttemeier, Ralf. "Literature Losing Legal Ground in Germany? The Case of Maxim Biller's 'Esra' (2003–2009)." In *Literary Trials: "Exceptio Artis" and Theories of Literature in Court*, edited by Ralf Grüttemeier, 141–158. New York: Bloomsbury Academic, 2016.

Gruzinski, Serge. *Les quatre parties du monde: Histoire d'une mondialisation*. Paris: Martinière, 2006.

Gumbrecht, Hans Ulrich. *Production of Presence: What Meaning Cannot Convey*. Stanford, CA: Stanford University Press, 2004.

Hall, Alaric. "Constructing Anglo-Saxon Sanctity: Tradition, Innovation and Saint Guthlac." In *Images of Sanctity: Essays in Honour of Gary Dickson*, edited by Debra Higgs Strickland, 207–235. Visualising the Middle Ages 1. Leiden: Brill, 2007.

Halleux, Robert. *Les textes alchimiques*. Turnhout: Brepols, 1979.

Hamburger, Jeffrey F. *Nuns as Artists: The Visual Culture of a Medieval Convent*. Berkeley: University of California Press, 1997.

Hamburger, Jeffrey F. *The Visual and the Visionary: Art and Female Spirituality in Late Medieval Germany*. New York: Zone Books, 1998.

Hamburger, Jeffrey F. "The Visual and the Visionary: The Image in Late Medieval Monastic Devotions." *Viator* 20 (1989): 161–182.

Hamerow, Helena. "Migration Theory and the Anglo-Saxon 'Identity Crisis.'" In *Migrations and Invasions in Archaeological Explanation*, edited by John Chapman and Helena Hamerow, 33–44. British Archaeological Reports International Series 664. Oxford: Archaeopress, 1997.

Hamilton, Bernard. "Knowing the Enemy: Western Understanding of Islam at the Time of the Crusades." *Journal of the Royal Asiatic Society* 7, no. 3 (November 1997): 373–387. https://doi.org/10.1017/S135618630000941X.

Hamilton, Bernard. *The Leper King and His Heirs: Baldwin IV and the Crusader Kingdom of Jerusalem*. Cambridge: Cambridge University Press, 2000.

Hamm, Berndt. "Heiligkeit im Mittelalter: Theoretische Annäherungen an ein interdisziplinäres Forschungsvorhaben." In *Literatur – Geschichte – Literaturgeschichte: Beiträge zur mediävistischen Literaturwissenschaft; Festschrift für Volker Honemann zum 60. Geburtstag*, edited by Nine Miedema and Rudolf Suntrup, 627–645. Frankfurt: Peter Lang, 2003.

Hamm, Berndt. "Die Medialität der nahen Gnade im späten Mittelalter." In Dauven-van Knippenberg, Herberichs, and Kiening, *Medialität*, 21–60.

Hamm, Joachim. "'Meister Umbrîz': Zu Beschreibungskunst und Selbstreflexion in Hartmanns 'Erec.'" In *Vom Verstehen deutscher Texte des Mittelalters aus der europäischen Kultur*, edited by Dorothea Klein and Elisabeth Schmid, 191–218. Würzburg: Königshausen & Neumann, 2011.

Hammerling, Roy, ed. *A History of Prayer: The First to the Fifteenth Century*. Leiden: Brill, 2008.

Hanna, Ralph. "Alliterative Poetry." In *The Cambridge History of Medieval English Literature*, edited by David Wallace, 488–512. Cambridge: Cambridge University Press, 1999.

Hansen, João Adolfo. "Máquina do Mundo." *Teresa*, no. 19 (13 December 2018): 295–314. https://doi.org/10.11606/issn.2447–8997.teresa.2018.149115.

Haraway, Donna J. *When Species Meet*. Minneapolis: University of Minnesota Press, 2008.

Harman, Graham. *Object-Oriented Ontology: A New Theory of Everything*. London: Penguin, 2018.

Hartmann, Jan-Peer. "Monument Reuse in Felix's *Vita Sancti Guthlaci*." *Medium Ævum* 88, no. 2 (2019): 230–264.

Hasebrink, Burkhard. "Selbstüberschreitung der Religion in der Mystik: 'Höchste Armut' bei Meister Eckhart." *Beiträge zur Geschichte der deutschen Sprache und Literatur* 137 (2015): 446–460.

Hasebrink, Burkhard, Susanne Bernhardt, and Imke Früh, eds. *Semantik der Gelassenheit: Generierung, Etablierung, Transformation*. Göttingen: Vandenhoeck & Ruprecht, 2012.

Hasebrink, Burkhard, and Peter Strohschneider. "Religiöse Schriftkultur und säkulare Textwissenschaft: Germanistische Mediävistik in postsäkularem Kontext." *Poetica* 46, no. 3–4 (2015): 278–291.

Haug, Walter. "Die Entdeckung der Fiktionalität." In *Die Wahrheit der Fiktion: Studien zur weltlichen und geistlichen Literatur des Mittelalters und der frühen Neuzeit*, 128–144. Tübingen: Niemeyer, 2003.

Haupt, Barbara. "Literaturgeschichtsschreibung im höfischen Roman: Die Beschreibung von Enites Pferd und Sattelzeug im 'Erec' Hartmanns von Aue." In *Festschrift für Herbert Kolb zu seinem 65. Geburtstag*, edited by Klaus Matzel and Hans-Gert Roloff, 202–220. Bern: Lang, 1989.

Heidegger, Martin. "The Thing." In *Poetry, Language, Thought*, by Martin Heidegger, edited by Albert Hofstadter, 163–184. New York: Perennial, 2001.

Heinz, Andreas. "Das marianische Te Deum des Trierer Kartäusers Dominikus von Preußen (†1461): Ein spätmittelalterlicher Lobgesang auf Maria als Vorlage für ein Marienlied Friedrich Spees." *Spee-Jahrbuch* 15 (2008): 93–114.

Heinzer, Felix, and Gerhard Stamm. *Die Handschriften der Badischen Landesbibliothek Karlsruhe XI: Die Handschriften von Lichtenthal*. Wiesbaden: Otto Harrassowitz, 1987.

Helffenstein, Iris. "Intermediale Verfahren im *studietto*: Zu Materialästhetik und Medialität von Verre églomisé und Goldgrund im italienischen Spätmittelalter bis Lorenzo Monaco." In Brahms and Krüger, *Gezeichnete Evidenz*.

Heng, Geraldine. *Empire of Magic: Medieval Romance and the Politics of Cultural Fantasy*. New York: Columbia University Press, 2003.

Herz, Randall. *Studien zur Drucküberlieferung der "Reise ins Gelobte Land" Hans Tuchers des Älteren: Bestandsaufnahme und historische Auswertung der Inkunabeln unter Berücksichtigung der späteren Drucküberlieferung.* Quellen und Forschungen zur Geschichte und Kultur der Stadt Nürnberg 34. Nuremberg: Selbstverlag des Stadtarchivs Nürnberg, 2005.

Hicks, Dan. "The Material Cultural Turn: Event and Effects." In *The Oxford Handbook of Material Culture Studies*, edited by Dan Hicks and Mary C. Beaudry, 25–98. Oxford: Oxford University Press, 2010.

Hilg, Hardo. "Mantel Unserer Lieben Frau." In [2]VL 5 (1985), 1221–1225.

Hilsdale, Cecily J. "Gift." *Studies in Iconography* 33 (2012): 171–182.

Hines, John. *Voices in the Past.* Cambridge: Cambridge University Press, 2004.

Hodder, Ian. *Entangled: An Archaeology of the Relationships between Humans and Things.* Malden, MA: Wiley-Blackwell, 2012.

Höffe, Otfried. "Thomas Morus' *Utopia:* Eine Einführung." In *Über Thomas Morus' "Utopia"*, edited by Joachim Starbatty, 11–35. Hildesheim: Olms-Weidmann, 2016.

Holsinger, Bruce, ed. "Medieval Fictionalities: An NHL Forum." Special issue, *New Literary History* 51, no. 1 (2020).

Honnefelder, Gottfried. *Der Brief im Roman: Untersuchungen zur erzähltechnischen Verwendung des Briefes im deutschen Roman.* Bonner Arbeiten zur deutschen Literatur, vol. 28. Bonn: Bouvier, 1975.

Howe, John, and Michael Wolfe, eds. *Inventing Medieval Landscapes: Senses of Place in Western Europe.* Gainesville: University Press of Florida, 2002.

Howe, Nicholas. "The Landscape of Anglo-Saxon England: Inherited, Invented, Imagined." In J. Howe and Wolfe, *Inventing Medieval Landscapes*, 91–112.

Howe, Nicholas. *Writing the Map of Anglo-Saxon England: Essays in Cultural Geography.* New Haven: Yale University Press, 2008.

Huber, Christoph. "Wilde Rede bei Hartmann von Aue? Beobachtungen zum 'Erec.'" In *"wildekeit": Spielräume literarischer obscuritas im Mittelalter; Zürcher Kolloquium 2016*, edited by Susanne Köbele et al., 119–134. Berlin: Erich Schmidt, 2018.

Hueck, Irene. "Ein umbrisches Reliquiar im Kunstgewerbemuseum Schloß Köpenick." *Forschungen und Berichte* 31 (1991): 183–188.

Hunter, Michael. "Germanic and Roman Antiquity and the Sense of the Past in Anglo-Saxon England." *Anglo-Saxon England* 3 (1974): 29–50.

Ingold, Tim. "The Temporality of the Landscape." *World Archaeology* 25, no. 2 (1993): 152–174.

Iovino, Serenella. "The Living Diffractions of Matter and Text: Narrative Agency, Strategic Anthropomorphism, and How Interpretation Works." *Anglia* 133, no. 1 (2015): 69–86.

Iovino, Serenella, and Serpil Oppermann. "Introduction: Stories Come to Matter." In Iovino and Oppermann, *Material Ecocriticism*, 1–17.

Iovino, Serenella, and Serpil Oppermann, eds. *Material Ecocriticism.* Bloomington: Indiana University Press, 2014.

Israëls, Machtelt. "'Sculpted Painting' in Early Renaissance Florence." In *The Springtime of the Renaissance: Sculpture and the Arts in Florence 1400–60*, edited by Beatrice Paolozzi Strozzi and Marc Bormand, 151–157. Florence: Mandragora, 2013. Exhibition catalogue.

Jahn, Bernhard. *Raumkonzepte in der Frühen Neuzeit: Zur Konstruktion von Wirklichkeit in Pilgerberichten, Amerikareisebeschreibungen und Prosaerzählungen.* Frankfurt: Peter Lang, 1993.

Jardine, Lisa. *Worldly Goods: A New History of the Renaissance.* New York: Doubleday, 1996.

Johnson, Barbara. *Persons and Things.* Cambridge, MA: Harvard University Press, 2008.

Johnson, Christine. *The German Discovery of the World: Renaissance Encounters with the Strange and Marvelous.* Charlottesville: University of Virginia Press, 2008.

Johnson, Geraldine A. "Touch, Tactility, and the Reception of Sculpture." In *A Companion to Art Theory*, edited by Carolyn Wilde and Paul Smith, 61–74. Blackwell Companions in Cultural Studies 5. Oxford: Blackwell, 2002.

Johnson, Jim [Bruno Latour]. "Mixing Humans and Nonhumans Together: The Sociology of a Door-Closer." *Social Problems* 35, no. 3 (1988): 298–310.

Johnston, Andrew James. *Performing the Middle Ages from "Beowulf" to "Othello"*. Turnhout: Brepols, 2008.

Jones, Lars Raymond. "Visio Divina? Donor Figures and Representations of Imagistic Devotion; The Copy of the 'Virgin of Bagnolo' in the Museo dell'Opera del Duomo, Florence." In V. Schmidt, *Italian Panel Painting*, 30–55.

Jung, Jacqueline E. "The Tactile and the Visionary: Notes on the Place of Sculpture in the Medieval Religious Imagination." In *Looking Beyond: Visions, Dreams, and Insights in Medieval Art and History*, edited by Colum Hourihane, 203–240. Index of Christian Art, Occasional Papers 11. Princeton, NJ: Index of Christian Art, Princeton University / Penn State University Press, 2010.

Kaelber, Lutz. "Spiritual Pilgrimage." In *Encyclopedia of Medieval Pilgrimage*, edited by Larissa J. Taylor et al., 693–695. Leiden: Brill, 2010.

Kaeuper, Richard W. *Holy Warriors: The Religious Ideology of Chivalry*. Philadelphia: University of Pennsylvania Press, 2009.

Kaeuper, Richard W. *Medieval Chivalry*. Cambridge Medieval Textbooks. Cambridge: Cambridge University Press, 2016.

Kanter, Laurence B. "Lorenzo Monaco." In Kanter, *Painting and Illumination*, 220–306.

Kanter, Laurence B., ed. *Painting and Illumination in Early Renaissance Florence 1300–1450*. New York: Abrams, 1994. Exhibition catalogue.

Karnes, Michelle. "Marvels in the Medieval Imagination." *Speculum* 90, no. 2 (2015): 327–365.

Karnes, Michelle. "Wonder, Marvels, and Metaphor in the Squire's Tale." *ELH* 82, no. 2 (11 June 2015): 461–490.

Kassell, Lauren. "Reading for the Philosopher's Stone." In Frasca-Spada and Jardine, *Books and the Sciences*, 132–150.

Kavey, Allison. *Books of Secrets: Natural Philosophy in England, 1550–1600*. Urbana: University of Illinois Press, 2007.

Keen, Maurice. *Chivalry*. New Haven: Yale University Press, 1984.

Kemper, Tobias A. *Die Kreuzigung Christi: Motivgeschichtliche Studien zu lateinischen und deutschen Passionstraktaten des Spätmittelalters*. Münchener Texte und Untersuchungen zur deutschen Literatur des Mittelalters 131. Tübingen: Niemeyer, 2006.

Kessler, Herbert L. *Spiritual Seeing: Picturing God's Invisibility in Medieval Art*. Philadelphia: University of Pennsylvania Press, 2000.

Khanmohamadi, Shirin A. *In Light of Another's Word: European Ethnography in the Middle Ages*. Middle Ages Series. Philadelphia: University of Pennsylvania Press, 2013.

Kiening, Christian. "Einleitung." In Dauven-van Knippenburg, Herberichs, and Kiening, *Medialität*, 7–20.

Kiening, Christian. *Fülle und Mangel: Medialität im Mittelalter*. Zurich: Chronos Verlag, 2016.

Kiening, Christian. "Gebete und Benediktionen von Muri (um 1150/1180)." In *Literarische Performativität: Lektüren vormoderner Texte*, edited by Cornelia Herberichs and Christian Kiening, 100–118. Zurich: Chronos, 2008.

Kiening, Christian. "Mediating the Passion in Time and Space." In *Temporality and Mediality in Late Medieval and Early Modern Culture*, edited by Christian Kiening and Martina Stercken, 116–146. Cursor Mundi 32. Turnhout: Brepols, 2018.

Kirokisian, Racha. *From the Material to the Mystical: The Vernacular Transmission of Gertrude of Helfta's Visions* (Cambridge: University Press, 2021).

Klinkhammer, Karl Joseph. *Adolf von Essen und seine Werke: Der Rosenkranz in der geschichtlichen Situation seiner Entstehung und in seinem bleibenden Anliegen; Eine Quellenforschung.* Frankfurt: Josef Knecht, 1972.

Klinkhammer, Karl Joseph. "Dominikus von Preußen." In ²VL 2 (1980), 190–192.

Klobucka, Anna. "Lusotropical Romance: Camões, Gilberto Freyre, and the Isle of Love." *Portuguese Literary and Cultural Studies* 9 (2003): 121–138.

Knape, Joachim. *Die Dinge: Ihr Bild, ihr Design und ihre Rhetorik.* Wiesbaden: Harrassowitz, 2019.

Knapp, Fritz Peter. "Heinrich von Neustadt." In *Die Literatur des Spätmittelalters in den Ländern Österreich, Steiermark, Kärnten, Salzburg und Tirol von 1273 bis 1439*, vol. 2, bk. 1, of *Geschichte der Literatur in Österreich: Von den Anfängen bis zur Gegenwart*, edited by Herbert Zeman, 280–297. Graz: Akademische Druck- und Verlagsanstalt, 1999.

Knappett, Carl. *Thinking through Material Culture: An Interdisciplinary Perspective.* Philadelphia: University of Pennsylvania Press, 2005.

Kohl, Karl-Heinz. *Die Macht der Dinge: Geschichte und Theorie sakraler Objekte.* Munich: C. H. Beck, 2003.

Köhn, Rolf. "Dimensionen und Funktionen des Öffentlichen und Privaten in der mittelalterlichen Korrespondenz." In *Das Öffentliche und Private in der Vormoderne*, edited by Gert Melville and Peter von Moos, 309–357. Cologne: Böhlau Verlag, 1998.

Köpf, Ulrich. "Kreuz IV: Mittelalter." In *Theologische Realenzyklopädie*, vol. 19, *Kirchenrechtsquellen–Kreuz*, 732–761. Berlin: Walter de Gruyter, 1990.

Kopytoff, Igor. "The Cultural Biography of Things: Commoditization as Process." In *The Social Life of Things: Commodities in Cultural Perspective*, edited by Arjun Appadurai, 64–91. Cambridge: Cambridge University Press, 1986.

Kornbluth, Genevra Alisoun. "Early Medieval Crystal Amulets: Secular Instruments of Protection and Healing." In *The Sacred and the Secular in Medieval Healing*, edited by Barbara S. Bowers and Linda Migl Keyser, 143–181. London: Routledge, 2016.

Kreytenberg, Gert. "Ein Tabernakel mit Kruzifix von Nino Pisano und Luca di Tommè." *Pantheon* 58 (2000): 9–12.

Krieger, Verena. "Die Farbe als 'Seele' der Malerei: Transformationen eines Topos vom 16. Jahrhundert zur Moderne." *Marburger Jahrbuch für Kunstwissenschaft* 33 (2006): 91–112.

Krüger, Klaus. "Bildandacht und Bergeinsamkeit: Der Eremit als Rollenspiel in der städtischen Gesellschaft." In *Malerei und Stadtkultur in der Dantezeit: Die Argumentation der Bilder*, edited by Hans Belting and Dieter Blume, 187–200. Munich: Hirmer, 1989.

Krüger, Klaus. *Bildpräsenz – Heilspräsenz: Ästhetik der Liminalität.* Figura 6. Göttingen: Wallstein, 2018.

Krüger, Klaus. "Bild und Bühne: Dispositive des imaginären Blicks." In *Transformationen des Religiösen: Performativität und Textualität im geistlichen Spiel*, edited by Ingrid Kasten and Erika Fischer-Lichte, 218–248. Trends in Medieval Philology 11. Berlin: Walter de Gruyter, 2007.

Krüger, Klaus. *Der frühe Bildkult des Franziskus in Italien: Gestalt- und Funktionswandel des Tafelbildes im 13. und 14. Jahrhundert.* Berlin: Mann, 1992.

Krüger, Klaus. "Mimesis als Bildlichkeit des Scheins: Zur Fiktionalität religiöser Bildkunst im Trecento." In *Künstlerischer Austausch: Artistic Exchange*, edited by Thomas W. Gaehtgens, 2:423–436. Berlin: Akademie Verlag, 1993.

Kruse, Christiane. *Wozu Menschen malen: Historische Begründungen eines Bildmediums.* Munich: Wilhelm Fink, 2003.

Kumler, Aden, and Christopher R. Lakey. "*Res et significatio*: The Material Sense of Things in the Middle Ages." Special issue, *Gesta* 51, no. 1 (2012): 1–17.

Kusukawa, Sachiko. "Illustrating Nature." In Frasca-Spada and Jardine, *Books and the Sciences*, 90–113.

Lakey, Christopher R. "The Materiality of Light in Medieval Italian Painting." In "Medieval Materiality," special issue, *English Language Notes* 53, no. 2 (2015): 119–136.

Largier, Niklaus. *Die Kunst des Begehrens: Dekadenz, Sinnlichkeit und Askese.* Munich: C. H. Beck, 2007.

Largier, Niklaus. *Spekulative Sinnlichkeit: Kontemplation und Spekulation im Mittelalter.* Zurich: Chronos, 2019.

Largier, Niklaus. "Zwischen Ereignis und Medium: Sinnlichkeit, Rhetorik und Hermeneutik in Auerbachs Konzept der *figura*." In *Figura: Dynamiken der Zeiten und Zeichen im Mittelalter*, edited by Christian Kiening and Katharina Mertens Fleury, 51–70. Würzburg: Königshausen & Neumann, 2013.

Latour, Bruno. "The Berlin Key or How to Do Words with Things." Translated by Lydia Davis. In *Matter, Materiality and Modern Culture*, edited by P. M. Graves-Brown, 10–21. London: Routledge, 1991.

Latour, Bruno. "From Realpolitik to Dingpolitik or How to Make Things Public." In *Making Things Public: Atmospheres of Democracy*, edited by Bruno Latour and Peter Weibel, 14–41. Cambridge, MA: MIT Press; Karlsruhe: Center for Art and Media, 2005.

Latour, Bruno. *An Inquiry into Modes of Existence: An Anthropology of the Moderns.* Translated by Catherine Porter. Cambridge, MA: Harvard University Press, 2013.

Latour, Bruno. *Reassembling the Social: An Introduction to Actor-Network-Theory.* Clarendon Lectures in Management Studies. Oxford: Oxford University Press, 2005.

Latour, Bruno. *We Have Never Been Modern.* Translated by Catherine Porter. Cambridge, MA: Harvard University Press, 1993.

Latour, Bruno. *See also* Jim Johnson.

Laube, Stefan. *Von der Reliquie zum Ding: Heiliger Ort – Wunderkammer – Museum.* Berlin: Akademie-Verlag, 2012.

Legassie, Shayne Aaron. *The Medieval Invention of Travel.* Chicago: University of Chicago Press, 2017.

Lehmann, Ann-Sophie. "How Materials Make Meaning." In *Meaning in Materials, 1400–1800*, edited by Ann-Sophie Lehmann, Frits Scholten, and H. Perry Chapman, 6–27. Leiden: Brill, 2013.

Lentes, Thomas. "Gebetbuch und Gebärde: Religiöses Ausdrucksverhalten in Gebetbüchern aus dem Dominikanerinnen-Kloster St. Nikolaus in undis zu Straßburg (1350–1550)." PhD diss., Westfälische Wilhelms-Universität Münster, 1996.

Lentes, Thomas. "Die Gewänder der Heiligen: Ein Diskussionsbeitrag zum Verhältnis von Gebet, Bild und Imagination." In *Hagiographie und Kunst: Der Heiligenkult in Schrift, Bild und Architektur*, edited by Gottfried Kerscher, 120–151. Berlin: Reimer, 1993.

Lentes, Thomas. "Inneres Auge, äußerer Blick und heilige Schau: Ein Diskussionsbeitrag zur visuellen Praxis in Frömmigkeit und Moraldidaxe des späten Mittelalters." In *Frömmigkeit im Mittelalter: Politisch-soziale Kontexte, visuelle Praxis, körperliche Ausdrucksformen*, edited by Klaus Schreiner, 179–220. Munich: Wilhelm Fink Verlag, 2002.

Levine, Caroline. *Forms: Whole, Rhythm, Hierarchy, Network.* Princeton, NJ: Princeton University Press, 2015.

Lloret, Albert. *Printing Ausiàs March: Material Culture and Renaissance Poetics.* Madrid: CECE, 2013.

Lloret, Albert, and Miguel Martínez. "Introducción: Poesía y materialidad / Introduction: Poetry and Materiality." *Calíope: Journal of the Society for Renaissance and Baroque Hispanic Poetry* 23, no. 2 (December 11, 2018): 7–19.

Lochrie, Karma. *Nowhere in the Middle Ages.* Philadelphia: University of Pennsylvania Press, 2016.

Löhr, Wolf-Dietrich. "Dantes Täfelchen, Cenninis Zeichenkiste: *Ritratto, disegno* und *fantasia* als Instrumente der Bilderzeugung im Trecento." *Das Mittelalter* 13 (2008): 148–179.

Löhr, Wolf-Dietrich. "Handwerk und Denkwerk des Malers: Kontexte für Cenninis Theorie der Praxis." In Löhr and Weppelmann, *Fantasie und Handwerk*, 152–177.

Löhr, Wolf-Dietrich. "Die Perle im Acker: Francesco di Vannuccios Berliner 'Kreuzigung' und die Eröffnung der Wunden." In *Zeremoniell und Raum in der frühen italienischen Malerei*, edited by Stefan Weppelmann, 160–183. Studien zur internationalen Architektur- und Kunstgeschichte 60. Petersberg: Imhof, 2007.

Löhr, Wolf-Dietrich, and Stefan Weppelmann, eds. *Fantasie und Handwerk: Cennino Cennini und die Tradition der toskanischen Malerei von Giotto bis Lorenzo Monaco*. Munich: Hirmer, 2008. Exhibition catalogue.

Löhr, Wolf-Dietrich, and Stefan Weppelmann. "'Glieder in der Kunst der Malerei': Cennino Cenninis Genealogie und die Suche nach Kontinuität zwischen Handwerkstradition, Werkstattpraxis und Historiographie." In Löhr and Weppelmann, *Fantasie und Handwerk*, 13–43.

Long, Pamela O. *Artisan/Practitioners and the Rise of the New Sciences, 1400–1600*. Corvallis: Oregon State University Press, 2011.

Long, Pamela O. *Openness, Secrecy, Authorship: Technical Arts and the Culture of Knowledge from Antiquity to the Renaissance*. Baltimore: Johns Hopkins University Press, 2001.

Löther, Andrea. *Prozessionen in spätmittelalterlichen Städten: Politische Partizipation, obrigkeitliche Inszenierung, städtische Einheit*. Norm und Struktur 12. Cologne: Böhlau Verlag, 1999.

Macedo, José Agostinho de. *Censura das Lusiadas*. Lisbon: Impressão Regia, 1820.

Maguire, Henry. *Rhetoric, Nature and Magic in Byzantine Art*. Aldershot: Ashgate, 1998.

Mann, C. Griffiths. "Relics, Reliquaries, and the Limitations of Trecento Painting: Naddo Ceccarelli's Reliquary Tabernacle in the Walters Art Museum." *Word & Image* 22, no. 3 (2006): 251–259.

Martínez, Miguel. "A Poet of Our Own: The Struggle for 'Os Lusíadas' in the Afterlife of Camões." *Journal for Early Modern Cultural Studies* 10, no. 1 (2010): 71–94.

Marzell, Heinrich. "Alraun." In Bächtold-Stäubli and Hoffmann-Krayer, *Handwörterbuch des deutschen Aberglaubens*, 1:312–324.

Matter, Stefan. "Zur Poetik mittelalterlicher Architekturbeschreibungen." *Mittellateinisches Jahrbuch: Internationale Zeitschrift für Mediävistik und Humanismusforschung* 47, no. 3 (2012): 387–413.

Mauss, Marcel. *The Gift*. Selected, annotated, and translated by Jane I. Guyer. Chicago: HAU Books, 2016.

McDonald, William C. "Wolfram's Grail." *Arthuriana* 8 (1998): 22–34.

McLoughlin, Kate. *Authoring War: The Literary Representation of War from the "Iliad" to Iraq*. Cambridge: Cambridge University Press, 2011.

Meany, Audrey. "Felix's *Life of Guthlac*: History or Hagiography?" In *Æthelbald and Offa: Two Eighth-Century Kings of Mercia; Papers from a Conference Held in Manchester in 2000*, edited by David Hill, 75–84. British Archaeological Reports, British Series 383. Oxford: Archaeopress, 2005.

Meiss, Millard. *Painting in Florence and Siena after the Black Death*. Princeton, NJ: Princeton University Press, 1951.

Meurer, Peter H. *Fontes cartographici Orteliani: Das "Theatrum orbis terrarum" von Abraham Ortelius und seine Kartenquellen*. Weinheim: VCH, 1991.

Miles, Margaret. "Vision: The Eye of the Body and the Eye of the Mind in Saint Augustine's 'De trinitate' and 'Confessions.'" *Journal of Religion* 63, no. 2 (1983): 125–142. Accessed 23 April 2021. http://www.jstor.org/stable/1202858.

Miller, William Ian. "Gift, Sale, Payment, Raid: Case Studies in the Negotiation and Classification of Exchange in Medieval Iceland." *Speculum* 61 (1986): 18–50.

Mittelstrass, Jürgen. "Nature and Science in the Renaissance." In *Metaphysics and Philosophy of Science in the Seventeenth and Eighteenth Centuries: Essays in Honour of Gerd Buchdahl*, edited by R. S. Woolhouse, 17–40. Heidelberg: Springer Science & Business Media, 2012.

Mixson, James. "Introduction." In *A Companion to Observant Reform in the Late Middle Ages and Beyond*, edited by James D. Mixson and Bert Roest, 1–20. Leiden: Brill, 2015.

Moore, Kathryn Blair. *The Architecture of the Christian Holy Land: Reception from Late Antiquity through the Renaissance.* Cambridge: Cambridge University Press, 2017.

Moran, Bruce T. *Distilling Knowledge: Alchemy, Chemistry, and the Scientific Revolution.* Cambridge, MA: Harvard University Press, 2005.

Mueller, Alex. *Translating Troy: Provincial Politics in Alliterative Romance.* Columbus: Ohio State University Press, 2013.

Mühlherr, Anna. "Einleitung." In Mühlherr et al., *Dingkulturen*, 1–20.

Mühlherr, Anna. "Nicht mit rechten Dingen, nicht mit dem rechten Ding, nicht am rechten Ort: Zur *tarnkappe* und zum *hort* im Nibelungenlied." *Beiträge zur Geschichte der deutschen Sprache und Literatur* 131 (2009): 461–492.

Mühlherr, Anna, Bruno Quast, Heike Sahm, and Monika Schausten, eds. *Dingkulturen: Objekte in Literatur, Kunst und Gesellschaft der Vormoderne.* Berlin: De Gruyter, 2016.

Muller, Norman E. "The Development of Sgraffito in Sienese Painting." In *Simone Martini: Atti del Convegno*, edited by Luciano Bellosi, 147–150. Florence: Centro Di, 1988.

Neil, Ketti. "St. Francis of Assisi, the Penitent Magdalen, and the Patron at the Foot of the Cross." *Rutgers Art Review* 9/10 (1988–89): 83–110.

Newhauser, Richard. "The Senses, the Medieval Sensorium, and Sensing (in) the Middle Ages." In *Handbook of Medieval Culture: Fundamental Aspects and Conditions of the European Middle Ages*, edited by Albrecht Classen, 3:1559–1575. Berlin: Walter de Gruyter, 2015.

Newman, Barbara. "What Did It Mean to Say 'I Saw'? The Clash between Theory and Practice in Medieval Visionary Culture." *Speculum* 80, no. 1 (2005): 1–43.

Newman, William R. *Promethean Ambitions: Alchemy and the Quest to Perfect Nature.* Chicago: University of Chicago Press, 2004.

Niesner, Manuela. "Das Wunderbare in der 'Conjointure': Zur poetologischen Aussage des Feimurgan-Exkurses in Hartmanns 'Erec.'" *Zeitschrift für deutsches Altertum und deutsche Literatur* 137, no. 2 (2008): 137–157.

Noetzel, Justin T. "Monster, Demon, Warrior: St. Guthlac and the Cultural Landscape of the Anglo-Saxon Fens." *Comitatus: A Journal of Medieval and Renaissance Studies* 45 (2014): 105–131.

Norris, Herbert. *Medieval Costume and Fashion.* Mineola, NY: Dover, 1999.

Nummedal, Tara. *Alchemy and Authority in the Holy Roman Empire.* Chicago: University of Chicago Press, 2007.

O'Brien O'Keeffe, Katherine. "Guthlac's Crossings." *Quaestio: Selected Proceedings of the Cambridge Colloquium in Anglo-Saxon, Norse, and Celtic* 2 (2001): 1–26.

Ochsenbein, Peter. "Deutschsprachige Gebetbücher vor 1400." In *Deutsche Handschriften 1100–1400: Oxforder Kolloquium 1985*, edited by Volker Honemann and Nigel F. Palmer, 379–398. Tübingen: Max Niemeyer Verlag, 1988.

Ohly, Friedrich. "Vom geistigen Sinn des Wortes im Mittelalter." In *Schriften zur mittelalterlichen Bedeutungsforschung*, edited by Friedrich Ohly, 1–31. Darmstadt: Wissenschaftliche Buchgesellschaft, 1977.

Oosterhoff, Richard J. "A Book, a Pen, and the *Sphere*: Reading Sacrobosco in the Renaissance." *History of Universities* 28, no. 2 (2015). https://doi.org/10.1093/acprof: oso/9780198743651.001.0001.

Oosthuizen, Susan. *The Anglo-Saxon Fenland.* Oxford: Windgather Press, 2017.

Oppermann, Serpil. "From Ecological Postmodernism to Material Ecocriticism: Creative Materiality and Narrative Agency." In Iovino and Oppermann, *Material Ecocriticism*, 21–36.

Oswald, Marion. *Gabe und Gewalt: Studien zur Logik und Poetik der Gabe in der frühhöfischen Erzählliteratur.* Göttingen: Vandenhoeck & Ruprecht, 2004.

Palazzo, Eric. "Art, Liturgy, and the Five Senses in the Early Middle Ages." *Viator* 41, no. 1 (2010): 25–56.

Passannante, Gerard. *The Lucretian Renaissance: Philology and the Afterlife of Tradition.* Chicago: University of Chicago Press, 2011.

Patch, Howard R. *The Goddess Fortuna in Mediaeval Literature.* Cambridge, MA: Harvard University Press, 1927.

Patterson, Lee. *Negotiating the Past: The Historical Understanding of Medieval History.* Madison: University of Wisconsin Press, 1987.

Pettegree, Andrew, and Malcolm Walsby. *Netherlandish Books: Books Published in the Low Countries and Dutch Books Printed Abroad before 1601.* 2 vols. Leiden: Brill, 2010.

Pettenati, Silvana. "Vetri a oro del Trecento padano." *Paragone: Arte* 24, no. 275 (1973): 71–80.

Pettenati, Silvana. *Vetri dorati e graffiti dal XIV al XVI secolo: Vetri rinascimentali.* Lo specchio del Bargello 20. Florence: Museo nazionale del Bargello, 1986.

Pettenati, Silvana. *I vetri dorati graffiti e i vetri dipinti.* Turin: Museo Civico, 1978.

Peuckert, Will-Erich. "Signatur." In Bächtold-Stäubli and Hoffmann-Krayer, *Handwörterbuch des deutschen Aberglaubens*, 7:1710–1712.

Philipp, Michael. "Vom Kultbild zum Abbild der Wirklichkeit: Zur Entwicklung der Malerei in Italien 1250–1500." In Westheider and Philipp, *Erfindung des Bildes*, 12–33.

Phillips, Dana, and Heather Sullivan. "Material Ecocriticism: Dirt, Waste, Bodies, Food, and Other Matter." *Interdisciplinary Studies in Literature and the Environment* 19, no. 3 (2012): 445–447. doi:10.1093/isle/iss064.

Plagnard, Aude. "A descrição da máquina do mundo: Francisco Garrido de Villena e Luís de Camões." *Criticón*, no. 134 (10 December 2018): 115–140. https://doi.org/10.4000/criticon.5056.

Poellinger, Michele. "Violence in Later Middle English Arthurian Romance." PhD diss., University of Leeds, 2013.

Pope-Hennessy, John. "The Interaction of Painting and Sculpture in Florence in the Fifteenth Century." *The Journal of the Royal Society for the Encouragement of Arts, Manufactures and Commerce* 117, no. 5154 (1969): 406–424.

Preising, Dagmar. "Bild und Reliquie: Gestalt und Funktion gotischer Reliquientafeln und -altärchen." *Aachener Kunstblätter* 61 (1995/1997): 13–84.

Price, Leah. "Introduction: Reading Matter." *PMLA* 121, no. 1 (2006): 9–16.

Principe, Lawrence M. *The Secrets of Alchemy.* Chicago: University of Chicago Press, 2013.

Quast, Bruno. "Dingpolitik: Gesellschaftstheoretische Überlegungen zu Rundtafel und Gral in Wolframs von Eschenbach *Parzival*." In Mühlherr et al., *Dingkulturen*, 171–184.

Rajewsky, Irina O. *Intermedialität.* UTB für Wissenschaft 2261. Tübingen: A. Francke, 2002.

Ramachandran, Ayesha. *The Worldmakers: Global Imagining in Early Modern Europe.* Chicago: University of Chicago Press, 2015.

Randolph, Adrian W. B. *Touching Objects: Intimate Experiences of Italian Fifteenth-Century Art.* New Haven: Yale University Press, 2014.

Rankin, Alisha. "How to Cure the Golden Vein: Medical Remedies as *Wissenschaft* in Early Modern Germany." In Smith, Meyers, and Cook, *Ways of Making and Knowing*, 113–135.

Renz, Tilo. "Utopische Elemente der Reiseliteratur des späten Mittelalters." *Das Mittelalter* 18, no. 2 (2013): 129–152.

Rimmele, Marius. "Memlings Mantelteilung: Der Marienmantel als Schwellenmotiv." In *Bild-Riss: Textile Öffnungen im ästhetischen Diskurs*, edited by Mateusz Kapustka, 101–126. Berlin: Edition Imorde, 2015.

Rimmele, Marius. *Das Triptychon als Metapher, Körper und Ort: Semantisierungen eines Bildträgers.* Munich: Wilhelm Fink, 2010.

Rimmele, Marius. "(Ver-)Führung durch Scharniere: Zur Instrumentalisierung kleinformatiger Klappbilder in der Passionsmeditation." In Dauven-van Knippenberg, Herberichs, and Kiening, *Medialität*, 111–130.

Ringbom, Sixten. "Devotional Images and Imaginative Devotions: Notes on the Place of Art in Late Medieval Private Piety." *Gazette des Beaux-Arts* 73 (1969): 159–170.

Rubin, Miri. *Corpus Christi: The Eucharist in Late Medieval Culture.* Cambridge: Cambridge University Press, 2006.

Rudy, Kathryn M. "Introduction: Miraculous Textiles in 'Exempla' and Images from the Low Countries." In Rudy and Baert, *Weaving, Veiling, and Dressing*, 1–35.

Rudy, Kathryn M. "Touching the Book Again: The Passional of Abbess Kunigunde of Bohemia." In *Codex und Material*, edited by Patrizia Carmassi and Gia Toussaint, 247–257. Wolfenbütteler Mittelalter-Studien 34. Wiesbaden: Harrassowitz Verlag, 2018.

Rudy, Kathryn M. *Virtual Pilgrimages in the Convent: Imagining Jerusalem in the Late Middle Ages.* Disciplina Monastica: Studies on Medieval Monastic Life 8. Turnhout: Brepols, 2011.

Rudy, Kathryn M. "Virtual Pilgrimage through the Jerusalem Cityspace." In *Visual Constructs of Jerusalem*, edited by Bianca Kühnel, Galit Noga-Banai, and Hanna Vorholt, 381–396. Cultural Encounters in Late Antiquity and the Middle Ages 18. Turnhout: Brepols, 2014.

Rudy, Kathryn M., and Barbara Baert, eds. *Weaving, Veiling, and Dressing: Textiles and Their Metaphors in the Late Middle Ages.* Turnhout: Brepols, 2007.

Ruh, Kurt. "Vorwort." In ²VL 1 (1978), v–vii.

Ryser, Frieder. *Verzauberte Bilder: Die Kunst der Malerei hinter Glas von der Antike bis zum 18. Jahrhundert.* Munich: Klinkhardt & Biermann, 1991.

Saraiva, António José. *Luís de Camões: Estudo e antologia.* Amadora: Bertrand, 1980.

Scafi, Alessandro. *Mapping Paradise: A History of Heaven on Earth.* London: University of Chicago Press, 2006.

Schama, Simon. *Landscape and Memory.* London: Harper Collins, 1995.

Schanze, Christoph. "Dinge erzählen im Mittelalter: Zur narratologischen Analyse von Objekten in der höfischen Epik." *KulturPoetik: Zeitschrift für Kulturgeschichtliche Literaturwissenschaft* 16, no. 2 (2016): 153–172.

Schiewer, Regina D. "Sermons for Nuns of the Dominican Observance Movement." In *Medieval Monastic Preaching*, edited by Carolyn A. Muessig, 75–96. Leiden: Brill, 1998.

Schmidt, Charles. *Historisches Wörterbuch der elsässischen Mundart: Mit besonderer Berücksichtigung der früh-neuhochdeutschen Periode.* Strasbourg: J. H. E. Heitz, 1901.

Schmidt, Victor M., ed. *Italian Panel Painting of the Duecento and Trecento.* Studies in the History of Art 61, Symposium Papers 38. Washington, D.C.: National Gallery of Art, 2002.

Schmidt, Victor M. "The Lunette-Shaped Panel and Some Characteristics of Panel Painting." In V. Schmidt, *Italian Panel Painting*, 83–101.

Schmidt, Victor M. "Der Maler und seine Kunst: Über Pietro Lorenzettis Diptychon in Altenburg." In Westheider and Philipp, *Erfindung des Bildes*, 46–57.

Schmidt, Victor M. *Painted Piety: Panel Paintings for Personal Devotion in Tuscany, 1250–1400.* Italia e Paesi Bassi 8. Florence: Centro Di, 2005.

Schmidtke, Dietrich. *Studien zur dingallegorischen Erbauungsliteratur des Spätmittelalters: Am Beispiel der Gartenallegorie.* Tübingen: Max Niemeyer, 1982.

Schneider, Almut. *Chiffren des Selbst: Narrative Spiegelungen der Identitätsproblematik in Johanns von Würzburg "Wilhelm von Österreich" und in Heinrichs von Neustadt "Apollonius von Tyrland"*. Göttingen: Vandenhoeck & Ruprecht, 2004.

Schnyder, André. *Die Ursulabruderschaften des Spätmittelalters: Ein Beitrag zur Erforschung der religiösen Literatur des 15. Jahrhunderts*. Bern: Haupt, 1986.

Schnyder, Mireille. "Der unfeste Text: Mittelalterliche 'Audiovisualität'?" In *Der unfeste Text: Perspektiven auf einen literatur- und kulturwissenschaftlichen Leitbegriff*, edited by Barbara Sabel and André Bucher, 132–153. Würzburg: Königshausen & Neumann, 2001.

Scholz, Susanne, and Ulrike Vedder, eds. *Handbuch Literatur & Materielle Kultur*. Berlin: De Gruyter, 2016.

Schreiner, Klaus. "Gebildete Analphabeten? Spätmittelalterliche Laienbrüder als Leser und Schreiber wissensvermittelnder und frömmigkeitsbildender Literatur." In *Wissensliteratur im Mittelalter und in der Frühen Neuzeit: Bedingungen, Typen, Publikum, Sprache*, edited by Horst Brunner and Norbert Richard Wolf, 296–317. Wiesbaden: Ludwig Reichert, 1993.

Schulz, Otto. "Die Wiederherstellung der St. Sebaldkirche in Nürnberg 1888–1905." *Mitteilungen des Vereins für Geschichte der Stadt Nürnberg* 17 (1906): 246–281.

See, Geoffrey. "'Wes möhten si langer bîten?': Narrative Digressions in Hartmann von Aue's 'Erec.'" *Neuphilologische Mitteilungen* 96, no. 4 (1995): 335–349.

Seibert, Jutta. *Lexikon christlicher Kunst: Themen, Gestalten, Symbole*. Freiburg: Herder, 1980.

Selmayr, Pia. *Der Lauf der Dinge: Wechselverhältnisse zwischen Raum, Ding und Figur bei der narrativen Konstitution von Anderwelten im "Wigalois" und im "Lanzelet"*. Frankfurt: Lang, 2017.

Serif, Ina. "'…wie dz ich ain súnderin bin: Überlegungen zu Text und Kontext eines spätmittelalterlichen Gebetbuchs aus einem franziskanischen Frauenkloster in Vorarlberg." In *Handschriften als Quellen der Sprach- und Kulturwissenschaft: Aktuelle Fragestellungen – Methoden – Probleme*, edited by Anette Kremer and Vincenz Schwab, 177–199. Bamberg: University of Bamberg Press, 2018.

Siewers, Alfred Kentigern. "Landscapes of Conversion." *Viator* 34 (2003): 1–39.

Siewers, Alfred Kentigern. *Re-imagining Nature: Environmental Humanities and Ecosemiotics*. Lewisburg, PA: Bucknell University Press, 2015.

Sigerist, Henry E. "Hieronymus Brunschwig and His Work." In *The Book of Cirurgia*, by Hieronymus Brunschwig, edited by Henry E. Sigerist. Milan: R. Lier, 1923.

Skaug, Erling. "Painters, Punchers, Gilders or Goldbeaters? A Critical Survey Report of Discussions in Recent Literature about Early Italian Painting." *Zeitschrift für Kunstgeschichte* 71, no. 4 (2008): 571–582.

Skaug, Erling. "Stippled Angels and 'Forgotten Haloes.'" In "Das Göttinger Barfüßerretabel von 1424," special issue, *Niederdeutsche Beiträge zur Kunstgeschichte*, n.s., 1 (2015): 395–402.

Smith, Pamela H. *The Body of the Artisan: Art and Experience in the Scientific Revolution*. Chicago: University of Chicago Press, 2004.

Smith, Pamela H. "Making as Knowing: Craft as Natural Philosophy." In Smith, Meyers, and Cook, *Ways of Making and Knowing*, 17–47.

Smith, Pamela H. "Making Things: Techniques and Books in Early Modern Europe." In Findlen, *Early Modern Things*, 173–204.

Smith, Pamela H., Amy R. W. Meyers, and Harold J. Cook, eds. *Ways of Making and Knowing: The Material Culture of Empirical Knowledge*. Ann Arbor: University of Michigan Press, 2014.

Smith, Pamela H., and Benjamin Schmidt, eds. *Making Knowledge in Early Modern Europe: Practices, Objects, and Texts, 1400–1800*. Chicago: University of Chicago Press, 2007.

Soares Amora, Antônio. *A prosopopéia, de Bento Teixeira, à luz da moderna camonologia*. Lisbon: Universidade de Lisboa, 1957.

Starkey, Kathryn. "From Enslavement to Discernment: Learning to See in Gottfried's *Tristan*." In *The Art of Vision: Ekphrasis in Medieval Literature and Culture*, edited by Ethan Knapp, Andrew James Johnston, and Margitta Rouse, 124–148. Columbus: Ohio State University Press, 2015.

Starkey, Kathryn. "Time Travel: Ekphrasis and Narrative in Medieval German Literature." In *Anschauung und Anschaulichkeit: Visualisierung im Wahrnehmen, Lesen und Denken*, edited by Hans Adler and Sabine Gross, 179–193. Munich: Fink Verlag, 2015.

Starkey, Kathryn. "Tristan Slippers: An Image of Adultery on a Symbol of Marriage?" In *Medieval Fabrications: Dress, Textiles, Clothwork and Other Cultural Imaginings*, edited by E. Jane Burns, 35–53. New York: Palgrave, 2004.

Starkey, Kathryn, and Horst Wenzel. "Visuality in German Courtly Literature." *Oxford German Studies* 37 (2008): 130–159.

Strasser, Ingrid. "Fiktion und ihre Vermittlung in Hartmanns Erec-Roman." In *Fiktionalität im Artusroman*, edited by Volker Mertens and Friedrich Wolfzettel, 63–83. Tübingen: Niemeyer, 1993.

Strässle, Thomas. "Pluralis materialitatis." In *Das Zusammenspiel der Materialien in den Künsten: Theorien, Praktiken, Perspektiven*, edited by Thomas Strässle, Christoph Kleinschmidt, and Johanne Mohs, 7–23. Bielefeld: transcript, 2013.

Strayer, Joseph. *The Albigensian Crusades*. Crosscurrents in World History. New York: The Dial Press, 1971.

Summers, David. *The Judgement of Sense: Renaissance Naturalism and the Rise of Aesthetics*. Ideas in Context. 1987. Reprint, Cambridge: Cambridge University Press, 1994.

Sussmann, Vera. "Maria mit dem Schutzmantel." *Marburger Jahrbuch für Kunstwissenschaft* 5 (1929): 285–351.

Swarzenski, Georg. "The Localization of Medieval Verre Eglomisé in the Walters Collections." *The Journal of the Walters Art Gallery* 3 (1940): 55–68.

Taape, Tillmann. "Distilling Reliable Remedies: Hieronymus Brunschwig's 'Liber de arte distillandi' (1500) between Alchemical Learning and Craft Practice." *Ambix* 61, no. 3 (2014): 236–256.

Tartuferi, Angelo, ed. *Giotto: Bilancio critico di sessant'anni di studi e ricerche*. Florence: Giunti, 2000. Exhibition catalogue.

Tartuferi, Angelo, and Daniela Parenti, eds. *Lorenzo Monaco: A Bridge from Giotto's Heritage to the Renaissance*. Florence: Giunti, 2006. Exhibition catalogue.

Thali, Johanna. "*andacht* und *betrachtung*: Zur Semantik zweier Leitvokabeln der spätmittelalterlichen Frömmigkeitskultur." In Hasebrink, Bernhardt, and Früh, *Semantik der Gelassenheit*, 226–267.

Thali, Johanna. "Strategien der Heilsvermittlung in der spätmittelalterlichen Gebetskultur." In Dauven-van Knippenberg, Herberichs, and Kiening, *Medialität des Heils*, 241–278.

Thomas, Alois. *Maria der Acker und die Weinrebe in der Symbolvorstellung des Mittelalters*. Trier: Habil., 1952.

Tipper, Jess. *The Grubenhaus in Anglo-Saxon England: An Analysis and Interpretation of the Evidence from a Most Distinctive Building Type*. Landscape Research Centre Archaeological Monograph Series 2, no. 1. Yedingham: The Landscape Research Centre, 2005.

Tobler, Titus. *Golgatha: Seine Kirchen und Klöster; Nach Quellen und Anschau; Mit Ansichten und Plänen*. St. Gallen: Huber, 1851.

Toesca, Pietro. "Vetri italiani a oro con graffiti." *L'Arte* 11 (1908): 247–261.

Tolan, John V. *Saracens: Islam in the Medieval European Imagination*. New York: Columbia University Press, 2002.

Tomasek, Tomas. *Das deutsche Rätsel im Mittelalter*. Tübingen: Max Niemeyer Verlag, 1994.

Tresch, John, and Bruno Latour. "Another Turn after ANT: An Interview with Bruno Latour." *Social Studies of Science* 43, no. 2 (1 April 2013): 302–313.

Tribit, Anthony. "Making Knighthood: The Construction of Masculinity in the *Ordene de chevalerie*, the *Livre de chevalerie de Geoffroi de Charny* and the *Espejo de verdadera nobleza*." PhD diss., University of Oregon, 2018.

Tripps, Johannes. *Das handelnde Bildwerk in der Gotik: Forschungen zu den Bedeutungsschichten und der Funktion des Kirchengebäudes und seiner Ausstattung in der Hoch- und Spätgotik.* Berlin: Mann, 1998.

Turville-Petre, Thorlac. *The Alliterative Revival.* Cambridge: D. S. Brewer, 1977.

van den Broecke, Marcel, Peter van der Krogt, and Peter Meurer, eds. *Abraham Ortelius and the First Atlas: Essays Commemorating the Quadricentennial of His Death, 1598–1998.* 't Goy-Houten, Netherlands: HES, 1999.

Wachinger, Burghart. "Heinrich von Neustadt, 'Apollonius von Tyrland.'" In *Positionen des Romans im späten Mittelalter*, edited by Walter Haug and Burghart Wachinger, 97–115. Tübingen: Max Niemeyer Verlag, 1991.

Wandhoff, Haiko. *Ekphrasis: Kunstbeschreibungen und virtuelle Räume in der Literatur des Mittelalters.* Berlin: De Gruyter, 2003.

Wand-Wittkowski, Christine. *Briefe im Mittelalter: Der deutschsprachige Brief als weltliche und religiöse Literatur.* Herne: Verlag für Wissenschaft und Kunst, 2000.

Webb, Ruth. *Ekphrasis, Imagination and Persuasion in Ancient Rhetorical Theory and Practice.* Farnham: Ashgate, 2009.

Weckwerth, Alfred. "Christus in der Kelter: Ursprung und Wandlung eines Bildmotivs." In *Beiträge zur Kunstgeschichte: Eine Festgabe für Heinz Rudolf Rosemann zum 9. Oktober 1960*, edited by Ernst Guldan, 95–108. Munich: Deutscher Kunstverlag, 1960.

Weilandt, Gerhard. *Die Sebalduskirche in Nürnberg: Bild und Gesellschaft im Zeitalter der Gotik und Renaissance.* Studien zur Internationalen Architektur- und Kunstgeschichte 47. Petersberg: Michael Imhof Verlag, 2007.

Weiss-Krejci, Estella. "The Plot against the Past: Reuse and Modification of Ancient Mortuary Monuments as Persuasive Efforts of Appropriation." In *The Lives of Prehistoric Monuments in Iron Age, Roman, and Medieval Europe*, edited by Marta Díaz-Guardamino, Leonardo García Sanjuán, and David Wheatley, 307–324. Oxford: Oxford University Press, 2015.

Wels, Volkhard. "Die Alchemie der Frühen Neuzeit als Gegenstand der Wissensgeschichte." In Alt et al., *Magia daemoniaca*, 233–265.

Wenderholm, Iris. "Aura, Licht und schöner Schein: Wertungen und Umwertungen des Goldgrunds." In *Geschichten auf Gold: Bilderzählungen in der frühen italienischen Malerei*, edited by Stefan Weppelmann, 100–113. Berlin: SMB-DuMont, 2005. Exhibition catalogue.

Wenderholm, Iris. *Bild und Berührung: Skulptur und Malerei auf dem Altar der italienischen Frührenaissance.* Italienische Forschungen des Kunsthistorischen Institutes in Florenz, I Mandorli 5. Munich: Deutscher Kunstverlag, 2006.

Weppelmann, Stefan. "Kollektives Ritual und persönliche Andacht: Kleinformate in der Tafelmalerei des Trecento." In *Kult Bild: Das Altar- und Andachtsbild von Duccio bis Perugino*, edited by Jochen Sander, 212–249. Petersberg: Imhof, 2006. Exhibition catalogue.

Wernli, Martina, and Alexander Kling. "Von erzählten und erzählenden Dingen." In *Das Verhältnis von res und verba: Zu den Narrativen der Dinge*, edited by Martina Wernli and Alexander Kling, 7–31. Freiburg: Rombach, 2018.

Westheider, Ortrud, and Michael Philipp, eds. *Die Erfindung des Bildes: Frühe italienische Meister bis Botticelli.* Publikationen des Bucerius-Kunst-Forums. Munich: Hirmer, 2011. Exhibition catalogue.

Wiederkehr, Ruth. *Das Hermetschwiler Gebetbuch: Studien zur deutschsprachigen Gebetbuchliteratur der Nord- und Zentralschweiz im Spätmittelalter; Mit einer Edition.* Berlin: De Gruyter, 2013.

Wilkins, David G. "Opening the Doors of Devotion: Trecento Triptychs and Suggestions concerning Images and Domestic Practice in Florence." In V. Schmidt, *Italian Panel Painting*, 370–393.

Wilkinson, Alexander S. *Iberian Books / Libros ibéricos: Books Published in Spanish or Portuguese or on the Iberian Peninsula before 1601 / Libros publicados en español o portugués o en la Península Ibérica antes de 1601*. Leiden: Brill, 2010.

Williams-Krapp, Werner. "Observanzbewegungen, monastische Spiritualität und geistliche Literatur im 15. Jahrhundert." *Internationales Archiv für Sozialgeschichte der deutschen Literatur* 20, no. 1 (1995): 1–15.

Williamson, Beth. "Matter and Materiality in an Italian Reliquary Triptych." *Gesta* 57, no. 1 (2018): 23–42.

Winston-Allen, Anne. *Stories of the Rose: The Making of the Rosary in the Middle Ages*. University Park: Pennsylvania State University Press, 1997.

Wittchow, Britta Maria. *Erzählte mediale Prozesse: Medientheoretische Perspektiven auf den "Reinfried von Braunschweig" und den "Apollonius von Tyrland"*. Berlin: De Gruyter, 2020.

Wittkower, Rudolf. "Marvels of the East: A Study in the History of Monsters." *Journal of the Warburg and Courtauld Institutes* 5 (1942): 159–197.

Wolf, Alois. "Hartmann von Aue and Chrétien de Troyes: Respective Approaches to the Matter of Britain." In Gentry, *Companion*, 43–70.

Wolf, Gerhard. "'bildes rehte brechen': Überlegungen zu Wahrnehmung und Beschreibungen in Hartmanns 'Erec.'" In *Beschreibend wahrnehmen – wahrnehmend beschreiben: Sprachliche und ästhetische Aspekte kognitiver Prozesse*, edited by Peter Klotz and Christine Lubkoll, 167–188. Freiburg: Rombach, 2005.

Wolff, Renata E. "Selected Marian Stories from *The Dialogue of Miracles* of Cesarius of Heisterbach." *Cistercian Studies Quarterly* 33, no. 2 (1998): 191–210.

Worstbrock, Franz Josef. "Dilatatio Materiae: Zur Poetik des 'Erec' Hartmanns von Aue." *Frühmittelalterliche Studien* 19, no. 1 (1985): 1–30.

Worstbrock, Franz Josef. "Wiedererzählen und Übersetzen." In *Mittelalter und frühe Neuzeit: Übergänge, Umbrüche und Neuansätze*, edited by Walter Haug, 128–142. Tübingen: Niemeyer, 1999.

Zarncke, Friedrich. *Der Priester Johannes: Erste Abhandlung*. Leipzig: Hirzel, 1879.

Zimmermann-Homeyer, Catarina. *Illustrierte Frühdrucke lateinischer Klassiker um 1500: Innovative Illustrationskonzepte aus der Straßburger Offizin Johannes Grüningers und ihre Wirkung*. Wiesbaden: Harrassowitz, 2018.

Contributor Biographies

Martin Bleisteiner is an editor and academic translator who lives and works in Berlin. His primary research interests are automata in late medieval English literature and medievalism in contemporary popular culture (e. g., *Game of Thrones*), with a special focus on issues of materiality, temporality, and transcultural entanglement. His publications include "Perils of Generation: Incest, Romance, and the Proliferation of Narrative in *Game of Thrones*," in *The Medieval Motion Picture: The Politics of Adaptation*, edited by Andrew James Johnston, Margitta Rouse, and Philipp Hinz (New York, 2014). Bleisteiner is an alumnus of the German Academic Scholarship Foundation (Studienstiftung des Deutschen Volkes) and a former member of the Collaborative Research Center "Episteme in Motion" and the Cluster of Excellence "Temporal Communities: Doing Literature in a Global Perspective" at the Freie Universität Berlin.

Björn Klaus Buschbeck is *Wissenschaftlicher Assistent* in medieval German studies at the University of Zurich. He is currently completing a book on the reception aesthetics of late medieval prayers and devotional texts, especially with regard to rosaries, textile craft prayer, and spiritual buildings. His research interests include religious literature and the Middle High German heroic epic. His articles include "Sprechen mit dem Heiligen und Eintauchen in den Text: Zur Wirkungsästhetik eines Passionsgebets aus dem *Engelberger Gebetbuch*," in *Das Mittelalter* 24 (2019); "Eintauchen und Einverleiben: Die Andachtsübung *Wirtschaft des Leidens Christi* aus dem Straßburger Dominikanerinnenkloster St. Nikolaus in undis," in *Vielfalt des Religiösen: Mittelalterliche Literatur im postsäkularen Kontext*, edited by Susanne Bernhardt and Bent Gebert (Berlin, 2021); and "Ein Held, der keiner mehr sein wollte: König Ortnits Tod und das Problem, eine Heldenerzählung zu beenden," in *Zeitschrift für deutsche Philologie* 136 (2017).

Jutta Eming is professor of medieval German literature at Freie Universität Berlin. Her research interests include romances from the High to the late Middle Ages, genre theory and gender, emotionality, performativity, and premodern drama. She runs a research project at the Freie Universität "Episteme in Motion" Collaborative Research Center called "The Marvelous as a Configuration of Knowledge in Medieval Literature." Her publications include *Funktionswandel des Wunderbaren: Studien zum "Bel Inconnu," zum "Wigalois" und zum "Wigoleis vom Rade"* (Trier, 1999); *Emotion und Expression: Untersuchungen zu deutschen und französischen Liebes- und Abenteuerromanen des 12.–16. Jahrhunderts* (Berlin, 2006); and *Der Begriff der Magie in Mittelalter und Früher Neuzeit* (Wiesbaden, 2020), coedited with Volkhard Wels. Eming has been the recipient of fellowships from the Alexander von Humboldt Foundation, the Social Sciences and Humanities Research Council of Canada, the Peter Wall Institute for Advanced Studies at the University of British Columbia in Vancouver, Canada, and the German Academic Exchange Service (DAAD).

Jan-Peer Hartmann is a fellow at the "Episteme in Motion" Collaborative Research Center at the Freie Universität Berlin. His articles on Old English poetry and early medieval Latin hagiography have appeared in *Leeds Studies in English* and *Medium Ævum*, and he coedited (with Andrew James Johnston) *Material Remains: Reading the Past in Medieval and Early Modern Literature* (Columbus, OH, 2021). He has just completed the manuscript for a monograph on early medieval English literature and archaeology.

Iris Helffenstein is an art historian specializing in the arts of medieval and early modern Italy, with particular focus on wall painting, devotional art, and interactions between different media. Her research interests include materiality, intermediality, allegory, and the relationships between artistic production, social practice, and aesthetic experience. Her publications include *Wissenstransfer in Bildprogrammen des Trecento: Allegorie, Imitation und Medialität* (Paderborn, 2021); and "Intermediale Verfahren im *studietto:* Zu Materialästhetik und Medialität von Verre églomisé und Goldgrund im italienischen Spätmittelalter bis Lorenzo Monaco," in *Gezeichnete Evidenz auf kolorierten Papieren in Süd und Nord von 1400 bis 1650*, edited by Iris Brahms and Klaus Krüger (Berlin, forthcoming, 2021). She is coeditor (with Anne Eusterschulte, Klaus Krüger, and Claudia Reufer) of *Figurales Wissen: Medialität, Ästhetik und Materialität von Wissen in der Vormoderne* (Wiesbaden, forthcoming, 2021/2022).

Christopher Hutchinson is assistant professor of German at the University of Mississippi, where he teaches courses on medieval and early modern German literature and culture. His research interests include book history, the history of disease, and the popularization of scientific discourses in literature. His current book project is on print and epidemic disease in German medical writing and literary texts at the turn of the sixteenth century.

Falk Quenstedt is a postdoctoral fellow at the "Episteme in Motion" Collaborative Research Center at the Freie Universität Berlin. His book on transcultural relations between medieval German and Arabic literature will be published in 2021, entitled *Mirabiles Wissen: Deutschsprachige Reiseerzählungen um 1200 im transkulturellen Kontext arabischer Literatur.* His research interests include late medieval courtly romances and early modern prose novels, with particular focus on their connections to Mediterranean literature and material culture. His articles include "Performing Knowledge Economies: Changing and Exchanging Goods in Pre-modern Ritual Communities" (coauthored with Martin Gehlmann and Lennart Lehmhaus), in *Wissensoikonomien: Ordnung und Transgression in vormodernen Kulturen*, edited by Niklas Pissis et al. (Wiesbaden, 2021); and "Mediation neuen Wissens: Anekdoten in Marco Polos *Divisament dou monde* und dessen deutschsprachigen Fassungen," in *Wissen* en miniature: *Theorie und Epistemologie der Anekdote*, edited by Melanie Möller and Matthias Grandl (Wiesbaden, 2021).

Mareike Elisa Reisch is a PhD candidate in the Department of German Studies at Stanford University. Her research interests include late medieval pilgrimage narratives, medieval perceptions of space, and reception practices, particularly with regard to reading and imagination. In her dissertation, she explores the different modes in which fifteenth-century pilgrimage accounts render pilgrimage experiences tangible to their audiences. She is the author of "*Sinne* and *sêlen kraft:* Medieval Models of Sensory Perception in a Mural of the Constance *Haus zur Kunkel*" (/postmedieval/ 12, 1–4 (2021)).

Tilo Renz is a postdoctoral researcher at the Freie Universität Berlin who currently holds a visiting professorship of medieval German literature at the University of Cologne. He works with medieval and early modern German literature, focusing on gender and embodiment, marvels, ideal communities, narrative constructions of space, and the relationship between literary and other forms of knowledge. His publications include *Um Leib und Leben: Das Wissen von Geschlecht, Körper und Recht im "Nibelungenlied"* (Berlin, 2012), for which he received the Tiburtius Prize (2011). He is coeditor (with Monika Hanauska and Mathias Herweg) of the handbook *Literarische Orte in deutschsprachigen Erzählungen des Mittelalters* (Berlin, 2018), and he recently finished his postdoctoral dissertation (*Habilitation*) on late medieval utopian narratives (*Utopische Entwürfe des späten Mittelalters*, 2020). Renz has been the recipient of fellowships from the German Research Foundation, the German Academic Exchange Service (DAAD), and the Fritz Thyssen Foundation.

Kathryn Starkey is professor of German in the Department of German Studies at Stanford University. Her primary research interests are medieval and early modern German literature and culture, with an emphasis on visuality, material culture, language, poetics, and manuscript studies. She is the author of *Reading the Medieval Book: Word, Image, and Performance in Wolfram von Eschenbach's "Willehalm"* (Notre Dame, 2004), and *A Courtier's Mirror: Cultivating Elite Identity in Thomasin's "Welscher Gast"* (Notre Dame, 2013); and she is the coauthor (with Edith Wenzel) of *Neidhart: Selected Songs from the Riedegger Manuscript* (Kalamazoo, 2016). Her coedited volumes include (with Fiona Griffiths) *Sensory Reflections: Traces of Experience in Medieval Artifacts* (Berlin, 2019). She is also the PI of the *Global Medieval Sourcebook* (sourcebook.stanford.edu). Starkey has been the recipient of fellowships from the Stanford Humanities Center, the National Humanities Center, the Alexander von Humboldt Foundation, and the Social Sciences and Humanities Research Council of Canada.

Leonardo Velloso-Lyons is a doctoral candidate in comparative literature at Stanford University, where he works with early modern texts in Spanish, Portuguese, Latin, Quechua, and Italian. He is particularly interested in the relation between literary, historical, and geographic discourses, the writing of global and local histories, the interaction between cartographic objects and literature, and comparative approaches to early modernity from the fields of trans-Atlantic, postcolonial, and decolonial studies. In his dissertation, he examines how historians from the Ibero-Atlantic world constructed knowledge of Africa via an ambivalent rhetorical framework, acknowledging the importance of African peoples and cultures for the Habsburg empire while at the same time limiting their symbolic influence by ascribing to them a flat continental identity—a single idea of "Africanness." Leonardo Velloso-Lyons is a recipient of the Stanford Humanities Center Dissertation Prize (2021/22) and the Lewis Award (2021/22).

Mae Velloso-Lyons is a doctoral candidate in comparative literature at Stanford University and a Stanford Data Science Scholar. Her primary field of research is Western European literature from 1100 to 1600 CE, with a secondary focus on quantitative methods for humanistic inquiry. In her dissertation, she combines close and distant reading techniques with manuscript analysis to reconstruct cultural understandings of the body from the Old French Lancelot-Grail Cycle. A keen collaborator, Mae Velloso-Lyons has coauthored articles on pedagogical approaches to the multilingual Tristan tradition and on scholar-led digital projects. Since 2016, she has edited the *Global Medieval Sourcebook* (sourcebook.stanford.edu), an online collection of premodern texts translated from more than twenty-five languages.

Color Plates

Plate 1: Gradual from Sta. Maria degli Angeli, Florence, Choir of Camaldolese Monks Chanting in an initial *C*, attributed to Zanobi Strozzi or Ballista di Biagio Sanguigni, dated to the 1420s. Tempera and gold leaf on parchment. Florence, Biblioteca Medicea Laurenziana, Ms. Corale 3, fol, 41v. Reproduced by kind permission of the MIBACT. Any reproduction in any form is prohibited.

https://doi.org/10.1515/9783110742985-017

Plate 2: Lorenzo Monaco, Christ on the Cross with Saints Benedict, Francis of Assisi, and Romuald, ca. 1405–1407. Tempera and gold leaf on poplar, 56.4 x 42 x 2.8 cm. Altenburg, Lindenau-Museum, inv. no. 23. © Lindenau-Museum Altenburg. Photo: Bernd Sinterhauf.

Plate 3a – 3c: Lorenzo Monaco, Christ on the Cross with Saints Benedict, Francis of Assisi, and Romuald, ca. 1405–1407 (details). Tempera and gold leaf on poplar, 56.4 x 42 x 2.8 cm. Altenburg, Lindenau-Museum, inv. no. 23. © Lindenau-Museum Altenburg. Photo: Bernd Sinterhauf.

Plate 4: Sienese or Pisan painter and Nino Pisano, Crucifixion, ca. 1365. Tempera and gold leaf on wood panel, polychrome wooden crucifix, 72 x 30 x 10.5 cm (overall). Florence, private collection. Photo: in Kreytenberg 2000.

Plate 5: Lorenzo Monaco, Reliquary Tabernacle with Saint, ca. 1400—1410. Gilded wood, *verre églomisé* (relics lost), 47 x 28.3 x 16 cm (overall). Lyon, Musée des Beaux-Arts, D698. © Lyon MBA. Photo: Alain Basset.

Plate 6: Florentine artist, Man of Sorrows, ca. 1315–1325. *Verre églomisé*, 24 x 30 cm. Fiesole, Museo Bandini. Photo: Museo Bandini.

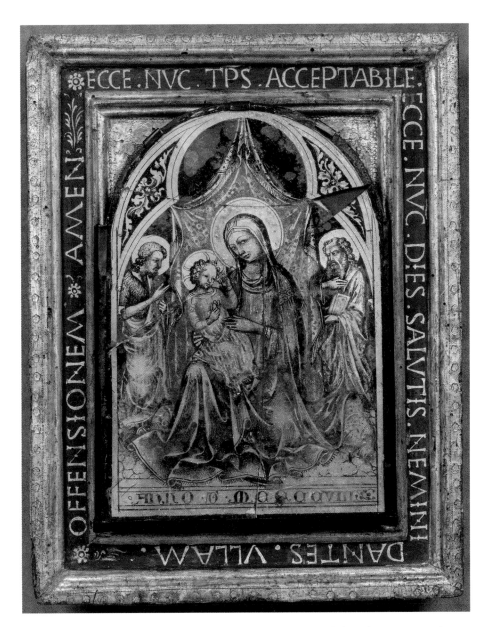

Plate 7: Lorenzo Monaco, Virgin and Child with Saints, 1408. *Verre églomisé*, 29.5 x 23 cm (overall). Turin, Palazzo Madama – Museo Civico d'Arte Antica, 0140/VD. Photo: Studio Fotografico Gonella 2020, reproduced by kind permission of the Fondazione Torino Musei, all rights reserved. Any reproduction in any form is prohibited.